Aristotelians and Platonists

Aristotelians and Platonists

A Convergence of the
Michaelic Streams in Our Time

LUIGI MORELLI

ARISTOTELIANS AND PLATONISTS
A CONVERGENCE OF THE MICHAELIC STREAMS IN OUR TIME

iUniverse books may be ordered through booksellers or by contacting:

iUniverse
1663 Liberty Drive
Bloomington, IN 47403
www.iuniverse.com
1-800-Authors (1-800-288-4677)

ISBN: 978-1-4917-8106-7 (sc)
ISBN: 978-1-4917-8107-4 (e)

Print information available on the last page.

iUniverse rev. date: 09/01/2016

CONTENTS

Part III: The New Age of Michael

Chapter 4: German Idealism 91

Chapter 5: Steiner's and Schröer's World Tasks 121

Chapter 6: Aristotelians and Platonists in the New Michaelic Age.... 161

Part IV: Michaelic Souls after Steiner's Death

Appendices and Bibliography

INTRODUCTION

Questions concerning Aristotelians and Platonists have engaged my attention for some twenty years now. They were life questions forming themselves before I knew it. They came with my biography and my relationship to anthroposophy itself. I lived the questions with curiosity, and confusion mixed with anguish. Somehow I felt this was immediately relevant, and that it was approachable even through direct experience.

I know that the same, or similar, questions live in other people. So the first questions could be "Why should these questions matter? And how do they matter?" It is a common understanding, from Steiner's spiritual heritage, that humanity is standing at the abyss of the death of culture. This is also the time in which a growing perception of the Christ in the etheric is made possible for more and more aware human beings. It is natural that at such an important turning point in history all the opposing forces are growing in intensity.

Platonists and Aristotelians prepared the advent of the Christ, whose incarnation was made possible in the Jewish stream, but whose understanding only Greek philosophy could foster. Again in the Middle Ages new evolutionary steps lay in store for mankind, and new dangers threatened the pursuit of knowledge and the development of individuality at the time of a growing estrangement from the spirit. Here again the Platonists of Chartres and the Aristotelian Scholastics added their efforts for the renewal of Christianity in order to lay the foundations upon which the Consciousness Soul could unfold and find its fulfillment.

And lastly, we come to modern times. Here the forces of renewal of civilization appeared first in classical German culture, then in the development of anthroposophy. It is only after this last preparatory stage that Aristotelians and Platonists have appeared in world history together. They have never before worked side by side. And their doing so is vital for the renewal of culture, as much as it is new to all of them and therefore a great challenge. Steiner knew that a step of this nature would be far from automatic, and he therefore warned us of the necessity of recognizing the streams as they manifest in ourselves and in the world, and of fostering their collaboration.

Anticipating the results of this research, one can say that it is the collaboration between the streams and their different orientations to anthroposophy, which render practical work and social impact stronger. It is only when the two streams fully integrate cultural consciousness that one-sidedness is avoided, and the work becomes therefore more sustainable. When we look at the social world, both streams hold one part of the equation, and here, more than anywhere else, only their joint efforts can offer solutions that are both inwardly coherent and fully viable.

My path to spiritual science came early in life but was not self-evident; no immediate recognition or lightning flash; rather a laborious step by step that took place over one year at Emerson College in 1982-83. Having been trained in sciences I struggled for a whole year to know anthroposophy to be a science. Certainly, being exposed to anthroposophy on a daily basis accelerated the process. And doubts were definitely dispelled by the end of that year.

It was some fifteen years after being introduced to Steiner's work that I came across *Karmic Relationships*, Volume 3, in a study group. I felt an immediate recognition in Steiner's description of old souls and young souls. And in the process, my initial difficulties, and the way I reacted to them, received an adequate explanation. I could clearly recognize myself as one of the soul types, which Steiner related to Aristotelians and Platonists.

Later in life, I have faced the tension of feeling a strong attraction to work done outside of anthroposophy, work done in the forefront of social renewal. I lived and worked through many important experiences (men's groups, support groups, interest in Twelve Step, Nonviolent

Communication, and later so-called "social technology" and Theory U). It was only in stages that I could integrate the experiences, and frame them within a plausible anthroposophical key of understanding. One experience made this possible at first: a three-month training I received in Adult Education at Engen, Germany in 2001 with Coen van Houten. A small part of the training was devoted to so-called Destiny Learning. The experience was important for me, and it seemed even more important for the other participants. What I felt was partly an echo of many things I had already known through my biographical interests; on the other hand much was completely new. This experience brought an intensification of many previous ones. For the first time what I had encountered in the various interests I mentioned above, was mirrored from inside anthroposophical practice through Destiny Learning. I was experiencing a bridge between the two worlds I belonged to.

What I saw in my own life-course seems to repeat itself in phenomena in the world, which I could characterize thus. When I look at people producing work in natural sciences, work in psychology or in the social field, it is again striking that two modalities are clearly recognizable. And it would be difficult, or simply impossible, to expect the same person to carry his work in the second modality if he works in the first, or vice-versa. I offer examples of these in the last part of the book.

I was starting to create bridges between the two worlds that I had carried in parallel for many years. A second key experience was the Global Presencing Classroom (an online training) in Theory U with Otto Scharmer. All the experiences that I was trying to integrate acquired new meaning. And everything I pursued afterwards became all the more readily understandable and easier to integrate.

The history of the development of anthroposophy first, and of the Anthroposophical Society later, offers us a microcosmos of world history. This statement should not surprise anyone who has studied Steiner's work at length. In parallel to the two turning points in my biography, I started noticing that what happens in the world at large and is reflected in modern trends, previously occurred in the lives of Steiner and the individuals more closely associated with him, and soon afterwards in the social laboratory that has been, and is, the General Anthroposophical Society. These were the revelations that came through *Karmic Relationships*, Volume 4, which closely follows Volume 3 in time. Here again, this came through a study group. What I had read on my own only acquired greater depth when deeper study and conversation enlivened it.

To sum up: first in Steiner's life, in the effort to offer the world anthroposophy, then in the life of the Society, the question of the whole of the Michaelic community is reflected, mirrored and set in motion for the world at large. And what we see today in the world reflects, for better or for worse, the path that pioneer anthroposophists have walked ahead of the times. It also reflects how and to what degree the Anthroposophical Society has integrated the two streams of the Michaelic Movement.

In my first book, *Karl Julius Schröer and Rudolf Steiner: Anthroposophy and the Teachings of Karma and Reincarnation*, I approached the matter of the world tasks of Schröer and Steiner. There the development of anthroposophy is contrasted with the spiritual-scientific understanding of karma and reincarnation. The goal of the writing was the characterization of the whole impulse of karma and reincarnation. The term that was adopted in the book in relation to karma and reincarnation is "spirit recollection," an expression that was first found in the Foundation Stone Meditation. The book contrasts spirit recollection with the more familiar spirit beholding, which refers to the study of the natural world, human being included, through spiritual science. Having done this, the book explores the whole extent and field of activity of the impulse of spirit recollection.

This book takes the thread further. It moves from Aristotle/Steiner and Plato/Schröer to Aristotelians and Platonists. The underlying question is one of integration. The goal is the understanding of Steiner's "culmination" at the end of the twentieth century, and what it means for all of us anthroposophists, and for those who could come to work with us, from wherever they are at present in the world.

The earlier book looked at Steiner and Schröer almost exclusively from the biographical perspective. This new attempt will look at the karmic history of Aristotelians and Platonists. Unavoidably it will look at Aristotle and Plato, their intermediate incarnations and those of Steiner and Schröer.

Before looking at the birth of the Michaelic movement, we will explore the historical conditions that moved world evolution from the ancient East to the West, through Greece. We will then look at three stages in the life of the Michaelic movement. The first is the earlier Age of Michael in Greece. The second will look at the Middle Ages, and offer a contrast between the School of Chartres and the Cistercians on one hand, and the Dominicans and Scholasticism on the other. The work of Alain de Lille will be contrasted with that of Thomas Aquinas. It is at this point in time that an important layer of the Aristotelians/Platonists polarity takes on a new light. This is simply the effect that the Christ impulse has over the initial twin impulses. In the Middle Ages, Aristotelianism and Platonism were Christianized. Chartres brought together the most various strands of culture and offered to the world the gifts of the cathedrals; the Dominicans renewed culture and set the stage for the time of the Consciousness Soul.

And we come finally to the New Age of Michael, with its preparation in German classical culture, and with the birth of anthroposophy itself. At that time, Plato's and Aristotle's eternal individualities reincarnated, respectively in Schröer and Steiner. Here their relationship will be examined again, but this time from a more epistemological perspective than was the case in my earlier book. This focus highlights the evolution of initiates themselves. The tasks that they embrace are those that humanity at large later embarks upon.

Chapters 6, 7 and 8 look at what is happening at present. The question of the differences between how Aristotelians and Platonists operate in the world, lived in me in an instinctive way. I could sense it, rather than bring it to clear expression. I placed it in perspective in the book *A Revolution of Hope*. What I intuited in that work is fleshed out in this work against a historical background.

A year ago I realized that what I was searching for in the present had constantly been the object of my interest and studies, though I could not yet recognize it and articulate it. Through this realization I could easily revisit very familiar material. It is clear that I have no insight into the incarnational paths of any of the individuals mentioned in Chapters 6, 7 and 8, other than what some rare ones disclose. What I offer is the perception of very different approaches to the same fields of inquiry that continue the trends of centuries and that present the polarities of Platonists and Aristotelians in ways that correspond to the characterizations of the two streams made by Steiner. Over the centuries these polarities have obviously metamorphosed.

I offer in Chapters 6, 7 and 8 three sets of contrasts of work done in psychology, natural science and social science. The first tableau compares the life and work of Willem Zeylmans van Emmichoven and Bernard Lievegoed, two contemporaries who interacted with each other for some thirty years. We have access to both their biographies and their literary estate. We can characterize their legacies as two complementary gestures. Bernard Lievegoed has exerted a continuous influence over my life and work. I came across Zeylmans van Emmichoven some ten years ago. I found his *The Foundation Stone* to be one of the most thorough, insightful and succinct overviews of the Christmas Conference. This motivated me to read his *Understanding of the Soul* and his biography.

The chapter will also look at something that came into my biography at important turning points: the question of forgiveness. I first met it in Prokofieff's *Occult Significance of Forgiveness*, a great source of inspiration, and a book that I have read three or four times and explored in a study group. The same question of forgiveness acquired another dimension in the work of Marshall Rosenberg known as Nonviolent Communication, in which I have trained, practiced for many years, and offered trainings.

Chapter 7 presents a second set of contrasts, in the work of Rudolf Hauschka and of Dr. Edward Bach. What made this comparison possible is the accessibility of their work and their biographies. Hauschka's work met my biography with one of the first anthroposophical books I read in natural sciences – *The Nature of Substance* – which captivated me; many of the most striking assertions, or experiments, have remained with me ever since as initial revelations of a different way of looking at the natural sciences. Bach's Flower Remedies have accompanied me for some twenty years. I both read as much as I could about them, and progressed in the understanding of their use. Dr. Bach's biography exerted a deep fascination that I also could not help but research.

Finally, I look at the expression of threefolding in the twentieth century. I met threefolding early on in my anthroposophical studies.

Immersed as I was in activist approaches to social change, I had initial difficulties in overcoming my biases and opening myself up to its concepts. Very soon, in the years that followed, the experience of running a business showed me how naïve were some of the assumptions I carried from my youth. I reread books on threefolding some ten years after my first attempts, and everything acquired new meaning.

Five years ago I deepened my interest in so-called "social technology," various approaches to facilitation that are used for processes of social transformation in organizations or communities. I completed a Mastery in Technology of Participation through the Institute of Cultural Affairs (ICA). I was simply pursuing my life interests a step further. In the middle of my training I came across the so-called "Social Process Triangles," in which familiar ideas about threefolding had emerged from a very unfamiliar place in the world, and in a seemingly unorthodox way. What ICA articulated is the equivalent of a threefolding that is born from experience. It is this that I contrast with the imaginations that Steiner has so eloquently left us.

In the previous chapters the contrast between Aristotelians and Platonists is brought into the present. This statement brings us to the concluding set of questions. What is it that Platonists need to learn from Aristotelians? And what is it that Aristotelians need to learn from Platonists? From these two emerge yet other questions. What is it that we need to do as members of the Michaelic Movement to bring its poles closer to each other? And what is it that needs to happen in order for the culmination at the end of the century to become a reality, even if with some delay?

It is my keenest wish that this book will inspire a sense of hope in those who read it that new efforts, literary and/or practical, will arise, addressing the question of the convergence of the Michaelic streams in our times.

PART I

THE PREVIOUS AGE OF MICHAEL

CHAPTER 1

SETTING THE STAGE:
FROM EAST TO WEST

In order to set the stage for our explorations it is important to understand the momentous transition that led to the passage of traditional Mystery knowledge from the East to the West. It led to the kindling of the cultural mission of Europe, the birth of philosophy, and some of the prerequisites for the events at the turning point of time and its understanding by the generations that followed. Although our exploration follows both Aristotelians and Platonists, it is clear that we have more material concerning Aristotle/Steiner's incarnations than we do of Plato/Schröer. We will therefore turn primarily to the first, and occasionally to the second, though we will look at the expressions of Platonism in depth. And when we speak of Steiner's eternal individuality's path in time, we cannot do so without looking at the soul who accompanied him every single step of the way.

It is remarkable how two individuals—Rudolf Steiner and Ita Wegman—have been closely associated in all their incarnations. Bernard Lievegoed defines these two as "sister souls" who reincarnate to further their world tasks and influence world karma.[1] These two souls, remarkable as they may be on their own, could not have achieved their tasks without each other. Steiner compares them to a blind man and

---

[1] Bernard J. Lievegoed, *The Battle for the Soul: The Working Together of Three Great Leaders of Humanity.*

a cripple: they could help each other because of their great differences and one-sidedness.[2]

Before beginning, we'll set the stage for Steiner's first incarnation in the post-Atlantean age.

Evolution of the Mysteries in the Post-Atlantean Age

After the Flood of Atlantis, the great Manu of the Sun oracle led those who had started to form the rudiments for the faculty of thinking first out of Atlantis, then toward Central Asia. Two major streams evolved from the Atlantean migrations, those that Steiner called the Northern and Southern Streams, characterizing two paths of knowledge: the path to the macrocosm and the path to the microcosm, respectively.

Maya (or illusion) has a twofold aspect. The first is met in the sense world, the second in the soul life. Behind the sense world (the world of space) are those beings who have their center in the Sun. The path to the soul life was taken under the guidance of Lucifer, by which is meant only a part of the luciferic beings. The two different paths were known at all times; and a distinction was made between the upper gods who lead beyond the sense world, and the lower gods who lead into the soul life. The path to the upper gods was taken by those following the Northern Stream; the path of descent to the underworld was taken by the people of the Southern Stream.

The Northern Stream moved through England, Northern France, Scandinavia, Russia, into Asia and India. This development led to the birth of the primeval Indian civilization of the first post-Atlantean epoch. The people who migrated along this route were more adapted to the use of the senses for external perception. Some cultures remained behind to take on tasks for later epochs of humanity. A group among these created the foundations for the Mysteries of Hibernia (the Mysteries of the West), which preserved ancient Atlantean wisdom; and another formed the "waiting culture" of northern Europe (Germany and Scandinavia) whose task would unfold only in later millennia.

---

[2] Rudolf Steiner, *Occult History: Historical Personalities and Events in the Light of Spiritual Science*, December 28, 1910, lecture.

Steiner called the Hibernian stream the last of the Great Mysteries because it preserved the unity of the inner and outer paths within one unified stream, as had been the case in Atlantis. These Mysteries were later continued in the Druid Mysteries. In the time after Christ they were preserved in the Arthur stream and in the Celtic Church. The second stream, which was waiting for the future, developed in the north of Europe. The Celts developed warrior qualities, in a culture emphasizing courage and the perfecting of the brain under the influence of external forces. From the Celtic culture the later cultures of Germany and Scandinavia developed.

The people of the Northern Stream worked at perfecting the outer bodily form, rendering it an image of the spirit. An example of the highest degree of initiation of the northern people is Zarathustra, who lived through every succeeding incarnation in bodies of higher moral, aesthetic, and intellectual qualities, until the process made possible the Jesus incarnation of the Solomon line. An incorporated spiritual being worked in Zarathustra's incarnations; thus what radiated through his individuality went beyond the boundaries of his ego and personal achievements.

The northern path leads the individual into the macrocosm. The fundamental number of space is twelve, and this is how time is manifested into space. This principle is reflected in the fact that at the time in which Christ descended from the world of time into the world of space, he was surrounded by the twelve Apostles, just as the world of space is surrounded by the twelve constellations of the zodiac. In these is represented what is above good and evil.

The people of the Southern Stream migrated through Spain, Africa, and Arabia. They followed what leads out of space into time, to the gods of the luciferic realms. Here the number seven reigns, the number that rules all cycles of time. The lower gods that one encounters along this path belonged to the underworld; they were rulers of the soul life, leading the human being to the acquisition of consciousness. Osiris, the divinity that man finds on passing through the gate of death, cannot live in the external sense world; in the world of the senses he was overcome by the powers of evil. Just as the people of the North developed their outer form as an image of the spirit, so the southern people created the invisible soul-image of the godhead in their inner life.

The spiritual world of the southern people is called the world of Lucifer, the Light-bearer. There are in fact two kinds of luciferic beings: those that led man into the path to the microcosmos and those that remained behind in their evolution and approached the human being not in his ego but in his astral body, called "the serpent" in biblical terms. The gods of the south inspire either fear and dread or trust and confidence, according to man's stage of development, and this is why the path to the inner world was fraught with many dangers.

The ancient Indians were still suited for pursuing paths to both the upper and lower gods: the path through the sense world and the path through the veil of the soul life. Piercing through both veils, they could recognize the same reality of the spiritual world.[3] The ancient Persians looked more to the outer world, to the sense world that they could behold in the outer Sun. Beyond it they could gaze at the spiritual Sun, at Ahura Mazdao, and from his realm the initiates received the inspiration for guiding Persian civilization in the second post-Atlantean epoch.

Things changed with the third post-Atlantean age, before and after the time of the beginning of Kali Yuga; this was a time of transition known as the "Twilight of the Gods," in which humanity had to progressively forsake all residual atavistic clairvoyance. Human etheric bodies were getting denser and contracting, particularly around the physical head. Kali Yuga marked the path toward materialism and the loss of clairvoyant faculties, starting around 3101 BC.

In the third epoch two tendencies were at work: the Egyptian to the south, the Chaldean to the north. The Chaldeans continued the Northern Mysteries. They developed an astro-theology, experiencing what lay beyond the world in which we live between birth and death. The Egyptian path to the inner world was fraught with dangers, and therefore possible only for the initiates. On the inner path the initiate met Ishtar, "a beneficent moon divinity who stood on the threshold that hides from man the spiritual element standing behind his soul life." "On

---

[3] Steiner, *The East in the Light of the West*, lecture of August 29, 1909.

4

the other side, where the door opening through the outer sense world into the world of spirit is situated, stood the guardian Merodach or Mardach. Merodach (whom we may compare with Michael) and Ishtar imparted clairvoyance to the soul, and led men by both paths into the spiritual world."[4]

The differences between Egyptian and Chaldean Mysteries were well known to the Greeks who followed them closely in cultural terms. The Greeks compared the Chaldean gods with their Apollonian realms. When they spoke about Osiris, they sought for illumination through the mysteries of Dionysus. They could understand both the Egyptian and Chaldean streams because they blended the two streams in their culture. Thus to represent a purified and spiritualized physical body, they used northern racial types. To represent the development of soul life, they used southern racial types; Hermes, the messenger to the lower gods, was represented as an African.

The path to the Apollonian beings was the path outward. These were the gods that were indicated to the masses. When they referred to Apollo, the Greeks were pointing to the general realm from which the Christ would come. "Apollo is an intimation of the Christ, but not the Christ Himself."[5] The path to the Dionysian gods (a name for the world of the luciferic gods) could not be trod as fully and openly, and was reserved for the highest initiates. Greek culture had as one of its goals to allow for the future apprehension of the full nature of Christ. However, at that time, the Christ could not be understood in his Dionysian nature, except by very few.

An interesting contrast between the northern and southern streams is made manifest in the key individualities whose sheaths prepared the descent of the Christ into incarnation: Gautama Buddha and Zarathustra, the two most exalted individuals representing respectively the southern path and the northern path. To Gautama (Prince Siddhartha) were revealed all his previous incarnations in the enlightenment experience under the Bodhi tree, in a meditation that lasted several days. Through this he ascended to the stage of Buddha. "Thus man discovers the path

---

[4] Ibid, lecture of August 30, 1909.
[5] Steiner, *The East in the Light of the West*, lecture of August 28, 1909.

to the former incarnations through submergence in his own being, and when his submergence is as intensive, powerful, and all-encompassing as was the case of the great Buddha, this insight into incarnations continues on and on."[6] Buddha represented the end-line of a stream of evolution, and the ideas of karma and reincarnation formed the apex of his teachings. To further this path, Buddha taught compassion, love, and the Eightfold Path.

In the case of Zarathustra, knowledge of previous lives played no part at all in the first stages. Zarathustra did not progress on the path of initiation solely on his own merits. He was actually chosen as the bearer of a spiritual entity that cannot incarnate but that can reverberate through the carrier's personality. Early in life the child felt like a stranger to all those around him, who could not understand the nature of the impulses that animated his soul.[7] Of Zarathustra, the legends speak of a life full of dramatic events, turmoil, persecutions, and so forth. Conflicts surged all around such a personality; the newness of the impulses that worked through such an initiate caused the environment all around to feel instinctive antipathy toward him. Buddha's life was much more serene.

The Stage of Rudolf Steiner's First Incarnation

To understand the setting of the sister souls' first common incarnation, it is necessary to indicate the changes in consciousness that occurred at this particular point, which marked the transition from the great wisdom of the East to the evolution of self-consciousness that emerged in the West at the time of the onset of Kali Yuga, the Twilight of the Gods.

Human consciousness has undergone many changes throughout the ages. To the human being of very early times, memory was associated with particular places. The erection of memorial monuments, stones or mounds (such as the dolmens) was performed with the goal of preserving memory of deeds and events. People of olden times did not have memory linked to experience, which we all take for granted now.

---

[6] Steiner, *Background to the Gospel of Saint Mark*, lecture of December 19, 1910.
[7] Ibid, lecture of December 19, 1910.

However, they could call back to memory what they associated with particular places; in particular, a memorial place. Dolmens or obelisks were erected for this purpose.

In later times, memory was acquired via the word spoken in a rhythmic way. For things to be remembered, it was necessary to preserve them in a certain way. This form later gave birth to poetry. We know from history that the first poetry adhered to very strict canons of meter and rhythm. Vestiges of this kind of consciousness remained in the way children were taught. The goal of nursery rhymes was initially to educate a child whose memory in early ages easily retains what is associated with rhythms and certain repetitions, for example in the sounds of objects and animals.

The transition from Asian civilizations to Greece, the turning point of the initial development of the West, occurred at a time when temporal memory, the one we currently know, was emerging in Greek consciousness. Another important change of consciousness occurred in relation to humanity's attitude toward death. To the Eastern man of old, death was a realm full of reality and merely a transition from one form of life to another. Western man started to regard death as a mystery, and to associate feelings of dread with it. The Greeks first coined the saying, "Better a beggar in the world of senses than a king in the realm of the shades," a feeling with which modern man still identifies almost exclusively.

Finally, all of these changes of consciousness were reflected in the way humanity received spiritual instruction in the Mystery Centers, or places of initiation. The Mysteries of the Orient retained a much more cosmic orientation. The people of the East had a consciousness that made them feel at home in the whole cosmos, much more so than on earth. Initiation occurred according to this form of consciousness. Certain experiences could be obtained only according to space and geography; experiences within a cave were of a different nature than those possible on a mountaintop. Other experiences could be obtained only according to the rhythms of earth, stars, and planets; therefore, only in winter or in summer; once every twenty-nine days for a full moon; once every twenty years for a conjunction between Jupiter and Saturn, and so forth.

7

The initiation centers of Greece moved on to a kind of instruction with which we are more familiar. The whole of the initiation process could be conducted in a single place. However, now the pupil's initiation depended upon personal effort, and was accompanied by corresponding exercises. According to the pupil's degree of development, certain experiences were possible for him that were no longer dependent upon place or time. The wisdom that fully emerged in Greece was less cosmic and more directed towards the personality.

From the Wisdom of the East to the Consciousness of the West

The first incarnations of Steiner and Wegman to which we will turn formed an important transition between East and West at the time of Kali Yuga, the time in which humanity progressively lost its old atavistic consciousness.[4] The original, natural clairvoyance had to undergo a process of withering that reached its culmination in the nineteenth and twentieth centuries. Loss of clairvoyant consciousness and development of individuality through the intellect can be seen, to a great extent, as interconnected processes.

The two sister souls appeared together for the first time in the city of Erech, during the Chaldean-Babylonian civilization about 5,000 years ago. Records of their deeds have survived in a way that modern humanity is no longer accustomed to understand—myth. The odyssey of Gilgamesh relates to the life of the individual who took the name Ita Wegman in her last life. Steiner defined this individual as a god-man, what the people of old called a demi-god. By this they meant someone through whom the divinity spoke on earth. Gilgamesh was the inaugurator of Chaldean-Babylonian culture. He had traits of old consciousness somewhere in between the East and the West. He still had a memory associated with rhythm, but he started to identify himself with his destiny on earth; therefore, with the physical body, rather than with his higher bodies and the cosmos. Gilgamesh was a conqueror at a time when the habit of conquering and imposing one's will upon other populations was beginning to be questioned. The city of Erech, which he had subjugated, resisted his rule at first.

We can imagine the tensions and contradictions that lived in this soul, which were projected outward in the situation the ruler had to face. The easing of these inner and outer tensions came from the king's encounter with the figure called Eabani, or Enkidu, the earliest known incarnation of Rudolf Steiner's eternal individuality. Eabani was a "primitive" man, a "wild" man. The myth depicts him as a being covered with animal skins, conveying in an image that Eabani was a very different individual from Gilgamesh. Eabani was coming to earth with very few incarnations behind him, and a very long time spent in the world of the spirit: what Steiner calls a "young soul." Saying that he was wild is tantamount to expressing that Eabani came to earth with all the cosmic knowledge normally acquired in the priestly precincts. That knowledge (added to the fact that he had little earthly experience) made him look quite different from everybody else—wild, says the epic. That is because he was completely new to earthly life, with no exposure to culture, no self-consciousness. Rather, he was more at home within cosmic reality.

Eabani was lured away from his task of herding animals into the city of Uruk, and seduced by a priestess of Ishtar, and in this act, he awakened into his astral body, to a deeper knowledge of himself and of the reality of life on earth. His encounter with the king occurred in a fight that led to a deadlock. From this episode came the friendship between Gilgamesh/Wegman and Eabani/Steiner, which we will follow in many other incarnations. What united the two in spite of their differences was the fact that they had souls of a very different complexion from any other in Asia at the time.

The myth indicates that the two fought against the Bull of Heaven, Khumbaba (the deity who brought destruction around himself), and defeated him. This is pointed to in the episode of Cedar Mountain, where a temple to the goddess Irnini (an aspect of Ishtar) was guarded by a monster who barred access to all mortals. After vanquishing Khumbaba, the two were able to inaugurate a rebirth of the social life of the city, which was rendered possible by Gilgamesh's experience and strong will, as well as by the fresh cosmic knowledge that lived in Eabani's clairvoyance. Gilgamesh's companion brought clarity to the ruler's choices and deeds. However, the tension between the king and the local initiation temple of Ishtar was not resolved. The sanctuary of Ishtar preserved much, in a syncretistic fashion, from the different sources of knowledge that had lived in the East; but it had entered a stage of decadence. Gilgamesh's consciousness was in many degrees already foreign to that kind of initiation knowledge. He did not understand the spirituality of the sanctuary, and in the myth he complained about the behavior of the goddess. Subsequently, the priests invoked the gods and these brought a punishment upon the city. There were troubles and illnesses, and, as an end result of these, Eabani died.

The friend's death was a heavy blow for the king. Having little connection left with the wisdom of the East, Gilgamesh still yearned to understand immortality of the soul. This question was awakened in Gilgamesh's soul by virtue of the new kind of connection that the king had with his physical body—an element that was foreign as yet to the culture of Asia. In order to get answers to his questions, he went west in search of other centers of wisdom. In his wanderings, the king arrived at a region that is now the modern Burgenland, in Austria. Here he met the school of wisdom of the high priest that the myth calls Utnapishtim, in whom lived the soul of the great initiate Manu. Steiner indicates that this school was an outpost of the Hibernian Mysteries, which preserved the remains of old Atlantean wisdom. Gilgamesh tried to undergo the process of initiation that was offered there. Owing to the particular kind of consciousness he had developed, this was no longer possible for him. A partial initiation was offered to him instead, a substitute, which could partly answer the questions that Eabani's death had stirred in his soul. As a result, Gilgamesh continued to receive inspiration from Eabani, which helped him continue his mission.

Gilgamesh's individuality initiated a new stage of development, which moved toward the later civilizations of the West. Previous to that point all inaugurators of a civilization had been initiates. Gilgamesh had remained, as it were, only on the threshold of initiation, which put a particular stamp on the Chaldean-Babylonian civilization.

During their joint incarnation, the sister souls brought a renewal of civilization to Asia Minor. Their budding new seed of individuality superseded the traditional Mysteries, which had emphasized physical inheritance, for example in the priesthood. A new element pervaded

SETTING THE STAGE: FROM EAST TO WEST

Chaldean-Babylonian civilization, which was an emerging culture of personality, barely at its beginning.

This first incarnation introduces us to what Lievegoed has called the "tragic element" of the succeeding lives of Steiner and Wegman. This consists of individuals who experience a consciousness that is either ahead of their time, or that retains qualities that have been lost by humanity at large. This is also the source of the inner tension that spurs them to bring into civilization elements that only their constitution of soul can offer. In their first incarnation, both Gilgamesh and Eabani carried an awareness that did not prevail in their environment, even though it expressed itself in such radically different ways in the two individuals. Together they took the first steps in moving from the wisdom of the East to the emerging consciousness of the West.

CHAPTER 2

THE EARLIER MICHAEL AGE:
ANCIENT GREECE

Greek civilization ushered in the important transition from the East to the West, and set the foundations for the birth of Europe. The sister souls of Gilgamesh and Eabani too transitioned from the Near East to the European ground, first by participating in the culture of the Greek Mysteries, then by bringing to maturation the whole of Greek philosophy. The eternal soul of Plato played a direct role in ushering in the transition from the culture of the oracles to the schooling of the Mysteries, where the pupil had to undergo the trials of the soul that gave him the necessary maturity for directly apprehending spiritual reality. At a second stage, when the Mysteries entered into a decadent phase, the Plato individuality brought, as it were, Mystery culture into the open, and created a path of individuation through thinking, which was later perfected by Aristotle. There is an important line of development between Socrates, who was Plato's teacher, Plato himself, and Aristotle, who was Plato's pupil. Before turning to these individuals however, it is useful to set the stage of Greek civilization, its history and the evolution of its culture.

I From the Oracles to the Mysteries

Greek civilization, as interpreted by Frederick Hiebel, can be seen as a succession of stages, rising from a mythical consciousness to an identification with the folk-spirit, and finally to individualism and cosmopolitanism.[8] The epochs indicated below are some of the signposts of this evolution.

Mythical Consciousness and Heroic Age: from the onset of Kali Yuga to the Trojan War. This stage refers to the early Aegean civilization, between 3,000 and 2,000 B.C., the Minoan epoch, from 2,000 to 1,600 B.C., and a Mycenean epoch, from 1,600 to 1,100 B.C. The latter was already connected with the half-historical Trojan War. During this age took place the transition from the use of stone to the use of metals. This is also the time of the Greek heroes or demi-gods, who were considered sons of mortal women and of gods, individualities directly inspired by the spiritual world.

After the Trojan War: 12th to 9th century B.C. The Age of Heroes ended with the Trojan War. The fall of Troy also marked the transition from the Bronze Age to the Iron Age, and the emancipation of Greece from the culture of the East. The Iliad and the Odyssey, the earliest records of Hellas, appeared at the beginning of the Iron Age. The historical stage begins after the fall of Troy.

Age of Homer: 9th to 5th century B.C. An important change of consciousness was ushered in when the sun rose on the vernal equinox under the sign of Aries, 747 B.C. This marked the beginning of the age of the Intellectual Soul, and coincided with the rise of the Greek polis (city-state). The polis gradually became a metro-polis, a mother-city with satellite colonies from southern Italy to Turkey.

Persian War: beginning to late 5th century B.C. The turning point in the history of the polis came during the time of Solon in Athens. He became archon—chief magistrate—of Athens around 594–593 B.C., and the reforms of the constitution he initiated laid the foundation for Athenian and Greek democracy. The war against Persia posed a test to the survival of the new consciousness.

---

[8] Frederick Hiebel, *The Gospel of Hellas: the Mission of Ancient Greece and the Advent of Christ*, Chapter 1.

<u>Civil war (Peloponnesian War) to the time of Alexander the Great: end of 5th century to late 4th century B.C.</u> The recognition of membership in the polis weakened, giving rise to the budding feeling of individuality. This transition ushered in the rise of the intellect, with the dangers of complete estrangement from the world of the spirit. It is this threat that Socrates effectively countered, paving the way for the next stage of Hellenic civilization.

Socrates' teachings countered the fall of the city-state and preserved the essence of its spirit in a way fitting the needs of the time. The self-sacrifice of Socrates is a watershed event in the transition from the Greek metropolis to the cosmopolis inaugurated by Alexander the Great under the inspiration of Aristotle. Through it the spirit of Hellas was allowed to travel abroad and was preserved as a gift to humanity in the worldviews of Plato and Aristotle.

The Age of the Heroes

With the fall of Troy, Greece started to emancipate itself from the old clairvoyance of the East, and to map the path towards individualism. The Greeks keenly felt the Twilight of the Gods at this stage, and started to doubt the immortality of the soul, which had been preserved in Eastern culture. Previous to the fall of Troy the heroes, considered sons of mortal women and of gods, paved the path for the Greeks towards individual consciousness and the experience of freedom. Among the heroes were Prometheus who brought the light of the gods to human beings and Hercules, a figure whose deeds prefigured the coming of Christ. Two other heroes we will refer to were Orpheus and Dionysus.

During this period Greek culture also transitioned from the old spirituality of the oracles to the schooling of the individual in the Mystery schools. Key to an understanding of this contrast is the distinction between the upper gods who acted as cosmic forces and the lower gods, who revealed themselves within the human soul. The first were interpreted by the oracles, the latter were apprehended inwardly through the Mysteries.

In early Greek civilization the human being felt the life of the elements around him. He had not developed an independent life of thought. "He did not as yet experience thought; instead of thought there unfolded within his soul a symbolic image… the symbolic picture rose in the soul of man when he contemplated the events of the world."[9] In this way the soul experience continued to be part of the life of nature. The ancient Greek still felt at one with nature, in which he experienced himself just as he would the lightning, the thunder, the life of the plants or the starry sky.

The oracles were consulted for the most important questions of life. The Greeks had recourse to them for prophecy, and for guiding their lives in accordance with the will of the spirit. And in the oracles spoke those individuals who were particularly fitted to converse with spiritual powers.

The revelations of the oracles were of a macrocosmic nature. Auguries were interpreted from doves on the branches of the oak tree or from the murmuring of waters in fountains. The oracles revealed various spheres of the macrocosm, coming progressively closer to earth. Just as Zeus followed Chronos (Saturn), so Apollo, the herald of the Sun, followed the oracles of his father, Zeus. The oracle of Saturn (Chronos) had seen its heyday during the prehistoric epoch in Olympia; the memory of the oracle of Zeus (Dodona) survived in the earliest records of history. The oracle of Apollo was connected with Helios, the Sun god, and reached its climax at the time of the city-state or polis.

In contrast to the oracles, there were the centers of the Mysteries of Hellas in the Cabiri in Samothrace, the temple of Artemis in Ephesus, the Mysteries of Delphi and the rites of Eleusis, which we will follow more closely. The way from Apollo's oracles to the Mysteries of Dionysus led from the polytheism of the early days to monotheism, from tribal consciousness to fuller individuality.

The being through whom the transition from the oracles to the Mysteries was finally accomplished is remembered as Orpheus, another Greek hero. His mission stood midway between Apollo and Dionysus. He was remembered as the inventor of the lyre and the hero who introduced the gift of music, but also as the teacher who brought medicine, writing and agriculture.

---

[9] Rudolf Steiner, *The Riddles of Philosophy*, Chapter 2.

At the time in which the Greek soul was starting to experience the twilight of the gods, music appeared as a compensation for the loss of the original state of communion, as the gift of the light of the cosmos. Orpheus implanted in the souls of men, who still lived within the feeling forces of clairvoyance, the first seed of a faculty which could later germinate and flower as logical thinking, as the power of intellectual discrimination.

The further humankind descended into the life of the senses, the more music, the gift of Orpheus, still granted human being access to the spiritual world. The highest expression of music helped to purify the soul for a higher union with the spirit. Music was the sum of the Mysteries of the weaving and living Logos, the Word of the world. Apollo's artistic impulse restored the distorted harmony between thinking, feeling and willing, allowing the development of the cardinal Greek virtues of wisdom, courage and temperance. And in the harmonized soul functions lay the seeds for the coming faculty of abstract and logical thinking. Furthermore, through Orpheus, the Apollonian oracles, which were exoterically accessible to all, opened the way to the Dionysian Mysteries which were esoteric, and only open to individuals considered fit.

Apollo, the god of the sun, brought the old spirituality of the oracles into relationship with the impulse of the human ego. And, quite significantly, the oracles of Apollo were placed in Delphi, at a central location in the life of ancient Greece. Apollo was the countenance of Helios as Michael was the face of Jehovah to the Hebrews. Just as the moon reflects the light of the sun, so the Delphic Apollo echoed the word of the Logos under the light of the moon. The Pythia received and communicated the word of Apollo at midnight, during nights of full moon.

With the onset of democracy, following Solon's reforms, Apollo became the spiritual leader of Hellas' polis. This was the dawn of geometry, mathematics, natural science and philosophy, all of which underwent a tremendous development in the sixth century BC. Apollo was the messenger and forerunner of the coming Christ impulse. And Apollo was closely allied with Dionysus; as one echoed Greece's past of the oracles, so did the other announce the future of the Mysteries. And Orpheus had created the link between them.

Dionysus the Elder and Dionysus the Younger

Greek myths speak of the transition from Dionysus the Elder (Zagreus) to Dionysus the Younger; this refers to an important change of consciousness. Steiner indicates that the conception of Dionysus the Elder was completely anchored in the life of feelings; it could not have been expressed in the life of thought.[10] The independent ego appeared first as clairvoyance, only later as individual thinking. And quite rightly, the myth presents Dionysus the Elder as the son of Persephone (daughter of Demeter, and therefore related to the earth) and Zeus. The forces of ancient clairvoyance, surging through the element of the Earth and through the forces of the body are, macrocosmically speaking, the elder Dionysus. The macrocosmic forces that accompanied the ego on the path of further incarnation in the human being produced the rudiments of an intellectual culture, but initially completely permeated with imagery. The receding of the type of consciousness associated with Dionysus the Elder was felt as a tragedy by the Greeks, who now faced the spiritual bereavement of life more and more confined to the senses.

The passage from the old clairvoyant consciousness to the new intellectual culture was indicated in Greek myth with the onset of the mission of Dionysus the Younger. Dionysus now stands through the trials of life, and is much more human; he is the macrocosmic representative of the forces of the soul, present within the Ego.[11] Steiner comments, "If he is the macrocosmic counterpart of our intellectual ego-forces, then he must be the intelligence that belongs to all the Earth and extends into the realms of space."[12] Therefore he was imagined as a being moving from land to land, and the legends say that he went to Europe, Egypt, and as far as Arabia and India.

Both Dionysus beings manifested their impulses through a living human being. Dionysus Zagreus carried out his work among the ancient Atlanteans. The legend of the younger Dionysus says he is born of a

---

[10] Rudolf Steiner, *Wonders of the World, Trials of the Soul, Revelations of the Spirit*, lecture of August 22, 1911.

[11] Rudolf Steiner, *Wonders of the World, Trials of the Soul, Revelations of the Spirit*, lecture of August 21, 1911.

[12] Ibid, lecture of August 22, 1911.

human mother, and that he is much closer to human beings than to the gods. Dionysus was one of the old heroes (demi-gods), one of those who set the stage for the transition from the mythical to the historical age. He belonged to the "dim past of prehistoric Greece," and the journeys of the legends really did take place. "At his earthly death, his soul flowed into the intellectual culture of humanity."[13] Plato in his dialogue *Cratylus* derives the etymology of Dionysus' name from didous oinon (oistai—to think): the bringer of thinking. Rudolf Steiner emphasized this characteristic of Dionysus when he pointed out that the Dionysian principle worked on the construction of the brain.[14] Furthermore, it was Dionysus who brought the gift of wine, whose mission was to break down the blood ties upon which atavistic clairvoyance depended, thereby loosening the forces of the earthbound brain.

Dionysus was considered the first teacher of intellectual civilization. However, Steiner indicates that for the Greeks Dionysus' ego had not yet taken full residence in a human being, but was only on the point of doing so. And further, the Greeks imagined that "Dionysus and all belonging to him had such human bodies as were bound to arise if no ego were in them, if the human body were only influenced by the physical, etheric and astral body."[15] These were in fact the forms of the followers of Dionysus, of Dionysus' master, Silenus, and of the satyrs, the forms that one would obtain by separating the ego from the other human sheaths. The satyrs, fauns and Pan represented the forms of Atlantean bodies carried into Greek times. Dionysus worked with those human beings whose bodies had the least of an ego in order to become the first teacher of the ego.

Dionysus, in contrast to the Greek gods, portrayed the adventures of the human soul in the pursuit of earthly knowledge, and in its attainment of spiritual knowledge. Knowledge of these trials was now only open to those who took the paths of the Mysteries, and Dionysus

---

[13] Ibid, lecture of August 22, 1911.

[14] Ibid.

[15] Rudolf Steiner, *Wonders of the World, Trials of the Soul, Revelations of the Spirit*, lecture of August 23, 1911.

was the inaugurator of such Mysteries in Greek civilization.[16] In the times following his physical incarnation, Dionysus became the most important teacher of those Mysteries. "Dionysus appeared as an etheric form in these holy Mysteries, and in connection with him things could now be perceived which were beheld not merely as reflections, by means of ordinary consciousness, but which sprang forth directly out of the inner being of Dionysus. Because Dionysus is in our own selves, each person saw himself in Dionysus, and learned to know himself..."[17] The mystics were taught by Dionysus in the Mysteries, and saw him as a spiritual form "which was entirely controlled by the most important, the most essential part of man's own nature, represented by the human self as it stands firmly planted on the earth." He appeared to the mystics as "a beautiful and dignified form, which outwardly represented man in a glorious manner..." And Dionysus remained the teacher of the Mysteries for a long time.[18]

Concerning the body in which he incarnated, Dionysus did not represent perfection; he did not possess the finest human form. Nor did his followers, the satyrs and fauns. And the teacher of Dionysus himself, Silenus, is said to have been a very ugly man, but a very wise individual. "And we should make a mistake, if we were to picture the teacher and master of this Dionysus—old Silenus—as otherwise than with an ugly snub nose and pointed ears, and not in the least handsome."[19]

Greek civilization recognized in its midst influences that expressed themselves through time and space in the human body. It beheld three archetypes: the Hermes type, the Zeus or Apollo type, and the satyr type. The satyr type, as we have seen, was a decadent remnant of Atlantis. The Zeus type was the racial structure which came from the north. The Hermes type came from the southeast.

The dark-skinned body and curly hair were characteristic of Hamitic populations of North Africa and Semitic populations in Asia Minor. And in Greek mythology Hermes led souls to the netherworld.

---

[16] Rudolf Steiner, *Wonders of the World, Trials of the Soul, Revelations*
[17] Ibid.
[18] Ibid.
[19] Ibid.

He led the soul on the path inward, and was therefore linked with the Dionysian principle. Plato continued to carry the body type of Dionysus; his face in many sculptures carries the features of the Hermes type.

The satyr type of Silenus was carried further in Socrates, the recognized lover of wisdom. The satyrs often appeared with a tail, goats' hooves, hairy skin and horns on their heads, reminiscent of atavistic clairvoyance. They could be recognized by their sensual lips, their short and upturned noses. In the satyr type the forces of the head and those of the limbs worked together, but in animal-like and decadent fashion.

In the Zeus type was found a harmonious blend of all racial features, which derived from Atlantis. The Zeus type is that of the Caucasian or European race, whose gaze is turned toward the external world, and whose forehead shows the development of thinking capacities. Aristotle, the thinker par excellence, or Alexander the Great, the man of action, were represented in the typical Zeus typology.

The polarities between the types of Zeus and Hermes were reflected in Apollo and Dionysus. Zeus and Apollo were the gods of the heights of Olympus, which mythology had assigned to the north of the country. Hermes-Dionysus came from the south, from where the Mysteries of the microcosm had been introduced into Greece. Zeus led to the wonders of the world of nature and the macrocosm; Hermes led the souls to the trials of the underworld.

The two different paths of initiation came together under the same roof, and lived as brothers in the sanctuary of Delphi, which for the Greeks was the navel of the earth. Here the oracle of Apollo and the Mystery school of Dionysus stood side by side. The oracle offered exoteric revelations in which everyone could participate. The Mysteries of Delphi were esoteric and open only to selected neophytes. Apollo stood for the day, the light of the sun and human reason. Dionysus opened the doors to the inner world of dreams and visions. Apollo was more strongly present in the nerves and senses, Dionysus in the blood. In Delphi, over time, the old Apollonian clairvoyance gave way to Dionysian initiation. While the Apollonian oracle was quintessentially Hellenic, the Dionysian Mysteries had a more cosmopolitan flavor, bringing together the wisdom of the Orient and the Occident.

Dionysus, Plato and the Mysteries

Silenus had been the teacher of Dionysus. The two individuals prepared the Greeks to acquire ego-consciousness. In reincarnating, Silenus returned as Socrates, Dionysus as Plato. Now, "...everything that Dionysus and the wise Silenus had been able to do for ancient Greece, was done anew by Socrates and Plato."[20] They returned at the time in which the mystics could no longer perceive clairvoyantly in the Mysteries, when the Mysteries were falling into decadence.

The Mysteries revealed the being of the Logos and foretold the approaching of Christ. The Pythian games at Delphi were devoted almost entirely to contests in music and poetry (the arts of the Word), in singing and playing the flute and the lyre. Through these arts Apollo revealed his mission as the bringer of harmony in the soul. The Logos was still more intimately understood at Ephesus, where it came nearer to the comprehension of the human mind. While music originated in Delphi, Ephesus became the spiritual birthplace of philosophy and natural science. Understanding of the human soul and revelation of the wonders of the world went hand in hand. Ephesus was most intimately associated with Athens, its mother city, and therefore philosophy was soon transplanted to the rising capital of Hellas.

Another Mystery center added to the growing importance of Athens. Eleusis—the most important Mystery center of the final epoch of Hellas—was located only twelve miles from Athens. The spiritual background of Eleusis' Mysteries were the realms of Zeus and Demeter— the Mysteries of the heavens and of the earth whose representatives appeared as their children, Persephone and Dionysus. The myth of Dionysus took a further step in its evolution. It concerned the birth, passions, death and resurrection of the human spirit. Eleusis concerned itself chiefly with the Mysteries of the Fall of Man. And the problem of death, always uppermost in Hellenic thought, acquired urgent relevance in the nocturnal rites of Eleusis.

Eleusis too had two sets of Mysteries. The lesser Mysteries, celebrated in February, recreated the drama of Persephone, aimed at reaching catharsis (purification) in preparation for the next stage.

---

[20] Steiner, *Wonders of the World*, lecture of August 24, 1911.

The Greater Mysteries, those of Dionysus, took place only every five years in September, over nine days. The outcry of Persephone in the lesser Mysteries awakened Dionysus. It was the cry for the birth of the Iacchus-child, or the reborn Dionysus. The drama prophetically depicted "the deity that was to descend into the material world and was buried therein, in order to rise again within man."[21] Iacchus-Dionysus became the bearer of the ego-consciousness, the inaugurator of the epoch of individualism. The anticipation of the Mysteries of the Christ-child planted its seeds in the Greek spirit, which was to play such an important role later in the spread of Christianity.

Athens became the city of Dionysus and incarnated the fullness of the impetus towards individualism. Dionysus had his temple in Athens, and at the foot of the Acropolis stood his theatre. Thus Athens became the stage for his dramas and the center of intellectual activity in Greece. One could say that the last of the Mysteries of Dionysus flowed together and reappeared as drama and philosophy. Due to the importance of these twin impulses Athens became the cultural center of Hellas. Many of the legacies of Greek culture, such as sculpture, painting, history, politics, rhetoric and grammar also originated in Athens or in its immediate hinterland.[22]

The word *theatron* is derived from *theaomai*, which contains the word god— *theos*—and means to admire or worship in devotion. The drama was conceived primarily as an interplay between chorus and monologue, which reflected the dialogue between the human soul and the world's spirit. The human soul became aware of what had been known in the Mysteries, the marriage of Dionysus with Persephone. The theater replaced the temple, and within it all the arts were present, architecture included.

As did its forerunner—Eleusis' drama of Persephone—the early Greek drama brought about catharsis, the purification of the soul. In the movement towards the macrocosm (the Apollonian pole) the

---

[21] Rudolf Steiner, *Aristoteles und das Mysteriendrama*, in Lucifer Gnosis, Berlin 1904, quoted in Frederick Hiebel, *The Gospel of Hellas*, Chapter 5.
[22] Hiebel, *The Gospel of Hellas*, Chapter 3.

overcoming of fear led to devotion and awe; the awareness of egotism in the soul (the Dionysian pole) made room for compassion and love. Thus the Apollonian and Dionysian principles that had accompanied the Greek polis historical phase were once more reunited. And the theater experience set the stage for the rebirth of the ego after the death experience. Greek philosophy became the ripe fruit of all the previous developments we have followed closely.

II The Birth of Philosophy

Dionysus' soul had accompanied the unfolding of Greek Mystery culture. When Mystery culture entered into a declining stage, the inaugurator of the Mysteries returned in the Plato incarnation to guide the next phase of evolution. It reentered Greek culture in close proximity to its old master, Silenus. Socrates and Plato played a crucial role in the evolution of Greek philosophy for the centuries to come.

Gilgamesh/Wegman and Eabani/Steiner followed these developments closely as well. They first reincarnated in the culture of the Mysteries of Ephesus under the guidance of the great Heraclitus. Later they brought Greek philosophy and culture to its blossoming in the form of Aristotelianism and Greek cosmopolitanism.

Greek consciousness was the most fit to offer the world philosophy and sharpen the tool of thinking, critical for the development of western civilization. This is because thinking had an intimately living quality. Both Greek words *theoria* and *idea* are connected with the activity of seeing. Theoria is derived from *horao* (to see) and idea from *oida*, which denotes simultaneous acts of knowing and seeing.[23] The idea was thus objectively apprehended at the same time as it was inwardly known. In Greece one could say thought was known as perception.

Another important change following the development of the personality was the awakening of conscience. The word for conscience, *synesis*, was first used by Euripides in his Medea, around 431 B.C.[24] This marked the time in which the individual awoke from the group

---

[23] Hiebel, *The Gospel of Hellas*, Chapter 1.
[24] Ibid.

consciousness of the polis. Up to that time individual and public morality were one and the same.

The birth of philosophy occurred in the 6th century B.C., a very important century, which marked the beginning of the Michael Age and saw the activity of Buddha in India. At that time the first statues of Apollo appeared in Greece, and Pythagoras became the pupil of Zarathustra in Babylonia. Individuals like Pherekydes of Syros, Thales of Miletus, Anaximander, Xenophanes, Heraclitus, Empedocles, all lived and worked between the 6th and 5th centuries B.C. The impetus for the philosophers' wisdom came from the Mysteries even though it evolved outside of them. And central among the Mysteries was the light that shone from Ephesus, in the form of the teachings about the Logos. Through these teachings a transition took place from the old image consciousness, as it still partly survived in Pythagoras, to intellectualism. However, with the death of the old clairvoyant consciousness came new dangers.

Anaxagoras was the first to formulate a mechanical theory of the universe, declaring that the moon reflected the light of the sun. Democritus only accelerated the movement towards a mechanistic and materialistic view of nature. In his philosophy nature is completely deprived of soul and life, and a wall is built between the inner world and nature. In essence this is the first time a completely materialistic worldview emerged to the surface of consciousness.[25]

The triumph of the dry intellect took a big step in the sophistry of Protagoras, Gorgias, Kritias, Hippias, Prodikus and others. The divine world gave way to the world of man. Logos became *dialogos* (dialogue), and it evolved into dialectic. Hiebel calls dialectic "spoken thought and thinking speech."[26]

This signified a further estrangement of Greek thinking from nature and the cosmos. The newly developing sophistry pushed dialogue to a simple exercise in thinking: arguing for arguing's sake, exalting the presumed capacity of the intellect to reach the living truth. Sophistry, pushed to its limits, led to skepticism and materialism.

---

[25] Steiner *The Riddles of Philosophy*, Chapter 2.
[26] Hiebel, *The Gospel of Hellas*, Chapter 10.

Socrates appeared at a time when Hellas faced the risk of falling into unrestrained individualism. He himself was a dialectician and a sophist. However, he elevated thinking and redirected it towards the pursuit of truth, rather than dispersing it into superficial inquiries. He called himself a "midwife of thought" and prepared the transition from the guidance of the gods towards the voice of conscience. He resolutely turned away from the Mysteries or oracles, for he deeply trusted what thinking alone could achieve. Through his supreme sacrifice, he preserved dialectic, and proved what he had achieved in his teaching: the immortality of the soul.

We will now follow the sequence of incarnations that led to the birth of Platonism and Aristotelianism and the beginning of our odyssey.

Cratylus and Mysa

The next incarnation of Gilgamesh and Eabani occurred in Greece in proximity to the temple of Ephesus. The wisdom taught in Ephesus formed the last link with the wisdom of the East. Its position in Asia Minor aptly symbolizes the nature of the transition occurring at the time. The Greeks were beginning to feel very much at home on earth, rather than in the whole cosmos. In Ephesus the instruction given to the pupils was independent of time and place. It already emphasized individual preparation through exercises assigned to the pupils. An example is the manner in which two individuals worked together to ascertain the properties of plants and their medicinal use. A teacher and a pupil would often go and study plants in nature together. One would observe the plants' outer aspect; the other observed the processes at work within it (for example, the flow of the sap). They would allow their respective experiences to mature through the night, and then compare each other's discoveries. The plant's use would thus be determined on the basis of the image the two individuals built together.[27]

In Ephesus for the first time, personal development and maturity completely superseded the previous role of heredity and blood. Ephesus

---

[27] Steiner, *True and False Paths in Spiritual Investigation*, lectures of August 14, August 15 and August 19, 1924.

was also the last Mystery Center to preserve retrospective knowledge of all earlier stages of cosmic evolution of the earth. This retrospective knowledge extinguished the yearning that arose, particularly in Gilgamesh, about the soul's origin and its immortality.

In the Greek incarnation, both souls we are closely following experienced consciously what had lived earlier in their unconscious. Consequently they fully apprehended the world of the spirit while also consciously beholding earthly reality. Both of them knew that what survived in Greece was now just a shadow of something far greater that had lived in the old East.

Eabani/Steiner returned to incarnate as Cratylus, whose name alone survives in history. We know that Plato wrote a book entitled *Cratylus, About the Correctness of Names.* Gilgamesh/Wegman was now a female pupil of his, called Mysa. Significantly, Mysa, or Misia, was the name of the earth-mother Demeter. Her daughter was Artemisia, also called Persephone. The name Mysa is one that Steiner later used affectionately in letters to Wegman. Cratylus and Mysa were disciples of Heraclitus, a fiery and passionate philosopher, a teacher born in Ephesus, who tried to fight with every fiber of his being against the decay of the Mysteries.

A word about Heraclitus is necessary here, given the importance of this individual and his teachings. The philosopher was still following the Mysteries, and he makes this clear when he says that his is "a path which is difficult to travel." Moreover, this is why he was called "the obscure."[28] Heraclitus, a choleric, stressed that becoming has more importance than being; this is because he experienced in his soul the world becoming. "The world soul pulsates in his own human soul and communicates to it of its own life as long as the human soul knows itself as living in it."[29] Out of this immersion in the world soul, Heraclitus spoke of the spirit as a consuming fire, albeit a fire of a higher order. As fire melts down matter, so the fire of the spirit melts sense-bound cognition and frees cognition of the eternal.

Because the universe is in perpetual motion, Heraclitus saw the

---

[28] Steiner, *Christianity as a Mystical Fact and the Mysteries of Antiquity*, 1902, Chapter "Greek sages before Plato in the light of the Mystery Wisdom."

[29] Steiner, *The Riddles of Philosophy*, Chapter 2.

creative role of strife that transforms and moves things to new stages of harmony. Man carries the spirit in himself, within the conflict of the elements that build him up. The spirit, which is freed in the human being, must be able to pacify the elements and their apparent strife. And, in the end, the same force that begets the conflict is able, through our cognition, to dissolve and resolve the conflict. The philosopher had fully experienced the transitory in light of the eternal, and could therefore see beyond the polarities at work in the world. He illustrated this in some of his fragments, like the following: "Living and dead are the same, and so are waking and sleeping, youth and age. For the one in changing becomes the other, and the other, changing, again becomes the one."[30]

Heraclitus is one of the first philosophers of the Logos. Richard Geldard points out that more than twenty of Heraclitus' known fragments refer to it, either directly or indirectly.[31] The Logos of Heraclitus was the moving principle of the created and constantly creating world. Through the Logos the will of the creator becomes visible. In the Logos the action of opposing forces reaches a higher goal. In the Logos time does not exist, and opposing forces are simultaneously in motion in a unity that is constantly in movement, yet also absolutely still. The physical universe would not come to manifestation without the presence and power to manifest of the Logos. We owe our existence to the Logos, we derive our sense of meaning through it, and we long for immortality because of the eternal nature of the Logos. Thus Heraclitus brought the Logos-idea into relation with the human soul.

Cratylus, the disciple of Heraclitus, had a role in developing new arts of speech and of healing. He taught the then very young Plato, who consequently went to Athens where he created his famous Academy. Mysa was now a disciple of Cratylus, and in her soul lived the shattering realization that the incarnated human being was becoming egotistical; this tendency had been foreshadowed in the soul of Gilgamesh. Mysa stood in time as a forerunner of later stages of development of the human race. The Mysteries of Ephesus brought upon its disciples the

---

[30] Steiner, *Christianity as a Mystical Fact*, Lecture: "Greek sages before Plato in the light of the Mystery Wisdom, 70.

[31] Richard Geldard, *Remembering Heraclitus*, 51.

depth of experience that surfaced in the soul as fear, anxiety, and terror. These experiences later awakened from within the ability to relate to all other human and living beings with compassion and understanding, thus tempering the egotistical tendency ushered in by the development of individuality.

The Ephesus incarnation served a particular purpose, as we hear in the *World History and the Mysteries* lecture cycle:

> And so these two personalities [Cratylus and Mysa] were able, on the one hand, to judge the spiritual of the higher world that came to them as a result of life experience, and that lived in them as an echo from their earlier incarnations. And now, as the origin of the kingdoms of nature was communicated to them in the Mystery of Ephesus under the influence of the goddess Artemis, they were able to judge how the things on the earth external to humanity came into being. ... And the life of these two personalities (which partly coincided with the last years of Heraclitus living in Ephesus, and partly with the period that followed) became inwardly imbued with the light of great cosmic secrets.
>
> The time of Ephesus was relatively peaceful; a time of digestion and assimilation of all that had passed through their souls in earlier, more agitated times.[32]

Another soul, intimately connected with the Eabani/Cratylus individuality, appears here as Plato; one that Steiner indicated as the previous incarnation of Karl Julius Schröer. This was an important relationship, which is demonstrated by the fact that Cratylus descended anew into incarnation very soon after his death, coming into contact with Plato once more. The reincarnated Cratylus is known to history as Aristotle. The sister soul of Gilgamesh/Mysa reappeared as Alexander the Great. The previous incarnation in proximity of the Mysteries of

---

[32] Steiner, *World History and the Mysteries in the Light of Anthroposophy*, lecture of December 27, 1923.

Ephesus had laid the basis for what reappeared subsequently in the souls of Aristotle and Alexander the Great.

A very significant event marked the stage upon which the twin souls returned. The birth of Alexander the Great in 356 BC occurred on the same day that Herostratus sealed the fate of the Mysteries of Ephesus by burning its temple. A transition into a new stage of consciousness emerged at this point. The last link with the Mysteries of the East was erased.

Plato: Spirit and Matter

Plato, an Athenian through and through, claimed Solon, the lawgiver and poet, as his ancestor. He embarked early on a career of drama, oratory, acting and poetry, becoming a successful playwright. A secure political career was open to him if he sought it, due to his aristocratic descent. In coming across Socrates and his teachings, however, Plato's life was completely changed. He decided to burn all of his plays and follow a soul with whom he had already been closely associated in his Dionysus incarnation.

When Socrates died, Plato decided to write down the *Dialogues*, in which he consecrated Socrates' dialectic. Plato the philosopher was born. The new quest set him on a long journey, first to Megara (Attica), where he worked with Euclid, then to Egypt, Cyrene, Magna Grecia, and Sicily. He returned to Athens at about age forty.

In his *Dialogues* Plato presented ideas which had their origin in the mission of Dionysus. But, whereas the Dionysian Mysteries previously led to clairvoyance, the *Dialogues* inaugurated the method of thinking. They were in fact dramas of knowledge, leading to a *catharsis*, to an early stage of awakening the force of conscience.

Plato's Dialogues

In the *Dialogues* Plato exalted the personality of Socrates, who appears as the master addressing his pupils. Socrates died in the manner of an initiate, and in so doing, he kept teaching his pupils about immortality. "His personality, knowing by experience the valuelessness of life, here acts as a proof of a quality very different from all logic and intellectual reasoning. It is not as though a man were conversing—for this man is at the point of crossing the threshold of death—but as though the eternal truth itself, which had made its abode in a transitory personality, were speaking."[33]

Socrates' choices represented the position of Plato. They both refused to belong to the Mysteries, because they wanted to discuss ideas publicly and develop the budding faculty of thinking. In the first dialogue (*Apology*) Socrates speaks about his mission, to help each man "take care of his soul." And in the *Apology* Socrates refers to God thirteen times.[34] His notion of a monotheistic God was new to the Greeks, and a departure from tradition of his time.

Many dialogues offer a review of the important stages of Socrates' heroic death. The *Euthyphro* portrays Socrates in discussion outside the court where he was to be prosecuted on charges of impiety and of corrupting youth. The *Apology* describes his defense before the Athenian jury, and the *Crito* a conversation during his subsequent imprisonment. Finally, this is brought to the conclusion in the *Phaedo*, which recounts the events and conversations that occurred on the day that Socrates was put to death and had to drink a mixture containing poison hemlock.

The dialogues are based on the Socratic method of question and answer. They portray how the students can make the effort of reaching their own conclusions. They offer directions for moral and ethical behavior, and provide a firm foundation for seeking higher truth and esoteric knowledge. Steiner argues that when the listeners had finished listening to a dialogue, they had found in themselves something they did not possess before. They had experienced a process of inner development, not just absorbed an abstract truth. They had in fact undergone something similar to an initiation. "As a teacher of philosophy, Plato wanted, insofar as possible through this medium, to be what the initiator was in the Mysteries."[35]

---

[33] Steiner, *Christianity as a Mystical Fact*, Chapter 3.

[34] Carol Dunn, *Plato's Dialogues: Path to Initiation*, 99.

[35] Steiner, *Christianity as a Mystical Fact*, Rudolf Steiner, Chapter "Plato as Mystic."

There is no absolute agreement among scholars about a detailed chronology of Plato's *Dialogues*. This is also the opinion of Carol Dunn, who only categorizes early, middle and late dialogues.[36] Let us look in more detail at the evolution of the content and teachings of the dialogues:

- First stage: definition and actualization of the virtues (*Euthyphro, Laches, Charmides, Ion, Hippias Major*). Putting the virtues into action in everyday life. The desire to live a virtuous life is the first rung of the ladder.

- Second stage: higher knowledge of the immortality of the soul, through the ideas of recollection, transmigration of the soul (reincarnation), and law of cause and effect (karma) found in the *Meno, Phaedo, Phaedrus, Symposium* and *Republic*. Such teachings change the pupil's perception of his place in the world. They deepen the motivation of the seeker in the pursuit of the virtues.

- Third Stage: higher esoteric truths reached through the *quadrivium*: mathematics, geometry, astronomy and music. The higher realms can only be approached by analogy and symbol. They can be contemplated from the realm of pure thought alone.

- Beyond these lies Socrates' experience of oneness with the "Good."[37]

At the lower levels we have to do with a "dialectic of division" ("elenchus dialectic") in which the philosopher continuously chooses between two possibilities in seeking a definition.[38] The definition will separate the object from all other objects and identify its uniqueness.

At the third stage, at the level of the *quadrivium*, we are dealing with a dialectic of union and inclusion. It separates the essences from all sensible objects. For Plato the sensible world is the embodiment of

---

[36] Dunn, *Plato's Dialogues*, xi.
[37] Ibid, PART I.
[38] Ibid, 61.

plurality; the supersensible world is a world of encompassing unity. Further on, in the attempt to apprehend the supreme Good, direct experience can only be communicated in images and symbols.

First Stage

Socrates discusses different virtues in specific dialogues: courage in *Laches*, piety in *Euthyphro*, temperance in *Charmides*, the beautiful in *Hippias Major*, etc. In each case Socrates first tries to define the essence of the virtue. Each participant offers his own views, and these can evolve as the dialogue progresses. Socrates seeks from all the participants the universal, the Form or Idea, which covers all manifestations of the virtue. In the early dialogues the participants do not reach the goal of finding a definition of the virtue. *Euthyphro* is named after the man of piety, a theologian. Even he cannot come up with a valid answer about piety. The same is true of Laches, a soldier, when he has to come up with a definition of courage in the dialogue of the same name.

No idea is found in the early dialogues, simply because the participants are not yet able to reach the goal, and Socrates can only go as far as they go. The students also fail because they need to seek understanding at a higher stage. This is just the beginning of their journey, and they are not equipped to offer the necessary answers.

The teaching of the virtues also has another goal, in addition to the immediately apparent one. Courage is what leads us, as in the case of Socrates, to disregard our body and follow the demands of the spirit, even when these demands endanger the body. The senses do not convey the eternal in its true form. Therefore what is eternal has to be apprehended by that which is eternal in us. And by living in the spirit (away from the senses) we immerse ourselves in the truth.

For Plato, thoughts stem from the spirit; they arise like memories, which are not gained from material reality. Thoughts are eternal: mathematical theorems will remain true even if the world were to collapse. Thought and truth are related to everything which is eternal and unchangeable; the body is ever-changing, mortal and dissoluble. So the path of the senses and the body, and the path of the spirit, are mutually exclusive.

Second Stage

At this stage are offered teachings that originated in the Mysteries. In *Meno* Socrates posits that the soul is immortal, and that if we tried hard, we would recollect what the soul knew in previous lives, or in the time before we incarnated. Thus for Socrates knowledge is an act of recollecting. He points to this by showing how a person with little formal education (e.g. a slave boy) can show great mental agility when given an opportunity, and surprise those around him.

The dialogue *Phaedo* captures Socrates' state of mind on the day of his execution. After some preparation, Socrates speaks of polarities: death and life, waking and sleeping, and how one generates the other (e.g. life generates death and vice-versa). Here immortality is linked to recollection, and knowledge acquired in the spiritual world before birth is shown as a proof of immortality of the soul.

Socrates outlines ideas that correspond to the existence of a heaven and a purgatory, by saying that the good soul will be in the presence of God in the afterlife; whereas the soul that has dwelt in earthly pleasures alone will remain close to earth, and be pulled back into physical existence earlier than the virtuous soul. The former needs education in the form of suffering, and therefore will return to life on earth sooner, where it can correct its mistakes.

The general theme of the dialogue *Phaedrus* is the relationship between the spiritual and material worlds, and the harmonizing role of love. The soul is likened to a "pair of winged steeds controlled by a charioteer." One steed seeks after the highest ideals; the other acts in an opposite way. The charioteer is torn between the two, and has to struggle to direct the chariot towards the good. In *The Republic* Plato goes a step further. He distinguishes a rational soul that lives in the life of ideas and becomes aware of itself in thought perception. But another part of the soul is not equally aware: the non-rational soul, in which thoughts are not active and ideas are not received. This is a twofold soul, which appears on one hand as the courage-developing soul that exerts the will, and on the other as the appetitive soul, turned to the senses. It is only in the immortal rational soul that we manifest our eternal nature in the life of the spirit. However, the human being lives in all aspects of the soul, and the philosopher educates all three of them. This education results from the ascendance of the rational souls over the other two souls. In the rational soul Plato felt called to develop *wisdom*, in the courage-developing soul *fortitude*, and in the appetitive soul *temperance*. The three virtues working in harmony with each other develop *justice*, which directs the human being towards the good.[39] The realization of the complexity of the life of the soul marks a milestone in philosophy; through Plato the soul reflects on its own nature. Thought ventures to express what the soul is, and feels itself at home in the eternal. It creates the yearning for the spirit.

The knowledge of karma leads to the idea, however corrupted from its earlier forms, of the soul's repeated lives on earth. The goal of the soul is to arrive at a place beyond the heavens, where true being dwells. It will take 10,000 years for souls on earth to return to the place from where they came. The exceptions are the philosophers who sought after wisdom, or those who truly loved each other with passion and yearned for the truth, who will not have to wait that long.

Third Stage

The Symposium is Plato's dialogue on love, and it describes an initiation. This is the dialogue that includes the Diotima/Socrates dialogue about the most transcendental experience of the divine (the Good).

In the Symposium different kinds of men speak of a love that corresponds to their stage of growth—the stage at which their *daimon* stands. Socrates speaks from the perspective of a man of cognition. For him love is more than Eros, which stands for the longing for beauty and goodness. But Socrates also wants to convey more than his thoughts. He speaks about "a revelation which a woman [Diotima] gave him." Diotima must be sought in the soul of Socrates himself. This is the force of the soul, the maternal principle, which gives birth to the Son of God, the Logos. The feminine element, as the unconscious force of love, allows the instreaming of the divine.[40] In Steiner's words, "If wisdom,

---

[39] Steiner, *Riddles of Philosophy*, Chapter 2.
[40] Steiner, *Christianity as a Mystical Fact*, Chapter 3.

the eternal Word (Logos), is the Son of the Eternal Creator of the world, then love has a maternal relationship with the Logos."[41]

The Republic is considered the crowning achievement of the *Dialogues*. It deals with the individual and collective levels (the state). While Book I examines what the city is and what its needs are, Book III contemplates the education of the "guardians," those who are trained to become its rulers. The guardians are people who need to be initiated, and in the attempt, renounce the appeal of the material world and turn their aspirations to the higher goals of the spirit. Basically Socrates wants the philosophers to be rulers, because they can recognize wisdom and beauty. And the knowledge of the person of wisdom is not opinion, but science.

It is also in this dialogue that Plato indicates the nature of the higher stage of learning. He harkens back to Pythagoras' *quadrivium* of mathematics, geometry, astronomy and music. In fact in this dialogue Pythagoras is mentioned by name, whereas he is hardly ever mentioned before.[42] And at this point Socrates wants to approach the highest realm of being, that of the Good. But he declares that he will only speak of the "offspring of the Good itself," not of the Good proper. Something comes to a conclusion that had not appeared in the previous dialogues. Until now the virtues had been approached as all separate from each other; now, Socrates invites us to see them as all part of a whole, of a unity. And he places us on the way towards identifying—or rather, experiencing— the Good, above the ideas. To do this one must turn away from the world of becoming, towards the world of true being. To reach this new level the four disciplines of the *quadrivium* must be approached in a way that transcends the sensible world. What is sought is the understanding of transcendental affinities, concordances, polarities.

In mathematics, the pupil grasps number through pure thought in order to arrive at its true essence. In geometry, through the contemplation of the Platonic solids he apprehends the nature of the elements and of the ether. In his *Timaeus* Plato associates four of the solids with the four basic elements—fire, air, water, and earth, through which matter comes

---

[41] Ibid, Chapter "Plato as Mystic."

[42] Dunn, *Plato's Dialogues*, 52.

into manifestation. Plato assigns the tetrahedron, with its sharp points and edges, to the element fire; the cube, with its four-square regularity, to earth; the octahedron and the icosahedron to air and water, respectively. For Plato the dodecahedron, with its twelve pentagonal faces, points to the heavens with its twelve constellations.

Astronomy deals with the movements of solids in the universe, which are patterns, illustrations of deeper truths of existence. Music shows much of what is at work behind the other disciplines. It must be approached in a way transcending audible sound, because the ultimate meaning of sound is found in its polarity, silence.

In arriving at the apprehension of the Good, Socrates tells us, we are at the limit of the intelligible. This is a second threshold, just as there is a threshold between the sensible worlds and the supersensible worlds. Beyond this second threshold lies the Good itself. If the pupil Glaucon wants to apprehend the last realities, he can only continue the road on his own, even if the required maturity could be only reached in a future incarnation. Socrates has shown Glaucon that it is possible.

All of Plato's philosophy still looked to what lived beyond the physical, in the realm of ideas, intended as the reality of living, spiritual beings. Plato felt his heart and limbs still united with the surrounding spiritual world, but his head and thinking starting to be isolated from it. He could still inwardly experience ideas full of content. In him an idea was a world-creative principle, a living, though diminished, perception of the creative power of the Logos. Ideas were like the shadows that light would cast on a cave wall, a shadow of the spirit.

New knowledge had to penetrate further into the reality of the physical world and be elaborated in clear thoughts. It was this mission that Plato entrusted to Aristotle, who was his disciple for eighteen years. Plato had been looking for the spirit *behind* matter; Aristotle needed to lead humanity to the understanding of the spirit *within* matter. In history, this episode has been transmitted as if Aristotle had been a contrary pupil, bent on doing things in his own way and causing Plato to retire from the Academy in Athens. This interpretation is understandable, because later on Aristotle was persecuted by the Athenians, who viewed with suspicion his new teachings; and they further resented him as a foreigner of the Greek diaspora. The truth of Aristotle's departure from his master, however, corresponded to the deeper necessities of world evolution.

Plato's soul was still able to behold the imaginations that the soul witnesses in life before birth. Aristotle could no longer make use of this; he confined his philosophy to what the soul could gather solely from earthly experience. Through entering this next stage of consciousness, the Greek soul lost access to the idea of pre-existence and hence to the reality of reincarnation and karma.

Aristotle: A Search for the Spirit in Matter

Plato's worldview was essentially dualistic. In perceiving nature as an insurmountable obstacle to the human spirit, he was unable to reconcile spirit and matter. Aristotle saw the path from matter to the spirit, while still sensing the roots of his thinking in initiation knowledge. Plato represented the sunset of a whole era; Aristotle formed the dawn of a new one.

Aristotle was born of mixed Macedonian and Thracian blood, and was what the Greeks considered a barbarian; he never acquired political rights in Athens. He was orphaned early in life, and joined Plato's academy at age seventeen. Throughout his life he was regarded with suspicion by the Athenians, who could not forgive his links to Philip and Alexander of Macedonia.

Plato recognized the higher stature of Aristotle among all of his students by calling him the "Nous of the Academy" (intelligence personified). And the two towering geniuses had a continuous impact upon each other. Hiebel indicates that Aristotle tried to Platonize his world conception while at the Academy. And at the end of his life Plato adopted a more methodological approach in his dialogues (*Theaetetus, Sophist, Statesman, Parmenides* and *Philebus*), attesting to the influence of the younger philosopher.[43]

Aristotle called his teacher "the man whom it is not lawful for bad men even to praise, who alone as first of mortals clearly revealed, by

---

[43] Hiebel, *The Gospel of Hellas*, Chapter 11

his own life and by the method of his words, how a man becomes good and happy at the same time..."[44] And the younger man made it a point to remain at the Academy until Plato's death. Even after his death, he continued to work closely with some of Plato's most conservative disciples.

At the end of Plato's life Aristotle and his patron conducted the famous "disputation" in Eleusis. It is from this event that Aristotle's two streams of writings originate. On one hand stood the works of natural science, in which Aristotle propagated the Mystery wisdom of the past (especially that of Eleusis) as it had been taught in Plato's Academy. These included teachings about stars, heavens, plants, animals, physiognomy, memory, sleep and dreams, geography, meteorology, ethnology,... The other stream included the logical works, which were later entrusted to Theophrastus.

After the death of Plato, Aristotle founded his own schools at Assos and Mytilene, but then abandoned these prestigious endeavors to become teacher of the thirteen-year old Alexander. A student of exoteric history might wonder what led him to give up all of his life's pursuits for a mere adolescent! Later, when Alexander launched his Eastern campaign, the philosopher located his school on the grounds of the sanctuary to Apollo Lyceus, inaugurating the famous Lyceum, which was the first university or school of knowledge independent of the Mysteries. It was also Aristotle who introduced the use of libraries, so important for any modern center of knowledge.

Frederick Hiebel recognizes three main phases in Aristotle's life, and their connection with the metamorphosed wisdom of the Mysteries.

- The first 20 years (ages 17-37): studying under Plato's guidance at the Athens academy. The first period was under the spiritual influence of the Mysteries of Eleusis.

- The middle 13 years: starting to travel, founding his own schools in Mytilene and Assos, instructing Alexander the Great (at ~ age 41). The second period received the spiritual impulses of the Mysteries of Samothrace.

---

[44] Aristotle, *De anima* III/ 3, quoted in Hiebel, *The Gospel of Hellas*, Chapter 11.

- The last 14 years: founding the Lyceum in Athens. In the third period, Hiebel estimates that Aristotle "rebuilt, spiritually, the temple of Ephesus." Among other things he transformed the teachings of the Logos into the new science of logic. In these last years he organized the presentation of all his work in treatises.[45]

To say that Aristotle received the spiritual influences of the Mysteries could be misleading. In his lifetime he strongly repudiated not only the oracles and the old clairvoyance, but also the Mysteries themselves, which he knew had fallen into decadence. He did, however, resurrect the wisdom of these Mysteries in new forms. He held on to the best influences that had previously emanated from the Mysteries, in whose final phase he had participated during his last incarnation. This he accomplished while emancipating man's thinking from the Mysteries through logic, metaphysics and natural science. Unfortunately, unlike all of Plato's writings, which have been preserved, that is hardly the case for Aristotle's opus. Let us look at the three main fields of Aristotle's work.

It is Steiner's estimate that "With [Aristotle] the process of absorption of thought life into the world conception has been completed and come to rest."[46] Plato had used thinking to move beyond what presents itself as object in the external world; in his judgment the idea hovered above the object, without fully penetrating it. Aristotle's thinking penetrated right into the object itself and revealed the idea within it. For him the ideas fully animated the objects in the physical world. Armed with this understanding, Aristotle went further than Plato in looking not only at the soul as object of knowledge, but looking at the act of knowledge itself. He can thus investigate the laws of thinking itself through the newly established logic.

In his very first works, Aristotle laid the foundations of logic, which he considered more of an art than a science. In his soul, thinking was still akin to perception. Mind had no less reality than the external

---

[45] Hiebel, *The Gospel of Hellas*, Chapter 11.
[46] Steiner, *Riddles of Philosophy*, Chapter 2.

world. Through the exertion of the mind beyond the surface appearance of the senses, the soul could reach to the immortal and eternal. The philosopher claimed that the experience of immortality was possible. In this effort the human being came in contact with his *daimon*, his genius, or conscience, which awakens to the knowledge of one's divine origin.

Logic allowed Aristotle to transform the knowledge of the Mysteries into the language of the intellect. Let us look at the well-known logical tool of the syllogism, such as the famous "All men are mortal; Socrates is a man; therefore, Socrates is a mortal." The above can be expressed in mathematical terms as $A = B$, and $A = C$; therefore, $B = C$. This example best illustrates how the rules of logic correspond to self-evident truths, just like a geometric axiom. In fact the syllogism has a geometric architecture. Its terms can be subdivided into:

Major premise: All men are mortal
Minor premise: Socrates is a man
Conclusion: Socrates is mortal

Socrates is the minor term; men the middle term, common to the two premises; mortal the major term. The middle term appears in each of the premises but not in the conclusion. The terms in the conclusion are called the extremes. In this movement from the minor to the major we are moving in three concentric circles (from Socrates, the minor at the center, men in the middle layer, mortal in the periphery). Thus Aristotle's logic (and the syllogism) can be represented geometrically.

The syllogism finds its last refinement in the idea of entelechy, concludes Hiebel.[47] Entelechy is composed of three words: *entos* (inner, or within), *telos* (aim, purpose) and *echo* (have). The whole means "I have within me the aim or purpose." *Telos* was used in the Mysteries to mean initiation. In entelechy the principle of initiation is transformed into the initiative of the free mind, which reaches the realization in the human being "having the aim within himself." Here the major premise is: "I am within me; the minor premise states: I am is the goal, aim or purpose; the conclusion is: the goal, aim, purpose (*telos*) is within myself."

---

[47] Hiebel, *The Gospel of Hellas*, Chapter 11.

For Plato the body was the prison of the soul; for Aristotle it was the instrument and organ of the soul. With this new understanding Aristotle could now look at the natural world, and study its evolution from the mineral to the plant and animal realm. Such an inquiry would not have felt meaningful to Plato.

After turning his gaze to plant and animal, Aristotle sees that beyond what is present in the plant and animal—the body-soul element—the human being carries a soul-spirit entity. The soul-spirit makes use of the body-soul element as of an instrument, but exerts its work well beyond the capacity of the body-soul complex. The human being has a conscience, which is lacking in the lower realms And Aristotle further elaborates the role of conscience, which is only embryonically present in Plato's metaphysics. In his *Ethics* he points to repentance as the psychological phenomenon aroused by conscience, and the springboard for virtue.[48] Not being able to experience repentance leads to a state of mind that is the opposite of moral virtue.

In parallel to the above, what Aristotle sees in the soul of man evolves in complexity in relation to what Plato had discerned. Aristotle defines other levels of the soul:

- *threptikon*, the vegetative, plant-like soul
- *aisthetikon*, the sentient, animal-like soul
- *oreptikon*, the soul that develops desire
- *kinetikon*, that part of the soul that lives in the will
- *dianoetikon*, the spirit-soul[49]

In the spirit-soul Aristotle recognizes further:

- *Nous pathetikos*: the passive thought
- *Nous poietikos*: the willing within thinking[50]

---

[48] Hiebel, *The Gospel of Hellas*, Chapter 1.
[49] Steiner, *Riddles of Philosophy*, Chapter 2.
[50] Hiebel, *The Gospel of Hellas*, Chapter 11.

More so than Plato, Aristotle clearly recognizes a spiritual element at the border of the soul, not just a soul element. The transition occurring in the human being marks the dividing line between a material world where idea and matter coexist, and a world above this, inhabited by beings and events of a purely spiritual nature; and the spirit-soul (*dianoetikon*) of man belongs to this world.

Aristotle has articulated a philosophy of the will, a philosophy of freedom. This is what Aristotle implies in his *Nicomachean Ethics*: "It is not possible to be good in the strict sense without practical wisdom, nor practically wise without moral virtue." His basic virtues—temperance, courage, justice, friendship—become avenues to freedom. Higher than these are the *dianoetic* virtues: art, reason, acting according to conscience. Conscience places reason in relation to wisdom (Sophia), the noblest of virtues. "Wisdom is pure reason and spirit united with knowledge." Reason is seen as pure *theoria*, which conceives the idea while perceiving it. And this is the basis upon which rests the unity of thought and action. "Mind must be related to what is thinkable, as sense is to what is sensible."[51] And it follows that mind itself must be able to think itself, just as objects are thinkable.

Aristotle's philosophy reached its pinnacle in the idea of human individuality, and the knowledge of immortality that the Greek soul, already so identified with the material world, was starting to doubt. Aristotle had to strengthen the idea of individual immortality at the expense of the last traces of knowledge of karma and reincarnation that survived in an already fragmentary and often confused fashion in Plato; those ideas would have hindered the human being's path toward further individuation and penetration of the physical world.

At the birth of Alexander the Temple of Ephesus went up in flames, but what had lived in Ephesus remained engraved in the cosmic ether. It's as if this wisdom with which Aristotle and Alexander had been so deeply connected in their last lives were now available in a new form outside of the temple. While Ephesus had been brought to an end, the Mysteries of the Kabiri at Samothrace were still a place for the active cultivation

---

[51] Aristotle, *De anima* III/ 3, quoted in Hiebel, *The Gospel of Hellas*, Chapter 11.

of the Mysteries. Through the influence of the Samothrace Mysteries there arose in Alexander and Aristotle something like a memory of the Ephesian time which both of them had lived through in their Cratilus and Mysa incarnations. And further, "Now when the cosmic sounding in the Moon [sphere through which the pupil of Ephesus received the spiritual revelations] was there again and Aristotle and Alexander recognized what the fire at Ephesus had signified, when they saw how this fire had carried forth into the far ether of the world the content of the Mysteries of Ephesus, then it was that there arose in these two the inspiration to found the Cosmic Script."[52] And this is the script that formed the thoughts spelled out as categories. In these categories, which encompassed the secrets of the spiritual and physical worlds, the ancient Greek could live within concepts, experience them in his soul, and read them in the cosmos.

In fact categories and concepts are interchangeable terms. "With the same justice one might say: all concepts are categories, as one might say: all categories are concepts."[53] A concept is constructed completely within the spirit. It does not derive from the observation. "The whole network of concepts that a man possesses… you may represent as a tablet, forming the boundary between the supersensible and sensible worlds. Between these two spheres the world of concepts forms the boundary."

When one approaches the world of the senses armed with concepts/categories, the external world is in agreement with the categories. And these can be corroborated through clairvoyant means. "From the other side the supersensible reality throws its rays as it were on the network of concepts, as on the one side does the sensible reality."[54] However, the formation of concepts is just as independent of clairvoyant abilities as it is of observation.

Steiner further compares concepts/categories to shadows. If we look at our hand illuminated from behind we see the shadow of the hand. The

---

[52] Steiner, *The Easter Festival in Relation to the Mysteries*, lecture of April 22, 1924.
[53] Steiner, *The Theory of Categories*, lecture of November 13, 1908 at http://wn.rsarchive.org/Lectures/19081113p01.html
[54] *The Theory of Categories*, lecture of November 13, 1908 at http://wn.rsarchive.org/Lectures/19081113p01.html

shadow is an obliteration of the light. Likewise, concepts can be seen as obliterations of supersensible reality. They resemble the spiritual world, as the shadow of the hand resembles the hand.

Pure concepts are formed in mathematics, which indicates that it is not necessary to ascend to spiritual reality in order to form concepts. To build a sum of concepts a human being must be able to build a concept upon other concepts. In this way Aristotle constructed an architecture of concepts, adapted to the sensible world and in agreement with spiritual reality. Through the studies of the categories the ancient Greek could form insights into the supersensible worlds, at a time in which the instruction of the Mysteries had fallen into the background.

Alexander the Great

When the young heir assumed the throne at age eighteen, Aristotle became Alexander's counselor. According to Plutarch, "He loved and cherished Aristotle no less than if he had been his father; giving this reason for it, that, as he had received life from the one, so the other taught him to live well."

Alexander is defined by Steiner as "the first man who was all personality." The quality of his life as Gilgamesh, and his experience of egotism in the life of Mysa, both contributed to this soul complexion. Alexander could naturally turn his attention to the East, based on the knowledge that lived deeply in his soul.

That Alexander was considered more than a mortal points to the fact that, unlike his teacher, he had been initiated into the Mysteries of Samothrace, the so-called Great Mysteries that offered the vision of earth's cosmic evolution, its past and future. He also set his residence in Ephesus at the place of the Artemision, the temple originally built to Artemis, which he offered to rebuild with his own money.

A spiritual event was associated with the founding of Alexandria: Alexander's visit to the oracle of Zeus-Ammon in the oasis of Siwah (northwestern present-day Egypt); there he was declared son of Zeus-Ammon, the sun divinity. Likewise, Alexander's interest led him in the same spirit to Jerusalem, where he intuitively recognized the importance of what lay there in preparation for the future.

In his expeditions Alexander had reached the two columns that Herakles had built at the boundaries of the North (the rock of Gibraltar), and he later led his armies to what was considered another boundary of the civilized world, India, where he traveled as far as the Ganges. Here once more Alexander had more of an initiation in mind than a conquest. He wanted to reach "the center of the earth," which pointed to the ultimate initiation.[55] Alexander's march must have brought back to mind the furthest extension of Dionysus' journey many centuries before. The ruler must have felt like a new Greek hero, a demi-god.

Contrary to his teacher, Alexander still stood with one foot in the Mysteries, and with the other under the discipleship of Aristotle. However, once more he did not reach complete initiation, and history rightfully perceives the most human side of his personality, which often fell short of his higher intentions. It is as if the shadow of Gilgamesh loomed large in the life of this ruler almost 3,000 years later.

The main thrust of Alexander's campaigns stemmed from his desire to disseminate into the East what it had lost, which had been re-elaborated in the form of Greek philosophy. His conquest was followed by the founding of academies, libraries, and museums in more than seventy cities, all of which played an important part in the later extension of Greek knowledge. The most important center of knowledge, Alexandria, was to play an important role in the spreading of culture and the rise of Christianity during the coming centuries. All the while the young ruler also kept the Lyceum alive with considerable financial contributions.

Alexander struggled in his brief life to integrate the promptings of his lower self with his highest ideals, but it came about in such a way that his triumph was mixed with tragedy. The ruler's expanded military campaigns already created an element of estrangement from Aristotle, who had advised him against the Indian campaign, at least. Another element of estrangement may have been his marrying into the local ruling class.

Alexander also let himself go into excesses. At one point, when drunk, he lost control of himself during events that led to the murder

---

[55] Hiebel, *The Gospel of Hellas*, Chapter 4.

of his general, Cleitus. Although he immediately regretted his rashness, the episode contributed to instilling a mix of fear and alienation into many of his close collaborators. To this was added the fact that for a time he adopted the Persian custom of "proskynesis," according to which the salute given to a noble or to the king denoted the social status of the person. Whereas a noble had to bend or bow to the monarch, a commoner was required to lie on the ground in order to pay homage. Such a practice was highly resented by the Greeks, who believed this obeisance was fit only for a god, not a mortal. Steiner too seems to point to Alexander's excesses in the following statement: "And even the outcome in the East of what Alexander carried back to it from the West— albeit in a way that from a certain point of view is unjustifiable..."[56]

The monarch's excesses played an important part in bringing about his early death, which endangered his legacy. It had other consequences in Greece as well. While in Babylon, the young king had recalled from Athens his general Antipater, whom he had left to protect Aristotle and the Lyceum, but in whom he had lost trust. This action unfortunately coincided with the time that the enemies of Aristotle mounted an attack against the Lyceum, and accused the philosopher of atheism and treason. The philosopher had to flee Athens and take refuge on the island of Euboea, where he lived in almost complete isolation. It was a tragic ending for Aristotle's endeavor and for the future diffusion of his teachings. The philosopher, however, became a mystic, further deepening his belief in the immortality of the soul.

Warned of the impending attack against the Lyceum, Aristotle managed to save his philosophical opus. However, his writings traveled two different paths. The logical-philosophical writings went to the West through his pupil Theophrastus. The teachings that concerned knowledge of cosmos and nature (including astrology, biology, physiognomy, geography, meteorology, ethnology, and others) went to the East.

Theophrastus is the person who played the greatest role in the preservation of Aristotle's legacy. The disciple was torn apart from

---

[56] Steiner, *World History and the Mysteries in the Light of Anthroposophy*, lecture of Dec. 27, 1923.

Aristotle, following the fortunes of the Eastern campaigns and Alexander's death. He became Aristotle's successor at the Lyceum, where he remained until his death in 287 BC. He is widely recognized as the spiritual heir of Aristotle, and he enlarged the teacher's legacy.

Theophrastus passed only Aristotle's logical works on to posterity, and decided not to publish the "esoteric portions" of Aristotle's work (mostly what related to nature-knowledge), because he wanted to preserve them; he did not mean for them to disappear, as happened subsequently. In consequence, the fate of these manuscripts colored much of the path of consciousness of future Europe, as we will see in the next chapters.

Alexander's shortcomings had immediate repercussions, not only on Aristotle and his work. They also played a part in the delayed meeting of Steiner and Ita Wegman, and in their collaboration.

Conclusions

Plato continued in a new way the tradition of the Mysteries, which were places for experience, not for intellectual knowledge. In a way Plato still played the role of what the hierophant was in the Mysteries. And Plato's dualism goes back to the past of the Mysteries. It is found in the Persian antagonism between Ahriman and Ahura Mazdao. This antagonism continued in the dichotomy between a natural soul and a spiritual soul in man's breast.

For Plato, God is spellbound in nature. The body of the world came into existence through a sacrifice of the Godhead. The soul of the world (the divine element) is crucified in the body of the world. It has met with death in the body of the world, in order to grant existence to it. And Plato calls nature "the tomb of the divine element."[57] It is the human being's task to raise nature from death. And this can only be done by the man who is initiated. The initiated human being sees in the Logoi (plural of Logos) the metaphysical archetypes of all things and the productive forces behind all perceptible objects. They are the mediators between universe and man.

---

[57] Steiner, *Christianity as a Mystical Fact*, Chapter "Plato as Mystic."

Plato's philosophy only enters the first stages of the process of thinking. In revealing words, Steiner sums up all of Plato's philosophy thus: "Plato's world-conception aims to be a form of cognition which in its whole nature is religion. It brings cognition into relationship with the highest man can reach through his feelings. Plato allows cognition to be valid when it completely satisfies man's feelings. Then it is not pictorial knowledge; it is the content of life. It is a higher man in man."[58] Aristotle understood Plato's mission in a convergent fashion when he stated that Plato "[revealed] by his own life and by the method of his words, how a man becomes good and happy at the same time…"

Plato was a rhetorician. He was a master of composition and style. Aristotle did not seek to convince with his style. Rather, he would say, "We should not try to delight them [hearers]: we ought in fairness, to fight our case with no help beyond the mere facts: nothing, therefore, should matter except the proof of those facts. Fanciful language is meant to charm the hearer. Nobody uses fine language when teaching geometry."[59] Plato's works are more akin to artistic compositions. Aristotle inaugurates science in the true sense of the word.

Aristotle's philosophy marked the great turning point within the history of the teachings of the Logos. The Logos doctrine of Heraclitus turned into the teaching of logic. Aristotle's Logos indicated the way to logical discrimination with regard to moral action. Later, through Aristotle's heritage, the teachings of the Logos joined with Hebrew tradition allowed philosophers to deepen the understanding of the Christ-Logos.

Aristotle further laid the basis for the evolution of consciousness. Socrates and Plato spoke of the *daimon* or the voice within. But they hardly spoke as yet of conscience. They made little distinction between subjective and objective knowledge of the true, the beautiful or the good. Aristotle spoke more fully of conscience and of the necessity to face it through repentance, the distinctive mark of the moral man. He laid the seeds for the coming of the Christ-Logos consciousness within the

---

[58] Steiner, *Christianity as a Mystical Fact*, Chapter "Plato as Mystic."

[59] Aristotle, *Rhetoric* III/1, quoted in Hiebel, *The Gospel of Hellas*, Chapter 11.

human breast, possible after the turning point of time. He differentiated thus between the objective Logos without and the conscience within, able to connect with the Logos.

Aristotle brought the understanding of the Logos to completion. He closed the loop that had been opened with the transition from the Oracles to the Mysteries. In the first instance knowledge was received from without, but in participation with the forces of nature that did not yet make full room for individuality. In the Mysteries the wonders of the world were replaced by the trials of the soul, to use Steiner's words. Aristotle emboldened thinking to penetrate not only the realm of the soul, but the Mysteries of nature. Thinking could further reflect upon itself through logic.

After Aristotle, Greek thought essentially did not generate anything new. The first seven to eight centuries of Christianity were mostly colored by Platonism. It was only when Aristotelianism was Christianized by Thomas Aquinas that the foundations were laid for the Christianity of the Consciousness Soul. Platonism allows preservation of the treasures of the past, and gives impetus to important revivals. It can give us a taste and foreknowledge of things to come, and the energy to prepare for them, but cannot generate the impetus forward for a new epoch. Aristotelianism engenders the new and paves the way for new impulses.

PART II

THE MIDDLE AGES

CHAPTER 3

THE SCHOOL OF CHARTRES
AND SCHOLASTICISM

Steiner recognizes four epochs in the evolution of philosophy, each of which lasted between six and eight centuries.[60]

We have surveyed the first epoch of the development of philosophical views in Greek antiquity. It goes back to the 6th century BC in Greece and it comes to an end at the time of Golgotha. The Greeks of this time received thought as we receive perception, giving the soul the capacity to orient itself in the world through its thought process.

After the time of Christ, thought reached the human being via a completely different experience. It was no longer perceived from without, but was felt as being generated from within the soul. The soul was now completely immersed in the experience of its own being; it explored the relationship between what this inner activity produces and what can be perceived in the external world. Thought was more focused towards self-knowledge than knowledge of the world. "This time [is] the 'Age of Awakening Self-Consciousness.'"[61]

The ego was now awakening within the life of the soul. And the relation of the human soul to the world was expressed according to the views gained from religious sources, which took center-stage in

---

[60] Rudolf Steiner, *The Riddles of Philosophy*, Chapter 1, Guiding Thoughts on the Method of Presentation.

[61] Ibid.

the consciousness of the times. The mystery of the birth of the ego, ushered in through the deed of the Christ, was contemplated through the revelation of the gospels. This trend continues up to the time of Scotus Erigena (815-877 BC).

The third period marks a time in which thought life is strengthened anew, and tested for its validity. And the leading question of the time is, "How can something be expressed in thought life that is not itself merely the soul's own product?"[62] It's as if Greek philosophy were reborn at a new stage. The faculty of thinking is now mastered at a stage in which it is placed in close relation to the experience of the ego. Anticipating what will come out of this chapter, we can say that Chartres continues the trend of the second period and brings it to a culmination; the worldview of Scholasticism forms the culmination of the third period.

Plato's writings always remained available to Western civilization. Aristotle's philosophical writings had spread to the West. The teachings concerning knowledge of cosmos and nature were thought lost for several centuries, until some of them reappeared in a monastery in Syria. They were translated into Syrian and other languages after that. This second kind of knowledge returned to the West in a variety of ways. The Crusaders, the Templar Knights among them, brought them back from the Middle East. Later on, the Arabs took Aristotle's teachings and disseminated them toward the West, into Spain. The thinker's work survived and acquired new forms in the hands of Boetius and Aquinas in the Middle Ages; and later on through Jakob Böhme, Paracelsus, and alchemists such as Basil Valentine and others. Traces of Aristotle's tradition lived on until the end of the nineteenth century, the time in which Rudolf Steiner and Ita Wegman incarnated. In his biography Steiner gives us an example of how such knowledge survived deeply in the soul of the herb-gatherer Felix Koguzki, with whom he had been acquainted in his youth.[63] Science at that time was utterly unable to

---

[62] Rudolf Steiner, *The Riddles of Philosophy*, Chapter 1.
[63] Steiner, *Self-Education: Autobiographical Reflections: 1861-1893*, lecture of February 4, 1913.

explain where such knowledge came from, and at best, would simply ignore it.

Aristotle's philosophical work survived until Steiner's time in the figure of the Benedictine Vincenz Knauer, whom Steiner had an opportunity to hear at the University of Vienna. In him, Steiner concluded, Aristotelianism still retained a certain vitality.[64]

At central turning points of time the individual, no matter how evolved, faces new challenges in order to carry the treasures that live buried in the soul to a new level. And no turning point had more importance for world evolution, and for individual development, than the Mystery of Golgotha. While Plato's and Aristotle's writings started to make their way into Europe, Aristotle and Plato themselves had to undergo the momentous initiation into the Christian Mysteries. We will now follow one and the other threads: the eternal individuality and the writings. We will alternate between the reincarnated Aristotle and Plato. Since Plato did not fully accomplish his mission in this epoch, we will complement his portrayal with that of the major Platonic representative of the Middle Ages: Alain de Lille.

The Experience of Christianity: Schionatulander and Sigune

Aristotle's knowledge needed to take on a new form, one that would be influenced by the rise of Christianity. It is for that reason that the two sister souls first reappeared in a much-fantasized, but little understood historical-cultural current (Grail Christianity), and later in the official Christianity of the Middle Ages. The Greek philosopher first reincarnated as the page/knight Schionatulander, and the Mesopotamian king as a woman by the name of Sigune. Here the roles are somehow reversed: the man of knowledge, Aristotle/Steiner, took on a role that related him to outer activity. The old soul/strong-willed Gilgamesh/Wegman entered a more receptive and subservient role as the woman Sigune in the only romantic, though brief, relationship we know of these sister souls. Both

---

[64] Steiner, *Karmic Relationships*, Volume 6, Lecture of July 19, 1924.

the abovementioned names appear only briefly in the epic poem *Parzival* by Wolfram von Eschenbach; written down in the twelfth century, it referred to events that had occurred in the ninth and tenth centuries. The names given in the epic are not those of the corresponding historical personalities; rather they are imaginative names that point to the essence of their beings, and to the roles they play in the Grail quest. The little we know from von Eschenbach's *Parzival* is usefully complemented by his later, unfinished epic, *Titurel;* and by another book completed about half a century later by Albrecht von Scharffenberg, *Der juengere Titurel.* In both later epics, Schionatulander takes the place of the main hero (rather than Parzival).

Let us review the links of destiny in this incarnation, according to the epics. King Titurel had a son Frimutel, who succeeded him. The latter had two sons (Amfortas and Trevrizent) and three daughters (Schoisane, Herzeloyde, and Repanse de Schoie). Schoisane died in childbirth, and her daughter Sigune was raised by the aunt Herzeloyde.

Schionatulander was the grandson of Gurnemanz, an Arthurian knight. When still a boy he served as a page to the French queen Anflise, and then later to Gahmuret. Schionatulander had been trained in the art of the troubadours, particularly in poetry and music. After Gahmuret married Herzeloyde, Schionatulander found Sigune at the court of the queen. The two grew up together and love unfolded between them.

Schionatulander fought as a page at the side of Gahmuret. He wanted to further Gahmuret's task, though he felt torn between accomplishing the task and his love for Sigune. Schionatulander had gone twice to Baghdad with Gahmuret, soon after the death of the famous caliph Harun-el-Rashid. Schionatulander was the one charged to announce Gahmuret's death by treachery, and Herzeloyde received the news just as Parzival was about to be born. Consequently Schionatulander became regent of Gahmuret's kingdom. He kept fighting knightly battles in the ideal of King Arthur's Round Table, and returned once more to Baghdad. In between fights, he returned to Sigune, who implored him to stay home. However, the knight felt inwardly compelled to complete what Gahmuret had started. Eventually he returned from his campaigns and the marriage was planned. Before the marriage could take place, however, tragedy struck. Schionatulander was killed by his enemy Orilus, after having tried to accomplish a mission entrusted to him by Sigune. Legend relates that Sigune sent Schionatulander to fetch the leash of a dog. Orilus mistook Schionatulander for Parzival, and killed him. Sigune later played a role in directing Parzival in his quest for the Grail.

The brief incarnation of Schionatulander allowed Aristotle/Steiner's soul to enter an esoteric Christian stream, in which Christianity was cultivated in the fashion of a modern Mystery schooling. However, since his life was cut short, he probably never reached the stage of initiation that would have been possible within Grail Christianity. But he played an important role in defending Parzival's life and mission, as Prokofieff points out on more than one occasion. Emil Bock comes to the conclusion that had Schionatulander not sacrificed his life, the impulses of the Arthur stream and those of the Grail would have been brought to an end.[65] At death, Schionatulander/Steiner took with him an impulse to unite the streams of pre-Christian and Christian wisdom. And this task was continued in the soul's return to incarnation.

Hroswitha of Gandersheim

We will first follow the thread of the reincarnated Plato, then look at the work the School of Chartres in which the whole of Christianized Platonism blossomed and offered its fruits for the future of Europe. We will then look at Alain de Lille, and the place of his writings in European culture. And finally, we will turn our attention to what took place in the Cistercian stream, which Alain joined in the last part of his life. In this stream the last traces of a living Platonism were carried into modern times. Even in later times, among the Cistercians great Platonic souls could at times communicate their wisdom to members of the order. And that order played an important part in Steiner's life, as shown in Chapter 5. From the Platonic stream we will then move to Scholasticism, the new expression of Aristotelianism within Christianity.

---

[65] Emil Bock, *The Life and Times of Rudolf Steiner*: Volume 2: "Origin and Growth of His Insights," 227.

While Aristotle was continuing his path into Christianity, Plato experienced difficulty returning to incarnate into the new conditions of Middle Europe. Nor could he incarnate in a position allowing him to significantly influence the further spread of Platonism. Ironically, Platonism developed without its main source of inspiration. If we want to look at the next most important Platonic exponent of the Middle Ages, this would no doubt be Alain de Lille. He came at the end of a line of development, and after him the role of the Platonists receded, and the task of the Aristotelians emerged fully.

Platonism was revived throughout the Middle Ages, most significantly in what was called the School of Chartres. However, it was difficult for Plato's individuality to look down at what survived on earth as Platonism. According to Steiner's research in *Karmic Relationships* Volume 4: "…it was for him only too frequently a dreadful disturbance in his supersensible life of soul and spirit."[66] He had great difficulty returning to earth and entering the Christian epoch, to find a body in which he might carry his former soul inclinations. This was because Plato had been a Greek, steeped in the artistic element. The subsequent civilization had acquired the Roman stamp through and through; and neo-Platonism lived on only in a pale copy of what Platonism had been. All of this explains the difficulty for Plato's soul in seeking re-embodiment. We also hear in the same lecture, "And there was also a certain difficulty for his nature to receive Christianity; for he himself represented in a certain sense the highest point of the pre-Christian conception of the world."[67]

Plato reincarnated as the tenth-century nun Hroswitha, who belonged to the convent of Gandersheim in Brunswick (Lower Saxony, Germany). Already at that time, she united strongly with the mid-European-Germanic spirit. However, she was reticent in receiving and working through the Roman coloring of the culture. This may have been a further cause for delay in her soul.

Little is known about Hroswitha's origin and life. The fact that she had been accepted at the royal abbey of Gandersheim implies that she

---

[66] Steiner, *Karmic Relationships*, Volume 4, lecture of September 23, 1923.
[67] Ibid.

was of noble descent. Under the reign of King Otto I (936–973), the abbey had been awarded autonomous power; it responded only to the control of provosts appointed by the king, not to any other secular or religious authority. The women living at Gandersheim agreed to regulate their conduct by a rule, but did not take permanent vows. As a result, people moved freely between court and abbey, promoting a lively exchange of ideas. Otto (Emperor ruling over part of Germany, Austria, Switzerland, and Northern Italy) had promoted a little renaissance at his court. Writers and artists came to see him from all over Europe, and Hroswitha enjoyed access to much of the written material of her time.

Hroswitha wrote from about 960 to shortly after 973. At the end of this period, she apparently organized her writing into three books in what was likely a chronological sequence. Book 1, *Historia,* mostly contains five legends; Book 2 centers around six dramas; in Book 3 are found two epic poems: *Gesta Ottonis* (The deeds of King Otto), and a narrative of the beginnings of the Abbey of Gandersheim. Nothing is known of Hroswitha's later life.

Hroswitha's dramas are narrated in a dialogue form that harkens back to Plato. Even though she portrayed dramatic stories, they were not written for the stage. The striving that runs through them could be expressed in terms of the question of how to Christianize art. This is what she did under the influence of the Roman dramatist Terence, whom she took as a model. She did not write comedies like her predecessor; rather, she used her stories as a means to educate the soul. Interestingly, she was also the first writer to introduce the theme of Faust, in her *Theophilus.* He is portrayed as a soul that struggles ever forward, and because of this he can find redemption in spite of each fall.

Although Hroswitha von Gandersheim had a certain influence upon her time, this incarnation was a considerable step down from what one would expect from the reincarnated Plato. One would naturally tend to seek the reincarnated individuality among the teachers of the School of Chartres. In effect, neo-Platonism received its major impulses without a meaningful contribution from its main protagonist. This element seems to explain the later difficulties in the incarnation of Karl Julius Schröer.

The School of Chartres

Until the seventh and eighth centuries, some characteristics of Mystery teachings were still retained in some centers of Christianity. This preservation was possible because the human soul still retained a connection with the spiritual world. Some human beings still received their thoughts from the cosmic intelligence, before it would turn earthly in the time following the 8th to 10th centuries. In those Mystery centers, the Goddess Natura appeared as a living being, with whom the pupils could converse. When the seeker after knowledge had been sufficiently prepared by the Goddess, he learned to know from her the nature of the four elements. Later he was introduced to the planetary system; with that arose knowledge of the human soul. At length he could approach what was called the Cosmic Ocean, which leads from the planets to the fixed stars, from the elemental to the spiritual world. One place where these Mysteries were taught was the Path of Santiago de Compostela in northern Spain. Chartres continued the tradition, and formed in fact its last cultural expression, though this type of knowledge remained, in isolated places, until the fourteenth and fifteenth centuries.

The "School of Chartres" preserved the open, intuitive conditions of soul that had been true when humanity still had access to the cosmic intelligence. In Chartres souls lived who still had access to the cosmic intelligence for a few more centuries than the rest of the culture around them.

In the School of Chartres, the pupils were taught the classical seven liberal arts: *Grammatica, Dialectica, Rhetorica, Arithmetica, Geometria, Astronomia,* and *Musica;* these were not just disciplines of knowledge as we would describe them now, but living goddesses, divine-spiritual beings. The teachings that took place in the School of Chartres were not just Platonism; "they contained the teachings from the old seership of the pre-Platonic Mysteries that had been imbued ever since with the contents of Christianity."[68]

---

[68] Steiner, *Karmic Relationships*, Volume 3, lecture of July 13, 1924.

Fulbert

The School of Chartres was founded by Fulbert, an individual coming from an obscure and poor Italian family, born sometime after 960. In Italy he was taught by an unknown bishop, who gave him the rudiments of sciences and theology. After being ordained he struck an important friendship with Gerbert, a Benedictine monk who became Pope Sylvester II in the year 999. Gerbert was a learned man far from ordinary, who had been taught by Arab teachers in Cordova. He had created an ecclesiastical school, and Fulbert was one of his most successful students. Fulbert was also a close friend of Robert II, king of France, a very pious soul dedicated to the arts.

Fulbert made two journeys to France, finally settling in Chartres, where he attended the medical lectures given by the famous doctor Heribrand, who had preserved the knowledge of Galen, Hippocrates and Oribase. He thus learned a medicine that had its origins in old Mystery knowledge. In Chartres he received recognition after recognition, becoming first master, then chancellor, and finally canon and bishop in 1006. Fulbert, who was called "Socrates" by his pupils, was both a scholar and a very pious Christian. His widespread reputation made him a counselor to princes and bishops throughout France, and even Europe.

Chartres, positioned in a very special meeting place of ley lines, had been a place of the Mysteries in Celtic times. The center of Chartres survived the closure decreed by Tiberius and Claudius and continued with alternating fortunes after that time. In Fulbert's time Chartres saw the construction of a first Romanesque cathedral in the year 1020. The school's fame grew rapidly and attracted some of the most brilliant minds of the time. Little is known of all the teachers who followed Fulbert, of people like Bernard of Chartres and his brother Thierry of Chartres, Bernard Silvestris, Gilbert de la Porrée, or William of Conches. It is only about the last great teachers of Chartres that we have some more, albeit sketchy, information: John of Salisbury and Alain de Lille in particular.

Alain de Lille was practically the last teacher of the school and after him Chartres lost importance, but the cathedral was erected which may be the most significant church of Europe. All of the knowledge of the School of Chartres found an expression in magnificent sculptural imaginations that convey to posterity the grandeur of Chartres' teachings.

The Teachers

A letter from Adelmann, Archdeacon of Liege, to his friend Berengarius of Tours, gives us an idea of how the teachings of Fulbert were viewed by his students: "And he guides our will to him through wishes and silent requests, calling upon us in those secret evening colloquia he often led in the small garden by the chapel; there he told us of that realm in which he, by God's will, lingers as a senator."[69] The historical record is amplified by Steiner, who in relation to all the teachers of Chartres states: "[They are] personalities who...with the characteristics of initiates went among people."[70] And further, in relation to Alain de Lille, Bernard Silvestris and Bernard of Chartres, "... [they] still went among other people with the character of an initiate, with the character of a person who knows much about the secrets of existence, like the great Joachim de Fiore, who was also initiated in the medieval sense."[71] Based on what had been initiations in previous incarnations, such individualities could fathom and intuit much that was missing from the culture of their times.

That little is known about the lives of the teachers of Chartres seems intentional. They lived in a simplicity of the past, consciously sacrificing personal recognition. They were dedicated to humility, poverty, quiet life and a desire to know. It is also very indicative that most called each other "brother" and that they lived close to nature, as was also the custom among the Cistercians, who included a large number of the teachers of Chartres. This spirit of Chartres was expressed in the recurring terms that one finds in the letters of the school: "stimulating friendship, love, wise kindliness, warm consideration," etc.

---

[69] Virginia Sease and Manfred Schmidt-Brabant, *Thinkers, Saints and Heretics: Spiritual Paths in the Middle Ages*, 51.

[70] Steiner, *Karmic Relationships*, Volume 8, lecture of August 14, 1924.

[71] Ibid.

The Teachings

Chartres' Platonic worldview embraced the whole of the Mystery traditions of humanity. Besides the Gnosis and Pythagoras, the people of Chartres drew from the free circulation of esoteric traditions, be they Christian Gnosis, Sufi, or Jewish. This eclecticism was not unusual at that time, as is known from the examples of Etienne Harding of the Cistercians or Hughes de Payens and André de Montbard, some of the founders of the Templar Order, who drew from the knowledge of the Middle East. However, in all of the teachings Plato took the central stage.

Plato took priority even over the Church Fathers, and some of the exponents of Chartres had to defend themselves from accusations of heresy. Gilbert de la Porrée was accused of Manicheism, and the same was true of ten disciples of Amaury of Chartres, who had brought Platonic thinking to its extremes, and were burned at the stake.

The Neo-Platonism of the School of Chartres brought to a culmination the union of the Platonic visionary spirit with the Christian worldview of the Middle Ages. The masters of Chartres could only speak through inspired imaginations, not in a rationalistic and abstract fashion. And the greatest expression of the teachings of Chartres finds its way in the sculptural forms of the cathedral, here too in images, rather than abstract concepts. Interestingly, Chartres cultivated the rudiments of music that later led to the use of musical harmony. Pierre Morizot indicates, "The lessons developed on the intellectual plane what had arisen in the heart … (through music, devotion, and the religious services)."[72] Overall, the Platonism of Chartres implied a life of thought imbued with imagination and an artistic mood.

The first three of the seven liberal arts are grouped under the name of *Trivium*, and are concerned with the Word: Grammar, Dialectic/Logic and Rhetoric. The *Quadrivium* comprised Arithmetic, Geometry, Astronomy and Music.

Grammar is the foundation for the grasp of language and for correct speech. Dialectic/Logic provides the framework for right thinking. Rhetoric modeled the forms of expression, seen as: structure,

---

[72] Pierre Morizot, *The School of Chartres*, 34.

invention (idea), presentation, style and memory (the fact that it can be remembered by others). Rhetoric could build upon the foundation of correct speech and right thinking.

Arithmetic, which reveals the laws and properties of numbers, was seen as intimately related to music through proportions and intervals. Geometry indicates how harmony arises in the physical world through equations and proportions. Astronomy applies proportions, equations, harmony and geometry to the heavenly worlds. Music concludes the work of astronomy by carrying the soul into the realm of the Harmony of the Spheres.

The spirit in the School of Chartres could not be approached through concepts, but through experiences. At that time, impressions of nature could still be received as spiritual experiences, at least for that part of the population that had retained earlier conditions of consciousness the longest. How that was the case will be seen when we turn to Alain de Lille's *Anticlaudianus* in more depth. In Steiner's words: "In Chartres... what entered, above all else, was a ray of the still living wisdom of Peter of Compostela who had worked in Spain, had cultivated a living Mystery-related Christianity in Spain that still spoke of the handmaiden Natura, still spoke about the fact that only when this Natura had led the human being into the elements, into the planetary world, into the world of the stars, only then would he be prepared to know by way of his soul... the seven handmaidens; these handmaidens, did not appear before the soul in abstract theoretical chapters in a book, but as living goddesses: Grammar, Dialectic, Rhetoric, Arithmetic, Geometry, Astronomy, Music. The pupil came to know them in a living way as divine spiritual figures." Further in the same lecture, this is what is added in reference to Peter of Compostela first and of Bernard of Chartres later: "Although, of course, he could no longer show them the Goddess Natura or the goddess of the Seven Liberal Arts, he still spoke with such liveliness about them that imaginative images were at least conjured up before these pupils and, in every hour of instruction, knowledge became a luminous art."[73]

The teachings of the School of Chartres spread throughout Europe

---

[73] Steiner, *Karmic Relationships*, Volume 3, lecture of July 13, 1924.

both north and south. It is significant that Steiner includes Joachim of Fiore as a representative of the School of Chartres, even though he lived and taught in southern Italy, and is not known to have been in Chartres.

Alain de Lille

To the best of modern scholarship it is believed that Alain de Lille was born sometime in the years 1116 or 1117, but this is just an estimate. Nor is his death determined with more certainty than the years 1202-03. Around the 1140s Alain attended first the School of Paris, then the School of Chartres, studying with the likes of Peter Abelard, Gilbert de Poitiers and Thierry de Chartres, as we are told by John of Salisbury. He lived and taught in Paris, then Montpelier, Southern France, and spent his last years in the monastery of Cîteaux, the mother abbey of the Cistercians. His stay among the Cistercians was one of the key moments in the life of the institution, and it marked the passing of the Platonic stream from Chartres, in its sunset phase, to the Cistercians.

The turning point leading to Alain's Cistercian experience is narrated in the form of a legend, which offers deep insight into this historical figure. At this important time in his life Alain was planning to deliver a sermon on the Trinity. Before the appointed time, he chanced upon a child who was spooning water out of the Seine into a hole. When asked what he was doing, the child answered that he wanted to empty the Seine into the hole. "But it will take you an eternity," retorted Alain, to which the child replied, "I will be done here long before you are finished with your explanation of the Trinity." Humbled by the experience, Alain reassessed his life and values, and decided to become the swineherd of Cîteaux.

Alain had entered the Cistercian order in which Platonism continued to live now that the sun had set over Chartres, and his presence among the Cistercians strengthened the order. Coincidentally, this was the time in which Chartres's heritage was cast in stone in its famous Gothic cathedral. A time was coming to an end, and Alain de Lille himself was aware of it. He was a last representative of a knowledge destined to fade in order to give way to the more intellectual pursuits of the Aristotelian-inspired Dominicans. Steiner reminds us that even the name by which

Alain is remembered, Alanus ab Insulis, points to the island of Hibernia, and to a legacy of its past Mysteries.[74]

Alain de Lille had a considerable literary output, consisting mostly of philosophical/moral allegories, theological treatises and sermons. Because of his wide knowledge he was known as Doctor Universalis. His most well-known works are *De Planctu Naturae* (The Complaint of Nature) and *Anticlaudianus*; both of them could be called moral treatises, and both are written in Latin verse.

From his days in Paris, Alain had acquired a deep knowledge of Aristotelian dialectic. Hints of it are present in his writing *Summa Quoniam Homines* in which Alain indicates a stage of the future in which humanity will reach direct spiritual vision. He sees this as a science that is also perception of the truth of things; a science that includes an inner resonance and knowledge of the deeper causes. Here Alain strives towards Aristotelianism, and what can later derive from it: an intuitive knowledge that means union between the knower and the object being known. He calls this "theophania," something that resembles the way in which angels know. For Alain this stage was first realized in Mary.

In his most famous and quoted opus, the *Anticlaudianus*, he comes back to his previous assessment of dialectic and logic, showing what he sees as their limits, and distancing himself from Aristotle, whom he previously admired. He now gives his preference to Plato. Let us see how.

Anticlaudianus

As in the *De Planctu Naturae,* the moral element weaves throughout the *Anticlaudianus*. Among the vices, continuous reference is made to homosexuality as the sin that for Alain de Lille most clearly exemplified going against Natura's union of the opposites. In fact, sexual imagery is used to the other extreme to exemplify the gifts of the Goddess Natura— witness these verses: "Her curved flanks, yielding to fit restraint, unite the upper and the lower parts of her body, the head and the feet. Who

---

[74] Steiner, *Ancient Myths: Their Meaning and Connection with Evolution,* lecture of Dec 30, 1917.

does not know that beneath these, other and better things lie hidden to which the quiet exterior serves but as an introduction."[75] The greatest bliss is reached in the union of opposites. Sexual innuendo points to that within the limits of earthly language, both in the positive and in the negative.

Before turning to the journey at the heart of the *Anticlaudianus*, let us consider some key ideas which summarize much of Chartres neo-Platonism: first the role of Natura in the scheme of creation, then the contrast between logic/dialectic and rhetoric, which is echoed in the characterizations of Aristotle and Plato respectively.

Logic and "Paintings"

God established the network of secondary causes, defined their domain and oriented their field of action, then gave autonomy to them and ceased intervening in it. Natura represents this system both in the physical and in the moral order. Thus all virtues spring from Natura. Among them are Concord, Laughter, Temperance, Reason, Decorum, Prudence, Piety, Sincerity, Nobility. Two key virtues are Reason and Prudence. Prudence is the only one to have also a Greek name, Phronesis.

Natura can perfect the human being in so far as he is of the earth. "The mortal body recognizes our [Natura's] anvil, calls for our artisans and our art; the birth of a soul demands other artisans."[76] And further, "However, the hand of God himself will make good what the norm of Nature leaves below the standard of perfection. What nature makes, the divine Artist will perfect. The Divine creates from nothing. Nature makes mortal things from some material..."[77] In the *Complaint of Nature* we hear, "He is the Creator of my work, I am the work of the Creator; He works from nothing, I beg work from another; He works by His own divine will, I work under His name."[78] This separation of tasks reappears clearly in the whole imagination that is the *Anticlaudianus*.

---

[75] Alain de Lille, *Anticlaudianus, or the Good and Perfect Man*, 57.

[76] Ibid, 60.

[77] Ibid, p. 68.

[78] Alain de Lille, *The Complaint of Nature*, Douglas M Moffat translator, 29.

Logic appears in clear contrast to rhetoric, and the same is amplified when Alain de Lille describes the role of imaginations, which are at the center of his rhetoric power. This is what makes him an orator and theologian, not a philosopher in the same way as Thomas Aquinas.

In many places logic is given its due in Alain's master opus, but hardly ever without a touch of irony, as in the following, which compares the role of imaginations (paintings) and logic: "Thus this art's [painting] power subtly checks logic's arguments and triumphs over logic's sophisms [and Alain has nothing positive to say about Sophists]. Logic gives proof, painting creates; logic argues, painting brings to pass everything that can exist. Thus, both wish the false [illusory] to appear true but painting pursues this end more faithfully."[79]

In the quote above we can recognize both Alain's appreciation of and bias against logic. Tradition incorporates logic into the liberal arts; Alain has a split mind about her. In his description of logic, an antipathy creeps in that is not present with the others. Just hear the words: "... the face suffered here and there of a certain leanness. The leanness entrenches it and, entrenched by this leanness, it is deep hollowed, and dry skin is wed to fleshless bones. ... Her hair, struggling in a kind of dispute, twists its way far down and unruly strands indulge in a tasteless sprawl. No comb restrains it, no clamping buckle holds it fast, no scissors' bite cuts it short."[80] It is a description in striking contrast to the other six liberal arts, in which Alain uses only imagery of harmony. One can definitely sense that he struggles in coming to terms with her. Compare the above description with that of rhetoric, which is central to Alain's work and art: "The maiden in like manner traces many a flower on the axle and with fresh blooms makes the steel grow young again. Though steel [of the axle that logic builds for the chariot] is usually rigid with stiffness of cold and reminds one of deep Winter's frost, this steel knows no Winter, leaves behind its congenial cold, establishes its claim to the smiling joys of Spring and with its pattern of flowers sets before us a view of meadow."[81]

---

[79] Alain de Lille, *Anticlaudianus*, 49.
[80] Ibid, 90.
[81] Ibid, 102.

Logic is contrasted with the role of "paintings," or imaginations. The virtues are represented imaginatively as maidens, and their robes or garments carry paintings (imaginations). The constant reference to Greek mythology serves the same purpose; it speaks of esoteric content imaginatively. And about the nature of the imaginations present in the home of Natura (in particular one portraying "men's character") it is said, "Oh painting with your new wonders! What can have no real existence comes into being and painting, aping reality and diverting itself with a strange art, turns the shadows of things and changes lies to truth." And again, speaking about the limits that Reason reaches in the realm of the fixed stars, the poet comments: "What the tongue cannot tell the picture does: how language, since it fails to reach the essence of God, grows senseless when it tries to express things divine, loses its power of communicating and tries to take refuge in its old meaning."[82]

What is said about logic continues in Alain's appreciation of Aristotle. Here again the contrast is still present, though it finds some higher degree of resolution: "Aristotle, the disturber of words, is here [in the painting of logic]; he disturbs many of us by his turbulence and rejoices that he is obscure. He treats logic in such a way that he gives the impression of not having treated it..."[(24)] And the superiority of Plato is finally expressed: "In that mural [one portraying "men's character" in Natura's home] Aristotle prepares arms for the logician and presents his school of logic, but Plato's profound mind has a more inspired vision of the secrets of heaven and earth and he tries to search the mind of God."[83]

The Journey

The *Anticlaudianus* is expressed in the form of a journey from earth to heaven conducted with the goal of fashioning the "new man." It starts with the building of the chariot that will carry the poet to the realm of the fixed stars and beyond.

The seven liberal arts fashion the chariot for the journey; Prudence/ Phronesis coordinates the work. Once the chariot is ready, Reason,

---

[82] Alain de Lille, *Anticlaudianus*, 141.
[83] Ibid, 95.

"reminded and instructed by mistress Natura," presents Phronesis with horses. These are the five senses: sight, hearing, smell, taste and touch. About hearing, Alain says that he is "inferior to the first [sight] and rates lower in appearance," but also "superior to the others, and first among them by his quality of beauty."[84] Here, and later in the poem, is a reference to the superiority of the power of inspiration, which comes through the sense of hearing, over that of Reason, which sees.

Now the chariot is fashioned by the seven liberal arts, represented as maidens, and it can start its journey. The *trivium* builds the chariot itself; the *quadrivium* shapes the four wheels. The travelers first move through the "regions of Air." Here they meet "an Angel, barred from the hall of the heavenly kingdom, dethroned from his seat, broken by his vaunting, cast down by his pride, ruined by his envy, pays for his sin by exile and for his guilt by suffering,"[85] a clear reference to Lucifer.

In a second step the chariot moves through the regions of Ether, "the higher realm where brightness [light] and fire hold sway." In this region Prudence can hear a sort of lower music of the spheres (the sound of the celestial harp). This is in fact the region of the Moon. This is followed by the region of the Sun, and the other planets follow. Mars is described as a region of strife. The sixth region, that of Jupiter, stands in stark contrast to Mars and is compared to the "happiness of unending spring."[86] The chariot proceeds to the seventh region, that of Saturn, again in sharp contrast to Jupiter: "There winter is feverish. ... Here grief groans, tears, discord, terror, sadness, wanness, mourning, injustice hold sway."[87]

Beyond Saturn, the eighth stage of the journey leads to the realm of the fixed stars, and the higher spiritual world. Here the constellations of the zodiac are named and "Phronesis' eye enjoys this view of the heavens which her sight cannot penetrate; she misses the familiar matter and is stunned by the wonder of so much light."[88] However, she is perplexed, and her spirit falters, not managing to find a fixed point of reference. The reader may remember that Alain had sought to dazzle with the intellect,

---

[84] Alain de Lille, *Anticlaudianus*, 49.

[85] Ibid, 129.

[86] Ibid, 134.

[87] Ibid, 135.

[88] Ibid, 138.

and, legend has it, a child had derided him along the banks of the Seine, before he turned back to the simple and modest life of the Cistercians. This is also borne out by the rest of Alain's comments in relation to what leads a man to understand what lies in this region: "Not nobility of lineage, not the charm of beauty, ...not unrestrained temerity leads thither but virtue of soul, constancy of mind, nobility attained not by birth but cultivated in the heart, interior beauty, a host of virtues, *rule of life, poverty in worldly goods, contempt of position*" (emphasis added).[89] In the last one or two lines Alain seems to speak of what happened to him in turning to the Cistercian life.

When the travelers try to move into the realm of the fixed stars, obstacles arise. First of all, the horses cannot move further; they refuse to draw the chariot. The senses cannot go any further, and Reason cannot rein them in. Phronesis herself is torn by conflicting feelings. A maiden approaches her; it is Theology. She describes how this realm lies far beyond the reach of reason, and expresses it thus: "He [God] is the just without justice, living without life, beginning without beginning, end without end, measureless without measure,..."[90]

Past the realm of the fixed stars the chariot enters the sphere of the Trinity. And here Phronesis meets with Noys (Nous), "Queen of the pole, goddess of heaven, daughter of the Master above..." Phronesis addresses in prayerful petition the queen of the pole, who asks her to leave the chariot and horses behind under the protection of Reason. If they were to attempt to go further "...Reason would falter and the chariot reel."[91] At this point lies an important change of consciousness of which Alain speaks thus: "But abandoning things petty, I now pluck a mightier chord and laying aside entirely the role of poet [rhetoric], I appropriate a new speaking part, that of the prophet." And at the same time he adds, "I will be the pen in this poem, not the scribe or the author."[92] He is in effect telling us that we are in the realm of Inspiration. This confirms that Alain has received inspiration and speaks from experience as to why what he knows as reason cannot apprehend reality in this realm.

---

[89] Ibid, 139.

[90] Ibid, 141.

[91] Ibid, 146.

[92] Ibid.

A very important step is taken here. Phronesis can continue to ride on the second horse, which can bear her aloft. This is the horse of hearing, for whose importance the poet has previously prepared us.[93] Now Phronesis is exposed to the highest secrets of creation, and "establishes [them] by deductions made on the spot," another reference to Inspiration.

Now Phronesis beholds the hierarchies, which are briefly described according to tradition. Further she is introduced to the Christ, to the realm of the saints, and to the Virgin Mary. In the Mystery of the virgin birth the mind again faces a challenge to understanding. Where Reason fails, Phronesis now calls on Faith to her aid. We are told that Faith comes before Reason; Faith anticipates and Reason can obey the dogmas of Faith and follow her, and later transfer the insights of Faith into writing.

In spite of the help she is receiving, Phronesis falls into a kind of lethargy. This cannot be compared to ordinary sleep, for it resembles an extinction of consciousness "which darkens life's light and deadens the vital element to a greater extent than ordinary sleep but less than death..." Phronesis is given a draught "prepared by heavenly hands."[94] She revives, regains consciousness and overcomes the fear that gripped her mind. Faith presents Phronesis a mirror, "equipped with images. In this mirror is reflected everything which the fiery region encompasses."[95] The mirror attenuates the fiery light and prevents it from burning her eyes.

Phronesis now stands in front of the Virgin Mary and beholds the Mystery of the virgin birth. Here once more Alain illustrates the dilemma of Logic (and Reason), which cannot reconcile virginity and motherhood. This only Faith can resolve. And, while Phronesis tries to understand, Faith reminds her of the futility of the attempt because here are at work higher laws that transcend earthly, or even lower spiritual laws.

The crowning effort of the journey is the creation of the New Man. The heaven/earth contrast is very apparent in Alain's description of

---

[93] Alain de Lille, *Anticlaudianus*, 146.

[94] Ibid, 159.

[95] Ibid, 160

this crowning achievement: "Through his soul let him dwell in heaven, through his body on earth," a typical Platonic dualism.[96]

Alain de Lille's most celebrated opus highlighted the Platonic nature of the School of Chartres. The whole work is a moral allegory, and we are reminded of it through the constant reference to the virtues. Rhetoric is emphasized at the expense of logic; in fact the whole work is a testament to the power of rhetoric. Though reason is given its due, it is ultimately contrasted with "...virtue of soul, constancy of mind, nobility attained not by birth but cultivated in the heart, interior beauty, a host of virtues, rule of life, poverty in worldly goods, contempt of position." And reason must give way to faith in the last stages of the journey. Likewise the goal of the journey is a moral goal, the attainment of the New Man, not the perfecting of a philosophy.

Rhetoric is explicitly and recurrently contrasted to logic, hearing to sight. Though recognized as one of the seven maidens, logic may be considered a poor sister to the others. And the attention to hearing is key in the passage from reason to inspiration that alone can guide the soul to the higher spiritual realms. Finally, this is rendered all the more explicit in the alleged superiority of Plato over Aristotle. In Alain's life this pull between the two philosophers lived with alternating fates within his biography, though finally the balance tilted towards Plato. All of this is very understandable given the soul makeup of the people of the School of Chartres, in whom the cosmic intelligence survived the longest, whereas everywhere around it had given way to the earthly intelligence.

The Cistercians and Platonism

What had been taught in the School of Chartres first found a continuation in the Order of Cluny, but there it became more exoteric. The abbey of Cluny was a Benedictine monastery in central-eastern France. As a church adhering to the reformed Benedictine rule from the late tenth century, Cluny had come to prominence; soon it became one of the most prestigious European monastic institutions.

---

[96] Alain de Lille, *Anticlaudianus*, 160.

The leading role of Cluny was later taken over by the Order of the Cistercians, who took their name from the village of Cîteaux, in eastern France. There, a group of Benedictine monks had founded their central abbey in 1098, where they adhered in strict manner to the Benedictine Rule. Bernard de Clairvaux, who joined the monastery in the early 1100s, helped assure the rapid expansion of the order. By the late twelfth century, there were Cistercian abbeys throughout all of western Europe and even in eastern Europe. In Steiner's assessment, among the Cistercians who broke off from Cluny were "the last relics of a striving to awaken Platonism—the Platonic world-conception, in unison with Christianity ...."[97] And here what had lived in the School of Chartres survived, although becoming more corrupted with time. Looking closely at the Cistercians we will find some of the motifs that have already appeared in the School of Chartres. Though quite metamorphosed, the Platonic thread appears quite clearly.

Etienne Harding, one of the pioneers who gave the order its firm structure, brought together an extraordinary culture and a talent for organization. He could be considered the true inspiration of the order, closely following its historical founder, Robert de Molesmes. During his early years Harding witnessed the banishment of Irish-Scottish Christianity. He left the Benedictine monastery of Sherbourne and found refuge in Iona, probably the center of Irish-Scottish Christianity. He also went at times to the school of the Celtic-druidic monastery of Lismore in Ireland. He later studied in the schools of Chartres, du Bec, Reims and Paris. After a pilgrimage to Rome, which seemed to have been at the root of an inner conversion, he decided to go to Cîteaux. Etienne asked permission from Robert de Molesmes to learn Hebrew and study under the famous rabbi Schlomo Jitzchaki in Troyes. He also studied Arabic together with Hughes de Payens and André de Montbard, two among the founders of the Templar Order. In essence, in true Platonic fashion, Harding brought together all the threads of antiquity, particularly Celtic and Middle Eastern, to converge into the new order. And those he wove closely with the new Chartres thread.

Another of the pillars of the order was Bernard de Clairvaux

---

[97] Steiner, *Karmic Relationships*, Volume 4, lecture of July 13, 1924.

(residing in Clairvaux from 1115 to 1153). For Steiner he was "perhaps the most outstanding personality of the twelfth century."[98] From early youth Bernard displayed a great sensitivity, a gift of prophecy, a strong link with the world of the departed, and great capacities for healing through prayer and the laying on of hands. He had an extraordinary charisma, witness the fact that he entered the Abbey of Cîteaux with some thirty relatives and friends, who had prepared themselves under his guidance for six months prior to their arrival. Harding entrusted Bernard to found the Abbey of Clairvaux in 1115, and this became the largest Cistercian abbey of the twelfth century. Although he declined the bishopric five times, Bernard managed to have a marked influence over the whole of Europe from the Abbey of Clairvaux. He was often called upon as mediator, and it was he who wrote the statutes of the Templar order. Not surprisingly, Clairvaux was considered a second Rome.

Bernard was first of all a mystic; he did not take the path of thinking, rather the path of feeling towards the Christ. His soul was a receptacle for the Logos. He could not be compared with any later figures, only with previous ones, Saint Francis in particular. Among other things, he was also a great lover of world history. Bernard's personality made it possible for the Platonism of the School of Chartres to unite itself with the Cistercian order, and that was even more the case after Alain de Lille's entry into the order. Steiner points out that the most remarkable teachers of Chartres belonged to the Cistercian order.[99] This means that the spiritual light of Chartres continued to live as Christian Platonism within the order.

Through Bernard, Cîteaux countered the stern Augustinian message that God would judge every deed that is found wanting, and that none of these would go unpunished. This worldview had manifested and intensified at the turn of the millennium with the great fear of Judgment Day. On the whole, the Old Testament view of a merciless God had been reinforced, and Bernard countered it with the New Testament message of a God of love. At first Bernard's ideas had impact within the

---

[98] Steiner, *A Sound Outlook for To-day and a Genuine Hope for the Future*, lecture of 16 July 1918.
[99] Steiner, *Karmic Relationships*, Volume 3, lecture of July 13, 1924.

Cistercian and ecclesiastical circles. A century later, they were embraced by great mystics such as Meister Eckhart and Tauler.

The earlier Platonism turned its gaze away from the earth and towards the Logos and the Sun. It had the character of reminiscence. The Platonism of Chartres, and later of Cîteaux, turned to service for the earth. It celebrated the metamorphosis of the Earth that will one day become the new Sun. The cult of Mary also took on a special role for this reason. She had been venerated in Chartres as a fertility goddess in Celtic times; she returned now as Mary who carries the savior.

The five initial Cistercian abbeys--very closely situated to each other in Burgundy--were to give birth, in less than a century, to a network that extended all over Europe. At the end of the Middle Ages the order counted some 1500 abbeys. No other order counted such a rapid expansion. This was due to the fact that Harding had envisioned that abbeys could not undergo unlimited growth. Once a number of sixty or so monks had been reached, the abbey had to create daughter abbeys. Some twelve monks were then sent to colonize a new area. The greatest expansion occurred during Bernard de Clairvaux's lifetime. And Clairvaux itself contributed 355 daughter abbeys, or 48% of all Cisterican abbeys in Europe.[100]

Wherever they went, the Cistercians put the land to use. Around each abbey were a varying number of farms, which introduced important agricultural innovations, such as the use of a plough with wheels, or the three-year soil rotation (pastures, followed by winter grains, followed by summer grains). Fields which had previously lain fallow were now planted with fodder and leguminous plants. The Cistercians used the farm as a closed system. There were always animals to produce compost for soil amendment. To the dung they added rock powder from their construction and calcium. It has been estimated that the Cistercians could multiply common yields by an average of five, and a maximum of fifteen times. Much of the extra yield was accumulated in the Cistercian

---

[100] Ekkehard Meffert, *Les Cisterciens et leur impulsion civilisatrice: L'ecole de Chartres, Alain de Lille*, 141.

warehouses. Thus, famines, following natural catastrophes or bad harvests, could be averted.[101]

The Cistercians often chose places between landscape features, e.g. where a river comes out of a wooded forest. Since they often started communities in the bottoms of valleys they had to drain excess water and reclaim land for agriculture. They often accepted donations of land deemed unusable because of drainage problems, since they were expert in the construction of waterworks. With the new bodies of water they developed fishing activity. For this reason they were dubbed the "human beavers of Europe."

The Cistercians chose the proportions of their buildings very carefully, going back to knowledge that had been accumulated since the Roman Vitruvius. And they paid great attention to acoustics, since song played an important role in their services. Their churches have between two and twelve seconds of echo, according to the materials used.[102] They also may have had other geomantic knowledge. E. Meffert discovered that in Pontigny, on June 21st the noon sun let some patches of light shine just in the middle of the nave, and that during the rest of the day, the light traveled from West to East towards the main altar.[103]

Cistercian churches are the expression of the passage from Romanesque to Gothic. The style was developed in parallel in the abbeys and cathedrals of Paris and its surroundings as far as Chartres, and among the Cistercian order in Burgundy and Champagne. It even appears that the key elements--lancet arches, flying buttresses--were used first among the Cistercians and then taken up in the architecture of the "Ile de France" (around Paris). All abbots, bishops and archbishops had attended the Council of Troyes, along with the Templars; then they all returned home, and somehow, the Gothic style emerged all at once. Suger of Saint Denis (Paris), who was very close to Bernard of Clairvaux, was one of the first to use the Gothic style during the reconstruction of the choir of his abbey. Soon thereafter, replicas of the style appeared in Reims and Chartres, followed immediately by the Cistercians, under

---

[101] Meffert, *Les Cisterciens et leur impulsion civilisatrice*, 196.

[102] Ibid, 281.

[103] Ibid, 277.

the guidance of Bernard. And they further introduced the Gothic style in Germany and Italy.

Alain de Lille keenly felt the reality of a transition to a new consciousness. He knew that what would follow the School of Chartres needed to be radically different. He carried this dichotomy in his soul and biography. His soul constitution made it possible for him to contact the cosmic intelligence that was fading from his environment, and rendered him a natural Platonist. Still, even in his youth, he had pored over the writings of Aristotle and intuited their importance. This tension in his soul echoed in his life after death. From the spiritual world Alain de Lille sent down to earth an unspecified pupil, whom he had instructed in the spiritual world, and who first became a Cistercian and then a Dominican. The goal of that pupil's mission is revealed in Steiner's words, "For in this pupil, he sent down on the earth all the discrepancies, it is true, which could arise between Platonism and Aristotelianism; but he sent them down so that they might be harmonized through the Scholastic principle of that time."[104] Alain's gesture of looking to the future and seeing the necessity of passing on the baton to the Aristotelians, reminds us of Plato's insight that only Aristotle would be able to carry his mission further.

The Cistercian order preserved a very important role until the time of Steiner. It continued to carry the Platonic impulse into modern times, though quite diluted.

Thomas Aquinas, Scholasticism and Aristotle

The next stage in the sister souls' progression sees the returning Schionatulander as the famous Saint Thomas Aquinas, incarnated in a family who lived in the town of Aquino, between Rome and Naples. Sigune was reincarnated not too far from there, as Reginald of Piperno. Thomas now entered the Christian life of the Catholic church in the order of the Dominicans, and became the most famous exponent of the school of thought called Scholasticism, teaching in Naples, Rome,

---

[104] Steiner, *Karmic Relationships*, Volume 4, lecture of July 13, 1924.

Paris, and Cologne. Aquinas's mission was to Christianize Aristotelian thinking. He was well acquainted with the body of Aristotelian thought and translated much of Aristotle's work from the Greek. In fact, he resurrected Aristotle's thought for the Western world, and turned him into the great philosopher of Christianity—so much so, that the Greek philosopher was often represented in Medieval art with the halo of the saints. Aristotle's ideas were integrated into Christian theology during the Middle Ages; hence the belief in newly created souls at every new incarnation. The same was true of the dogma of eternal punishment. According to Aristotle, the souls of the departed kept forever looking back at their lives and deeds on earth.[105]

When Thomas was a young child, his sister, who had been standing beside him in the room, was struck and killed by lightning, which spared him. This is the episode that led to the imprinting of the astral body of Jesus in Thomas's astral body. According to his biographer, Karl Werner, Aquinas was then five years old.[106] At around the same age, the only instance in which the child resisted his mother's requests, is reported to have occurred. His mother was asking Thomas to return to her a sheet of paper with the words "Ave Maria," which he was holding in his hands while taking a bath. Instead he swallowed it. At the same age he was brought to the Dominican abbey of Monte Cassino, where his Uncle Sinibald was the abbot. Here Thomas asked the abbot, much to his surprise, about the nature of God.

From an early age, Thomas knew where his destiny lay. At age nineteen he resolved to join the Dominican Order in Naples. This displeased the family, especially his mother, Theodora, who wanted him to become a Benedictine. While he was traveling on the way to Paris, his brother held him captive for eighteen months in their father's castle in Roccasecca; there Thomas had the opportunity to study Aristotle. One or two of Thomas's brothers tried to change his mind about his

---

[105] Steiner, *Polarities in the Evolution of Mankind: West and East, Materialism and Mysticism, Knowledge and Belief,* lecture of June 13, 1920.
[106] Thomas H. Meyer, *Rudolf Steiner's Core Mission: the Birth and Development of Spiritual-Scientific Karma Research,* 72.

vows through the wiles of a courtesan. To overcome the temptation, Thomas frightened her with a burning stick. In the process, the flame left the imprint of a cross on the wall of the dungeon where Thomas lay captive. Karl Werner wrote, "While he was still praying, a gentle sleep overcame him, during which he was enraptured by a gentle vision. He saw angels float down toward him, and gird his loins with the belt of chastity, arming the pure one as the knight of heaven. This armoring was connected with a vivid, sensory feeling of pain, which made him awake with involuntary sighs."[107] This is what Thomas confided on his deathbed to Reginald of Piperno alone, telling him that this was what rendered him completely insensitive to desires of the flesh.

Soon after that episode, in 1245, Thomas went to study in Paris, where he met Albertus Magnus, and followed him to Cologne. This meeting was very important to Thomas; as a result, he declined Pope Innocent IV's offer to make him abbot of Monte Cassino. Together, Albertus and Thomas studied the texts of Dionysius the Areopagite. In Albertus lived the soul who later returned as Marie von Sivers.

Gilgamesh/Alexander's soul accompanied Aquinas in the last fourteen years of his life, as the Cistercian monk known as Reginald of Piperno. Aquinas met him in the convent of St. Sabina (sacred to Artemis in olden times), where he stopped on his way from Paris to Rome. This casual encounter evolved into a deep reciprocal friendship. What is peculiar and striking about this association is that the pupil, Reginald, also turned out to be Thomas Aquinas's confessor. Reginald accompanied his master with devotion in every practical way in which he could support his work. At times Thomas Aquinas became so engrossed by his spiritual experiences that he would forget the practical necessities of life. At those times Reginald was always at his side.

Thomas traveled and moved frequently. Stops on the way were Naples, Orvieto, Rome, and again, Paris. But his task remained constant: teaching and writing. The years in Paris, between 1268 and 1272, were devoted to doctrinal matters directed against the rise of Averroes's brand of Aristotelianism. On December 6, 1273, Aquinas had what seems to have been an important spiritual experience with the Christ. Of this he

---

[107] Thomas H. Meyer, *Rudolf Steiner's Core Mission*, 127-128.

never spoke with anyone except his trusted Reginald of Piperno; and after that Aquinas stopped writing. Reginald asked him why; Aquinas is reputed to have said, "I cannot, because all that I have written seems like straw to me."

To understand the mission of Aquinas and his importance for Western thought we must take a step back, to view the evolution of Christianity and its body of knowledge in the time leading to the Middle Ages. In 529, the Emperor Justinian had closed the Athens School of Philosophy and banned its philosophers. The school was the original source of Mystery knowledge, which had allowed Saint Paul in his time to lay the foundations of a new theology. All the wisdom preserved from ancient Mysteries, and what they could offer to Christianity, was closed once and for all. This step undermined the attainment of a coherent Christian theory of knowledge; and the question had acquired more and more urgency by the time of Thomas Aquinas. The surviving Christian Mystery knowledge had survived only in secrecy, and could not benefit exoteric Christianity.

Saint Augustine (354–430 AD), ahead of his time, had already grappled with the early stages of the intellectual soul. He could already live in the growing dimension of individualism, but there was no frame of reference in the body of thought at that time, within which to place his experiences and growing awareness. He resorted to marrying Christian faith with Neo-Platonist thought, particularly from the perspective of Plotinus. Augustine fashioned the theory of predestination, in which half of humanity was predestined to salvation—regardless of personal merit—and the other half to damnation.

Opposite Augustine stood Pelagius, who promoted the view of individualism. He asserted that humanity could find in itself the power to oppose inner temptation and thus have a part in its own salvation.[108] In effect, at this stage of development, humanity was starting to feel that ideas originate from within. The Church took a convoluted position in between Augustine and Pelagius, asserting that the human being has

---

[108] Steiner, *The Redemption of Thinking: A Study in the Philosophy of Thomas Aquinas*, lecture of May 23, 1920.

some share in becoming a sinner or finding salvation of the soul, but God knows beforehand what the outcome will be. Church doctrine was sustained by, and embedded, in the postulate of this "double truth." This postulate further argued that an idea could be theologically true while philosophically false. In the face of this dilemma, one simply had to rest content with accepting the contradiction, and ultimately abide by faith in dogma. This compromise did not hold that there was an inherent and insurmountable abyss between the two; rather that it was so for the present level of understanding in which humanity lived. Obviously, this subtle mental gymnastic was not tenable in the long run.

At the time of Thomas Aquinas, the important step to be accomplished in individual thinking was threatened from yet another corner. Averroes and Arabic thinking held a kind of universality of mind that denied individuality. Their worldview argued that we have individual bodies, but that all have a common universal mind, which corresponds to a spiritual communion of humanity, rather than to the expression of individuality. This line of thought implied, further, that there is no individual immortality, only immortality of humanity. In this light, the vehement external opposition between the Scholasticism that Aquinas represented, and the exponents of Arabism, acquires a deeper meaning. What was at stake was the idea of the human being itself.

In the time of Aquinas, individuals felt truly individual in their feelings and in their impulses to action. They did not feel that their thoughts belonged to them. Rather, they could say that the thoughts filled the ether from the Earth to the Moon and that they breathed them in, received them into themselves.[109] They truly felt that they lived in a common atmosphere of thought, and they held the thoughts a little as we hold breath, releasing them at death when they passed into the cosmos again. This perception was preserved and deepened in the Aristotelianism that came to Europe from Asia through Islamic civilization. The Arabs conceded that at death the thoughts were out-breathed with an "individual human coloring," but this minor concession would have allowed only the slightest, most feeble feeling for the ego to

---

[109] Steiner, *Karmic Relationships,* Volume 1, lecture of July 1, 1924.

arise. Arabs who thought thus, felt themselves through their thinking to be intimately connected to the earth, but did not feel themselves to be individualities in the same way as the people of Europe were starting to do. The Arab and Spanish Moors held that the most important part of human knowledge did not remain with the individual being after death. This view did not deny immortality per se; rather personal immortality. The Dominicans declared human beings to be personally immortal. This explains the vehemence with which they opposed Averroes's ideas.

At the opposite extreme of Averroes stood Nominalism, a tendency that can be much more easily understood at present. To the representatives of Nominalism, thoughts were no more than empty abstractions; names were empty shells with no spiritual counterpart. Through this worldview, individualism could indeed develop, but also progressively sever itself from the spirit. The conflict of ideas played itself out both within the Dominican Order and between the Dominicans and Franciscans (Nominalists). Thomas Aquinas stood as the point of balance between a spirituality pointing to the past, such as in Averroes, and an early materialism pointing to the future, in Nominalism. Through Aquinas both individualism and a living, meaningful spirituality could survive.

Aquinas continued the existing stream of Scholasticism because he carried within himself the urge to reconcile philosophy and theology with the question of individualism. Ancient philosophers had not considered individuality, but only humanity as a whole, so Aquinas could not rest his edifice of thought on that basis. The recourse to "understanding" and "intellect" originated in Scholasticism, and is the product of the growing consciousness of individuality.

Aquinas wanted to further Aristotle's work; but he did so from a purely earthly perspective, not having the instinctive link that Aristotle kept with the world of the spirit, nor the proximity of the Mysteries. The incarnation of Aquinas was placed by the wise guidance of spiritual hierarchies in such a way that he experienced the very exceptional condition of the complete separation between the physical and spiritual worlds, which lasted for a time during the twelfth and thirteenth centuries. Even initiates at that time were unable to establish the connection with the spirit, and experienced the same darkness that befell all human souls of the time. This condition lasted until around the year 1250, when the first, short incarnation of the child Christian Rosenkreutz occurred. However, Aquinas later reestablished contact with the spiritual world, as Steiner tells us in *The Principles of Spiritual Economy*. This is how Steiner characterizes the philosopher in those lectures: "Being no less a scholar than a mystic, Thomas was able to give us such vivid descriptions, similar to those of the seer Dionysius the Areopagite, because he saw the spiritual hierarchies; and thus he was able to solve the most difficult problems during his long nightly meditations in front of the altar. Therefore, we find combined in him the qualities both of a mystic and of a brilliant thinker who is not influenced by the senses."[110]

The precision of thinking, for which Aristotelianism had laid the foundation, was now applied to an understanding of the spiritual being of Christ, along with his life and deeds. Whereas Aristotle had reached the culmination of the art of philosophy, Aquinas was the first modern thinker relying solely on his faculty of thought. Steiner says that we find in Scholasticism "the perfect flowering of logical judgment and of logical technique."[111] In fact, he argues, thought has never again attained such a pinnacle of precision and rigor.

Thomas Aquinas wanted to preserve Aristotle's philosophy and adapt it to the changed conditions of consciousness. He wanted to encourage individuals to elaborate their own ideas. He evolved the whole notion of percept and concept in great detail and exactitude. The Nominalists spoke of "universals" merely as an abstraction used to define the world. They said that in looking at the world, they found not the concept of "wolf," but examples of wolves; never the concept itself. This abstraction spilled from philosophy into theology. Thus Roscelin had reached the conclusion that "Trinity" was just a name of convenience for an unfathomable reality of Father, Son, and Holy Ghost.[112] Here lay

---

[110] Steiner, *The Principle of Spiritual Economy*, lecture of March 31, 1909.
[111] Steiner, *The Redemption of Thinking*, lecture of May 23, 1920.
[112] Ibid.

the task of Aquinas: to offer a philosophy that could reach to ideas that would soon be nothing more than abstractions.

Realists (Scholastics) had a differentiated approach to the matter of "universals" and their relationships to objects they stood for. Since Aquinas also harkened to the Christian tradition of the hierarchies, he held to the belief that above the concepts there was a whole spiritual world. He also knew that the soul and spirit work upon the formation of the body and that when this is completed, "the soul becomes a mirror to itself"; that is, the soul acquires capacities that emancipate the human being from the body.

Aquinas argued that for what we observe in nature with our thinking, we can come to the realization that it is the manifestation of something higher, something spiritual. What shines from behind the objects in the thought world is what Aquinas and the Scholastics called *universalia ante res* (universals before the objects). They are the universals issuing from the creative activity of the hierarchies. What is present to our senses he called *universalia in rebus* (universals in objects). These are what we perceive when we turn to the world with the activity of our senses. This activity is the stage of perception.

After perceiving with our senses, we turn to mental activity via the power of memory. What we have apprehended outwardly becomes a mental image that we can conjure up and, through it, form concepts within ourselves. The reflection within our soul of what is apprehended outwardly is what Aquinas calls *universalia post res* (universals after the object). Through the development of the power of thinking, the human being can stand before an outer object (such as a cat) and then turn away from it and experience the reality that is manifested in the object: the reality of what is present invisibly behind the cat. He does this by observing and studying deeply the object in front of him until he experiences the *universalia post res*, the concept behind the percept. The universals present in the objects (*universalia in rebus*) differ from the universal we experience in our soul (*universalia post res*) after we have perceived. Nevertheless, they are the same in their essence. Through intense thought and logical processes, the Scholastic found his way back from the concept to an understanding (not a direct apprehension) of the spiritual reality of a thing (*universalia ante res*). "The problem, which formerly was solved by direct vision, was now brought down into the sphere of thought and reason. That is the essence of the teachings of Aquinas, the essence of Scholasticism."[113]

Aquinas had to accomplish his task at the expense of the temporary division of external knowledge, leading to a science that could still in the future find its way to the spirit, and to the sphere of revelation concerning the divine and inner worlds. He recognized that revelation had streamed in earlier times from the world of the spirit itself, but human beings of his and later centuries would not be able to corroborate it. Aquinas paved the way by which these higher ideas could be shown to stand to reason, even though they could not be proved. This was a departure from the prevailing doctrine of the "double truth." The Christian philosopher bequeathed us elaborate concepts through which modern humanity could grasp the truth in revelation. In essence, he recognized that the intellect could not directly apprehend the suprasensory, but could still successfully strive to gain an understanding of it.

What Aquinas ultimately achieved was the building of a bridge between Reason and Faith. Although Reason, through logic and dialectic, could offer us an understanding of the created world, what lay beyond it was the domain of Faith. However, thinking could offer us an understanding of the domain of Faith, even though it could not prove it. "...after exercising his reason to the utmost to prove the existence of God, Aquinas has to admit that he arrives in the end at the same picture of God as the orthodox picture given in the Old Testament as Jehovah," Steiner tells us; and he continues, "To arrive at the Christ, however, he holds that one must pass over to the sphere of faith. In other words, in the view of Thomism, man cannot reach the Christ by the inherent power of his own intellect."[114] Ultimately, the question which Aquinas was not able to answer was, "How can human thinking be imbued by Christ? How can it be Christianized?" This question still confronted Aquinas on his deathbed in 1274. For this reason, he ceased writing and argued that "I cannot, because all that I have written seems like straw to me." It

---

[113] Steiner, *The Redemption of Thinking*, lecture of May 23, 1920.
[114] Ibid.

is of some interest for our further explorations that Aquinas died in the Cistercian monastery of Fossanova; and that Reginald was a Cistercian.

The breadth of Aquinas's work can be measured by the fact that by the second half of the thirteenth century, his teachings were used in all institutions of learning, particularly in monasteries. The importance of his legacy can be measured in contrast to the fact that the Franciscan Roger Bacon (1214–1294) was setting the stage for a purely materialistic science, which gained further ascendancy over the centuries. This movement was continued and brought to a whole new level by Francis Bacon (1561–1626).

Aquinas carried to his deathbed the question, "How can thinking be Christianized?" He would be able to answer it only in a later incarnation. Aquinas's philosophy, which had absorbed some of Aristotle's thinking, continued to play a role until the modern times. So did Aristotle's legacy.

In following the fate of Aristotle's work, one can distinguish two streams: nature knowledge on the one hand, and logic and philosophy on the other. The stream of logic and philosophy was elaborated by the Scholastics, as we have seen. The nature knowledge was carried to the Middle East and Egypt through Alexander's expeditions. Europe could not receive it; it only wanted external knowledge for the time being. The nature knowledge needed souls of the old Asian Mysteries, or what remained of them at the time following the burning of the temple of Ephesus. This kind of knowledge could be received in Asia Minor or Egypt. Later, it spread from the Middle East to Europe, often in a diluted way: either directly from the East, through the Crusades, or via Spain through the Moors.

Steiner talked about the nature stream of Aristotle's teachings in his lecture cycle *World History and the Mysteries in the Light of Anthroposophy:* "We find it in every corner of Europe, inconspicuous, flowing silently in hidden places."[115] And it was there that it was taken up by people like Jakob Böhme, Paracelsus, Valentin Weigel, Basil Valentine, and in the true alchemy of the cloisters of the Middle Ages.

---

[115] Steiner, *World History and the Mysteries in the Light of Anthroposophy,* lecture of December 29, 1923.

By the nineteenth century, modern human beings could no longer approach Aristotle in the right attitude of mind; they approached him, rather, as they would any other book. There were still isolated remnants, however, up until the 1860s and 1870s. And even as late as the last decades of the century these remnants could be found "within certain orders and in the life of a certain narrow circle," even if "sadly diminished and scarcely recognizable." So the last traces survived up until the time in which Steiner started his activity. "The two streams [of Aristotelianism] have lasted up to the very moment when it is possible to begin a renewed life of the Spirit."[116]

The last traces of Platonism and Aristotelianism survived until the standard-bearers of both philosophies reappeared on the world stage to continue the evolution of both streams. The souls of Aquinas/Steiner and Hroswitha/Schröer did not reincarnate until the 19th century, and this is what we will turn to next.

---

[116] Steiner, *World History and the Mysteries in the Light of Anthroposophy*, lecture of December 29, 1923.

PART III

THE NEW AGE OF MICHAEL

CHAPTER 4

GERMAN IDEALISM

The Recurring Ages of Michael

Michael alternates his time regency with six other archangels; each rules
for a period of about 350 years. Michael is the only one of the archangels
that fully believes in human beings, in spite of their being at a stage
lower than what God had initially destined them for. "This is indeed
the relation of Michael to the other *Archangeloi*. He has protested most
strongly against the Fall of Man."[117] Raphael, Zachariel, Anael, Oriphiel,
Samael, and to a lesser extent Gabriel, have stopped completely believing
in humanity; that is, believing that humanity will be able to see beyond
the *maya* in which it is mired at present. Living in a Michael age means
that humanity has access to a renewed hope that it can ascend to the
divine.

Before the time regency of Michael, despair and discouragement
had reigned in the Greek Mysteries, which were entering a period of
decadence. A feeling of resignation permeated the Mysteries, as people
believed that humanity could no longer ascend to knowledge of the
spirit. Then came the age of Michael, which culminated at the time
in which Aristotle founded his school of philosophy and Alexander
the Great conducted his campaigns in Asia and Africa. Alexander
responded to the cosmopolitan and universal call that is the impulse
of Michael.

---

[117] Steiner, *Karmic Relationships*, Volume 4, lecture of August 1, 1924.

During that Michaelic age, there was no such thing as personal intelligence; nor was there any "cleverness" in its modern form. The human being had no notion of such a thing as a thought produced by himself. When a thought emerged, a person knew it to be an inspiration of the spiritual world, not something he could possibly have generated on his own. These were thoughts raying down from the realm of Michael, who administered the cosmic Intelligence. And here a word is necessary about what cosmic Intelligence is. Steiner defined Intelligence as "…the mutual relationship of conduct among the higher Hierarchies. What they do, how they relate themselves to one another, what they are to one another—this is the Cosmic Intelligence."[118] Alexander the Great knew this, and considered himself only the envoy of Michael; and this gave him the strength to accomplish deeds of such daring and impact. But already at that time, and even more so later, Michael and his hosts saw that the cosmic Intelligence was slipping from Michael's grasp; they could foresee a future time when cosmic Intelligence would find itself on Earth, no longer in the realm of the Sun.

A further reality acquires importance here for our exploration. In the last Michaelic age, the idea of immortality differed from what is currently possible, chiefly because the Greeks had lost access to the idea of reincarnation. For either Aristotle or Alexander, immortality meant that their souls were sent down to Earth from the Sun, and that they would be received again into the Sun sphere by Michael.

At the time of Golgotha, the Michaelites witnessed Christ's departure from the Sun sphere, and they saw him uniting his destiny with Earth evolution. Most of them descended to earth for their first Christian incarnation between the third and fifth centuries; some incarnated later, even as late as the seventh and eighth centuries.

By the time all these souls had returned to the spirit world after a Christian incarnation, an important transition was occurring. Since human beings were starting to form thoughts on their own, the Michaelites saw that Michael could no longer administer the part of cosmic Intelligence that had in fact become earthly intelligence; and

---

[118] Steiner, *Karmic Relationships*, Volume 4, lecture of August 4, 1924.

this would progressively be the arena of the fight between Michael and Ahriman.

Because of the "fall" of cosmic Intelligence, human beings listened for, and received, inspirations for their life of soul in new ways after about the ninth century. They were starting to develop the ability to form a personal understanding from within themselves, rather than through a divine inspiration. Before the eighth or ninth centuries, human beings could be influenced through the warmth of enthusiasm of one who spoke and carried impulses of the spirit. The listener would actually slightly excarnate as far as her etheric body. She had the feeling of being "transported," or carried away. She could experience with sympathy beyond the words, into the liveliness that animated the god-inspired human being. This could be called a simple "elemental listening."[119]

After the ninth century, however, the listener could not be taught in the same way. Another kind of instruction arose in the Church, given through the interplay of question and answer, as it was found in the catechism. This was a substitute for the simple elemental listening that had lived before the fall of the cosmic Intelligence. Something else started to change as well. Previous to that time, the Mass had preserved an esoteric component. Not all Christians were allowed to attend the whole service. Some could be present only until the reading of the Gospels; others, who had received a considerably longer inner preparation, could witness the Mystery of transubstantiation, the esoteric aspect of the Mass. The first group was called the *Catechumenoi;* the second, the *Transubstantii.* Around the same period in which the catechism arose, the Mass became completely exoteric.

Another event, in addition to the rise of the catechism and the exoteric nature of the Mass, left an important imprint in the souls of the Michaelites as they were following world evolution from the spirit realm. This was the abolition of the idea of the threefold human nature in body, soul and spirit, at the eighth Ecumenical Council of Constantinople in the year 869. There it was said that the human being possesses only body and soul, even if the latter may have some attributes of the spirit. From the Sun realm, the hosts of Michael witnessed the vanishing of the whole

---

[119] *Karmic Relationships*, Volume 3, lecture of July 11, 1924

idea of the human being; they foresaw the impact that this would have for the future of humanity.

The decision made in Constantinople was itself the consequence of the fact that many angels were departing from the realm of Michael and moving closer to the Earth. Since angels are the beings that lead us in this life and into others, and participate in human karma, human destiny as a whole ended up being affected. The angels that had taken an earthly orientation would not be able to participate in the Michael School in the spiritual world from the fifteenth to the nineteenth centuries. The decision of the angels, which is naturally interwoven with individual karma, affected human beings for later incarnations. Referring to the choices of the angels, Steiner commented that "this...is one of the most difficult questions that can possibly be raised in connection with the modern evolution of mankind."[120]

Michael works from the Sun in relation to the other planetary Intelligences—Mercury (Raphael), Venus (Anael), Mars (Samael), Jupiter (Zachariel), Moon (Gabriel), and Saturn (Oriphiel). But it is Michael who rules over the whole of the cosmic Intelligence. The other planetary Intelligences emancipated themselves from the Sun under the leadership of Oriphiel, and from that moment on they worked at cross purposes with Michael. Those angels who turned to the other planetary Intelligences, rather than that of the Sun, also turned their gaze earthward, while the other angels remained faithful to Michael, the only archangel who completely retained trust in humanity. Ever since that time, a great deal of disorder has entered the karma of humanity, because some individuals' angels followed Michael, and others turned earthly. In the following incarnations many human beings could no longer find their way to everything their karma preordained. And this is one of the roots leading to the present state of social chaos worldwide. This situation could be addressed only with the return of a new age of Michael in the nineteenth century. At the turn of the millennium all Michaelites are deeply affected in their karma by all of the above events. The matter is explored in depth in Appendix 3.

---

[120] *Karmic Relationships*, Volume 4, lecture of August 8, 1924.

German Idealism

During the Middle Ages, and especially through Scholasticism, leading philosophers had reawakened the energy of thought life. Thinking did in fact reach a maturity hardly matched since. Thought was felt as something the soul had to produce out of its own depth. "How can something be expressed in thought life that is not itself merely the soul's own product?" had become the central question of the age.[121] The Scholastics had strengthened the life of the intellect and tested thought's inner power.

The rise of the Consciousness Soul is marked by the emblematic words, "I think, therefore I am," spoken by Descartes (1596-1650). He expressed the conviction that thought life can rest on its own foundation and be a secure source of knowledge. However, this worldview was now completely immersed in and conditioned by the emerging natural sciences. A picture of nature emerged that severed its ties with the inner soul life. The soul was losing all connection with nature, and it now confined its inquiries to a subjective inner world. There arose the challenge of a picture of nature that could no longer integrate any element of self-consciousness. These prevailing tendencies were challenged by classical German culture, as humanity was moving closer to another important moment of spiritual awakening, the dawn of the new Michael Age. We will now turn to four of the most prominent exponents of German idealism: Fichte (1762–1814), Schelling (1775–1854), Schiller (1759–1805) and Hegel (1770–1831).

Fichte

Johann Gottlieb Fichte was short and heavy-set. About his temperament Steiner offers that "He was all will, and will and will again, and his will lived itself out in the description of the most abstract concepts."[122] The strength of his speech is compared to a thunderstorm, and its delivery to strokes of lightning. His imagination had in strength and power what

---

[121] Rudolf Steiner, *The Riddles of Philosophy*, Chapter 1: "Guiding Thoughts on the Method of Presentation."

[122] *Karmic Relationships*, Volume 4, lecture of June 1, 1924.

it lacked in grace.[123] Continuing the description of a person of the will, Steiner calls him an "enthusiast of world conception."[124]

From early childhood, Fichte took on very definite life choices and displayed unusual capacities; here are two examples from his childhood. At age seven, his father wanted to reward Johann, a good student, by giving him the book of legends, *The Horned Siegfried*. The child became completely engrossed in the reading, and the father was thus very surprised when he saw his son throw the book into a creek. Though completely attached to the book, the child questioned a passion that could lead him to neglect his duties. This denotes the stamp of mind of a person who lives in an impulse towards a higher duty, a duty that wants to express itself beyond passing interests.

At age nine, an anecdotal event shows another unusual capacity in the boy. One day a neighbor from his father's village came to town for Mass, but arrived too late to hear the sermon. At the instigation of the local folk, who knew of Fichte's unusual skills, the neighbor was brought into the presence of the child, who was able to repeat the content of the whole sermon, showing that he had completely immersed himself in the experience of its delivery. Not only could he render the words, but he spoke out of the spirit of the sermon, as if he were still living in it.

Years later Fichte became a professor in Jena. One of his lectures was described by the scientist Steffens. During the lecture, Fichte called on the engagement of his audience. He asked them to "Think about the wall," and later "And now think about the one who thought about the wall."[125] He was thus engaging with his audience and asking them to undertake an immediate soul activity, so that they found themselves stimulating new capacities and exploring a new relationship towards the world.

Fichte sees the world as constantly changing, both within and without. He cannot conceive of any force that has permanence, nor of a way to come to know oneself or any other being. For him the world offers only pictures of an illusory nature, pictures living in a state similar to

---

[123] Steiner, *The Riddles of Philosophy*, Part 1, Chapter 6: "The Age of Kant and Goethe."
[124] Ibid.
[125] Steiner, *Karmic Relationships*, Volume 4, lecture of June 1, 1924.

that of a dream. And there is no way out in thinking. "Seeing—this is the dream; thinking—the source of all beings, of all reality, which I imagine, of my being, my strength of my purposes. This is the dream of that dream."[126] In this world of thinking he finds no way of awakening self-consciousness. This dream of thinking is contrasted by the moral world order, and the inner activity of the will.

Beings in the external world tell us what they are, through the qualities we can detect in them. Of these the human being can say "they [qualities] are." Things stand in a wholly different relationship in regard to the human being's existence. Man is the only one who can say "I am," not "It is." This denotes the presence of individuality, and this is the point of departure of Fichte's worldview. What he doesn't find in the world of thought, he seeks in the will and expression of individuality. At this point Fichte finds something with respect to which he sees himself completely independent of every other entity.[127] "This is how I live and this is how I am; this is how I am unchangeably—firm and complete for all eternity; for, this being is not taken on from outside; it is my own one true being and existence."[128] The soul that recognizes itself as an "I," becoming aware of the inner power that is activated in that recognition, engages in a process of self-awakening. Since this is so, in facing external objects and recognizing their being, these become part of the human being, for he perceives these objects are there for him.

For Fichte in the last analysis, all reality, even that of thinking, receives its certainty through the expression of that light that shines in the soul when the world-will works its revelations within it. And the human being can only know his highest being by engaging in living action. An eloquent example: "The surest means of convincing oneself of a life after death is to lead one's present life in such a way that one can wish an afterlife."[129]

---

[126] Steiner, *The Riddles of Philosophy*, Chapter 6: "The Age of Kant and Goethe."

[127] Ibid.

[128] Johann Gottlieb Fichte, *Vocation of Man*, quoted in Steiner, *The Riddles of Philosophy*, Chapter 6: "The Age of Kant and Goethe."

[129] Rudolf Steiner, *The Riddle of Man: from the Thinking, Observations, and Contemplations of a Series of German and Austrian Personalities: What They Have Said and Left Unsaid*, Chapter: "Idealism as an Awakening of the Soul: Johann Gottlieb Fichte."

Insofar as the "I" awakens itself in its experience of the world-will, it attains firm support for certainty about its being. This affirmation of the will leads Fichte to posit the existence of a moral world order, which has an order of reality independent of human existence, something outside of the "I." Admitting the impossibility of knowledge, Fichte steps into the realm of belief. "Because knowledge is a dream and the moral world order is the only true reality for Fichte, he places the life through which man participates in the moral world order higher than knowledge, the contemplation of things."[130] And this belief implies the necessity of an unconditional surrender to the moral world order for human life to attain the highest value and meaning. This finds the expression in the words "I, myself, and my necessary purpose are the supersensible."[131]

Fichte is a personality who believes that, in order to walk life's course, he has no need of the real world and its facts; rather, he keeps his eyes riveted on the world of ideas. He holds in low esteem those who do not understand such an idealistic attitude of spirit. To this vigorous personality, whose eyes are entirely directed to the inner life, it is repugnant to search anywhere else for a world conception, the highest aim man can obtain, except in his inner life. Fichte's striving is turned wholly to the world of ideas. He completely disregards the external world and its constraints.

Fichte's gaze is completely turned inward, and he cannot understand seeking higher meaning other than in the inner life. He believes that in so doing each human being can become aware of himself as living in supersensible reality. It is only through knowing the "I" within himself that one can truly become a philosopher. But he doesn't expect that one can become a philosopher unless he meets some preconditions. "The gift of a philosopher is inborn, furthered through education and then obtained by self-education, but there is no human art to make philosophers. For this reason, philosophy expects few proselytes among those men who are already formed, polished and perfected. . . ."[132] Fichte dethrones knowledge in order to open the way for living action

---

[130] Steiner, *The Riddles of Philosophy*, Chapter 6: "The Age of Kant and Goethe."
[131] Ibid.
[132] Ibid.

and moral activity. He wants the self to express its greatest degree of independence, but in so doing he denies a place to the external world. This means that knowledge of the external world becomes for him secondary, and that knowledge of nature does not seem to have any power to reveal the reality of the "I."

Fichte's philosophy left quite an imprint upon his generation. We will now turn to Schelling, whom Fichte admired, especially in the early years.

Schelling

Steiner describes the philosopher thus: "Schelling, who really always made a significant impression whenever he appeared again in public—the short, thick-set man, with the immensely impressive head, and eyes which even in extreme old age were sparkling with fire, for from his eyes there spoke the fire of Truth, the fire of Knowledge."[133] And he further mentions the charm of Schelling's speaking style, lively words and inspiring power. Another thinker, Gotthilf Heinrich Schubert, recalling the impact of Schelling's presence in Jena, compares reading or hearing Schelling to the effect of a new Dante, whose eyes are open into another world. He refers to his words as "measured, mathematically precise" and elegant.[134]

Friedrich Wilhelm Joseph Schelling began his career under the influence of Fichte's impulse, offering clear ideas in which lived his immense will.[135] However, fairly soon he took on new dimensions of his own, especially when he wrote *The Foundations of Human Freedom*, which Steiner calls "a kind of resurrection of the ideas of Jakob Böhme."[136] This was possible because, contrary to Fichte, whose will expressed itself in strength, Schelling tended more towards imagination, albeit an imagination that produced not artistic images but concepts and ideas.[137]

---

[133] Steiner, *Karmic Relationships*, Volume 4, lecture of September 16, 1924.
[134] Steiner, *The Riddle of Man*, Chapter: "Friedrich Wilhelm Joseph Schelling."
[135] Steiner, *Karmic Relationships*, Volume 6, lecture of June 1, 1924.
[136] Steiner, *Karmic Relationships*, Volume 4, lecture of September 16, 1924.
[137] Steiner, *The Riddles of Philosophy*, Chapter 7, "The Classics of World and Life Conception."

Not very differently from Fichte, Schelling sees himself at first with the awakening of the self in the soul, confronting the riddle of nature, which cannot offer him immediate answers. He sees that the soul awakens out of nature, and the relationship between the two is at first hidden. However, here is where he departs from Fichte's trajectory, in as much as he sees the possibility of awakening human cognitive capacities so that they acquire a tangible experience of what is at work as soul and spirit in nature, hidden behind its appearances. He can move beyond Fichte because of the imaginative capacity the latter lacked.

Schelling is thus attempting to move from the fulcrum of the "I" awakened in his soul through thoughts which are imbued with life and meaning. He believes that he can create a bridge between the natural world and the moral world. Discovering the realm of thoughts alive in his imagination, he calls these "intellectual imagination." He postulates with conviction that nature expresses and brings to manifestation the laws of the spirit. "Nature is to be the visible spirit: spirit the invisible nature." And further, "Nature and spirit, then, are not two different entities at all but one and the same being in two different forms."[138] This realization comes from the intuition that what lives as "intellectual imagination" in his soul is also the power at work in nature's process. Spiritual forces are at work in nature, and everything that later looks dead to human eyes, originated from the spirit. And he sees present-day nature as the product of a long evolution, in which what appears as mineral, plant or animal, is only the hardened end-product of what was much more ensouled at one point, the process of evolution having come to an end. Everything in nature is a manifestation of the spirit. The spirit that hides behind natural objects and phenomena shows itself more fully in the life of the soul.

Nature only shows itself as an end-product, but the human being has the ability to decipher how the spirit led to these end-products. Thus Schelling attempts through his worldview to offer ideas on how the creative spirit has power to produce in nature. Steiner summarizes the philosopher's views thus: "What preceded the things and what

---

[138] Steiner, *The Riddles of Philosophy*, Chapter 7, "The Classics of World and Life Conception."

created them is what emerges in an individual human spirit as thought. This thought is to its original real existence as a memory picture of an experience is to the experience itself."[139]

In referring to the "intellectual imagination" that makes the apprehension of the creative spirit at work in nature possible, Schelling is pointing to an awakening of the soul, to something that goes beyond ordinary cognitive faculties. This power of the soul can reveal the workings of nature by living into the soul element of nature; this predicates a soul participation, rather than the fresh creation of concepts. Steiner concludes: "Fichte had taken everything into the ego; Schelling had spread this ego over everything. What he meant to show was not, as Fichte did, that the ego was everything, but that everything was ego. Schelling had the courage to declare not only the ego's content of ideas as divine, but the whole human spirit-personality."[140]

Schelling's views extend further than those of Fichte into what we could see as the beginning of a cosmology centered around the question of good and evil, and the creative and evolving relationship between creator and creature. Just as Schelling places the striving for knowledge squarely within the evolving faculties of the soul and of the awakened "I," so does he see in the human race the capacity to co-create with God in freedom. He cannot accept the idea of an imperfect and helpless humanity subjugated to a perfect deity. The world that God creates must of necessity carry in itself perfection, or at least the ability to reach perfection. Schelling sees God revealing his work in a creature that is similar to himself, in beings that are endowed with the same freedom, beings who are like God and have their existence in God.

What is created by God is divine itself. However, something new enters Schelling's cosmology here. He sees the divine born of the non-divine. Light is born out of darkness, and from this non-divine darkness issue evil and selfishness. And freedom lies in the fact that God doesn't have all beings under his spell, that these must strive from the darkness

---

[139] Steiner, *The Riddles of Philosophy*, Chapter 7, "The Classics of World and Life Conception."

[140] Ibid.

to the light. Evolution is a continuous process through which the divine is born out of the non-divine. This exploration leads Schelling to questions about Christ, whom Schelling sees as letting the light of the divine penetrate the non-divine at a central point of human evolution. Christ's passion and resurrection are thus seen as a completely free act. His deeds appear in order to oppose the personal form that evil has assumed in the world. This is why he presented himself in human shape. Christ became the mediator between the creation and God; he was the one who enabled the human being to become divine once again.

We are fortunate to have more background knowledge about Schelling's eternal individuality than we have about Fichte, particularly his relationship with the Greek Mysteries. And it is interesting to preface these with a deep insight of Schelling that matches Steiner's revelations, and that concerns the evolution of philosophy. Schelling reveals that during Greek civilization the human being himself was an integral part of nature and therefore did not need to seek nature. Things changed after the time of Golgotha: humanity's earlier state of innocence faded out, and a polarity appeared between the divine and the natural—the first considered as divine and good, the second as evil, standing in opposition to the good. We see here that Schelling's insight matches what has come to light through spiritual science.

Steiner considered that Schelling had an inspired connection to the world of the Greek Mysteries, and he considered Schelling's work on the Samothracian Mysteries "extraordinarily deep and significant." He reveals that this work was written under the inspiration of Julian the Apostate/Herzeleide/Tycho Brahe. "…if we enter deeply enough into the curious language he uses in these passages, then presently we hear, no longer the voice of Schelling but the voice of Tycho Brahe!"[141] At other times other individualities inspired him as well, as for example in *Philosophy of Revelation*.

In his lectures in Berlin, Schelling predicates a departure from the philosophy of his day. He states the limits of rationalistic worldviews, in favor of what he seems to know dimly from experience: the need for

---

[141] Steiner, *Karmic Relationships*, Volume 4, lecture of June 1, 1924.

something that penetrates the soul from the outside, imbuing it with direct inspirations from the spiritual world. Steiner offers comments about Schelling's transition from the earlier rationalistic to the later inspired philosophy: "Then we see almost a kind of Platonism springing up in Schelling's soul. He writes a philosophic dialogue entitled *Bruno* which is truly reminiscent of Plato's Dialogues, and deeply penetrating."[142] This step in Schelling's work marks a reawakening of ancient Greek mythology and philosophy, "a reawakening of the old gods in a very modern way, and yet with old spirituality quite evidently working in it."[143] Of such power are his inspirations, particularly concerning Christianity, that Steiner sees them as harbingers of what is to come into the world as anthroposophy, directly out of spiritual vision rather than from sources of inspiration.

In the second stage of evolution of his thinking, Schelling qualifies all rationalistic knowledge as "negative philosophy." Another kind of knowledge can be attained when the human being immerses himself in the life of the creative spirit. He will then be able to transcend reason, through a more intuitive knowledge. He is thus complementing knowledge through reason, with knowledge deriving from inspiration. And this is what he calls "positive philosophy." "[The negative philosophy] will remain the preferred philosophy for the school; the positive philosophy, that for life. Only if both of them are united will the complete consecration be obtained that can be demanded of philosophy."[144] And Steiner's conclusion is quite revealing of what lives in Schelling's soul as a reverberation of the Greek Mysteries. He reminds us in effect of the difference between the minor Mysteries (Apollonian) and the major Mysteries (Dionysian). Schelling's negative philosophy corresponds to the minor Mysteries, the positive philosophy to the major Mysteries, and thus positive philosophy forms the crowning of the negative philosophy, upon which it can build.

---

[142] Steiner, *Karmic Relationships*, Volume 4, lecture of June 1, 1924.

[143] Ibid.

[144] Steiner, *The Riddles of Philosophy*, Chapter 7, "The Classics of World and Life Conception."

Schiller

Friedrich Schiller responded to Fichte in yet other ways from Schelling. Fichte distrusted knowledge's ability to reach beyond mere appearance, and opened the gates for living action, for moral activity. The importance of action in Fichte's case was replaced by imagination and inspired knowledge by Schelling, by beauty in Schiller.

Schiller's work can be divided into earlier and later phases. What separates the two is the important watershed of his encounter with Goethe. Schiller's worldview had to struggle against the main currents of thinking of the time: the materialism of the French Revolution and the estrangement of culture from life that lives in Rousseau's philosophy. Schiller's personality had to assert itself against these two oppressive views. And his youthful dramas were one of the first responses to this soul struggle. It was the poet Christian Gottfried Körner, a strong promoter of cultural life, who introduced Schiller to philosophy. From this point on, the main question with which his soul lived was "How can the interrelation of the sensuous with the spirit be found again?"[145]

In a treatise written after he completed his study of medicine, Schiller explores the life of the soul in the body, and how the body conditions the mind. The treatise ends on the question of the afterlife, with Schiller arguing as a matter of fact that death is not the end of life; after death, the soul simply moves on into another reality, another vantage point from which to look at its past life. And from there he quite naturally explores the possibility that the soul needs to repeat this experience a number of times, therefore implying reincarnation.[146]

The above view is amplified in his philosophical letters, where Schiller looks at natural phenomena and equates them to hieroglyphs that can be deciphered. An example is that of the chrysalis that changes into a butterfly. Here, what at first looks like death is only a metamorphosis. This is more than an analogy for Schiller; it is a guarantee that the human soul undergoes a similar evolution. It is a guarantee of human immortality.

---

[145] Steiner, *Origin and Goal of the Human Being*, lecture of May 4, 1905.
[146] Ibid.

After Schiller evolves his art and thought to this point, an event takes place which changes and shapes his further work: his friendship with Goethe. After a lecture given by the botanist Johann Karl Batsch, Schiller expresses to Goethe his dissatisfaction with what he sees as a fragmented way of looking at nature. Goethe, who points to another science of nature, could see the archetype or etheric body of the plant and could represent it to the puzzled Schiller in a schematic drawing. The philosopher of beauty now set out to attain an understanding similar to Goethe's encompassing viewpoint, which, however, he could achieve only to a degree.

A new stage of Schiller's thinking is reached in his *Letters upon the Aesthetic Education of Man*. His first effort lay in moving beyond Kant, who had inspired his youth, but who also presented formidable obstacles to his common sense. Immanuel Kant had affirmed the spirit against the sensuous nature of the body; he saw that only by denying the body could one hear the voice of the spirit in the call to duty, and thus be virtuous. Schiller rebels against this statement, because he sees it as a limiting view on human nature. He wants not to suppress, but to educate and transform.

Schiller recognizes two main drives, and one mediating drive. On one hand lies the drive toward the sensual; by surrendering to this, man falls in danger of egotism. On the other hand, he can resolve to lead his life according to the imperative of reason, with its stern logic and duty. Here lies a seemingly insoluble dilemma. If the human being follows the sensual without restraint, he silences reason; if he listens only to the imperative of reason, he mortifies his sensuality. There would seem to be no way out.

Logic and duty deny us freedom: we can only decide to submit to them. By following the urges of nature, the human being becomes a slave to them. How can harmony be found between the two extremes? Schiller wants duty to align itself with human desire, and morality to become something natural. He wants the human being to desire and enjoy what is his task. And where can such a path be found? Schiller looks for that state in which sensual and spiritual meet halfway, and he recognizes it in the creation of the beautiful. When producing a true work of art, as he knows from his own experience, he follows his natural inclinations without being driven by passion. He is led by imagination and the spirit. But this state is not limited to the one who produces the work of art; it applies equally to the one who enjoys it, since the artwork satisfies both his senses, without awakening passion, and his spirit. And Schiller compares the enjoyment of the beautiful to the child's impulse to play. He sees in play the possibility of satisfying moral imperatives while following sensual inclinations. He sees the possibility of the human being realizing virtue in the same way as he can pursue beauty. He concludes, "I am certain of this at least: The poet is the only true man and, compared to him, the best philosopher is merely a caricature."[147] Note that the philosopher he is referring to is mostly Kant, whose philosophy divorces humanity from nature.

Reflecting on the moral world, Schiller sees this as encompassing both the realms of reason up to where pure spirit reigns, and nature where necessity and compulsion hold sway. In a society in which morality is seen as an aesthetic question, human beings will forgo the rule of law and find spontaneous collaboration. They embody the laws that make possible harmonious living together.

Schiller bridges considerable divides in encountering Goethe's artistic worldview. When Goethe presents him with the archetypal plant, with the concrete experience of an idea, Schiller shows his surprise. He cannot fathom an experience corresponding to an idea. For him the very nature of an idea excludes the possibility of a full embodiment in an experience: the world of ideas and the world of experience are two separate realms. Experience takes place in space and time; the realm of ideas is apprehended by reason beyond space and time. And therefore man's knowledge flows from two different sources: externally through observation, and inwardly through thinking.[148] Steiner concludes, "One must seek in Greek antiquity for the underlying mental pictures which have given this [Schiller's] philosophy its stamp, and which have become driving forces of our entire Western spiritual development. .... [in contrast to Goethe's views, Schiller's views reflect] that way of picturing things which, originating from one aspect of Hellenism, sees an abyss

---

[147] Steiner, *The Riddles of Philosophy*, Chapter 6, "The Age of Kant and Goethe."
[148] Rudolf Steiner, *Goethe's World View*, Chapter "Goethe and Schiller."

between sense experience and spiritual experience."[149] There could not be a clearer reference to Platonism, which Goethe led out of a dead end. One can see to what extent the spirit of Greece lives in Schiller as in Schelling.

We have some inkling about Schiller's karmic biography. One pivotal incarnation took place around Rome in the 2nd century AD, during which he perceived and was stirred in his soul by the meek attitude of the Christian martyrs trying to uphold their faith against persecution. To this form of evil were added those of extreme injustices, perversity, degradation and corruption. The examples of good on one hand and evil on the other formed as questions in his soul. "[In this individual] there arose a kind of realization which was also a question: Where is the balance, the mean? Is there only the wholly Good and the wholly Evil in the world?"[150] In this incarnation he lived a long life, and he subsequently reincarnated as a woman in the attempt to balance the hard-edged sharpness of soul caused by the anxiety of the question he lived with. He could now turn this anguish into a detached, thoughtful understanding of good and evil. This quiet contemplation was further elaborated in his life between death and rebirth in the Saturn sphere. In Schiller's new life, this knowledge allowed both an encompassing and serene understanding of the past, and great idealistic enthusiasm for the future.

In coming closer to the essence of Schiller's work, Steiner calls the *Letters upon the Aesthetic Education of Man* "… a heart-balm; … they appeal to the core of the human being and want to raise this core a stage higher." And further he recommends that one not simply read the letters, but let them accompany one's life like a meditation book, "so that he wants to become as Schiller wanted to become."[151]

We have seen the links between Fichte, Schelling and Schiller. Things stand quite differently with Hegel, who is the purest thinker of the four.

---

[149] Steiner, *Origin and Goal of the Human Being*, lecture of May 4, 1905.

[150] Steiner, *Karmic Relationships*, Volume 6, lecture of June 1, 1924.

[151] Steiner, *Origin and Goal of the Human Being*, lecture of May 4, 1905.

Hegel

"With Hegel it is a matter of shaping the life of this soul in such a way that its thinking becomes a revelation of world thinking."[152] Alone among German Romantics, Georg Wilhelm Friedrich Hegel sees the possibility of raising thinking by emancipating it from its connections to the sense world. In his *Phenomenology*, this kind of knowing is called "absolute knowing," the thinking that goes from the finite to the infinite, which is reached through a severance from sensual content, but also from human feeling. These are "thoughts that reveal themselves in the soul when the soul makes itself into an onlooker of the process by which a *thought, free of everything of a non-thought nature*, unfolds into further and ever further thoughts. Then it is not the soul that thinks; the world-all thinks within the soul…"[153] In characterizing Hegel's capacity to build concepts upon concepts that are free from sense impressions or human feeling, Steiner compares them to Aristotle's "categories." A category is interchangeable with a concept that lives at the boundary between the sensible and supersensible worlds.[154] Concepts are in agreement with the nature of the sensible world, and their correctness can be perceived clairvoyantly. However, the formation of concepts is as independent from clairvoyant knowledge as it is from sensory observation. Hegel wants to build his philosophy on human reason completely devoid of mysticism; but living in his world of ideas can become a true mystical experience.[155]

Not unlike Schelling, Hegel sees the thought process at its culmination in the human being. Thought is first present in the natural world, but it is unconscious of itself. Thought is then present in the human being when he turns his attention to the life of the soul. For Hegel, thought is the essence both of nature and of the human being, but in the human being thought finally has the possibility of looking at itself. Nowhere else than in the cognizing human being is the possibility

---

[152] Steiner, *The Riddle of Man*, Chapter: "German Idealism as the Beholding of Thoughts: Hegel."

[153] Ibid.

[154] Ibid.

[155] Rudolf Steiner, *The Theory of Categories*, lecture of November 13, 1908, published in *Das Goetheanum* of November 13, 1908.

of thought's self-awareness possible. Thought is merely contained in nature; the human renders it active by directing it towards itself. Only the human being can accomplish the thoughtful comprehension of thought. Hegel's ultimate goal is to allow his consciousness to enter into the world's creative process, which manifests in thought. Once this process is present in his consciousness, the philosopher, Hegel believes, can let the spirit of the world reveal its own being.

Through his architecture of concepts, Hegel wants to bring order to and find harmony in the results obtained by scientific research. He wants to supersede the science of nature with a science that organizes and orders thoughts about nature.

For Steiner, "German idealism has expressed through Hegel this affirmation of the spiritual nature of the sense-perceptible."[156] However, Steiner's assessment of Hegel's success in this attempt stands in contrast to Hegel's stated goal. "Hegel at first seeks to find the circumference of all the supersensible thoughts that arise in the human soul when the soul lifts itself up out of all observation of nature and all earthly soul life. He presents this content as his *Logic*. But this logic contains not one single thought leading out of the region encompassed by nature and earthly soul life."[157]

Hegel is firm in his belief that the spiritual thought world expresses itself in the physical world, and that therefore everything in the world of the senses derives its being from a spiritual origin. However, in his attempt to decipher spiritual reality he does not make a departure from the sense world, nor does he offer another clear point of departure. Thus, he cannot approach supersensible reality from nature, nor approach it clearly from another perspective. And although he affirmed the supersensible nature of thinking, he was not able to lead his thinking to the supersensible.[158]

Steiner assesses that in spite of his "supersensible idealism," Hegel remained confined to the world of the senses. But he cautions: "One can

---

[156] Steiner, *The Riddle of Man*, Chapter: "German Idealism as the Beholding of Thoughts: Hegel."
[157] Ibid.
[158] Ibid.

acknowledge all this to oneself and yet not seek to judge the expression of German idealism in Hegel's worldview *negatively* ... One can arrive at a *positive* judgment and can find the essential thing about this worldview to lie in the fact that it contains the affirmation: Whoever observes in its true form the world spread out before our senses recognizes that it is in reality a spiritual world."[159]

We will now attempt to round off an understanding of Hegel's personality and work by referring to his other views, on theology first and on social questions later. As referred to above, Hegel saw in the human being the crown of God's creation. It is in the human being that thought can reflect on itself, and that God can know of himself and reach perfection. In saying this, Hegel is moving away from the idea of a perfect, immutable "first being" to the idea that the spiritual world itself is in the process of continuous unfolding

Hegel sees the first being as the agent that created the realms of nature and the human being. But he has left to humanity the task of creating thoughts about the created world. And, in so doing, the human being has become co-creator alongside the godhead.

Being able to co-create brings up the question of freedom. It is not surprising that given his views, Hegel holds freedom not as an innate gift, but as something to strive for. This means elevating our own being from a pure satisfaction in the sensual world to a progressive understanding of our spiritual nature, an active apprehension of the inner world. And the ultimate attainment of freedom means making oneself independent of the material world. "...gradually the individual wrests himself loose from this world of moral convictions that is thus laid down in the external world and penetrates into his own inner life, recognizing that he can develop moral convictions and standards out of his own spirit. ... For his moral commandment, he no longer looks to the external world but within his own soul."[160]

---

[159] Steiner, *The Riddle of Man*, Chapter: "German Idealism as the Beholding of Thoughts: Hegel."

[160] Steiner, *The Riddles of Philosophy*, Chapter 7: "The Classics of World and Life Conception."

Hegel's views about the relationship of the human to the divine carries consequences in the social world. According to Hegel, the eternal being is the "eternally real truth in which the eternally active reason is free for itself, and for which necessity, nature and history only serve as forms of manifestation and as vessels of its glory."

Here is first expressed the subordination of the human being to a world of necessity, in this case the world of the spirit, one that circumscribes the notion of freedom, even within the glorious concept of co-creation. These limitations come to light in Hegel's views about history and about the place of the individual in relation to the state.

For Hegel the world spirit realizes itself inexorably in the course of history, and the individual is merely a tool in its actualization. In great historical figures appears the coincidence of individual will and the will of the world spirit. These individuals are fortunate to have become agents of a greater will and act for the progress of humanity. Steiner concludes that in such a view, "The particular is mostly negligible in comparison with the general; the individuals are sacrificed and abandoned."[161]

In effect, Hegel sees the individual as fulfilling a role in history and society only in as much as reason or supersensible thought animate her, for thought is the central agent of world evolution. And Hegel sees in the state the realization of such thought in society, and quite naturally holds that the individual needs to subordinate himself to the state, not the reverse. With this Hegel denies the individual's capacity to determine his goals and direction in life; only if he acts in accordance with the dictates of the state is the human being acting in freedom.

In conclusion, we can say that Hegel sees the highest activity of the human spirit in thinking and strives to apprehend supersensible reality in thought, whose highest expressions are to be found in art, religion and philosophy. He cannot lead thinking from the sensible to the supersensible; however, his attempt lays foundations that will reach maturity in spiritual science. It seems appropriate that Steiner gives this final assessment of Hegel: "Hegel is in the modern world what Plato was

---

[161] Steiner, *The Riddles of Philosophy*, Chapter 7: "The Classics of World and Life Conception."

in the world of the Greeks. Plato lifted his spirit-eye contemplatively to the world of ideas so as to catch the mystery of the soul in this contemplation. Hegel has the soul immerse itself in the world-spirit and unfold its inner life after this immersion."[162]

An Assessment of German Idealism

The philosophers just reviewed expressed their personality and approached the gates of the spiritual world from very different perspectives: more typically in the will in Fichte, in the feeling in Schiller, and in thought in Hegel.

Steiner sees that in German idealism "the close alliance ...between poetic imagination and world conception has freed this conception from the lifeless expression that it must take on when it exclusively moves in the region of the abstract intellect."[163] The four philosophers in this chapter bring a personal element into their world conceptions. They believe that it is possible to build a world conception, that it is possible to reach an understanding of the world in agreement with their own nature, or, conversely, that by really trusting their soul they can build an understanding of the world within themselves. They believe that in this way they can reach an objective understanding of the world, not merely a personal fantasy. And each of them does it in markedly different ways.

Fichte forgoes all knowledge that is not gained from an inner source and experienced in daily life. Schiller feels he is at the utmost of his humanity when he can creatively play and experience beauty. His outlook is emblematic of many others of his generation. Steiner summarizes that "Romanticism wants to make the whole world into a realm of the artistic."[164] And further, "With them [Romantics], thinking was entirely absorbed by poetic imagination."[165] This, however, did not mean depending on belief. Only Fichte postulated a moral world

---

[162] Ibid.

[163] Steiner, *The Riddles of Philosophy*, Chapter 6: "The Age of Kant and Goethe."

[164] Ibid.

[165] Ibid.

independent of the human being; the others after him cultivated artistic imagination and unreservedly trusted the powers of the soul.

An artistic outlook in German idealists is closely allied with qualities of "intuition." Recall the impressions left by Fichte or Schelling, their very personalities, the fire of their convictions, the power of their speech. And add to this what Steiner calls "...powerful thought structures of Fichte, Schelling and Hegel were expressed aphoristically as strokes of lightning..."[166] We hear more from Steiner about the reason for these "strokes of lightning" in *The Mission of Folk-Souls in Connection with Germanic-Scandinavian Mythology*. However, in order to best understand the matter we need to look at the nature of the consciousness acquired by Germanic and Scandinavian souls in the centuries following the Mystery of Golgotha.

The people of northern Europe were closest to the state of consciousness of old Atlantis, and they experienced the transition from the old vision to the new kind of vision. While the "I" was not yet awake, they could contemplate spiritual beings. In this state of consciousness they witnessed the "I" being bestowed upon them and gradually awakening.

Until the 8th to 10th centuries AD, they could see how the soul forces started to work in the body. They could still perceive the imprinting of the soul forces into the body, and also the incorporation of the "I." "[The Germanic-Scandinavian] was present when the 'I' membered itself into the body and took possession of each single human being."[167] The Germanic people awakened to the "I" at a stage in which the folk-spirits still worked upon their souls, a stage corresponding to old Atlantis. They could literally perceive the "I" as a being among other entities; they saw it clairvoyantly. In fact they "developed the vision of the 'I' long before they became conscious of the real inner striving towards the 'I.'"[168] Through the "I" they could more consciously direct their relation to the outer world and form varied relationships with it. It was thus in

---

[166] Ibid, Chapter 9: "The Radical World Conceptions."
[167] Steiner, *The Mission of Folk-Souls in Connection with Germanic Scandinavian Mythology*, lecture of June 14, 1910.
[168] Ibid.

Europe that the human being first began to speak of the relation of the "I" to the world.

The people of northern Europe still carried the memory of an earlier stage of life, a time when they perceived everything as if in an ocean of mist, the time of old Atlantis. They remembered the gods that were still active at the time of Atlantis (whom they called the Vanas). And they perceived the later working of the Angels and Archangels (Asas) upon their souls. This second set of gods they saw still at work, forming the soul's forces and impressing them upon the body, as if this were happening in the moment, as late as the 8th, 9th and 10th centuries after Christ. The memory of the spiritual world did not lie in a far distant past, as it did for the old Indian or successive civilizations.

The philosophies of Fichte, Schelling and Hegel are "the result of the most penetrating old clairvoyance, acquired by man when he worked in cooperation with the divine spiritual beings. It would otherwise have been impossible for a Hegel to have looked upon his ideas as realities." And further, "Hegel's world of ideas is the final, the most highly sublimated expression of the spiritual soul, and contains in pure concepts that which the Northman still saw as sensible-supersensible, divine spiritual powers in connection with the 'I.'"[169] This also explains how all of Fichte's philosophy takes its start from the idea of the "I," which was a gift from the God Thor to the old people of the north.

Based as it is on the substratum of the Northern Mysteries, German philosophy does not fall into empty abstraction. German idealism shows that German culture is in essence ready to receive the ideas of spiritual science, once the times allow for them. And the German soul is also the best suited to understand the revelations of the coming of the Christ in the etheric.[170]

German classical philosophy is built upon the "idea-experience." In Steiner's assessment, "In Goethe, Fichte and Schiller, the experienced idea—one could also say, the idea-experience—forces its way into the

---

[169] Steiner, *The Mission of Folk-Souls*, lecture of June 16, 1910.
[170] Ibid, lecture of June 17, 1910.

soul.[171] Remember Fichte's emphasis on soul activity: "Think about the wall" and "Now think about the one who thought about the wall." It is this idea-experience that creates the solid ground for a worldview that sees the human being as perfect and as free as possible.[172]

The fruit of German classical culture is a world of ideas in which one can awaken consciousness of self. "With Fichte, world conception is ready to experience self-consciousness; with Plato and Aristotle, it had arrived at the point to think soul consciousness."[173] And further, "Goethe, Schiller, Fichte, Schelling and Hegel conceived the idea of the self-conscious soul to be so comprehensive that it seemed to have its root in a higher spirit nature."[174]

All of the above could remind us of the School of Chartres, in particular of what has been said of Alain de Lille, but also of all other people of the school, who lived in the fire of a world of ideas to which they could relate intuitively, and which they could still perceive in imaginations. Whereas Chartres gathered the fruits of the ancient Celtic Mysteries and the Mystery knowledge and traditions of the Middle East, German idealism gathered in a similar fashion the experience of German-Scandinavian initiation, and rendered in ideas the experiences that had taken form in the German soul and given shape to its mythology.

In the philosophers we have outlined in this chapter, as in Alain de Lille, rhetoric occupies a greater place than logic. Even in Hegel, the thinker par excellence, logic falls short of the mark. It seems the time is not yet ripe for the redemption of thinking. The German idealists counter, with all their energy, the foundations of the natural scientific outlook. But they cannot do so on epistemological grounds. Goethe, whose thinking goes the farthest in this direction, can only express himself in aphoristic and artistic terms. The others each contribute their brick to the building of a new worldview.

---

[171] Steiner, *The Riddles of Philosophy*, Chapter 6: "The Age of Kant and Goethe."
[172] Ibid.
[173] Ibid.
[174] Ibid, Chapter 9: "The Radical World Conceptions."

It is important to keep in mind that the fruit of German idealism would have found its fullest expression and culmination in the social sphere in German liberalism, had it not been for the effective counter-impulses of the western brotherhoods. Whereas British liberalism had its roots in economic thinking, German liberalism had a broader scope. It embodied a larger vision of the human being, as we have partly seen when Schiller's views from his *Letters upon the Aesthetic Education of Man* were taken into the social realm. Schiller considered the work of the politician to be the highest kind of art, the social art. Wilhelm von Humboldt's (1767-1835) *The Sphere and Duties of Government* is, according to Steiner, "... the first attempt at constructing an independent life of rights or of the state, an endeavor to find independence for the political realm."[175] The attempts that took shape in central Europe were founded on impulses that could evolve into the ideas of the threefold social order.

The elaboration of ideas that took shape in German liberalism could have found political expression through someone like Kaspar Hauser (1812-1833). Count Polzer-Hoditz recorded a conversation he had with Steiner, in which the latter indicated that Hauser's reign would have ushered in a "new Grail castle" in Southern Germany, in the area of Baden-Württemberg, Bavaria, and also Austria.[176] The united principalities could have resisted the rise of materialism and the threat of Prussian hegemony.

Materialism countered liberalism in Marxism. In 1848 Karl Marx wrote *The Communist Manifesto*, continuing the impulse of the denial of the spirit of the Constantinople Council of 869, and furthering it with the denial of the existence of the soul. For Marx only the struggle for economic well-being occupied center stage; culture mirrored this trend, becoming a mere "superstructure." From 1848 on, the liberal impulse fought against both the Bismarckian central state and socialist impulses. Repression of the liberal impulse occurred as early as the year 1850, and this was followed by the restoration of the German Confederation, bringing the reactionary Bismarck to power against the

---

[175] Steiner, *Ideas for a New Europe: Crisis and Opportunity for the West*, lecture of December 15, 1919.
[176] Sergei Prokofieff, *May Human Beings Hear It*, 711.

wishes of the liberals. By 1871, when Wilhelm I was crowned German emperor, Germany had turned its back on the legacy of Goethe and on its spiritual task. "Since that event, the throat of the German spirit has indeed been well and truly cut" is Steiner's assessment.[177]

Classical German Culture and Anthroposophy

There is a relationship between classical German culture and anthroposophy, about which Steiner wanted us to reach the greatest clarity. Steiner was emphatic that one will not find the sources of anthroposophy anywhere in the nineteenth century. In essence, Steiner made a great distinction between spiritual continuity and historical contributions. Anthroposophy is not in spiritual continuity with German classical culture; however, anthroposophy most naturally flowed within the stream the latter created.

Goetheanism survived in Steiner's time in a "somewhat petrified form," but it was a form that could be rejuvenated. Materialistic science overwhelmed the achievements of German idealism. The thrust of ahrimanic culture rendered Goethe's work all but unintelligible for the new German generations. At that time, Steiner judged it was anomalous to immerse oneself in the Goethean worldview. What German people received from their background (mostly Protestantism) did not prepare them to assimilate Goetheanism.

Germany repeated what had previously occurred in Greece and the whole of Europe, with the sequence of Platonists and Aristotelians. Modern times leading to anthroposophy were preceded in Germany with the Platonism of Goethe's time. Emil Bock saw Platonism not only in Goethe, but in the whole of the Goethean era; and the present work has corroborated him.[178] Indeed, the whole stamp of classical German culture is an echo of old wisdom now formulated in intellectual abstractions derived from large intuitions. We see here a situation analogous to what had happened with the transition from the School of Chartres to Scholasticism. The School of Chartres had offered a vista

---

[177] Steiner, *Ideas for a New Europe*, lecture of December 15, 1919.
[178] Emil Bock, *The Life and Times of Rudolf Steiner: Volume 1: People and Places.*

117

over the Mysteries of the past, via the preservation of the last vestiges of cosmic Intelligence. Then the time of the Consciousness Soul all but erased the last remnants of the old consciousness; they would survive only as seeds for future impulses. The Aristotelian Dominicans had to lay new foundations, even though the Platonists could still inspire them from the spiritual world. The German philosophers of the 19th century preserved inspired knowledge that could only enter intellectual abstraction with a certain degree of discomfort. Everywhere its intuitions seem larger than what words can convey; they find a more artistic and poetic expression than a scientific one.

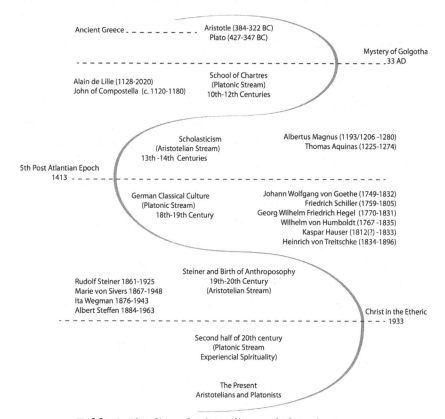

Table 1: Timeline of Aristotelian and Platonic streams

Although Austria was Catholic, Catholicism seemed not to directly affect the Austrian soul; it was as if it were not relevant. Austrians could still access the heritage of Goethe, Lessing, Schiller, Hegel, and others; and Austria played a role for the German soul similar to the role that Macedonia had played for Greece, in disseminating Hellenism toward the East in the time of Alexander the Great. Through Austria, the German legacy of Romanticism was passed on to the people of the Hapsburg Empire. Goetheanism, which had died in Germany, found a sort of refuge in Austria. "Austria in the second half of the nineteenth century unobtrusively provided a Platonic environment for the progress of humankind" is Bock's assessment.[179]

It is interesting to note that in Austria Plato/Schröer arrived at the end of an impulse, with the mission of lifting it up to a new level. That is precisely what he could have done had he, the returning Plato, brought Platonism to a new level, starting from Goethe who had been one of its pupils. Table 1 summarizes part of our findings and announces what is to come in the following chapters.

---

[179] Emil Bock, *The Life and Times of Rudolf Steiner: Volume 1: People and Places*, 98.

CHAPTER 5

STEINER'S AND SCHRÖER'S
WORLD TASKS

After Germany the focus of cultural renewal shifted to the Austro-Hungarian Empire at the end of the 19th century. It was there that Karl Julius Schröer and Rudolf Steiner incarnated in order to continue and further their world tasks. It is interesting to note that Schröer/Plato came at the end of the line of Platonists that had incarnated in Germany. He clearly was meant to carry Platonism, and particularly the work of Goethe, to a new level. And Steiner/Aristotle returned again in proximity to his old teacher to build upon what the former was meant to offer.

The interweaving of the karmas of Rudolf Steiner and Karl Julius Schröer has already been explored in *Rudolf Steiner and Karl Julius Schröer: Anthroposophy and the Teachings of Karma and Reincarnation*. This was done primarily from the perspective offered in the lectures known under the title *Karmic Relationships*, Volume 4, the last cycle of lectures given by Steiner. Let us briefly return to some of the threads developed in that book: Steiner's earlier discovery of his Thomas Aquinas incarnation; the destiny that united him with the Cistercians; what he said about Karl Julius Schröer in relation to anthroposophy; and a full characterization of the impulses that would have been representative of Schröer and Steiner.

Steiner's Initial Steps in Karmic Research and the Cistercians

The year 1888 was clearly a turning point in Steiner's life in relation to his faculties of karmic perception. Steiner had been touched by the poems of Fercher von Steinwand, and had an opportunity to meet the reclusive poet. In him he recognized someone whose strong individuality could not be explained by his environment. Steiner felt that, although advanced in age, Steinwand was the youngest in spirit of all the people around him. "His facial expression and every gesture revealed to me a soul being who could only have been molded at the time of Greek paganism and its influence on the development of Christianity at the beginning of the Christian era," is Steiner's comment in his autobiography.[180]

Steiner had another decisive encounter, this time with Wilhelm Anton Neumann, a learned Cistercian priest, in November of the same year. With Neumann Steiner had already had many long conversations, including a seminal one on reincarnation. Though interested in the topic, Neumann was of two minds. His personal interest lay at odds with everything that dogmatic Catholicism declared outside the faith.

On November 9, 1888, Steiner gave a lecture on "Goethe as the father of a new aesthetics." Neumann, who had listened with interest, shared his intuition with Steiner that "The seeds of this lecture you gave today are to be found already in Thomas Aquinas!" Referring to this conversation in the lecture of July 18, 1924, Steiner commented, "And then came the remarkable thing that I was giving a lecture on one occasion in Vienna. The same person [Neumann] was present and after the lecture he made a remark that could be understood as the fact that at this moment he had full understanding of a modern human being and his relationship to his former incarnation. And what he said at that moment about the connection between two lives was correct, not wrong.

---

[180] Rudolf Steiner, *Autobiography*, Chapter 20. Friedrich Zauner has continued the poet's characterization and come to the conclusion, agreed upon by T. H. Meyer, that he was the reincarnation of Dionysius the Areopagite. This had played an important part in Aquinas' education. See *Rudolf Steiner's Core Mission: the Birth and Development of Spiritual-Scientific Karma Research*, T. H. Meyer, 2009 (translated 2010) (Forest Row, UK: Temple Lodge, 2010) 44.

But he understood nothing at all and was only saying it."[181] Concerning this same lecture, Steiner told Friedrich Rittelmeyer, "...my own former incarnation dawned on me."[182] This indicates that Steiner knew nothing of this beforehand. Knowledge of a previous incarnation came to him via a Cistercian priest.

In Karmic Relationships, Volume 4, Steiner makes repeated references to the Cistercians and the role they played from his early childhood. The reader may remember that they were also present in the incarnation of Aquinas, who died in the Cistercian monastery of Fossanova with Reginald of Piperno, himself a Cistercian, at his side. In relation to the Cistercians, Steiner said, *"From my earliest youth, until a certain period of my life*, something of the Cistercian Order *again and again* approached me. Having gone through the elementary school, *I narrowly escaped*—for reasons which I explained in my autobiography, *The Story of my Life*—becoming a pupil in a gymnasium or grammar school conducted by the Cistercian Order. *Everything seemed to be leading in this direction*; but my parents, as I have explained, eventually decided to send me to the modern school [Realschule] instead" (emphasis added).[183]

The Cistercian presence continued in Steiner's life in the years immediately following. Steiner recalls, "But the modern school that I attended was only five steps away from the Cistercian grammar school. Thus we made the acquaintance of all those *excellent Cistercian teachers* whose work was indeed of a high quality at the time." Where this relationship went is commented upon later, when Steiner tells us *"I was deeply attracted to all these priests*, many of whom were extremely learned men. I read a great deal that they wrote and was profoundly stirred by it. *I loved these priests..."*(emphasis added).[184] And he concludes, *"In short, the Cistercian Order was near me.* And without a doubt (though these of course are hypotheses such as one uses only for purposes of illustration), if I had gone to the Cistercian school *I should, as a matter of course,*

---

[181] Steiner, *Karmic Relationships*, Volume 8, lecture of July 18, 1924 (London: Rudolf Steiner Press, 1977).

[182] T. H. Meyer, *Rudolf Steiner's Core Mission*, 52.

[183] Steiner, *Karmic Relationships*, Volume 4, lecture of September 12, 1924.

[184] Steiner, *Autobiography*, Chapter 14.

have become a Cistercian."[185] It is worth adding a similar statement from *Karmic Relationships,* Volume 6: "*I should have become a priest in the Cistercian Order.* Of that there is no doubt whatever. ...*I loved these priests* and the only reason why I passed the Cistercian Order by was because I did not attend the Gymnasium" (emphasis added).[186]

Later, in the years in Vienna, key friendships were formed in the circle of Maria Eugenia delle Grazie, where many important Cistercian figures gathered. Here it was that Steiner came to understand the karma of the Michaelic movement and the fate of the souls of the School of Chartres. "And to me those things were most important which revealed to me: it is indeed impossible for any of those who were the disciples of Chartres to incarnate at present, and yet it seems as though some of the individualities connected with that School became incorporated, if I may call it so, for brief periods, in some of the human beings who wore the Cistercian garment."[187] In the circle formed around delle Grazie lived people intimately connected with Steiner, therefore most likely Aristotelians. The inspiration they received from the Platonists on the other side of the threshold reminds us in fact of what happened among the Scholastics. At the time of their work on earth the souls of Chartres had departed the physical plane, but were still actively inspiring their fellow Michaelites from the spirit world.

The circle of delle Grazie also formed an important link to Schröer, though one that could not play out its role. That leaving this circle of people was a difficult decision is indicated in Steiner's words: "I was now divided between this house [delle Grazie's], which I so much liked to visit, and my teacher and fatherly friend Karl Julius Schröer, who, after the first visit, never again appeared at delle Grazie's."[188] Steiner is here referring to the task that he had to take from Schröer and advance as his own—the further elaboration of Goetheanism, establishing the basis for spiritual science itself. We will now look at this last, most important karmic connection.

---

[185] Steiner, *Karmic Relationships,* Volume 4, lecture of September 12, 1924.
[186] Steiner, *Karmic Relationships,* Volume 6, lecture of June 18, 1924.
[187] Steiner, *Karmic Relationships,* Volume 3, lecture of July 13, 1924.
[188] Steiner, *Karmic Relationships,* Volume 6, lecture of June 18th, 1924.

Schroer, Steiner, Platonism and Aristotelianism

Schröer's soul carried a deep respect for all that Goethe had achieved. He intuitively felt that his scientific work was far ahead of what science professed in the nineteenth century, but he recoiled from inquiring more deeply into the matter. Steiner had noticed that Schröer formed his ideas from a certain level of intuition, but had little interest in structuring his world of thoughts.[189] "Had he attained intellectuality, had he been able to unite it with the spirituality of Plato, Anthroposophy itself would have been there," is Steiner's revealing conclusion in the last lecture of *Karmic Relationships*, Volume 4. A similar conclusion is reached in his *Autobiography*: "Anthroposophy would really have been his [Schröer's] calling.... The very thing which he bears within him from a former incarnation, if it could enter into the intellect, would have become Anthroposophy; it stops short; it recoils, as it were, from intellectualism."[190]

Noticing that Schröer shrank from his task, Steiner could only conclude, "But as I said, what else could one do, than loose the congestion that had taken place, and carry Goetheanism really onward into Anthroposophy." And he added, "I resolved at that time to live Schröer's destiny as my own, and relinquish my own path of destiny."[191] Walter Johannes Stein, who published his memory of one of his conversations with Steiner in 1922, indicates that Steiner could return to his mission only after the Christmas Conference, "whereas everything that lay between was taken over from the path which Schröer should have trodden." This was made more explicit in reply to the question of what would have been Schröer's task. "The whole teaching of Imagination, Inspiration, and Intuition, and everything up to the forms of the Goetheanum building," was the answer.[192]

---

[189] Steiner, *Autobiography*, Chapter 9.
[190] Steiner, *Karmic Relationships*, Volume 4, lecture of September 23, 1923.
[191] Ibid.
[192] Steiner, *Autobiography*, Chapter 27.

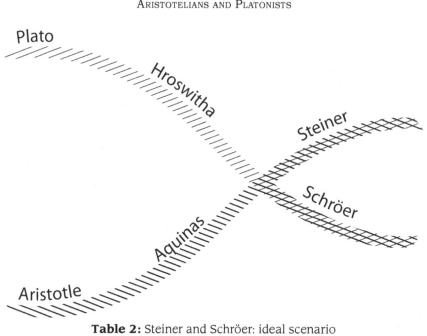

Table 2: Steiner and Schröer: ideal scenario

In various private conversations Steiner indicated what would have been his central life task. This is what was recorded by W. J. Stein: "Rudolf Steiner regarded it as his mission to bring the knowledge of repeated earthly lives to humanity—not in the form of a principle proclaimed in vague generalizations, but as a concrete knowledge that must be protected with a full sense of responsibility, tact, and insight."[193] Very early in life, Steiner had already built up all the soul faculties that equipped him for the fulfillment of his world task, offering the new spiritual-scientific teachings of karma and reincarnation from a Christianized perspective. He was in fact able to spiritually research a given individual's previous lives as early as 1888, if not sooner. But signs of destiny had already shown him that something else lay in store for him: something requiring his willingness to sacrifice. Had world karma proceeded in an optimal way, Schröer would have had to redeem the fallen intellect. He would have had to thoroughly school his thinking faculties to build the foundations for spiritual science. Steiner would simply have brought forward what he could directly perceive in the spiritual world, like a new Plato working out of a world of ideas.

---

[193] Walter Johannes Stein, *Rudolf Steiner's Life and Work*, 20.

His schooling of the faculties of the intellect had been achieved in his Aristotle and Aquinas incarnations.

Had Schröer proceeded normally to developing the task that world karma had entrusted him, the situation would have been as presented in table 2. In the diagram, the crossover indicates that Schröer would have had to work in a more Aristotelian way, whereas Steiner could have worked in a more Platonic way. However, world history unfolded otherwise.

Steiner's Path of Sacrifice: The Hague Document

The first step in Steiner's path of sacrifice was brought to him from the external world. Schröer's shortcomings affected more than one individual destiny, as well as world destiny. The most directly affected was Steiner. This meant, first of all, taking the way of the Realschule instead of the Gymnasium; and relinquishing the company of his most intimately and karmically connected circle of the Cistercians.

We have a crucial understanding of Steiner's task in the Hague Conversation that Steiner had with Walter Johannes Stein in 1922 (See Appendix 1). To the German anthroposophist Steiner confided how he had accepted Schröer's destiny as his own. He had decided for the time being to relinquish his own task in order to do what the world needed; he took on Schröer's mission. "By coming to that decision at that time, I experienced true freedom. I was able to write my *Philosophy of Freedom [The Philosophy of Spiritual Activity]* because I experienced what freedom is." And elsewhere, to indicate how personal had been the path to the writing of the *Philosophy,* he commented that the book did not aim at describing the only path to truth, but a path upon which walked one soul in search of the truth.[194]

In the same Hague Conversation, Steiner described the three levels of the experience of freedom in Imagination, Inspiration, and Intuition. At one time, they may be experienced as a unity; later in life, three

---

[194] Steiner, *From Symptoms to Reality in Modern History,* "Brief Reflections on the Publication of the New Edition of 'The Philosophy of Freedom,'" lecture of October 27, 1918.

different phases in the ways of knowing may emerge. "To immediate experience, they [Imagination, Inspiration, Intuition] appear as a unity, but, with the passage of time, they can enter into consciousness as separate entities." Following are the three stages described in the letter:

> Because one loves it, what one decides to do appears as a true Imagination. The second element that is woven into this unified experience is that higher powers admonish us to follow the impulse that is arising within us. "Do it," the inner voices say, and becoming aware of this is a perceptible Inspiration. Yet there is still a third element woven into this unified experience: through this free deed one places oneself within outer arenas of destiny into which one would otherwise never have entered. One encounters other people, is led to other places; what was first grasped inwardly through Intuition now approaches one externally as new destiny. This occurs when true Intuition unfolds.

Thomas Meyer concludes that after the meeting with Neumann and his karma revelation, Steiner left Vienna with a heavy heart, and moved to Weimar. There he met different people, and entered into newly chosen activities; different activities from what would have been in line with the normally intended world karma. As outcome of his detour through the Goethe work, Steiner said, "Because my destiny brought me the Goethe task as part of my life, this [normal] development was slowed considerably. Otherwise, I would have pursued my spiritual experiences and described them exactly as they presented themselves to me. My consciousness would have widened into the spiritual world more rapidly, but I would have felt no need to work hard at penetrating my inner being."[195] Had Steiner not met Schröer's destiny along the way, he could have brought forth his knowledge in a more Platonic way, directly out of the sphere of revelation. He would have been an even better Platonist

---

[195] Steiner, *Autobiography*, Chapter 27.

than Plato, because he could have perceived much more exactly what lived in the spirit world.

In his autobiography, Steiner indicated that had Goethe's task not met his path, he would have presented scientific research in a different way. "Initially, it was not my intention to attempt an interpretation of them [the words of Goethe], as I did soon after in my introduction to Goethe's scientific writings in Kürschner's *German National Literature*. It was my intention to present independently some field of science, just as that science appeared to me in accordance with the spirit."[196] Hella Wiesberger completes this line of thought. Steiner renounced the state of being through which the spirit world revealed itself through grace. A natural state of grace, which had endowed him with special faculties ever since his childhood, is contrasted with the other state of soul "in which, step-by-step, the soul develops an affinity with the spirit in order to stand within the spiritual of the world once it has experienced itself as spirit. Only in this actual participation does one experience how intimately the human spirit and the world's spirituality can grow together in the human soul."[197] The "detour" in Steiner's destiny occurred between 1882 and 1889 at first; then from 1889 to 1896. In the first period, Steiner was working on the Kürschner edition of Goethe's works. In the second he worked on the Sophien standard edition and published *The Philosophy of Freedom*.

Steiner stepped into the Weimar period, meeting there what Schröer should really have made of his Plato karma. And this is how Steiner characterizes the step he took: "I arrived in Weimar still influenced by the mood of my thorough study of Platonism. I believe that this helped me greatly to find my way into my work at the Goethe-Schiller archives. How did Plato live in the world of ideas, and how did Goethe? This question occupied me as I made my way to and from the archive building; it occupied me also, as I studied the papers of the Goethe estate."[198] This quotation is reflected in Steiner's writing of *Goethe's World View* in 1897. In Chapter 1, "Goethe's Place in the Development

---

[196] Steiner, *Autobiography*, Chapter 15.

[197] Ibid.

[198] Ibid, Chapter 31.

of Western Thought," some thirty pages are dedicated to characterizing the Platonic worldview in relation to the development of modern philosophy, and especially its theories of knowledge. And all of it is contrasted with Goethe's worldview. In essence, Steiner, who stepped into the Schröer/Plato karma, had to thoroughly delve into Platonism, and into the relationship that had existed between Plato and the young artist who worked within his circle of influence, the future Goethe.

What Steiner said about embarking on Schröer's task, he confirmed thus: "In a way, *Intuitive Thinking as a Spiritual Path* [*The Philosophy of Freedom*] freed me of what destiny had demanded of me in terms of forming ideas during the first part of my life, and placed them into the external world; this took place through my experience of the natural scientific mysteries of existence. My next task could only be a struggle to form ideas of the spirit world itself" (emphasis added).[199]

When he compared his own views with those that formed themselves in Schröer's spirit, Rudolf Steiner found more than the difference between the thinking of two individuals. He saw the individual standing within the great relationships of historical streams, and he recognized Goethe's spiritual "type" as that of the Platonic school. Just as Goethe thought about the primal plant, so Plato had thought about the ideas that underlie sense perceptions as their spiritual essence. And Rudolf Steiner found that Schröer, who, as a scholar of Goethe, lived in the realm of Platonic ideas, was no longer capable of finding the bridge that led from the realm of ideas to reality. He saw in Schröer the lonely heights of this super-worldly soul disposition. And that became for him a greater problem of humanity; he felt that finding a new bridge between the sensible and the supersensible was a necessity.

Such were the thoughts that stimulated Steiner to occupy himself with Goethe's *Fairy Tale of the Green Snake and the Beautiful Lily*. He saw the realm of the lily, that is, of the spirit, as existing within the Platonic stream in such a way that contact with the present time could not take place in a living way. He saw the Green Snake, whose task is to form the bridge between the world of the spirit and the world of the

---

[199] Steiner, *Autobiography*, Chapter 25.

senses, driven to the decision to sacrifice herself. The thought of this sacrifice lived in Steiner's soul.

In the end, one could say that the conundrum of "following my task/taking up someone else's task" disappeared, though not all the karmic consequences for humanity. In fact, the conditions were present in Steiner's sacrifice for a deeper apprehending of the polarity of freedom and destiny so central to the task that was his own—offering a spiritual scientific understanding of karma and reincarnation. Steiner concluded:

> Because of my connection with the Goethe work, I was able to observe vividly "how karma works in human life." There are two aspects of destiny that become unified in one's life. One arises from the soul's longing, and is directed toward the outer world; the other comes toward a person from the outside world. My own soul impulse was directed toward conscious experience of the spirit, and the external world's spiritual life brought me the Goethe task. I had to harmonize the two streams in my consciousness.[200]

The conclusion to this line of argument brings us back to the initial parting of the ways in Steiner's karma at the time in which he chose to go to the Realschule, and to the conclusion that "this was also for very good karmic reasons."[201] Steiner knew that had he not received a scientific education, he would not have been able to rescue Goethe's heritage and to write *The Philosophy of Freedom*. We can thus come to understand that much of the tragic karma of the Anthroposophical Society results from the fact that Steiner had to embrace both Schröer's and his own task (table 3).

Steiner's task in relation to Schröer appears even more clearly placed in perspective if we look at some of Steiner's indications concerning the ways individual tasks—most clearly those of initiates—evolve across incarnations. We will look at this aspect next.

---

[200] Steiner, *Autobiography*, Chapter 27.
[201] Steiner, *Karmic Relationships*, Volume 4, lecture of September 12, 1924.

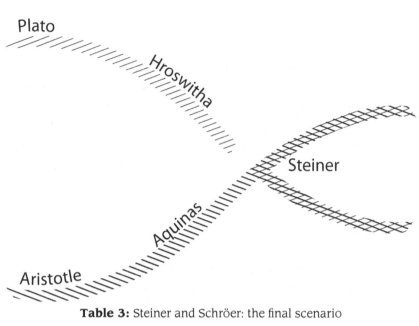

Table 3: Steiner and Schröer: the final scenario

The Evolving Tasks of World Initiates

The interplay and intersection between Steiner's and Schröer's lives has a deeply mysterious quality. When we follow the line of Steiner's incarnations, there is a natural progression between three incarnations in particular: those of Aristotle, Aquinas, and Steiner. Here lies the basis for the development of thinking in the whole of Western civilization. In anthroposophy, this thinking is redeemed and re-spiritualized. In this sense, Steiner's incarnation reaches a culmination in full congruence with the developments that preceded it. So why then does Steiner claim that his task lay in furthering the teachings of karma and reincarnation?

We have looked at this question from biographical and historical perspectives. We can find supplemental understanding on this issue if we look at what Steiner said in a lecture on *The Second Coming of Christ in the Etheric World*. Here we are told:

> Just as the spirit of Moses prevailed in the epoch that is now over, so in our time the spirit of Abraham begins to prevail, in order that after men have been led to the

consciousness of the divine in the material world, they may now be led out and beyond it. For it is an eternal cosmic law that each individuality has to perform a particular deed more than once, periodically—twice at all events, *the one as the antithesis of the other.* What Abraham brought down for humanity into the physical consciousness he will bear upward again for them into the spiritual world (emphasis added).[202]

To understand how the words just quoted apply to Steiner, we will look at the individuality of a teacher of mankind, whose role it was to lead humanity through the loss of a primeval state of being. Such was the case of Adam/John the Baptist, the "oldest soul" of humanity, the one whose earliest life covers the beginning of the process of incarnation. Adam led humanity through the Fall, out of its primeval communion with the spiritual world. At that time the human being had to sever its state of union with the Godhead, and that process reached its lowest point at the time of Golgotha. The reincarnated Adam, as John the Baptist, was the one who asked us to change our ways because the kingdom of God was at hand. Through preparing for the event of Golgotha—which occurred at the deepest point of humanity's incarnation and estrangement from the spirit—the same individuality who had taken the plunge away from the bosom of the gods also prepared the way for a gradual re-ascent from the physical to the spiritual. Having been the first to descend, he could now show the way to inaugurate the path of ascent.

When looked at from the perspective offered in the abovementioned lecture, the two figures of Plato and Aristotle appear in a new light. Plato's philosophical work promoted a consciousness of the divine outside the precincts of the Mysteries. He spoke about the Mysteries, but outside of these. Dionysus had inaugurated the way of the Greek Mysteries; Plato, the reincarnated Dionysus, brought his philosophical teachings to Greece at a time in which the Mysteries were turning decadent. Even if his knowledge was still rooted in the revelations of the Mysteries, he

---

[202] Steiner, *The Reappearance of Christ in the Etheric World*, lecture of March 6, 1910.

showed humanity the way toward the new consciousness embodied in philosophy, which was emancipating itself from the atmosphere of the Mysteries. Plato also left the world the legacy of a divided worldview: matter and spirit now severed from each other.

Aristotle was never part of the Mysteries. In him the evolutionary process was continued in a much more specific way through rigorous cultivation of the faculty of thinking. To achieve this goal, Aristotle had to forgo knowledge of reincarnation and karma. He originated the concept of the new formation of souls at birth and the idea of eternal salvation or damnation. The last traces of knowledge of reincarnation still survived in Plato, although in a corrupted manner. Aristotle had to consciously close the doors to this knowledge because the faculty of thinking had to develop within the exclusive boundaries of life on earth.

More than two millennia later, the same two individuals could undertake a deed that is an antithesis of what they had done earlier: a restoration of a condition of humanity that had been lost earlier. Schröer could have re-inaugurated the Mystery knowledge to which he closed the doors in his Plato incarnation, and this would have led to the inauguration of the path of spiritual science. In so doing, he also would have healed the inner rift that lived in his soul where matter stood at odds with spirit. That rift is healed in anthroposophy, but Schröer recoiled from fully entering intellectualism. Steiner, the new Aristotle, restored the way to a conscious knowledge of our eternal individuality, rooted in the reality of reincarnation and karma. He could now Christianize these teachings. This was the knowledge on which Aristotle had to turn his back, by virtue of the necessities of world evolution.

A closer look at Goethe and the development of modern philosophy and thinking will further highlight Plato/Schröer's destiny and life task in relation to world karma. Much of this was presented by Steiner at a critical turning point of his life, in his book *Goethe's World View*.

The change that preceded Plato in Greek philosophy was introduced when philosophers started to mistrust their sense perceptions as a means to attain knowledge. Steiner traced this change to the Eleatic school of philosophy and to Xenophanes, its first representative, who was born in 570 BC. Plato expressed this inability to trust the senses by saying that the things we perceive have no true being. He describes them as in a process of "becoming," but never "being." Thus there is a schism between the mental picture of a world of semblance and the world of ideas in which eternity is found. Plato could not ascribe real being to the sense world on its own. The schism between a world of semblance in front of the senses, and a true world to be found in ideas, is what Steiner called the "one-sided aspect of Platonism," which was to color all of Western philosophy.

In the evolution of Western thought, the Platonist one-sidedness is present in one form or another up to the days of Kant. It was present even in the materialistic antitheses. Francis Bacon did not see anything but subjectivity in the realm of ideas; reality, he believed, stood in front of the senses and nothing else was needed. His was "Platonism in reverse" and the foundation of modern science.

David Hume saw in ideas nothing more than habits of thought. Finally, Kant re-elaborated past philosophy without adding much that was new. He started from the premise that there are ultimate truths independent from experience, and a proof of these truths is given to us through mathematics or physics. Like Hume, Kant believed that thoughts do not stem from experience, but are added to it by the human being. He trusted scientific thinking up to the point where the human being asks the ultimate questions about freedom, immortality, and the divine. In the latter realm, he posited that only faith could offer us a response. This elaborate thought system was nothing more than an attempt to preserve a place for the highest aspirations of the human soul. Until the days of Kant, one-sided Platonism had been continued through the centuries. Even when the reverse stance was taken, as is most noticeably the case in Bacon and Hume, it was still the separation between idea and sense perception that unified different worldviews.

One-sided Platonism was completely foreign to Goethe's nature. According to his deepest feeling, what arose in his spirit was what surged within him by virtue of nature's power. He lived in the instinct that told him that all he needed to do was to live into things in order to extract from them what is present as the idea. There was no need to raise himself above them. He could not imagine perceiving an object in nature without the accompanying idea. "The reciprocal working of idea and perception was for him a spiritual breathing."[203] And nature proceeded from the whole in the idea to the particular manifestation of it that presented itself to the senses.

The attitude Goethe had toward nature was carried into artistic ideation. He felt that artistic creation comes forth in the same way in which a plant is the expression of an idea. For him, art was inseparable from the spiritual element. That explains why he was often willing to wait a very long time in order to complete a work of art, rather than rush to finish it through some artifice of fancy. Goethe's *Faust* could not be completed until the artist lived to sufficient inner maturity to grasp the spiritual ideas he had been struggling so long to bring into a perceptible form. And this is what Goethe wrote about art: "The great works of art have at the same time been brought forth by human beings according to true and natural laws, as the greatest works of nature."[204] In his journey to Italy, he was able to behold the spiritual component of the plant world—the primeval plant—just as he beheld the archetypes of great art from the Italian museums. Insight into nature basically did not differ for him from what he attained in art. And Steiner said about this process, "Goethe attains his worldview, not on a path of logical deduction, but rather, through contemplation of the being of art. And what he found in art, this he seeks also in nature." In this realm, Goethe was erasing the sharp boundaries Plato had erected between art and nature, art and science. Art was for Plato the realm of fantasy and feeling; science resulted from concepts free of fantasy. For Goethe, the difference between art and the scientific perception of nature lay in the fact that art makes the idea perceptible, and through it, the artist seizes the ideas of nature that lie concealed within it. And Steiner concluded, "It is one and the same truth which the philosopher presents in the form of thought, the artist in the form of a picture. The two differ only in their means of expression." However, ideas were not brought to consciousness in the form of clear concepts in Goethe's mind.

In all of this, we can see how important Goethe's work was for

---

[203] Steiner, *Goethe's World View*, Mercury Press, chapter "Goethe and the Platonic World View."
[204] Ibid.

the redemption of Platonism. The ground for German classical culture had been prepared by the reincarnated Platonic souls themselves. We can fathom how important furthering this task would have been for Schröer/Plato himself. It would have brought balance to what lived in his soul, which manifested in his unwillingness to immerse himself in the intellectualism of the age, and whose ultimate consequence was feeble-mindedness in old age.

We can also see a gesture of complementarity between the two main philosophers of Greek times. Plato's soul lived in the soul gesture of a comprehensive spiritual reality, best expressed in the notion of Platonic love. In Schröer this gesture had to find a complement in the passage through the crucible of the intellect. Aristotle had already acquired a rigorous training of the mind, and the same was continued in Aquinas. This rigorous training led Steiner, more naturally than was the case with Schröer, to the contrary condition, in which he could now apprehend the pure world of the spirit as a given reality. Yet in order to take up Schröer's task, he did not make full use of this condition of soul.

We can notice in the above soul gestures that initiates show the way to the soul-spiritual integration of human faculties that all human beings will have to achieve in future. That this is not an easy task is shown by the fact that even an initiate can fail at it. One could say that Steiner needed to integrate Platonism into his soul and world-mission, and managed to do so quite naturally and very early in his biography; whereas Schröer failed to do the same with Aristotelianism. This is what is shown in Illustrations 1 and 2, with the crossover between the two streams.

In light of the above, we can hypothesize that Schröer would have been more fit to meet his life task in theosophy. The whole ancient Mystery wisdom of the East that lived in Plato's soul could have been Christianized in a Theosophical Society that naturally linked back to the primeval fount of wisdom of the East. Within theosophy Schröer could have brought anthroposophy to fruition, and done so earlier than Steiner could, being his elder. Moreover, Schröer could have worked within the Theosophical Society when Christian Rosenkreutz's original impulses still influenced the course of events. In that case, Steiner could have unfolded his mission within the Christian stream, taking his departure from the people in the Cistercian order, deeply anchored in western traditions, and moreover with deep links of karma to him. No doubt this could not have been achieved within the Cistercian order itself, given its Catholic grounding; the individuals who followed him would have had to abandon their Catholic allegiances. Within the bounds of the old Cistercian order, Steiner would have found a link between Aristotelianism

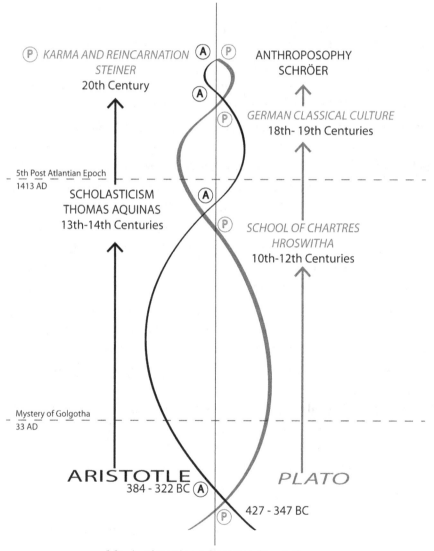

Table 4: Platonic and Aristotelian Influences
from Ancient Greece to the Present

and Platonism, since on occasion Platonic souls inspired the Cistercians from the spiritual world. Nothing would have been more natural than for Steiner to insert his task into such fertile ground.

We offer the conclusions of this work in graphic form in Table 4, where the successive Platonic and Aristotelian impulses are shown in their interweaving in time. The reader should keep in mind that the illustration is true for Platonists and Aristotelians as a whole; however, only some Aristotelians and Platonists may have incarnated in each successive stage of their respective stream. The illustration also indicates the stages of incarnation of Aristotle and Plato. (In the Middle Ages Plato did not carry on his work within the School of Chartres, but independently from it as the nun Hroswitha.)

We will now relate the original tasks of Steiner and Schröer to the panels of the Foundation Stone Meditation, and in particular to what the first panel calls "Spirit Recollection" (or "Spirit Remembering") and the third panel calls "Spirit Beholding" (or "Spirit Vision"). Spirit Recollection is the practice which ultimately allows us to apprehend the reality of our individual previous lives. Along the path of Spirit Beholding we behold the idea at work in matter; we tread the path from Goetheanism to spiritual science. About this, much has been said in *Schröer and Steiner: Anthroposophy and the Teachings of Karma and Reincarnation*. It was in fact the whole thesis of the book. Here, we will express enough of the basics in order to turn our gaze to Aristotelians and Platonists in the present.

Spirit Beholding and Spirit Recollection

The terms Spirit Beholding and Spirit Recollection only appeared at the end of Steiner's life, within the Foundation Stone Meditation at the end of the year 1923. The same polarity was expressed in other terms in 1923 with the characterization of the Saturn path and the Moon path, or respectively the path to the macrocosmos and the path to the microcosmos.

Why this only happened towards the end of Steiner's life is understandable when we return to Steiner's personal destiny and the interplay of his life with that of Schröer. Only towards the end of his life was Steiner able to bring the teachings of karma and reincarnation to complete fruition. Only in 1924 was he able to remind us that understanding karma and reincarnation in our lives means working on specific exercises. Only then could he reveal esoteric teachings that the forces of opposition had prevented from spreading. These new circumstances explain why all of a sudden the whole of anthroposophy is expressed in terms never used before, particularly the three practices indicated in the Foundation Stone Meditation.

The Foundation Stone Meditation brings to full expression three paths or impulses: Spirit Recollection (or Spirit Remembering), Spirit Mindfulness (or Spirit Awareness) and Spirit Beholding (or Spirit Vision). We will look at the expression of the two terms that form a polarity in Spirit Recollection and Spirit Beholding. The central term lies midway between the two, or rather forms a higher synthesis. It becomes more understandable in light of the other two paths.

In the year leading to the Christmas Conference, Steiner introduced the contrast between the "path of Saturn" and the "path of the Moon."[205] In relation to the Saturn path, Steiner took his start from *The Philosophy of Freedom*. Abstract thinking, which gives free rein to association of ideas, is resurrected from a passive activity into a path of perception of the spiritual in matter, when the thinker tries to apprehend the relationship between thinking and himself; when he looks at the activity of thinking itself. This is what leads to pure thinking, or spiritualized thinking. Steiner described "how the will strikes into the otherwise passive realm of thought, stirring it awake and making the thinker inwardly active." This is the path through which the human soul eventually reaches beyond Saturn into the universe (the path to the macrocosm). Steiner continues, "in that book [*Philosophy of Freedom*] I limited the discussion entirely to the world of the senses, keeping more advanced aspects for later works, because matters like these have to be gradually developed." The Saturn path is then contrasted with the Moon path, on which "one can advance on the opposite side [microcosm] by entering deeply into the will, to the extent of becoming wholly quiescent, by becoming a pole of stillness in the motion one otherwise engenders in the will." Instead of

---

[205] Steiner, *Awakening to Community*, lecture of February 6, 1923,

becoming an unconscious part of world movement, one can consciously come to a standstill. Through this "one succeeds in keeping the soul still while the body moves through space; succeeds in being active in the world while the soul remains quiet; carries activity, and at the same time quietly observes it; then thinking suffuses the will, just as the will previously suffused thinking." The Moon path allows one to separate the will from the physical body, just as the Saturn path offers body-free thinking. On the Moon path, "One learns to say 'You harbor in your will sphere a great variety of drives, instincts and passions. But . . . they belong to a different world that merely extends into this one, a world that keeps its activity quite separate from everything that has to do with the sense world.'"

Sense-free thinking on one hand; sense-free willing on the other. This is as much as was said before the Christmas Meeting. We can now take this further with the Foundation Stone Meditation, the *Leading Thoughts*, and the *Letters to the Members*.[206]

The third panel of the Foundation Stone Meditation contains the mention of Spirit Beholding, in which we are told:

Soul of Man
Thou livest in the resting Head
Which from the ground of the Eternal
Opens to thee the Thoughts of Worlds.
Practice *Spirit-vision*
In Quietness of Thought,
Where the eternal aims of Gods
World-Being's Light
On thine own I
Bestow
For thy free Willing.
Then from the ground of the Spirit of Man
Thou wilt truly *think*.

---

[206] Steiner, *Anthroposophical Leading Thoughts: Anthroposophy as a Path of Knowledge; The Michael Mystery.*

For the Spirit's Universal Thoughts hold sway
In the Being of all Worlds, beseeching Light.
Archai, Archangeloi, Angeloi!
(Spirits of Soul!)
Let there be prayed in the Depths
What from the Heights is answered,
Speaking:
Per Spiritum Sanctum reviviscimus.
(In the spirit's Universal Thoughts the Soul awakens.)
The Elemental Spirits hear it
In East and West and North and South:
May human beings hear it![207]

Here, it appears quite clearly that it is through thinking that we can apprehend the working of the spirit, in the quiet of the head. Key words are World Thoughts and Light of the being of Worlds. Through the "quietness of Thought" the "Eternal aims of Gods" grant us "World-Being's Light." This is the activity penetrated through and through by the will, which allows us to truly think "in grounds of the spirit in Man." It is the activity that leads us to "truly think" which connects us to the World of the Holy Spirit, or the Spirit's Universal Thoughts, through which the soul resurrects into eternity ("Per Spiritum Sanctum Reviviscimus" or "In the Spirit's Universal Thoughts, the Soul awakens.")

Leading Thought 66 expresses, "The Beings of the Third Hierarchy reveal themselves in the light which is unfolded as a spiritual background in human Thinking. In the human activity of thought this life is concealed. If it worked on in its own essence in human thought, man could not attain freedom. Where cosmic thought-activity ceases, human thought-activity begins." In Letter 17 of July 6, 1924, "Understanding of the Spirit and Conscious Experience of Destiny" (see Appendix 2), the path of thinking through the will (Saturn path) is such that the human being can say, "I am forming thoughts about what my senses reveal to

---

[207] Sergei O. Prokofieff *The Foundation Stone Meditation: A Key to the Christian Mysteries*, 210-212.

me as the world," and he can experience himself in his thinking, and therefore become conscious of the self.

The path of Spirit Recollection or Spirit Remembering resounds in the words of the first panel of the Foundation Stone Meditation.

Soul of Man!
Thou livest in the limbs
Which bear thee through the world of Space
Into the ocean-being of the Spirit.
Practice *Spirit-recollection*
In depths of soul,
Where in the wielding
World-Creator-Being
Comes to being
Within the "I" of God.

Then in the All-World-Being of Man
Thou will truly live.

For the Father-Spirit of the Heights holds sway
In Depths of Worlds, begetting Being
Seraphim, Cherubim, Thrones!
(Spirits of Strength!)
Let there ring out from the Heights
What in the Depths is echoed,
Speaking:
Ex Deo nascimur.
(From God, Mankind has Being.)
The Elemental Spirits hear it
In East and West and North and South:
May human beings hear it![208]

---

[208] Sergei O. Prokofieff *The Foundation Stone Meditation: A Key to the Christian Mysteries*, 210-212.

Here we can gather that Spirit Recollection addresses the realm of the Father and the activity of the will through the limbs. The activity of Spirit Recollection leads us back in time (through the stream of memory) to the time in which our "I comes to being within the I of God," which is later addressed in the same stanza in the voices of the Rosicrucian motto of "Ex Deo Nascimur," or "From God, Mankind has Being." This refers to, among other things, the time in Lemuria in which the Fall and the stream of earthly incarnations took place. The end of the activity of Spirit Recollection is not to truly will, but to "truly live in the All-World-Being of Man." The limbs mentioned here should be seen as limbs in motion, as the limb activity that moves us through the world of space in search of our destiny. These active limbs stand in contrast to the lungs and heart, whose activity is a rhythm (second panel), and in even further contrast to the head, which has to be brought to a complete standstill in Spirit Beholding (third panel).

Leading Thought 95 (September 21, 1924) reads: "In the manifestation of the Will, Karma works itself out. But its working remains in the unconscious. By *lifting to conscious imagination what works unconsciously in the Will*, Karma is apprehended. Man feels his destiny within him" (emphasis added). Central to this sentence are the words "lifting to conscious imagination," to which we will return later. The above finds a continuation in the formulation of Leading Thought 68: "The beings of the First Hierarchy manifest themselves in spiritual creation beyond humanity—a cosmic world of spiritual Being which indwells the human Willing. This world of cosmic Spirit experiences itself in creative action when man wills. It first creates the connection of man's being with the Universe beyond humanity; only then does man himself become, through his organism of Will, a freely willing human being."

Finally the elements we have explored come to a culmination in Letter 17 of July 6, 1924, "Understanding of the Spirit and Conscious Experience of Destiny" (see Appendix 2). Here Steiner again contrasts the two paths previously defined as Saturn (macrocosmos) and Moon (microcosmos) paths. In the Moon path—corresponding to Spirit Recollection—we direct our attention to the life of the soul; then those events emerge into consciousness that belong to our life's destiny, the events towards which our ego has gone back in the effort of memory. The human being who experiences this enhanced memory can tell himself, "I with my own self have experienced something that destiny brought to me." In this path an awareness awakens that I am not alone in my destiny, and that the world enters into the expression of my will. In relating to myself through an enhanced memory, I move from experiencing myself to experiencing the world.

Developing Imaginations of Self and Others: Steiner's Karma Exercises

We will take a step further in characterizing the effort of *lifting to conscious imagination what works unconsciously in the Will* before we attempt the contrast between the path of Spirit Recollection and Spirit Beholding.

Especially in the last years of his life, Steiner indicated that human beings are antisocial in their conscious life, and social in their sleeping life. This conundrum of conscious antisocial impulses and unconscious social impulses would seem to tend towards an entropic dissolution of the social world by the antisocial forces. The reality of this phenomenon is not difficult to intuit when we look at the present. The way out of this false dilemma lies precisely in "lifting to conscious imagination what works unconsciously in the Will."

To help us be more conscious in our encounters or in the script of our life, Steiner formulated many exercises designed for awakening interest, acquiring objectivity, and increasing our understanding of people and events in our lives. Central to Steiner's attempt were the exercises that can awaken a sense for individual recognition of the forces of destiny in our biography, and ultimately the reawakening of memories of previous lives. Steiner's effort never received the consecration or ultimate form that the path of thinking finds in *The Philosophy of Freedom*. The reason for this could be that Steiner barely managed to complete laying out important blocks of this edifice in the last year of his life. Nevertheless, a whole, coherent direction emerges once we look at some of these exercises, arranging them from the most immediate to the most demanding or far-reaching. This review is in no

145

way exhaustive; it is merely indicative of the breadth of Steiner's work in the matter. A more detailed analysis of the exercises appears in *Karl Julius Schröer and Rudolf Steiner: Anthroposophy and the Teachings of Karma and Reincarnation.*

Karma Exercise I: Gratitude Recollection

The name for this exercise has been chosen by the author. The exercise is designed to awaken gratitude and a sense of perspective concerning our personal achievements.[209] In it, Steiner asks us to review our life and see what part other people have played in it, by detecting how much we owe to our parents, relatives, friends, teachers, colleagues, and so forth. Each person we remember should be portrayed vividly. The exercise should lead to the realization of how much in our life we owe to others. Repeated over time, it allows us to develop imaginations of those people who play an important part in our life, imaginations that point to their deeper being. A variation on this exercise, offered in the lecture "Social and Anti-Social Forces in the Human Being," goes a step further.[210] We are asked to bring before our mind's eye images of those who have played a role in our lives, either directly and positively, or indirectly through hindrance and opposition, and see them as vividly as possible. We should be able to develop an objective sense of our indebtedness. Steiner has this gripping comment to offer: "It is extremely important, for the ability to inwardly picture another individual without love or hate, to give space to another individual within our souls, as it were; this is a faculty which is diminishing week by week in the evolution of humanity. It is a capacity which we are losing completely, by degrees; we pass one another by without arousing the slightest mutual interest." By invigorating this ability, we develop a truer picture of the people in our lives: in effect, an imagination of them. This will develop further in the ability to "relate ourselves imaginatively to those we meet in the present."

---

[209] Steiner, *Inner Aspect of the Social Question,* lecture of February 4, 1919.
[210] Steiner, "Social and Anti-social Forces in the Human Being," lecture December 6, 1918.

Karma Exercise II: Basic Lesser Karma Exercise

Another simple exercise, the Lesser Karma Exercise, consists of looking back to one single event in our life, one that is seemingly due to chance, or to something we did not wish to happen. Steiner spoke of this exercise in more than one place.[211]

The example that Steiner offers is that of a shingle falling from a roof onto our head. He asks us to imagine the deed of the "second person in us" who loosens the shingle from the roof just in time for it to fall on our heads when we pass under it. In other words, he wants us to picture that we have planned our lives before our birth in such a way as to come to certain critical turning points on earth. When we enter the exercise for the first few times, this second man is clearly seen as an invention, something artificially conjured up. However, he grows and evolves in us to the point that we cannot escape the feeling that he really is within us, accompanied with the growing realization that we really wanted these events to come to pass. The memory of the fact that we wanted these events has been all but erased from our consciousness; and the exercise, repeated over many life events, serves to awaken it. We can thus deepen an inner conviction and feeling for our karmic biography. Cultivating this feeling bestows deep inner strength, and modifies our attitude toward events we may have previously confronted with fear. We acquire a certain peacefulness and acceptance, together with the feeling that everything in our life has a purpose. This can even go further, as Steiner points out in a lecture of 1912.[212] "Through such mental pictures— that we ourselves have willed the chance events in our life—we arouse, in the life of feeling, memory of our earlier incarnations. In this way we understand that we are rooted in the spiritual world, we begin to understand our destiny." Whether or not we attain more than a simple feeling for the tenor of our past lives, something else becomes apparent: we start taking responsibility for our destiny, and stop blaming parents,

---

[211] Steiner, *Karma and Reincarnation*, lecture of January 30, 1912. See also *Esoteric Christianity and the Mission of Christian Rosenkreutz*, lectures of January 29, 1912 and February 8, 1912.

[212] Steiner, *Esoteric Christianity*, lecture of January 29, 1912.

friends, adversaries, or random events for those things that cause us unhappiness.

Karma Exercise III: Greater Karma Exercise

A final exercise is the so-called four days/three nights exercise or the Greater Karma Exercise.[213] This involves bringing back to memory an event from daily life that may or may not involve other individuals. It is a matter of depicting it inwardly, or "painting it spiritually," as Steiner puts it, by recreating in greatest detail all the impressions received by our senses. If the memory includes a person, one recreates inwardly the way she moved; the quality, pitch and tone of her voice; words used, gestures, smells, and so forth. This experience is taken into the night and repeated the following two days. The image is first given shape by the astral body in the external ether. From there, the next morning the image is impressed into the etheric body. One awakens with definite feelings and the impression that the image wants something from us. It grows real in us. The etheric body continues to work on the image. On the third day, the image is impressed into the physical body. There the image is spiritualized. Steiner describes the experience of the day as a cloud in which the person moves. We acquire the feeling of being part of the picture itself: at first with our will paralyzed, frozen, so to speak. This experience then evolves and becomes sight, an objective image. This will be the image of the event of the previous life that is most immediately connected with the event in the present incarnation. An experience of this kind will most likely not arise until the exercise is carried out a great number of times.

Before moving further, we can look at the contrast between Lesser and Greater Karma Exercises. The distinction is significant. The first stage is one of "taking responsibility for our lives"; the second leads to precise knowledge. The first stage is emblematically reached by the character of Strader in Steiner's Mystery Drama, *The Souls' Awakening,* with the words "And yet will come what has to come about" (*The Souls'*

---

[213] Steiner, *Karmic Relationships*, Volume 2, lecture of May 9, 1924.

Awakening, Scene 1). Strader has acquired an unshakeable faith in the wise guidance of karma, one that leads him to accept bitter opposition, and even complete paralysis in his life pursuits, with the knowledge that other doors will open to him after death. Quite differently from him, Thomasius encounters tremendous challenges with an aspect of his double, called "the Spirit of Johannes' Youth," and only manages to redeem him through knowledge of his previous incarnation as an Egyptian woman (*The Soul's Awakening*, Scene 10). This second instance illustrates a stage that can be attained through the Greater Karma Exercise.

We can graphically present the evolution of Steiner's exercises of Spirit Recollection in Table 5. All of these imply a strengthening of our powers of observation, and of our memory. The quintessential exercise that forms the foundation and prelude for all of them is the Rückschau. The activity of the Rückschau is one of pure review, in which we retrace the events of the day in reverse order, even in reverse motion. As we move towards the other exercises, significant concepts are added to the pure review, concepts the soul has to struggle to individualize. Only the Rückschau is pure observation and memory.

Preliminary Exercise	Exercise I	Exercise II	Exercise III
Rückschau	Gratitude Recollection	Lesser Karma Exercise	Greater Karma Exercise
Review of daily events in reverse order.	Developing imaginative pictures of self and others.	Taking responsibility for our lives.	Perceiving the origin of present events and patterns in previous life events.

Table 5: Exercises of Spirit Recollection

Let us return now to the contrast between Spirit Recollection and Spirit Beholding. It is clear that we are looking at a contrast between thinking and will in panels one and three of the Foundation Stone Meditation. However, the terms "thinking" and "will" evoke simplistic characterizations, and such are not applicable in this instance. Rather, one has to see thinking and will as interpenetrated activities; there is thought in the will, and will in the thinking.

At one end our thinking is penetrated through and through by the act of will implied in the act of cognition, in the act of directing the thinking towards an object without any external distraction, and without swerving into associative thinking. This is the path of thinking through the will: the Saturn path, and the path of Spirit Beholding.

At the other end, the activity of will is penetrated through and through by the thinking evoked by memory. This is what allows one to be a spectator of one's own deeds; to act and at the same time perceive our actions as spectators. This is the path in which the activity of the will is penetrated by thinking: the Moon Path, and the path of Spirit Recollection. Because we are used to calling the first the "path of thinking," the second should be called the "path of the will." A more complete characterization of either impulse would be the "path of thinking through the will," Spirit Beholding, and the "path of the will through thinking," or Spirit Recollection. The path of Spirit Beholding is the path of thinking transformed by the will. The path of Spirit Recollection is the path in which the will is transformed through thinking. This latter transformation is made possible by recollection, the activity that consists in looking back in the course of time.

On the path of thinking through the will (Spirit Beholding), the exercises in *Knowledge of Higher Worlds*, meditation, and the whole of anthroposophy form the essential foundation, which accompanies the pupil in his higher understanding of how the spirit permeates everything we behold through the senses.

In Spirit Recollection, the exercises we have just described, and other similar ones, form the essential core of the path. The whole of anthroposophy and even knowledge of karma and reincarnation form the complement. In fact, to walk at least the first stages on the path of the will, as Prokofieff's study confirms, it is not necessary to know anthroposophy.[214] And the attitude of soul necessary on this second path also differs greatly from what is needed on the path of Spirit Beholding.

---

[214] Prokofieff, *Occult Significance of Forgiveness*, Chapter 5. See the example of Bill Cody, pp. 54-55.

This difference is clearly stated in *Philosophy of Freedom's* Chapter 12, "Moral Imagination." In contrasting natural-scientific knowledge (and all external knowledge) with knowledge that leads to moral action, Steiner said:

> The confusion arises because, as natural scientists, we already have the facts before us and afterwards investigate them cognitively; while for ethical action, we must ourselves first create the facts that we cognize afterward. In the evolutionary process of the world order, we accomplish something that, on a lower level, is accomplished by nature: we alter something perceptible. Thus, initially, the ethical norm cannot be cognized like a natural law; rather, it must be created. Only once it is present can it become the object of cognition.

Only when I have acted in the world can I perceive what I have done and how it has affected the world. And only when I have acted can I go back in thought to review and evaluate. This appeals to a strengthening of observation and especially of memory.

The contrast between the two paths appears emblematically when we look at the polarities between the "pencil exercise" (control of thoughts) and the Rückschau as expressions of Spirit Beholding and Spirit Recollection respectively. In the pencil exercise we focus all our attention on an object, such as a pencil, by discerning our sense impressions of the object, thinking about its component parts and their relationships, imagining the steps of the process that created it, and so forth. During the few minutes of the observation all thoughts foreign to the object are carefully kept at bay, which requires a tremendous effort of the will. It is truly an education of thinking through the will.

Its polar opposite, though this may not be immediately apparent, happens in the Rückschau exercise, whose intent is to focus inwardly upon the whole of the day or parts of it, picturing events in the reverse order of their occurrence, and even in reverse motion. Instead of looking outward, we turn our focus inward with an effort of memory. What our will has brought about throughout the day, all of which would remain unconscious or semi-conscious, is raised to awareness. This is also a conscious effort of the will, but here thinking imposes order on the • course of the will's unfolding during the day, reminding us of Steiner's precondition for ethical action, in which "we must ourselves first create the facts." Looking outward in the pencil exercise becomes looking inward in the Rückschau; the first addresses the thinking through the will, the second the will through thinking.

It is quite symptomatic that at the end of his life Steiner was able to articulate the great polarity between the paths of Spirit Beholding and of Spirit Recollection. This could not come to the fore without the full revelations of karma, mostly brought forward in the *Karmic Relationships* lectures. Spirit Recollection is the path that is most natural to the Platonist; Spirit Beholding is what Steiner taught for most of his life, and the path that he outlined for the Aristotelians of his time. It is not surprising that, with the impending arrival of more Platonic souls, Steiner had to accelerate the spread of the teachings of karma and reincarnation. The future of the convergence of the two streams depended on it.

The contrast between Aristotelians and Platonists receives great attention in Walter Stein's "Hague Conversation" with Steiner in 1922 (see Appendix 1). After alluding to the tragedy of the Beautiful Lily and the necessity of the sacrifice of the Green Snake, Steiner indicated that the polarity between Schröer and him was more than a personal matter. And here he leads us to another polarity, that between "natural-scientific knowledge" and "historical-literal knowledge." To Stein, who inquired about the difference between the two, Steiner replied:

The actual knowledge in these domains is this: Natural science comprehends ghosts with its thoughts. You only have to take the word in its original sense. What the cosmos spins, what the planets weave, this is what natural-scientific thinking comprehends. Historical thinking, on the other hand, comprehends "demons," but this word is also taken in its noble sense: in the way that Socrates speaks of his daimonion, as a guiding spirit, a spirit such as Plutarch speaks of as a good star that men can follow. Each historical fact is a demon in the sense of the Greeks. And when one grasps the two forms of knowledge together, approaches both in their most noble form, then a path opens up. Yes, a true path. Historical thoughts are tentative thoughts, thoughts of an experimental nature. One must ask the spiritual beings to ensoul them. Then they correct themselves, and become truth over the course of time. And natural-scientific thoughts are also thoughts that are thought by way of experiment. One must present them to the cosmos, then they become artistic pictures, Imaginations. And then, then when one treads both these paths simultaneously, and achieves natural-scientific Imagination and historical Inspiration, then life itself undergoes change; destiny is transformed. Then, sacrificing, and celebrating one's destiny, one places oneself into the stream. That is the path; that is anthroposophic knowledge; that is anthroposophic life.

In these last words recorded by Stein, we have an impression of what the "culmination" at the end of the twentieth century would be: "a celebration of destiny," not only for the individual, but also for the Michaelic Movement as a whole; and further, a way to bring together "anthroposophical knowledge and anthroposophical life." The first is the gift of the Aristotelians, the second of the Platonists. The last statement echoes at a global level what has been said about the individual, particularly in relation to the path of Spirit Recollection in contrast to the path of Spirit Beholding, and of the Saturn path in polarity to the Moon path. It is only through the integration of these two paths (representing, respectively, the attainment of Imagination and Inspiration) that we will be able to walk into the next cultural epoch. Likewise, the culmination of the Michaelic Movement in the twentieth and twenty-first centuries derives from the ability to recognize and validate Aristotelian Imagination and Platonic Inspiration, which together will bring anthroposophical knowledge and anthroposophical life for the renewing of civilization. We can summarize our findings in Table 6.

SPIRIT BEHOLDING	SPIRIT RECOLLECTION
Saturn path (macrocosm)	Moon path (microcosm)
Path of thinking through the will	Path of the will through thinking
Pencil observation exercise: looking at the outer world	Rückschau: looking at the inner world
Preparation through study of anthroposophy	Preparation through the karma exercises: review exercises going first to Lesser Karma and then to Greater Karma exercises
Furthering through meditation, and deepening of the study	Furthering through study of karma and reincarnation teachings: eventually, karmic research
Third panel of the Foundation Stone Meditation: Spirit Beholding	First panel of the Foundation Stone Meditation: Spirit Recollection
Understanding of the Spirit	Conscious experience of Destiny
Facts are given	Facts (deeds) need to be created in order to be known and understood
Natural-scientific thinking (The Hague Conversation)	Historical-literary thinking (The Hague Conversation)
Imagination	Inspiration
Anthroposophical thought	Anthroposophical life

Table 6: Spirit Beholding and Spirit Recollection

The path of Spirit Recollection is the path that is most naturally followed by Platonists; the path of Spirit Beholding is more natural to Aristotelians. Not surprisingly, Aristotelians feel most at home within the natural sciences. The Platonists tend to gravitate towards the humanities. This, however, is an overly broad characterization. Reality is far more nuanced, as we will see in Chapters 7, 8 and 9, in which we will investigate the polarities between Aristotelians and Platonists when we look at complementary ways of working in natural sciences, in psychology and around the social question.

Spirit Recollection and the Seven Life Processes

Spirit recollection connects us to our being in time, to the unfolding of our biography on earth, and further to our eternal being as it repeatedly incarnates. The realm of time is that of the number seven. As the twelve senses connect us to the world of space, so the seven life processes underlie everything unfolding in time, such as the building of our bodily and soul sheaths.

The seven life processes are: breathing, warming, nourishing, secreting, maintaining, growing and reproducing. The life processes in the etheric body are closely associated with the senses in the physical body. There is a process of breathing, of warming, of nourishing, and so forth, for the sense of sight, hearing, balance, and each one of the twelve senses. The first three processes, breathing, warming and nourishing, connect living beings with the external world. In the middle stands the process of secreting, which covers assimilation, absorption and excretion. It is the turning point, which individualizes what the organism receives from the environment. The remaining three processes are inner ones. First comes maintenance, the ability to sustain the life of the organism; growth, the ability to bring about quantitative and qualitative changes in the organism, and finally reproduction, leading to the formation of new, independent organisms.

The life processes build the human organism in its sheaths before the completion of ego maturity: first the physical, then the etheric and the astral, up to the birth of the ego. What is devoted to the building of our adult form is then freed first for soul processes, then for spiritual processes. Naturally, these are not strictly sequential processes, but ones that keep overlapping each other.

In a human being the life processes are at work in the first three cycles of seven years in the respective building up of physical, etheric, and astral bodies, up to the birth of the ego at age twenty-one. At this point, the life processes are further freed from the body and made available for a new process of learning led by the conscious ego. Different kinds of learning are called into account depending on what the human being turns her attention to. Coenraad van Houten has developed the so-called "Adult Learning" and "Destiny Learning." The two approaches call on us to consciously enhance the life processes for the purpose of learning; the first concerns what we can learn from the study of anthroposophy, the second one what we can learn at the hand of biographical events.[215]

The example of Destiny Learning closely follows the exercise of the Greater Karma Exercise. The path of Destiny Learning explores our inner being and what approaches us in the events in our lives. Whereas in Adult Learning we start from what is universal and objective, in Destiny Learning we turn to what is utterly personal and subjective. Ultimately we know that we can reach the objective ground that forms the bedrock of a biography, or what we know from spiritual science as our previous incarnations. In that light, we are no longer merely the product of our physical environment and social and cultural forces. We are not only unique manifestations of individuality, but also the result of discernible forces at play in the universe and in our souls. The Mystery Dramas can serve as a blueprint for this perspective. No life in those plays follows the supposedly universal pattern of development outlined in *Knowledge of Higher Worlds*. Who we are now derives from a higher karmic logic: from who we were in the distant past, from what we set in motion in the present life, and from what others contribute to our personal development. Let us see how that is the case from the perspective of Destiny Learning, as a complementary approach to Adult Learning (see Table 7). We will look here at Destiny Learning as it is conducted in a workshop lasting three to four days (Destiny Learning Workshop 1). Steps 1 to 4 are part of this process. Steps 5, 6 and 7 cover Destiny Learning Workshops 2 and 3, and will be mentioned only briefly.

---

[215] For the contrast between Adult Learning and Destiny Learning see Coenraad van Houten, *Awakening the Will: Principles and Processes in Adult Learning*. For an in-depth understanding of Destiny Learning see *Practising Destiny* and *The Threefold Nature of Destiny Learning* by the same author.

Step	Life Process	Learning to Learn Process	Destiny Learning Process	
I	Breathing	Observing	Observing an event out of life, finding the gesture	
II	Warming	Relating	Placing single event in biography, finding the symptoms of the being	Destiny Learning I
III	Nourishing	Digesting, assimilating	Finding the karmic cause and learning task for this life	
IV	Secreting	Individualizing	Acceptance, saying yes to destiny	
V	Maintaining	Exercising, practising	Practising transformation of your Double	Destiny Learning II
VI	Growing	Growing faculties	Transforming relationships in the network of destiny	
VII	Reproducing	Creating something new	Ordering karma	Destiny Learning III

Table 7: From *The Threefold Nature of Destiny Learning*, C. van Houten, p. 3.

Once again we start by educating the activity of our senses. We can do this by looking at a significant event in our biography as clearly and objectively as possible. We bring to mind every possible detail of setting, persons and environment, as well as feelings, sensations, thoughts, and so forth. We "breathe in" the event. In the second step, we place this event in the flow of our biography. In doing this, we recognize it as something that belongs to us, even when it seems to belong to the random caprices of chance. It actually has a place in our biography, and has contributed to shaping us into who we are. In fact, many times the event forms a cluster with other similar events in our lives, and we can recognize a gesture common to all of them. This is why recurring events, rather than the one-of-a-kind, are taken as points of departure for Destiny Learning. The next step is that of digesting; that is, finding the causes and the learning task that emerge from this cluster of events. In this step we try to reach the deeper, originating causes in a previous life; we wrestle for self-knowledge. This stage is best supported through conversation, art, and exercises, and through the help of a facilitator. In addition to the earlier question ("What are the deeper causes of events in my destiny?") there is another that goes closely in hand with it: "What is this event trying to tell me, and what inner forces do I need to develop in order to integrate it into my life?"

The next stage of individualizing/accepting our destiny pushes us to a step of determination of the will, toward a complete identification with the event. Whereas before I may have looked uncomfortably on the event, or even turned away from it, at this stage this is no longer possible. We now face all the ways in which the double hides from our consciousness, such as in anger, denial or guilt. We can basically recognize the nature, on the one hand, of Luciferic doubles that promote our love of self and estrange us from our real task. On the other hand are the Ahrimanic doubles that harden us and keep us as if imprisoned in the reality of the five senses, in hardbound concepts, and in recurrent patterns of behavior. We are in fact coming to a closer recognition of what lies beyond both of them, the "second person in us," who orchestrates the events in our biography.

The next stage of work consists in maintaining/working at transforming our double. Through daily commitment, we learn to recognize the ways through which we limit our freedom in meeting new situations. We can take on the practice of transforming our double in small increments, with what Destiny Learning calls "freer deeds"; actions we may plan carefully, knowing how much we can reasonably expect of ourselves. In fact, initially we could work at transforming the way in which we think of a person with whom we have hostility or difficulties. A next step may be confined to not avoiding him, but greeting him, refraining from commenting at the first sentence, and so forth. In so doing, we may notice how the double reacts in us. At this stage, journaling offers support for observation and knowledge of our inner dynamics, and hence supports the ability to affect the dynamics and transform them.

The next steps move into the abilities that humanity will evolve more fully in the future: developing faculties of karmic perception, and bringing harmony into one's karma. In the first instance we develop the ability to sense from our hearts the forces of destiny. At this stage we have acquired enough familiarity with our double that it gradually takes on the role of guide, letting us know or sense what is possible to carry out in our deeds and what is not yet ripe for action. In the last two stages we can become true agents for social change: first by developing a deeper sense for what a situation calls for, and later by perceiving the deeper links of destiny, and developing the ability to work outside of the karmic ties created from the past (our "Moon karma"). In other words we can truly act freely, and create new "Sun karma."

Destiny Learning moves in stages from the individual to his/her karmic connections, and from the fabric of relationships to the social process. We will return to the seven life processes and see how they underlie many other social processes in Chapter 9.

CHAPTER 6

ARISTOTELIANS AND PLATONISTS
IN THE NEW MICHAELIC AGE

We are coming to the end of our explorations, and are now connecting everything of which we have spoken, and relating it to the present. Steiner began to speak about Michaelites and differentiated them into two streams, Aristotelians and Platonists, only in 1924. In fact, as Steiner was coming toward the end of his life, he did more than enjoin us to take up the karma exercises. He also asked us to discern whether we are young or old souls, and whether we are Aristotelians or Platonists (the two polarities are intimately connected, as we will see below).

During the first lecture offered on the themes of karmic relationships, in which Steiner explored the karma of the anthroposophical movement, he noticed a resistance from the members. At the end of this lecture he said: "But in some minds this may cause great anxiety over the consequence, when they see many things brought to light of which they would prefer to remain more or less ignorant. For are we now to decide whether we belong to one group or the other?"[216] Knowing the difficulties members might face, Steiner encouraged them to attitudes of wonder and courage, in order to stay clear from the temptation to spin fantasies about previous lives (a Luciferic temptation), or the tendency to be afraid to even attempt karmic research (an Ahrimanic temptation).

Bernard Lievegoed reminds us of both extremes in the history of

---

[216] Steiner, *Karmic Relationships*, Volume 3, lecture of July 8, 1924.

the Anthroposophical Society. In the thirties many people in Dornach spoke freely about karma; later on, and especially after the expulsions of members that took place in 1935, talk of karma became somewhat taboo.[217] It is also true that after Steiner's death, karma revelations were mishandled and became a source of strife and disharmony. On one hand the identification of Ita Wegman as the reincarnated Alexander the Great incarnation served to fuel in some members the hope of a direct succession to Steiner; on the other hand, the assertions were turned by a vast majority of members into the "Alexander legend," and they were used to discredit Wegman.[218] In light of such excesses one can understand why karmic investigation was later handled with discomfort. But it remains, nevertheless, all the more urgent.

Because the question of streams in the anthroposophical movement is fraught with numerous layers and various risks of misunderstanding, we will turn our attention to overlapping matters; then we will return to the polarity of Aristotelians and Platonists. We will present various strands of polarities and later separate the strands that matter most.

Acquiring Perspective on the Streams

Aristotelian and Platonist streams were initiated at the time that the Mystery School tradition originating in the East was coming to an end. We followed in Chapter 1 how the Mystery streams differentiated after the fall of Atlantis into a Northern Stream and a Southern Stream. The bulk of the Northern Stream gave the impetus for the Mysteries that inaugurated the post-Atlantean age through the Indian civilization first, the Persian culture later. During the third post-Atlantean age, the Southern Mysteries joined their influences to the Northern Mysteries in the double civilization of Egypt and Chaldea. The Northern Mysteries expressed themselves more fully in Chaldea, the Southern Mysteries in Egypt. In Greece both of them were present and expressed in the contrast between the Sun Christ/Apollonian path to the macrocosmos

---

[217] Bernard Lievegoed, *The Battle for the Soul: The Working Together of Three Great Leaders of Humanity*, 25.
[218] Thomas Meyer, *Rudolf Steiner's Core Mission*, 260.

(northern), and the Lucifer/Dionysian path to the microcosmos (southern). This was the prelude to the turning point of time and the incarnation of the Christ. It is within this context that we can now look at the matter of Aristotelians and Platonists.

First of all, however, we will try to clear the field of possible confusion. This is useful because Platonists and Aristotelians can be compared to or amalgamated with the Shepherds and Magi polarity; with the Grail Knights and Arthurian Knights; and with old souls and young souls. Let us look at these groups of polarities, one after the other, to differentiate among them and acquire clarity.

Shepherds and Magi

The question of Magi and Shepherds was extensively treated by Steiner in *The Search for the New Isis, the Divine Sophia*.[219] Steiner introduced them as "the last heirs of two different modes of clairvoyance." And in this respect he referred to "primeval faculties of vision in man" coming from the Turanian highlands of Asia, from the forerunners of what would later become the Egypto-Chaldean and Greek cultures. It was there, in Central Asia, that the Northern and Southern Streams first united.[220] Shepherds and Magi constitute the culmination of what we have seen respectively in the Northern and Southern paths after the collapse of Atlantean civilization. Let us see how.

The Shepherds, as we know them from the Gospels, were simple souls completely united with the Earth. They carried an "inner perception ... spontaneous and inspirational, related to the will." And they received the revelation of the approaching Christ in hearts which had clairvoyant capacities. The Magi continued the tradition of the wisdom of the East that translated into an imaginative vision of an intellectual nature, although completely different from what intellectualism is today. They knew of the Christ from what they could read in the glyphs of the cosmos. There is no more striking contrast between the two groups

---

[219] Steiner, *The Search for the New Isis, Divine Sophia*, lectures of December 23 to 26, 1920.
[220] Ibid, lectures of December 19 and December 26, 1910.

than their presence at the birth of the two Jesus children. The Shepherds accompanied the primeval soul of the Nathan Jesus child of the Luke Gospel in all its innocence—the youngest soul of the world. The Magi lent their wisdom by witnessing the birth of the Solomon Jesus child of the Matthew Gospel—the reincarnated Zarathustra, one of the most mature individualities in Earth evolution.

The Shepherds could perceive the forces that emanated from the earth. They could experience inwardly the various kinds of landscapes and sense whether there was granite, sandstone, limestone or chalk in them. In Steiner's words, these perceptions "... arose inwardly like colors or clouds inwardly felt, inwardly experienced. Thus man experienced the earth's depths; thus too, the soul in his fellow man and the life of animals."[221] Through these enhanced perceptions the Shepherds received intimations of what forces were at work in social life or in the animal world.

The Magi, on the other hand, could experience what the spiritual world manifests in the world of the stars, and in the minerals and plants, through the cosmic memory of what they had experienced in life before birth. "And this cosmic memory enabled them to behold the spiritual in the whole external world as well, to see the destiny of man on earth."[222] At the time of Christ, the Shepherds could feel that the earth was changing, whereas the Magi could read in the script of the stars that the Christ was drawing near.

The difference between the two kinds of consciousness lies in the fact that the Magi's knowledge was what survived of their life before birth; the Shepherds' consciousness found its fulfillment only in the life after death. They carried the youthful qualities that will fully develop only in the life after death. Whereas the Magi can perceive the forces at work in the cosmos, the Shepherds have the perceptions of the forces at work in the earth's depths. All of the above confirms that the Magi are forerunners of the Northern path to the macrocosmos, the Apollonian stream of the Greeks. The Shepherds plumb the depths

---

[221] Steiner, *The Search for the New Isis, Divine Sophia*, lecture of December 25, 1910.
[222] Ibid.

of the soul's journey to the underworld, the Greek Dionysian path. What the Shepherds accomplished in the will, the Magi followed in their thinking, and Steiner concluded "...what the shepherds of the field, without wisdom, experienced through the piety of their hearts is the same as what stimulated the Magi of the East as the highest wisdom."[223]

The Shepherds and Magi marked the end of the Abel line of initiation; the rise of the Cain line of initiation is most aptly represented by Lazarus/John, the reincarnated Hiram Abiff, himself descending from the line of Tubal-Cain. What Steiner said in a lesson of the Esoteric School of the Theosophical Society held true for all old initiates, whether from the Northern Stream (Magi) or the Southern Stream (Shepherds): "At the time of initiation, the etheric bodies of these leaders (Moses, Hermes, Zarathustra, Buddha, and so forth) were outside their physical bodies, and observed the nature of the whole race."[224] This is how the initiates were able to impart wisdom to their people in the laws and dispositions that they could give. But this also meant that the initiates carried the responsibility for the transgressions of the folk-soul, and had to reincarnate in the line of racial inheritance "until the folk-karma of that people had been expiated." The initiate was becoming responsible for the carrying out of the laws. In the same lesson, Steiner added, "In the case of these old initiates, the group-soul of the nation united with their etheric bodies during the ceremony [of initiation]. It continued to live on in them afterward, too." All the old initiates were from the Abel line; they received inspirations through the Moon forces, the forces of Yahve, which they received at night. These were the very same forces connected with birth and procreation, the forces that worked through the blood. At the time of Christ, the Magi and the Shepherds were the final expressions of these streams.

In his time, Hiram Abiff (who had worked with Solomon at the

---

[223] Steiner, *The Search for the New Isis, Divine Sophia*, lecture of December 25, 1910.

[224] Steiner, *Freemasonry and Ritual Work, the Misraim Service: Letters, Documents, Ritual Texts, and Lectures from the History and Contents of the Cognitive-Ritual Section of the Esoteric School: 1904-14*, (CW 265), 379-432, "The Further Evolution of the Abel and Cain Races at the Time of Christ" (from an Instruction Lesson given in Berlin, April 15, 1908) text according to the original handwriting of Rudolf Steiner, no date offered.

building of the temple) came to the outer boundary of initiation; but his true initiation arrived only in his later, Lazarus incarnation. The Spirit-Sun had to descend to Earth, into physical incarnation in Christ. And only Christ could initiate Hiram Abiff in his Lazarus/John incarnation. Steiner emphasized that this initiation was a moving away from blood ties. "What Hiram Abiff had acquired through his life on the physical plane had to remain. Not the life of the group, but that of every single incarnation was now of importance. Every single incarnation was to add a page to the Book of Life..." There was a transition from the working of the forces of the Moon to the working of the forces of the Sun. After the deed of Golgotha, initiation was freed from the forces of heredity, which worked through the blood.

We can thus not find a direct relationship between Shepherds and Magi on one hand, and Platonists and Aristotelians on the other.

Grail and Arthurian Streams

In two lectures in Volume 8 of *Karmic Relationships*, Steiner spoke of the Arthurian and Grail knights, of the karma of the two streams, and of their relation to the School of Chartres. There we learn that the Arthurian knights continued the impulses of Hibernia, which preserved the Atlantean unity of inner and outer Mysteries in later times. In effect, the Arthurian knights worked longer than any other stream at preserving the cosmic intelligence of Michael. The initiates of the Mysteries of Hibernia, and later the Arthurian knights, perceived Christ's life spirit in the Earth's own life spirit, through the interplay of the elements in light and air.[225] They knew Christ as the Sun Hero, and by reading the book of nature, they perceived the Mystery of Golgotha as a fact. Their impulses spread from West to East.

The Grail stream traveled from East to West: from Palestine to Greece, northern Africa, Italy, Spain, and across Europe. It emanated from a more inward understanding of the Christ event. Here too, as in the Arthurian Mysteries, twelve disciples were united around the initiate. In the Grail stream the individuals struggled to come to grips

[225] Steiner, *Karmic Relationships*, Volume 8, lecture of August 27, 1924.

with an intelligence that is no longer cosmic; witness the celebrated foolishness of Parzival. In so doing, the Grail knights wanted to prepare a way for the Christ in the hearts and minds of men.

The Arthurian knights sought the Christ in the Sun sphere, which was for them the fount of Christianity. Steiner characterized the Arthur stream as bearers of the "pre-Christian" Christ; this is contrasted by the directly Christian stream of the Grail knights ("the Christian Christ stream") who knew Christ as the Brother of Humanity. The knights of King Arthur were those who strove the longest to preserve Michael's cosmic intelligence. The Grail knights' representative, Parzival, is the fool, the ordinary man who strives to find his way to Michael's intelligence from the ground of human intelligence.

The two streams met each other in the year 869. This was above all a spiritual event, rather than something that can be found on Earth, and it can be characterized as the meeting of Christ the Brother of Humanity with Christ the Sun Hero; of Christ with his "Image," what the Arthurian knights knew of Christ's life spirit. "And then the meeting takes place—the meeting between the Christ Who had Himself come down to Earth and His Own Image [life spirit] which is brought to Him from West to East. This meeting took place in the year 869. Up to that year we have two streams, clearly distinct from one another."[226] The year 869 was also the year in which the Council of Constantinople repudiated the threefoldness of body, soul, and spirit, in effect assimilating soul and spirit into one.

The men of Chartres (the Platonic stream of the tenth to twelfth centuries) held a position in between that of the Grail and Arthur streams. They saw the Christ both in the impulse that poured in through Earth evolution, and also in the impulse that emanated from the Sun. "In a remarkable way this School of Chartres stands midway between the Arthur-principle in the North and the Grail-principle in the South."[227] In Chartres the attitude of the Arthur stream was still present. The teachers of Chartres referred to the old traditions in which nature was not yet seen intellectually, but felt and known as a being full of life.

---

[226] Steiner, *Karmic Relationships*, Volume 8, lecture of August 27, 1924.
[227] Ibid.

They still held on to preserving Michael's cosmic Intelligence, while all around them most of European civilization struggled to come to grips with human intelligence. Here too, we do not find a direct connection between Arthur and Grail streams on one hand and Platonism and Aristotelianism on the other.

The polarity "young souls/old souls" is more closely connected with the Aristotelian/Platonist duality than the previous ones.

Old and Young Souls

Steiner invited us to discern to which of the two groups we belong. In his words: "Are we now to set to work and think, whether we belong to the one type or the other? My dear friends, to this I must give a very definite answer."[228] He answered the question by asking whether it would be unthinkable to reveal to a child that he is a Frenchman, a German, a Russian, a Pole, or a Dutchman. Since that is not the case, he concluded, "We must grow just as naturally and simply into self-knowledge, which is to realize that we belong to the one type or the other." As a precaution, he also added that this cannot be done in a simplistic way.

Steiner spoke of old and young souls at length on July 8 and 11, 1924 in Dornach, and again in Arnhem on July 18, 1924. During Lemuria, because of a tendency toward solidification that was later forestalled by the separation of the moon, souls departed from the Earth and dwelt on other planets of the solar system. At a certain time during the Lemurian and Atlantean times they returned to Earth; some came relatively soon and others comparatively late. Young souls, when looking back in time, reach their earliest incarnations comparatively soon. Old souls incarnated relatively early, during Atlantean times. The oldest of all souls is that of Adam/John the Baptist; the youngest soul is that of the Nathan Jesus; both these souls played a critical role in the incarnation of the Logos.

Souls from both groups incarnated into Christianity. For most, their first such incarnation was between the third and fifth centuries, and more rarely, as late as the seventh or eighth centuries. The experiences

---

[228] Steiner, *Karmic Relationships*, Volume 3, lecture of July 8, 1924.

of this first Christian incarnation were "fastened or confirmed" in a later incarnation. At the time, both sets of souls had characteristics that differentiated them from the non-Michaelic souls around them. This had to do with how their sheaths integrated into each other upon waking and falling asleep. Upon waking, they could sense the ego and astral penetrating first the etheric, then their physical bodies, in a way that human beings no longer can at present. Something similar happened upon falling asleep, because astral and ego separated gradually, not simultaneously as they do at present. Because of this gradual reentry into their sheaths, the souls could still bring into waking consciousness images of the experiences they had undergone in the spiritual world at night. And, especially in the early hours of the morning, they could perceive the astral aura of living beings, both in plants and in animals. In other words, they could still perceive how the spiritual was present in nature.

Young souls experienced as their most important incarnation the one in the early centuries before Christ, and returned to incarnations "of importance" only after the seventh century. Old souls experienced most deeply the incarnation which occurred in the centuries immediately after the event of Golgotha. Steiner further differentiates between two subgroups of old souls. One group experienced the kind of Christianity that had spread in Southern Europe, but also to some extent to Middle Europe, in the first centuries.[229] In this Southern spirituality, Christ was presented as a "mighty Divine Messenger," and was still seen as the Sun God. This picture was part of an ancient clairvoyant perception, but one that was starting to fade. After this point in time, no one could tell with certainty whether the Christ was completely divine or if he had been both man and God; nor how the divine element related to the human. Eventually dogma replaced vision.

The second subgroup of old souls, those who were known as "heretics" in a Christian incarnation, retained the perception of Christ as a Sun Being, and continued to do so until the eighth century. The heretics themselves became, in Steiner's words, "weary of Christianity,"

---

[229] Steiner, *Karmic Relationships*, Volume 6, lecture of June 18, 1924, and *Karmic Relationships*, Volume 8, lecture of August 21, 1924.

because they could no longer recognize Christianity in the teachings of their time. And in this mood of soul they passed through the gate of death. Their most important incarnation remained for them the one they had experienced in the early centuries of Christianity. About this subgroup Steiner said, "Those belonging to it were fired still by what had been alive in the Platonism of ancient Greece. So fired were they that when through the tidings emanating from ancient times their inner vision opened, they were always able, under the influence of a genuine, albeit faint Inspiration, to perceive the descent of the Christ to the Earth and to glimpse His work on the Earth. This was the Platonic stream."[230]

After the seventh and eighth centuries, the traditions perpetuated by the heretics had largely faded out. However, their knowledge survived in small circles until the twelfth century. "These circles were composed of Teachers, divinely blessed Teachers, who still cultivated something of this ancient knowledge of spiritual Christianity, cosmological Christianity. There were some amongst them, too, who had directly perceived communications from the past, and in them a kind of Inspiration arose; thus they were able to experience a reflection—whether strong or faint, a true image—of what in the first Christian centuries men had been able to behold under the influence of a mighty Inspiration of the descent of the Sun God leading to the Mystery of Golgotha."[231] Without mentioning them in this lecture, Steiner is talking about people like the teachers of Chartres, who still had access to the cosmic Intelligence, when most everybody had reached the stage of earthly intelligence.

Young souls had their most important incarnation in the few centuries before the event of Golgotha, not in the early Christian centuries. They brought memories of the ancient Pagan Mysteries, not of the Christian Mysteries, through which they had known that the Christ was going to incarnate. Their truly Christian incarnations started only after the seventh century AD.[232] In contrast to the old souls, they were not weary of Christianity, but longed for it; longed for a form of it that had the

---

[230] Steiner, *Karmic Relationships*, Volume 6, lecture of July 18, 1924.
[231] Ibid.
[232] Ibid, lectures of July 18 and August 21, 1924.

cosmic element of Paganism, but had the Christ at its center. Rudolf Steiner and Ita Wegman, both young souls, only met with a deeper esoteric Christianity in their respective tenth-century incarnations of Schionatulander and Sigune.

The task of the young souls was to prepare the intellect for the epoch that had its beginning in the first half of the fifteenth century. All those who propagated Aristotelian teachings until well into the fifteenth century were souls who had passed through their last most important incarnation in ancient Pagan times, especially in the world of Greek culture.

When speaking about himself and Ita Wegman, the quintessence of Aristotelianism, who reincarnated among the Dominicans, Steiner said: "I may remind you of what I said at the Christmas Foundation Meeting, when I spoke of those individualities with whom the epic of Gilgamesh is connected. I explained certain things about such individualities. We find, as we look backward, that they had had comparatively few incarnations."[233] Moreover, the two souls had their most important incarnations in the time before Christ and did not incarnate in the early centuries of Christianity. Thus it seems reasonable to conclude (in line with what Steiner says elsewhere, as well) that the Aristotelians were exclusively young souls, and Platonists exclusively old souls.

The difference between old and young souls can be most clearly understood in the way in which they took up and related to Christianity. In fact, this is a root differentiation. Old souls had many incarnations behind them when they dove into the Christian stream. In Steiner's time, and at present, these souls, as anthroposophists, long to call themselves Christians. They would feel ill at ease if they did not find the Christ at the center of anthroposophy. Many of the old souls coming back to incarnation in Christianity, somewhere between the third and eighth centuries, could no longer grasp the Sun nature of the Christ— the fact that he dwelt on the Sun before descending to the Earth. They could not fathom Christ's divine nature, and they could no longer turn to the cosmos in order to behold him. They knew of him but could not find him or understand him fully. After death they experienced great

---

[233] Steiner, *Karmic Relationships*, Volume 3, lecture of July 8, 1924.

uncertainty about him, and in the next incarnation they tended to become heretics.

Young souls find the greatest satisfaction in anthroposophical cosmology, and from there they are naturally led to Christianity. They do not place the Christ in the central place at all costs. These souls, however, have the predisposition to take in the Christ as a cosmic being. Their challenge lies in moving straight forward in the direction of the anthroposophic ideas, avoiding being sidetracked. The forces of this group, Steiner said, will play an important part in spreading an atmosphere of continuous progress; but the forces may emerge with difficulty. However, among the young souls are those who work and cooperate with anthroposophy most actively. The souls who come well adapted to the present times are often young souls. These had not reached a weariness of Paganism in the first centuries of Christianity; thus the impulses of Paganism were still strongly working in them at that time. Not having formerly grown into Christianity, they have been waiting to become real Christians.

After the onset of the time of the Consciousness Soul in the fifteenth century, both old and young souls in the spiritual world found themselves part of the School of Michael, which ended in the great supersensible *cultus*, or ritual, in the eighteenth and nineteenth centuries. The ritual consisted of mighty Imaginations in which the great Sun Mystery of Christ was enacted in relation to the Mysteries of the past and the future. What later became anthroposophy on Earth, took on its initial form in the spiritual world. The young souls took in the impulses from the imaginations of the supersensible School, primarily in their will. And on Earth at the time of Steiner, "...it was as though they remembered a resolve that they had made during that first half of the nineteenth century: a resolve to carry down on to the earth all that had stood before them in such mighty pictures, and to translate it into an earthly form."[234]

On the other hand, the old souls had participated in the supersensible ritual with great longing, but reached it from an undefined mystical mood; they carried only dim recollections upon incarnating again.

---

[234] Steiner, *Karmic Relationships*, Volume 4, lecture of July 11, 1924.

This relieved them of many doubts, and gave them a memory of what they had received about the Christ. The ritual reawakened an immense devotion and warmth of feeling toward Christianity, which translated into the longing to be truly Christian. However, it was difficult for these souls to find a place in anthroposophy on Earth, because anthroposophy studies the cosmos first, and leaves consideration about the Christ to a later stage. It can be surmised that this is still the case.

Finally, we can recognize "transitional souls" in those who cannot help bringing into anthroposophy the habits of non-anthroposophic life. In their case neither of the impulses of young or old souls is very strong.

Gathering All the Strands

The sets of streams (Magi/Shepherds, Arthur/Grail, old souls/young souls) that we have seen here cannot be confused or equated with one another. In the rest of this chapter we will be speaking exclusively of the Platonists and Aristotelians, or old and young souls.

An orientation toward the will or toward thinking expresses itself in many variations in all the polarities explored above. The theme of polarity is present as a thread throughout post-Atlantean evolution, starting from the contrast between the Southern path (to the microcosm, tending toward the will) and the Northern path (to the macrocosm, tending toward thinking). However, at the time thinking was hardly an independent human activity as it is intended to be today. The polarity persisted up until the time of Christ, in the difference between the Magi (macrocosm, tending toward thinking) and Shepherds (microcosm, piety and the will). After the time of Christ, the polarity continued, in a sense, on one hand with the knights of King Arthur (macrocosm, Christ as the Sun Hero, "thinking"); and on the other hand, the knights of the Grail (microcosm, Christ as the Brother of Humanity, will). And finally, when we refer to Aristotelians and Platonists, we can trace the same thread, assigning thinking to the first group and willing to the second. Obviously, no pair of characterizations completely matches any other.

Finally, the contrast between thinking and willing appears within the same stream in the example of the twin souls, Steiner and Wegman. Wegman most often played the role of a will-person in respect to her teacher. This appears clearly in the incarnations as Alexander the Great, Reginald of Piperno, and Wegman. Thus the basic polarity of thinking/ will reappears in ever-evolving modalities, and cannot be used as a criterion for differentiating Platonists and Aristotelians, though it is part of it.

Before concerning ourselves with the incarnation of Platonists and Aristotelians at the end of the twentieth century and their possible collaboration in what Steiner calls the "culmination," it is useful to review what we have surveyed, and to fully characterize Platonists and Aristotelians.

Platonists and Aristotelians: Some Characterizations

We have now gathered enough of an imagination to be able to differentiate between the Platonic and the Aristotelian impulses. Plato looked back to the past of the world's existence; at the personal level this culminated in the anamnesis, the soul's remembrance of existence before its birth in the world of ideas. Aristotle confined his gaze to the present, and consequently he closed the door to memory of previous lives. The Platonists of Chartres looked into the past of the world Mysteries, and they preserved conditions that held true in the past. The Aristotelians of Scholasticism prepared for the future that would fully materialize only in our fifth post-Atlantean age. And we can see how the Platonism of German classical culture brought to life after their time, the last vestiges of ancient northern European wisdom. This is why Steiner said of Hegel (another Platonist) that "...he was one who brought the final glimpse of the ancient spiritual light into an era when spirit is veiled in darkness for human cognition."[235]

An orientation toward the past or future is thus a first element that differentiates the two streams. Another contrast is found in the respective soul moods. The School of Chartres was characterized by Steiner, "not so much [for] the actual content of the teachings, as [for] the whole attitude and mood-of-soul of the pupils who gathered with glowing enthusiasm in the 'lecture halls'—as we should say nowadays—of Chartres."[236]

---

[235] Steiner, *Autobiography*, Chapter 58.
[236] Steiner, *Karmic Relationships*, Volume 8, lecture of August 21, 1924.

Steiner described thus the coming together of Platonists and Aristotelians in the spiritual world in the thirteenth century: "All these souls afterward came together again—those who with fiery lips had declared ancient and sacred teachings in the School of Chartres, and those who had wrestled in the cold and clear, but heart-devoted works of Scholasticism, to master the true meaning of Intelligence."[237] And in describing a conversation he had with a priest of the Cistercian Order, Steiner blended the attributes of both streams thus: "...with Aristotelian clarity and definition of concept, and yet at the same time with Platonic spiritual light."[238] Of Schröer, the reincarnated Plato, Steiner said, "Our souls were lifted by his wonderful idealism and noble enthusiasm."[239] And another important differentiation between Aristotelians and Platonists lies behind the thinking of its two major representatives:

Schröer was an idealist; for him, the driving force in everything created, whether by nature or human being, was the world of ideas itself. For me [Steiner], on the other hand, ideas were shadows cast by a living spiritual world. I found it difficult, even for myself, to say what the difference was between Schröer's way of thinking and my own. He spoke of ideas as the forces driving history. He felt that ideas have life. For me, the life of spirit was behind ideas, which were only manifestations of the spirit within the human soul.[240]

All of the above speaks of a contrast between a way of looking at things from a global perspective and with a certain mood of soul pervaded with enthusiasm among the Platonists; and of an attitude of detached devotion, great clarity and smaller-scale focus among the Aristotelians. Overall, the Platonists have a more general orientation to the will, the Aristotelians to thinking. But most of all the contrast

---

[237] Steiner, *Karmic Relationships*, Volume 3, lecture of July 28, 1924.
[238] Ibid, lecture of July 13, 1924.
[239] Steiner, *Autobiography*, Chapter 12.
[240] Steiner, *Autobiography*, Chapter 14.

between Aristotelians and Platonists will be made clear through the evolution and metamorphosis of their gestures over the centuries. To this we turn next.

The evolution of the Michaelic streams has taken us from ancient Greece into the times and lives of Steiner and Schröer. Before proceeding to the present we can review the stages of incarnation of the Michaelic impulses, up to the time in which they can work together, and no longer in succession.

In ancient Greece the oracles were followed by the Mysteries. The state of union of inner world and nature still held sway at the time in which the oracles spoke to the ancient Greek and offered indications about the life of the individual and of the social body. The ancient Greek of that time had not developed a life of thought; he experienced the surrounding world in images, and felt himself a part of the life of nature. He experienced what Steiner called the "wonders of the world." From this original state of union of microcosmos and macrocosmos Greece moved into the time of the "trials of the soul." This meant moving from oracles to Mysteries, with the transition most clearly played out in the sanctuary of Delphi with its oracle of the Sun and its Dionysian Mysteries. Dionysus opened the way for a more individualized connection to the spiritual world through the stages of trials that found the individual worthy of being initiated into the spirit. Along this path Dionysus himself was the hierophant, first in the body, then as a disincarnated entity.

The life of the Mysteries came to a state of decadence roughly around the 6th century BC. It was then Plato, the reincarnated Dionysus, who led the way out of the Mysteries and disciplined the faculties of thinking from which philosophy developed its early rudiments. Plato still acted like the hierophant of the new faculty of thinking. He helped in the transition from the culture of the Mysteries into the newly evolving faculties of the intellect.

Aristotle perceived that the human being needed a complete severance from the realm of the Mysteries. He turned his gaze to the life between birth and death. In his categories, or in his logic, lived concepts that mirror the reality of both spiritual and physical worlds, and can be confirmed through clairvoyance. Nevertheless one need not be clairvoyant in order to elaborate such concepts, and anyone with healthy thinking could verify their lawfulness.

Here we may see a first gesture/contrast between Plato and Aristotle. Plato gathers everything from the past. He carries memories from his life before birth, centuries after these had faded from the experience of most Greeks. He gathers all the wisdom of the Mysteries, both from Greece and from Egypt, and makes it available to the pupil. In the process some of this knowledge is corrupted and can no longer be entirely trusted; it is like a long-gone memory. Through Platonism, conditions are gathered for the environment to take on a new evolutionary step. The Athenian *polis*, of which Plato is the proud son, can soon become the *cosmopolis* under Alexander the Great and Aristotle. The fruits of Plato's Academy, and especially of Aristotle's Lyceum, can now be disseminated from the West to the East. They have reached ripeness in a thinking that can apprehend the reality of both the natural world and the soul, a thinking that can even reflect upon itself. After Aristotle no philosophy reaches the pinnacles of the master for centuries to come.

Plato gathered the fruit of the past and created a space in which a solid platform for the future could be built. Aristotle alone, at the time of Michael's last regency before the present age, could sow the seeds of the future and create the conditions for a cosmopolitan and universal culture.

The Middle Ages recreate and metamorphose this gesture anew. The School of Chartres gathers the fruits of the Mystery traditions of the Middle East and of Europe. Chartres recapitulates and extracts the essence of the past, and most of all it recaptures the impulses of Plato and Christianizes them. Chartres' teachers live in a condition of consciousness that has long disappeared from the immediate environment. They can perceive the cosmic Intelligence and communicate it with enthusiasm to their pupils, who can lift themselves to a higher level of perception and live in the imaginations their masters have conjured up. The teachers offer their pupils glorious echoes of the past. Chartres and the Cistercians do something else: they tame the landscape of Europe, they reclaim the wetlands, they put untamed lands under cultivation, they increase agricultural yields and help prevent famines. Theirs is an eminently social impulse. In essence the Platonic impulse once more prepares the ground and the conditions for a momentous change, and no more fitting image could be mentioned than that of the great cathedrals, whose secret dies with the end of the Chartres impulse. The teachers of Chartres live anonymous lives; they do not yet feel the impulse towards stronger individualism that comes from the cosmic Intelligence turning earthly. This is also why they cannot repulse the dangers looming in the near future, especially in the cultural realm—they who live in conditions rather reminiscent of the past.

The School of Chartres also brought to its end a great revival. It preserved everything from the past that was worth saving. It linked Christianity with the philosophy of Plato. It created the social conditions under which new evolutionary steps could be taken. Just imagine the landscape of Europe without the cathedrals and without the network of economic activity created by the Cistercians.

The Dominicans show an essentially different gesture. Their sphere of activity moves from the frontiers of nature, dear to the masters of Chartres and the Cistercians, to the growing urban environments. They want to place themselves center-stage in the growing culture of the Middle Ages. They live in the cities and promote the cultural life of the emerging universities. They tackle the questions of knowledge that are so central at a time in which the cosmic Intelligence, growing earthly, runs the risk of falling prey to Ahriman.

The Scholastics' role in the Michaelic movement is less conspicuous, but more critical for the future. They fight cultural battles on two fronts. They fight a return to the past in the Arabism of Averroes, who predicates a human intelligence deprived of individuality, and who distorts the heritage of Aristotle and directs it to purposes it was never devised for. They fight against Nominalism, that tendency to see a world devoid of meaning, a dissociation between the world of the senses and the concepts used to understand it. Nominalism would have created many of the negative conditions for the Consciousness Soul, visible at present, before its time. Thomas Aquinas resurrects the thought of Aristotle and preserves the realms of reason and faith in a manner that still allows their reunification in modern times.

In this second stage we see again the gesture of collecting everything from the past, even if for a short interlude, and creating the cultural and social conditions for a more cosmopolitan future. This is what the Platonists can offer to culture. On this solid foundation a truly cosmopolitan cultural impulse can take root that sets the tone for the culture of the Consciousness Soul and averts the main threats to its blossoming.

We now come to the 19th and 20th centuries, to the doorstep of our own world. German idealism leads the way, but one should not forget Great Britain's Romantic literature, and the transcendentalist movement in the United States, among others. The German Platonists counter the rising materialism and scientific outlook of the age with the innate feeling that the human soul can find from within answers to the world riddle, that nature need not live at odds with the human soul. Each of the German Platonists knows he can reach this goal, even from very different points of departure. The new worldviews struggle to find expression in the growing world of abstraction, which, however, they German idealists imbue with poetic imagination. Steiner reminds us that here too we see an echo of the past; that Hegel, Fichte, Schelling and the others carried in their souls the memory of a time in which the human being perceived spiritual beings at work in the soul. And the ideas of German classical philosophers are better described as "idea-experience" or the experienced idea, which live with a certain elemental vigor in the soul.

German idealists have in common the striving for a worldview in which self-consciousness forms the center and ground. The movement reaches a pinnacle in Goethe in what the artist and scientist reveals in deep poetic insight. He cannot transform his insights into clear concepts, but he nevertheless lays the basis for the transformation of thinking.

Schröer and Steiner arrive on the scene at the culmination of this Romantic movement, when the focus is moving from Germany to the Austro-Hungarian Empire. Steiner carried both his and Schröer's tasks in parallel, ensuring that from Goetheanism anthroposophy would be born. From a new understanding of karma and reincarnation he developed the impulse for a new way of seeing the place of the individual in the world, and of carrying pre-birth intentions into the world. This impulse has been explored in depth in *Rudolf Steiner and Karl Julius*

Schröer: Anthroposophy and the Teachings of Karma and Reincarnation. From both impulses that Steiner developed we can recognize archetypes at work in the natural and social worlds. What lived in Goethe under the inspiration of the German folk-soul is now expressed in universal fashion in anthroposophy. What came from inspirations carried by the great German philosophers is now becoming the fruit of direct vision in the spirit. The teachings of karma and reincarnation, which only survived as memories from the East, are now articulated in such a way that each human being who truly desires it, can ascend in a deeply experiential way from the subjective dimension of individual life to an objective ground beyond the veil of maya spread before the human soul.

Between German idealism and anthroposophy there is, once again, no direct continuity. But here too, the former sets the basis for the latter. And between the two lay the momentous watershed of Michael's new time regency. The German idealists had to set the conditions for a spiritual ascent and light the flame at the time of the growing darkness of materialism. They could do so with the power of the inspirations they received from the spiritual world. They set the tone for another Platonic revival of German culture. They also strove to create the foundations for a new social reality, which would have developed under the impulse of German liberalism and found a culmination under the guidance of Kaspar Hauser. These developments, however, were thwarted by the Western brotherhoods. The inspiration of the spiritual world becomes, ideally, direct spiritual vision in spiritual science. And what was present in some discrete pockets of culture—Germany, Austria, Great Britain, United States primarily—now becomes a universal impulse which can ray from the spiritual Goetheanum. The fruits of anthroposophy can be grasped universally, regardless of local cultures.

The German idealists had to set the conditions for a spiritual ascent and light the flame at the time of the growing darkness of materialism. They could do so with the power of the inspirations they received from the spiritual world. They set the tone for another Platonic revival of culture.

We will see the twin Michaelic impulses at work in the modern world when we turn to individuals of the twentieth century working in the natural sciences, in the humanities and in the social sciences.

Anticipating what is to come we will see that the contrast between German idealists and anthroposophists of the time of Steiner is still at work in the present.

Towards the Convergence of the Michaelic Streams in Our Time

In the words recorded by Walter Johannes Stein from his conversation with Steiner (Appendix 1), we are reminded that the "culmination" at the end of the twentieth century would be "a celebration of destiny," not only for the individual, but also for the Michaelic movement as a whole; and further, a way to bring together "anthroposophical knowledge and anthroposophical life." The first is the gift of the Aristotelians, the second of the Platonists. The last statement echoes at the global level what has been said about the individual, particularly in Chapter 5, under the heading "Spirit Recollection and Spirit Beholding." It is only through the integration of these two paths (representing, respectively, the attainment of Imagination and Inspiration) that we will be able to walk into the Sun path of the next cultural epoch. Likewise, the culmination of the Michaelic movement in the twentieth and twenty-first centuries derives from the ability to recognize and validate Aristotelian Imagination and Platonic Inspiration, which together will bring anthroposophical knowledge and anthroposophical life for the renewing of civilization. In Volume 6 of *Karmic Relationships*, Steiner characterized this culmination in the following terms:

> For according to the agreement reached in the heavenly conference at the beginning of the thirteenth century, the Aristotelians and Platonists were to appear together working for the ever-growing prosperity of the Anthroposophical Movement in the twentieth century, in order that at the end of this century, with Platonists and Aristotelians in unison, Anthroposophy may reach a certain culmination in earthly civilization. If it is possible to work in this way, in the way predestined

by Michael, then Europe and modern civilization will emerge from decline.[241]

In the appraisal of many anthroposophists, the culmination has not occurred. In the estimation of this author and from the perspective of what is accessible to him in North America, the Michaelic forces are present and active in the world. What is missing is a recognition of each other's presence and endeavors, and a way of bringing these efforts into synergy. But this harmonization is possible, and in fact it has started here and there. So the goal of this book is to render clear the presence of other forces beyond those that we recognize within the anthroposophical movement. And ultimately, the goal is to see how we can achieve the collaboration that Steiner intended, so that "modern civilization will emerge from decline." This is what we will turn to in the next chapter. At present we can turn to the question of the number of Michaelic souls in the world.

About the Number of Michaelic Souls

A first question of relevance in approaching the destiny of the Michaelic movement concerns the number of Michaelic souls that we may expect to see incarnated at the end of the twentieth century and the beginning of the twenty-first. This is because we are waiting today for the coming together of the Michaelic souls, many of whom were present at the turn of the twentieth century, according to Steiner.

When the Free Anthroposophical Society was created in Germany in 1923, Steiner hoped it could draw one million members. Already then he thought (or most likely knew) there were that many Michaelic incarnated souls in Europe alone.[242] Something similar is restated in *Earthly Knowledge and Heavenly Wisdom*: "One only advances forward when he represents the truth as strongly as possible, so that as many predestined souls as possible—who are present today in greater numbers

---

[241] Steiner, *Karmic Relationships*, Volume 6, lecture of July 19, 1924.
[242] Hans Peter von Manen, *Twin Roads to the Millennium: The Christmas Conference and the Karma of the Anthroposophical Society*, 119.

than one generally supposes—come to find the spiritual nourishment that is necessary."[243] Concerning why this would be so, Steiner confided to Rene Maikovski: "The souls that seek Anthroposophy are incarnated; but we don't speak their language!" And in referring to these souls, Steiner told Maikovski that there were a few million of them.[244]

Many other indications to the same effect come from Steiner's lectures, for example in the *Karmic Relationships* cycle. "There are many human beings... truly predestined by their pre-natal life for the Anthroposophical Society; and yet, owing to certain other things, they were unable to find their way into it. There are far more of them than we generally think."[245] In referring to old souls and young souls Steiner offered that "...we find the souls who had come from one or the other of the two streams of which I spoke here in the last few days [old and young souls]. It is a large circle of human beings, for many are living in this circle who have not as yet found their way to the Anthroposophical Movement."[246] In another lecture of the *Karmic Relationships* cycle, Steiner spoke of the great difficulty for souls in modern times to express the potential of their previous incarnations; preserving the treasures of wisdom of previous incarnations while having to pass through the crucible of intellectualism can be a trial.[247] Many very developed souls fail in this effort. Schröer is only one case in point.

On one hand, the challenge of the times makes it difficult for individuals to express their full karmic potential. On the other, anthroposophy does not yet speak the language that many more souls could understand. An illustration of how this difficulty relates to a single individual is offered in Steiner's lecture of January 18, 1924, and it concerns Henry Ford.[248] "So he [Henry Ford] knocks at the door (of legitimate and urgent desires, but 'not

---

[243] Steiner, *Earthly Knowledge and Heavenly Wisdom*, lecture of February 18, 1923.
[244] R. Maikovski, *Schicksalswege auf der Suche nach dem lebendingen Geist* 27; quoted in Jesaiah Ben Aharon, *The Supersensible Experience of the Twentieth Century*, 40.
[245] Steiner, *Karmic Relationships*, Volume 3, lecture of July 6, 1924.
[246] Ibid, lecture of July 13, 1924.
[247] Steiner, *Karmic Relationships*, Volume 4, lecture of September 23, 1924.
[248] Steiner "The Organic Development of the Anthroposophical Society and Its Future Tasks," lecture of January 18, 1924, in *The Constitution of the School of Spiritual Science; Its Arrangements into Sections* Rudolf Steiner, 15-16.

exactly spiritual needs'), knocks urgently—invents all manner of devices to thunder out what he desires." And further, "When I read Ford's book, I feel almost as though I myself were the door...And there behind that door is Anthroposophy. Hitherto, however, it has been so constituted in a Society as to make it quite impossible for that which stands before the door to come near to that which is behind. It is simply impossible. To this end we need something quite different."

Ford, who was a Freemason, had a deep intuitive grasp of reincarnation, and a high dedication to the ideal of service. It was precisely his grasp of reincarnation—what he called the "larger view"—that turned his life around. In his words, "I was forty when I went into business; forty when I began to evolve the Ford plant. But all the time I was getting ready. There is one thing the larger view does for you. It enables you to take time to get ready. Most of my life has been spent in preparation."[249]

---

[249] The idea of reincarnation was something Ford sensed all around him in his life. He believed that genius and intuition were derived from who we were in previous lives, and he was not shy about articulating his beliefs in numerous interviews. "I adopted the theory of Reincarnation when I was twenty six. Religion offered nothing to the point. Even work could not give me complete satisfaction. Work is futile if we cannot utilise the experience we collect in one life in the next. When I discovered Reincarnation it was as if I had found a universal plan I realised that there was a chance to work out my ideas. Time was no longer limited. I was no longer a slave to the hands of the clock. Genius is experience. Some seem to think that it is a gift or talent, but it is the fruit of long experience in many lives. Some are older souls than others, and so they know more. The discovery of Reincarnation put my mind at ease. If you preserve a record of this conversation, write it so that it puts men's minds at ease. I would like to communicate to others the calmness that the long view of life gives to us." (Henry Ford, interview in the *San Francisco Examiner* of August 26, 1928) Ford felt he did not depend on historical precedent, nor on present culture; just on himself, because he was willing to take full responsibility for everything in his life. In his thinking, Ford wanted to "read the signs of the times," or "read... what is yet not written." And he wanted to be remembered as an original thinker. His independence of mind allowed him to place his business venture in a deeply rooted ideal of service, which he saw as the only secure root for success; people all around him, even his associates, believed he was taking an immense gamble; they who operated in the belief of profit as the driving machine of the economy. And he did not embrace the idea of service as altruism, but just as sound business.

We can surmise that, like Ford, there were many others who were knocking at the door of anthroposophy in Steiner's time, as Steiner indeed confirmed. And this could have changed; should have changed, according to Steiner's best wishes. "Now at last, however, we may find the possibility for Anthroposophy herself to open the door from within. To this end, however, it must be made possible for anthroposophic matters to come before the world in such a way that men who grow out of the civilization of our time with the type of mind possessed by Henry Ford, the Automobile King, will say to themselves: 'Here I have written that modern science itself is, after all, something that points to the past. There must be something that guarantees life for the future.'" And to the soul who would articulate this question, anthroposophy would become the "door that opens from within."[250]

Platonic and Aristotelian souls meet us all the time; Aristotelian and Platonic impulses likewise. This is unavoidable given the sheer numbers of Michaelic souls who incarnated at the end of the twentieth century and are around us at present. We are simply failing to recognize each other and validate our impulses. We will return to this matter when we look at modern times.

---

[250] Steiner "The Organic Development of the Anthroposophical Society," lecture of January 18, 1924, in *The Constitution of the School of Spiritual Science*, 15-16.

PART IV
MICHAELIC SOULS
AFTER STEINER'S DEATH

CHAPTER 7

ARISTOTELIANS AND PLATONISTS IN PSYCHOLOGY

Aristotelians and Platonists operate in similar occupations, often cover similar interests, and work side by side. Because each field of operation is bound to its own logic and laws, we would make vague generalizations and broad mistakes if we offered blanket statements about the ways Aristotelians and Platonists worked in various fields. Only a differentiated approach can lead us to significant understanding. Wanting to approach the matter by degrees and uncover its layers gradually, we will start by looking at the inner world of psychology, then turn to the world of natural sciences, and finally look at work done in the social world.

At this point a word of caution is due. The author does not know of the karmic past of the individuals that will be explored in this chapter and the next ones, other than what some rare individuals themselves have revealed about it. This chapter and the next two will highlight different approaches to the same field that closely match Steiner's characterizations of the streams, and additionally, the predominant orientation towards either the path of Spirit Recollection or that of Spirit Beholding. The approach will be purely phenomenological, resorting to biography and literary estate of the individuals in question.

We will be looking at biographies and literary work, bringing one in relation to the other. And these will be some of our questions: What are the significant influences in an individual's biography? What are its turning points? What is unique about an individual's way of working? What can we see that unites biographical themes and work/literary output? What can we tell about the individual's mission and how it was carried out in the world?

We will turn first of all to the life and work of two remarkable Dutch anthroposophical doctors. They were contemporaries and close friends for over thirty years. Both of them worked very publicly. Both managed to bring anthroposophy into the mainstream. And both were well received, even if only partly understood. The first filled lecture halls wherever he went, and the newspapers reported what he had to say. He addressed the needs of the times with surprising new directions of thought. The second offered cultural initiatives in response to requests from Dutch society. He was presented with many opportunities to address pressing needs of the times and offered responses coming from anthroposophy, even though the source of inspiration may not have been explicit to all who made use of them. Both individuals started anthroposophical cultural institutions for healing. Both wrote a doctoral work on the effect of art on the soul: the first in regard to color, the second in regard to music.

We are talking of Willem Zeylmans van Emmichoven and Bernard J. Lievegoed. And everything said above applies first to van Emmichoven, the elder of the two, then to Lievegoed. Van Emmichoven challenged people of all persuasions to see that there is a whole other way of approaching important cultural matters (medicine, health, science) and that a paradigm shift is needed in order to apprehend reality more fully. Lievegoed offered sensible concepts that could be apprehended by his culture; he rendered anthroposophy relevant to the times, and visible through its effects upon culture. Both of them made anthroposophy very visible in the world, but in markedly different ways. Both were good diplomats, able to find common ground and defuse conflicts. Finally, both van Emmichoven and Lievegoed felt at home in the spoken and written word. They lectured extensively, and wrote numerous books. This gives us tools to compare their styles and worldviews.

In 1961 van Emmichoven asked Lievegoed to succeed him at the helm of the Dutch Anthroposophical Society, which he had steered for thirty-seven years. To his friend, Lievegoed had already previously said that it would have been difficult to combine his more worldly pursuits with that of the Society, because of the gulf between the tasks. Van Emmichoven replied that he was acting out of the old maxim of giving power to those who were not seeking it. Lievegoed continued to ponder the idea, then saw that it was unavoidable. He could not say no to van Emmichoven.

This important responsibility was offered to Lievegoed a few days after his fifty-sixth birthday. In September 1961, before going to South Africa, van Emmichoven told his friend, "I am going to Africa very shortly, and when I return in the New Year I shall resign as Chairman; and I expect you to take over the Chairmanship of the Dutch Society!" As we said before, for Lievegoed this was a shock, and the thought did not appeal to him, mindful as he was of the dimension that politics played in the Dutch Society. Van Emmichoven added, "You know, I shall then withdraw [after you take the Chairmanship] and from somewhere up above I shall look down at you, going about things in quite a different way from how I would have approached them! And I shall be pleased to see things done differently!" True to his word, van Emmichoven died six weeks later.[251]

To give us a flavor of the difference between the two doctors, let us first look at it through the eyes of Lievegoed. "We were very different people and were conscious of that. He had a strong imaginative life and was able to put deep truths into words. He was also a bit of a loner, he was at his most creative when he was alone with himself. I was more a will person, more oriented towards doing things and flourished especially in cooperation with other people." Lievegoed greatly treasured this key destiny link with his colleague; witness what he said on the same occasion: "Willem Zeylmans remained my teacher to the last moment of his life."[252] Let us now see van Emmichoven through his biography and writing, before doing the same for his colleague.

---

[251] Bernard C. J. Lievegoed, *Developing Communities*, 78-79.
[252] An Interview with Jelle van der Meulen, *The Eye of the Needle: Bernard Lievegoed; His Life and Working Encounter with Anthroposophy*, 34.

Willem Zeylmans van Emmichoven

Van Emmichoven wrote an autobiography of his youth, giving himself the fictional name of Bender Bole. There he recalls that his first memory came in the second year, when the shadow of the neighbor's small girl fell between himself and the light in which he was basking. To this first memory of flooding light many similar ones followed. He experienced pain with the darkness and joy with the light, in fact almost rapture. "He [Bender Bole] has countless memories of giving himself up entirely to the light," but soon after that "Returning to earth everything seems to him blacker than before."[253]

Frederik Willem Zeylmans van Emmichoven was born on November 23, 1893 in Helmond, North Brabant, the second boy of the family. At the child's birth his father was working as a bookkeeper and running an insurance agency. Then he attached himself to the cocoa confectionery venture of his father-in-law. This latter enterprise was very successful. The father, a fiery idealist, was among the first to introduce social security for his workers in the Netherlands.

Early Years: Light and Darkness

The young child had a very strong imaginative life, and great love for the gardens. In contrast he was shocked by the bleak world of the factories and tenements that surrounded him. Living close to factory workers' houses, the contrast between the beauty of the gardens and the ugliness of people and buildings marked his soul. He felt the need to protect himself from this ugly reality, by imagining a world of lovely young people, a world "where only young, radiant people lived" and "everything there was perfect, except that he did not have yet a queen."[254] Predictably, the boy experienced school as a prison. Once more he found refuge in his inner world. In this world he was a king on a white horse. He would defy his teachers by telling the other children that they could do what the teachers told them not to, a way to test his kingly powers,

---

[253] Emanuel Zeylmans, *Willem Zeylmans von Emmichoven: An Inspiration for Anthroposophy. A biography,* 7.
[254] Ibid, 8.

though the result was predictable. And he imagined all sorts of great adventures.

Not only was his inner life imaginative; it also opened up to direct spiritual perception. Demons appeared for the first time when the boy was five. They waited until it was evening. "The moment everything was quiet they emerged from these shadows. They appeared from all the dark places, from under the cupboard, from under the bed. It was no use shutting his eyes--they still came." They looked like animals and yet different from them. "They were all as frightful as each other, and he could feel himself going rigid with fear."[255] There was a particularly frightening being carrying a white coat, and a yet more frightening black man with a covered face.

Only years later did his inner voice enjoin him to look the beings in the eyes because this would make them vanish. When he did this he experienced great dread, but the demons effectively started to dissolve. These visions went on for years, especially when he was tired or ill at ease. Still, he could face the beings and dispel them.

The young boy could also experience the elementals of the animal world. One day he observed a crow at very close range, and from that day he started looking at animals with great interest, being fascinated by their mystery. He could perceive the elemental dimensions of animals, a "'something' that was both friendly, gentle, delicate, … and eerie and frightening."[256] He was a little frightened, and most of all fascinated by the mystery. Van Emmichoven mentions something else of interest, though only in passing. In his neighborhood he could see many drunkards, and he could recognize whether they were affected by wine, beer, or other liquors quite precisely, based on the elemental beings that accompanied them.

His imaginative life soon also had a romantic-idealistic dimension. At age seven, he mentions there was a girlfriend with whom he also took dancing classes. He took this experience very seriously, and was dismissive of criticism of puppy-love. "In these years love for him [Bender Bole] was something which belonged completely to the world

---

[255] Emanuel Zeylmans, *Willem Zeylmans van Emmichoven*, 10.
[256] Ibid, 12.

of light. Nothing bad or common, ugly or dark, was able to obscure it."[257] And he could not find light anywhere else. Gradually he also started to feel attracted by bad things, but not often, and always with revulsion, once he went through them. Curiously, he was also a fighter, and could pick quarrels with older boys. But most of all, he liked to tell stories, especially romantic ones about beautiful girls. Still, there was no forestalling growing up and "a mood of sadness, mixed with longing for a return to paradise, increasingly took root of his soul. Mourning for lost paradise, unquenchable longing to live there."[258]

With the beginning of adolescence, an unexpected twist of fate brought a new world to Willem, one that offered much relief to the young idealistic soul. When the factory went through a hard time, his father was dismissed. And when Willem was fifteen, the family moved to Amsterdam, where the father started a confectionary business. In the effervescent city the young boy met ambitious and talented young men, and he was taken into their circles. When at school he had the first opportunity to write a story, the teacher declared that the class had found a poet. From that moment on his inner life was fired. What he had done in his imagination, he could now put on paper. He started writing long essays, reading stories, poems, novels, world literature. Another absorbing world was that of light and darkness that he found in painting. In a museum he had a deeply significant experience. After feeling overwhelmed by the amount of paintings, "... suddenly, like a flash of lightning, he saw what was around him; deep shimmering colors, radiant bright colors, fiery blazing colors, colors that quietly drew him into the distance. Slowly he began to see the paintings themselves, to distinguish one from another and at last to know them."[259] And something else offered him relief. He could now see the demons he knew so well in the paintings--he in fact recognized most of them--and knew by this that others had experienced them.

---

[257] Emanuel Zeylmans, *Willem Zeylmans van Emmichoven*, 13.
[258] Ibid, 14.
[259] Ibid, 18.

Facing The Inner Darkness

Adolescence faced Willem with a few other tests. At age sixteen, he fell ill with typhoid: he had high fever with hallucinations. At its peak, he was so weak that he could hardly raise a hand. Once recovered, he had to go through a long convalescence.

Soon after he briefly felt the need to join organized religion, via a Christian community, but it did not feed his soul. What did, however, was the world of music, particularly since he lived close to the Concertgebouw, Amsterdam's main concert hall.

To help us understand his soul life at the time, van Emmichoven spends quite some time telling us about his adolescent love for a beautiful girl named Christie, who did not return his love. The youthful infatuation lasted for more than three years, and pain engulfed him. Connecting to the world through this experience, he realized the role of pain in the world. By going through his pain fully, he cleansed himself of all his attachment for Christie. The elder man later recalled, "I had experienced something which, from that time on, I could carry with me as a treasure. The power of suffering endured..." And further, "Joy is like a great light that streams in from without. Suffering, in contrast, awakens an inner light that begins to shine in the soul: small to start with, but *stronger than the other light.* And it was with this inner light that I wanted to meet my future wife, and become one with her, as the human spirit strives to become one with the world-soul itself..."[260]

When Willem's parents moved to The Hague, the youth moved from the University of Amsterdam to that of Leyden to continue his medical studies. The young van Emmichoven elected to specialize in psychiatry. He had a natural aptitude for this field. Even in his early days people used to confide to him their emotional and mental problems. And he knew these phenomena from up close. His mother had suffered from anxiety, and was subject to "some degree of mental stress."

In the years of his studies, cynicism was van Emmichoven's inner foe. "...sometimes he [Bender Bole] fell into a cynical, bitter mood and then liked to speak in paradoxes. He felt himself completely at odds with the world, even above it all, like an observer who gazes down

---

[260] Emanuel Zeylmans, *Willem Zeylmans van Emmichoven*, 25.

from a high, bare cliff—interested in what he sees, but without any real involvement. Then, in contrast, he was filled with a mood similar to the one he had felt in his childhood years, when he discovered that paradise had vanished and only darkness and ugliness remained on earth. A deep melancholy held sway in his soul."[261] He also continued to deepen the theme of knowledge of pain. He suffered about the war, about poverty and illness. It was a relief to work in the editorial department of the college's *Minerva* publication and publish the story "The Golden Girl" in its pages. He also joined a small literary circle, which became very important for him. He met with very highly gifted individuals, learned to discuss, form judgments, and write critical essays. His piece "The Mirror" speaks about an encounter with the double which had been reported to him by a friend, and shows quite some insight for a psychiatrist-to-be.

Yet another source of relief was nature, particularly the sea. Walking along the dunes on a warm summer day, he saw his future wife, an adolescent playing with other children along the beach. He felt spellbound. "He [Bender Bole] stood there motionless, without breathing, and a cold shiver ran through him. Now he could see her face from close-up. This face…it had something of the still inwardness of the Madonna faces of the great masters of the Renaissance….Did he recognize her? Her face seemed so familiar, so intimately known. But how could that be. He had never seen her before. And yet it was like seeing her again, a holy reunion. As though he ought to run to her with arms flung wide and call: 'At last, at last!' He stood there rooted to the spot, motionless as a statue."[262] He waited for her three years until she reached adulthood.

The World of Color and the Meeting with Rudolf Steiner

Van Emmichoven recalls first hearing about Steiner from Jan Buys, a member of the circle of the painter Arthur Briët, and from Pieter de Haan, a publisher who was very enthusiastic about Steiner. When he

---

[261] Emanuel Zeylmans, *Willem Zeylmans van Emmichoven*, 29.
[262] Ibid, 38.

first saw the portrait of Steiner in a painter's studio, he had the feeling of knowing him intimately. Upon hearing who it was, he realized he had not met him. He was then twenty-three. At this time he started visiting two anthroposophical painters—Jacoba van Heemskerck and Marie Tak van Poortvliet—who had a collection of modern painters he liked and admired. When he told them that he was intending to go to the West Indies at the end of his studies, they were disappointed because they already felt he would be the future leader of the Dutch Anthroposophical Society. In fact the ladies later offered to pay for him to stay in the country, rather than go to the West Indies. Van Emmichoven accepted the offer, and the course of his destiny would be significantly altered.

Though the young man was starting to form a friendship with the two ladies, he was put off by the way they spoke of modern science. They were the first ones to give him Steiner books to read. He read the books without yet being touched to the core, but feeling that their content was credible. Something else was needed, that would follow very soon.

Van Emmichoven's interest in the world of colors was deepening; it met him on many fronts. While engaged in his medical studies, he continued to explore color in modern paintings together with his two painter friends. He had already awakened his interest in modern art and had been touched by Kandinsky, Kokoschka, Mondrian, Franz Marc, and Paul Klee, among others. From July 1920 he started to conduct experiments on color. In a darkened room he exposed people to different colors. The subjects were simply asked to beat a regular rhythm on an electrical apparatus, and the resulting tempo was recorded in relation to clock time. The results showed the fastest rhythms between yellow and orange, the slowest ones between blue and violet, and the middle ones in the green part of the spectrum. But what was of further interest was that at the other side of the spectrum, there was a point of balance similar to green in the color crimson. The results were further corroborated by the participants' verbal input; there was agreement in their responses. At this time he wrote: "Newton's theory may not be perfect, or explain everything...but I believe that it contains a useful core of truth. In my view Goethe's color theory does not have such a core, yet it can have a very fruitful influence on one's thinking about this subject, through the many important observations and remarks he makes…so that my reading was not wasted."[263]

He was getting ready for a breakthrough, and what came next were Steiner's writings on Goethe, which helped him cross the threshold of his hesitations. He had an epiphany: "So I went to the university library and asked for Goethe's scientific writings, and began to read Rudolf Steiner's introduction, and suddenly, lo and behold, a whole bundle of light flashed down from the heavens and struck through me, as I read Rudolf Steiner's sentence: 'Our image of the visible world is the sum of perceptions metamorphosing independently of underlying matter.'" And further, "A whole world opened and showed me color as a living being." This led to the unavoidable conclusion: "I went to Frau Wolfram, the group leader, and told her I would like to join the Society."[264] This he did because he wanted to study an as yet unpublished medical course cycle now given to members of the Society.

On December 1920 van Emmichoven traveled to Dornach, where his wife Ingeborg was already studying eurythmy. He heard Steiner lecture for the first time on December 17 evening; it was the first of three lectures on "The Bridge between Universal Spirituality and the Physical Constitution of Man." This experience completed his breakthrough. It was a turning point in his biography. When Steiner appeared he remembered later, "At this moment I had a clear experience of recognition. This was so strong that a whole series of images surfaced in me at the same time, vaguely recalling former situations––as though I recognized him as my teacher through the millennia. It was the most powerful experience I have had in my whole life. For a long time I sat, lost in thought, and only later did I realize that the lecture had begun."[265] We can sense that van Emmichoven is cautiously pointing to the images of previous lifetimes. Not only were memories stirred; he was also deeply touched by Steiner's appearance, which for him personified the full human being in its whole potential. Something else left an imprint on his soul: the quality of Steiner's voice, the impressions that his words left

---

[263] Emanuel Zeylmans, *Willem Zeylmans van Emmichoven*, 48.
[264] Ibid.
[265] Ibid, 49.

long after being spoken, and the strength of the ideas expressed, whether he understood them or not.

Ingeborg then introduced him to Steiner, who said: "I have been waiting for a long time for you to come." Steiner meant he had waited for van Emmichoven to join the common work, confirming in a way the young doctor's inklings about previous lives. And Steiner offered to speak to him the very next day. To Steiner van Emmichoven talked about his work with the color spectrum. He explained that "green was a zero-point because all the feeling responses were there in equilibrium; and crimson was, because it represented a balance between the greatest will activity and the highest intensification of thoughtful and reflective activities." Steiner, impressed, showed him that the spectrum of colors is really a circle. "In one stroke he had answered all the questions that I could not even put."[266] The two had been sitting all along, their back to the wooden sculpture of the Representative of Mankind that was still unfinished at the time. "I felt freer than ever, taken into another world into which only important things matter; in which what one otherwise considers unimportant falls away. That gave me a wonderful sense of joy and freedom. The feeling of freedom was helped by the fact that we sat next to one another, not opposite."[267]

Career and Dutch Anthroposophical Society

At age twenty-seven, van Emmichoven started his career. His first position in Maasrood, Amsterdam's city mental asylum, was very short-lived. He was soon germinating the idea of moving to The Hague and opening his own practice in order to have more time to devote to anthroposophy. This he did in 1924, and by the end of 1927 he had opened his Rudolf Steiner Clinic, located between The Hague and Scheveningen. Here he could realize one of his cherished dreams: painting all of the thirty-five patients' rooms in different colors. He also carried the concern of being able to treat people regardless of financial ability to pay. And by 1937 the demand exceeded the clinic's capacity.

---

[266] Emanuel Zeylmans, *Willem Zeylmans van Emmichoven,,* 53
[267] Ibid, 54.

Van Emmichoven's medical career ran in parallel with his involvement within the Dutch Anthroposophical Society and his lecturing activity, which continued from 1922 to the end of his life. He soon became accustomed to large audiences. In November 1922 Steiner was lecturing in Holland and, no doubt, starting to rethink the structure of the General Anthroposophical Society. He was particularly deploring the sectarian element of the Society everywhere, the Netherlands included. And on that occasion he asked whether someone could lecture on anthroposophy. When van Emmichoven mentioned that he had just started, Steiner replied: "Well, then all you need to do is make Dr. Zeylmans free for anthroposophy and offer him a generous salary."[268] Van Emmichoven was also asked to lead the Dutch Society since it was perceived that that was also the wish of Steiner. When van Emmichoven told Steiner he had less interest in working for the Society than in anthroposophy itself, Steiner's reply was quite emphatic: "That's your karma and there's nothing to be done about it." And soon after: "You see, the tasks on behalf of the Society are simply your karma." A third time he repeated basically the same. And to this he added: "As a doctor, you are particularly fitted to be General Secretary, for the Society will increasingly need the therapeutic aspect."[269] When he accepted the task, Steiner warned him against sectarianism once more.

Christmas Foundation Meeting and Inner Darkness

Zeylmans van Emmichoven was one of the first to realize the crucial importance of the Christmas Meeting and of the Foundation Stone Meditation. He attended everything that happened in Dornach between December 23, 1923 and January 9, 1924.

In 1935 van Emmichoven, Ita Wegman and many others were expelled from the General Anthroposophical Society. Lievegoed reveals that Van Emmichoven had a heart attack in the train leaving Dornach, and that he suffered deeply under this tragedy. Lievegoed saw him as an eagle with clipped wings. And van Emmichoven had reason to

---

[268] Emanuel Zeylmans, *Willem Zeylmans van Emmichoven*, 59.
[269] Ibid, 91.

feel wounded. He believed that "What Rudolf Steiner meant with the Christmas meeting of 1923 is now going to be delayed for decades."[270] Lievegoed himself, at that point, felt that the worldwide Society had lost its right to speak on the world arena. The anthroposophical movement in Dornach further split around the personalities of Albert Steffen and Marie Steiner. Van Emmichoven countered by writing a booklet entitled "Development and Spiritual Conflict."

After the events of 1935 van Emmichoven dedicated much of his life to healing the rift that had occurred within the Anthroposophical Society. But at the same time he had to struggle with his own demons. Inwardly he kept hearing a voice telling him to resign from the Society as a general secretary, and even as a member. He had restless nights, and such an intense inner struggle that Emanuel, his son and biographer, says, "We know that he woke up every morning for three years asking: 'God let me die now!'"[271] The writing of a book about Rudolf Steiner may have helped him to overcome his inner doubts.

In 1948 van Emmichoven was trying different ways to approach Dornach. Emil Bock, who was also attempting the same, had conceived the plan of a "Friendship Conference" that would gather a small number of friends to discuss the world situation, and how it needed to be addressed. Through van Emmichoven and Karl König's input a Weleda hall, close to Arlesheim, was chosen for the meeting in June 1948. There were fourteen participants, from the Netherlands, Germany and the United Kingdom, and one American. They spent a week together, occupying the first three days with a study of the Arnhem *Karmic Relationships* lectures that Steiner had offered in 1924. After that, other Dornach members were invited to join, and in the last day and a half the executive committee of the Goetheanum. Progress took the form of collaboration between lower-level groups in the respective countries. A December 1948 conversation also took place, but it was marred by Marie Steiner's death, which caused a bit of disarray. On New Year's Eve van Emmichoven gave a lecture; then a small group of fifteen people

[270] An Interview with Jelle van der Meulen, *The Eye of the Needle: Bernard Lievegoed*, 46.
[271] Emanuel Zeylmans, *Willem Zeylmans van Emmichoven*, 125.

worked together for three days. The theme of the Christmas Foundation Meeting and its impulse was the thread that united them.

The initial group enlarged, and it supported the Dutch summer conferences in the following years. This culminated in a 1953 European conference, held in The Hague and attended by 1200 people. The chosen theme was "The Birth of Europe: A Spiritual Question." There was a conference the following summer, but nothing of import occurred until 1960. By then van Emmichoven took the last steps in order to ensure that reconciliation would happen. In a letter of September 1959 (presumably addressed to the Goetheanum) he announced: "If we [Dutch Anthroposophical Society] are ready to reintegrate with the General Anthroposophical Society, this is because we believe the time is pressing, and that we ought at least to make our contribution to building up a General Anthroposophical Society which deserves the name 'General' because it includes all who see themselves as honest students of Rudolf Steiner." At the Annual General Meeting the following year on Easter Saturday, April 16, 1960, he changed this slightly to "And if people should ask us why we are reintegrating with the General Anthroposophical Society, we can only give one reply: because we wish and have the will to!"[272] Van Emmichoven had accomplished one of his most important tasks just before dying.

Van Emmichoven's Literary Work: a Look at the Soul

According to his son Emanuel, in his lecture notes van Emmichoven fixed "in his mind what he first saw as images before him." And he concludes, "It was probably his lectures' vivid imagery which chiefly struck his audience."[273] Unique among his literary output was a short attempt at poetry titled *Mysteries*. Though unfinished, it is very symptomatic of van Emmichoven's outlook. The poem was conceived in three parts: "Images," "Being," and "Word," and it sounds like a fairy tale. Only the first part was ever written. Of interest to us here is what van Emmichoven says about images/imaginations: "The human

[272] Emanuel Zeylmans, *Willem Zeylmans van Emmichoven*, 248-49.
[273] Ibid, 106.

202

being is surrounded by the mystery of images. Everything that his eye perceives is image, that his ear hears, that is revealed to his soul in taste and fragrance. The cosmos veils itself in images! …. So earth too, and all its creatures, are an image."[274] And further, "Thus everything which the human eye perceives and human senses experience on earth is image. An image of divine will, divine wisdom and divine love, woven from heavenly light. In eternal alternation the images pass before the soul."[275]

Central among van Emmichoven's books are *The Anthroposophical Understanding of the Soul* and *The Foundation Stone*. Of the first, his son Emanuel says, "This book, subtitled *Introduction to Knowledge of the Nature, Activity and Development of the Soul,* was van Emmichoven's first and only book on the nature of the human soul."[276] The author approaches the topic from the realm of the Word, and concludes it by returning to the importance of the Word. In fact, the book contains detailed linguistic studies that introduce most major headings. Van Emmichoven was also fluent in English and German and able to lecture in both without notes, and could thus draw from these languages as well. Looking at the book in some detail will allow us later to compare van Emmichoven's approach to that of Lievegoed, who wrote abundantly about the soul.

The book follows a clear Goethean approach. Van Emmichoven looks at pure phenomena without allowing himself to be led astray by preconceived hypotheses. He starts by explaining that it is possible to have direct observation of the souls of others through gesture, sound, tone, word or thought (sense observations). And that the soul can perceive itself through the I.

Van Emmichoven invites us into the soul at deeper and deeper levels. He delineates key concepts and then goes further into them. As Lievegoed would say, he circles the topic like an eagle moving closer to the earth. Chapter I is titled *The Nature of the Soul*; Chapter II, *The Forces at Work in the Soul*; Chapter III is *A More Detailed Description of the Forces at Work in the Soul.* (See Table of Contents in Appendix 4) Ideas are

---

[274] Emanuel Zeylmans, *Willem Zeylmans van Emmichoven*, 176-77.
[275] Ibid, p. 180.
[276] Ibid, 158.

built up very patiently and progressively: through etymology, polarities that are reintroduced after each new key concept, and exploration of the soul's boundaries with the world and with the body. In addition, here and there are developmental comparisons between plants, animals and human beings, and considerations about human development.

The author opens the first chapter by outlining the field of activity of the soul. He looks at the soul in relation to the world and in relation to the self; how the two realities communicate to the soul, and the soul to them; the world of perceptible phenomena and the world of inner spiritual phenomena; the rhythms of the soul (opening to the world, closing in self); the polarities it experiences (light and dark, major and minor, sweet and sour…); the soul's relationship to time and space; the soul's urge to development; its need to act as a whole; and so on.

In Chapter 2 we are led from the realm of feelings into the forming of judgments through the act of separating from the world. The forming of mental images is contrasted with the polarity of desiring. This basic polarity will be re-explored and deepened in the following chapters.

Intensifying the previous ideas, in Chapter 3 judgment is defined in relation to thinking (cognitive judgment), feeling (aesthetic judgment) and willing (moral judgment). And the importance of mental images is underlined in the attainment of spiritual and moral judgments for pure thinking. The life of the senses and the forming of mental images is contrasted with the life of desires. An important concept appears: the drives that animate desiring at its lowest level are forces of nature; they originate from the unconscious life of the organs.

The key concept of consciousness is introduced in Chapter 5. Consciousness is defined as a state of being determined by an inner knowing. There are different stages of consciousness: from knowing what lives in the soul and where the soul indwells, to a knowing that arises in the soul itself. The second stage is a "knowing about knowing." Consciousness can address what comes to the soul from the world, or what arises inwardly from the soul itself. And it is deepened through life experience, sorrow and pain.

We come then to a central concept. Life and consciousness stand in opposition. When we live in positive feelings we are carried by the life forces that reveal themselves in the life processes. In negative feelings the soul withdraws from the universe and makes possible the emergence and development of its cognitive functions (judgments and mental images). The different degrees of consciousness are expressed in relation to sleeping, dreaming and waking: the work of the soul in the body processes in deep sleep; the activity of the soul in the feeling realm in dreams; and the conscious experience of thinking in day consciousness. Where the soul is unconscious the body processes are built up; where the soul is most conscious, as in thinking, sense perception and mental images, the soul works in the destructive forces.

Another key concept is introduced in Chapter 6, showing the polarity of mental images, which through their link to memory look to the past, and desires, which express the urge of our individuality, and lead us into the future of our evolving personality. A stream coming from the past meets the other, coming from the future. They meet in the present in which consciousness dwells. Mental images are objective; they leave us free. Desires continuously express the drives of our personality that want to be satisfied. Mental images are placed as "image" in contrast to desires which express "being." And van Emmichoven points to the central role of the I beyond the streams of time: "...I-hood remains beyond the framework of space and time, beyond the cognitive and experiencing functions of the soul. In this context its real nature cannot be discerned, for it is rooted in eternity."[277]

The book closes on a variety of themes. One that is symptomatic of the whole of van Emmichoven's outlook is that of sounds, word, concepts and ideas. The author goes to considerable length in looking at all of these terms. He first delineates the difference between vowels (connected with being) and consonants (connected with cognizing and the pictorial element). The word is defined as a "sound-picture in which we express our encounter with a reality in the world or within ourselves." The birth of the personality is linked to the ability of uttering the word. And van Emmichoven points to the tragedy of our time, where the word is currently a corpse bereft of soul and spirit. He points to concepts, through which we inwardly grasp spiritual content, and

---

[277] F. W. Zeylmans van Emmichoven, *The Anthroposophical Understanding of the Human Soul*, 131.

ideas that "connote that this spiritual content has become a picture and indeed a purely spiritual picture."[278]

Van Emmichoven returns with more depth to the Word, its genesis, the role of vowels and consonants; the erect posture of the human being; the place of the brain in emancipating the human being from gravity and from the body, and forming the basis for the cognitive function. He then elaborates the difference between intellect, which can see everything that has come to a halt (everything from the past) and reason (in Goethe's terms) which comprehends development, and what comes from the future. The intellect keeps everything fixed in order to make use of it. Reason, or that thinking that is able to encompass the very processes of becoming in nature, becomes an organ of perception.

The author now returns to a theme that is central to his whole way of being. "The force active in human thinking is of the same kind as the force that creates the manifold forms in nature. To our sense-perception, nature appears in pictures, in percepts. The picture-forming force itself, however, works in our soul as a thinking-force that makes possible the forming of ideas."[279] Quite naturally, this progression leads to the evolution of consciousness on the path of knowledge, through Imagination, Inspiration and Intuition. The three types of consciousness are placed in relation with the threefold human body.

Van Emmichoven concludes the book by pointing to love as the force that works both in feeling and willing; the force that forms the soul from within; the force that unites feeling and willing. "In love we have to do with a merging of two archetypal forces: feeling and willing; the soul unfolds its strongest activity in the realm of the spirit, where the 'I' works into the soul. ... This is why love has the characteristic of inexhaustibility."[280]

Some other themes appear in addition to the main ones presented above. A first thread is woven within the others: that of the boundaries of the soul between body and world (spirit). It is developed and deepened

---

[278] F. W. Zeylmans van Emmichoven, *The Anthroposophical Understanding of the Human Soul*, 145.

[279] Ibid, 155.

[280] Ibid, 162-63.

through the chapters. Van Emmichoven places desires (drives) at the border between soul and body, and mental images at the border between soul and spirit. The impulse to act is in the soul; with action we enter the world. In perception an opposite movement is reached: "A movement in the soul is withheld in a certain sense, creating a space for the instreaming world."[281] Perception is made possible through the qualities of the world entering our souls through the gates of the senses.

Another example of these boundaries appears in the realm of feelings. Pleasure and displeasure are found at the border between feeling and desiring and in connection with the body (hunger, thirst, sexual drive). Sympathy and antipathy take place in the soul itself; they have more lasting significance than pleasure and displeasure. Joy and sorrow also belong to the soul: they express something of a more objective nature than sympathies and antipathies. Love and hatred are more complex than the above and also deeper; they touch on the moral-spiritual, at the boundary between soul and spirit.

A second theme, that of evolution and development, completes the palette of approaches to the topic of the soul. Van Emmichoven looks at how the soul deviates in order to return to the norm (for Goethe the exception indicates the norm). Quite often van Emmichoven refers to the young child to illustrate how soul and world are united at the beginning, and how soul functions differentiate and evolve. The evolution from plant to animal to human being completes the developmental tableau. An example is the evolution of desire. The plant does not desire. It reveals in its entire form the complexity of the growth forces. The animal form exemplifies the animal's dominating desire. Life forces are alone in the plant; desire appears in the animal. If the soul can effect a certain liberation of the forces of desire, then wish and longing appear, pointing to the spiritual element in the human being.

A certain gesture has started to emerge so far from the being of Zeylmans van Emmichoven. The reader may recall that in seeing Steiner lecture for the first time in his life, "a whole series of images surfaced in me at the same time, vaguely recalling former situations—as though I

---

[281] F. W. Zeylmans van Emmichoven, *The Anthroposophical Understanding of the Human Soul*, 46.

recognized him as my teacher through the millennia." We are fortunate to be able to trace two of these personalities at crucial points in time, and further the emerging picture.

Looking Back to "Former Situations"

In 1932 Ita Wegman wrote to van Emmichoven about her extensive journey through Greece: "For me, the finest experience was to let the landscape of each Mystery site work on me in such a way that one could recall that Aristotle, Plato, Alexander had seen the same landscape and found great joy in their beauty. Thus the present started to fall away, and one could live completely into ancient times, could experience Ptolemy's enthusiasm for the great Cabiri spirits to which he gave expression in his Ptolemy temple, whose foundations and pillars still lie around, as well as in the Arsineium. And it made a strange impression on me to read, in Greek, on a great gable stone, the clear words: "Here Ptolemy and Veronica honor the great Cabiri."[282] Notice here the insistence on Ptolemy, a general of Alexander the Great, not to be confused with the mathematician and astronomer who lived four centuries later. Ita Wegman was knowingly referring to the individual with whom van Emmichoven knew himself united in the course of time.

Van Emmichoven went to Greece in 1957 and was inspired for an in-depth study of the ten Aristotelian categories, "which he linked, among other things, to a spiritual figure who meant much to him... This was Raimundus Lullus, the zealous missionary of Majorca" with whom van Emmichoven also saw himself connected.[283] He is the one whom he mentions three times in his book on the Foundation Stone in relation to alchemy.[284]

Ptolemy was a contemporary of Alexander the Great/Ita Wegman and Aristotle/Steiner. Ramon Lull lived in the 13th century, after all

---

[282] F. W. Zeylmans van Emmichoven, *The Anthroposophical Understanding of the Human Soul*, 238.

[283] Ibid, 239.

[284] F. W. Zeylmans van Emmichoven, *The Foundation Stone*, 52, 57, 64.

Platonists had accomplished their mission and returned to the spiritual world. The two incarnations together form an important linchpin to the personality of Zeylmans van Emmichoven, on both sides of the Mystery of Golgotha. We will now look at them more closely.

Ptolemy I Soter

Ptolemy I Soter (367 BC-c. 283 BC), also known as Ptolemy Lagides, was one of Alexander the Great's most trusted generals, who became ruler of Egypt (323-283 BC), and founder of the Ptolemaic Dynasty. His mother was Arsinoe of Macedon; his father is not known with certainty. Ancient writers assign the fatherhood to either Lagus, a Greek Macedonian nobleman, or to Philip II, King of Macedon, of whom he would have been the illegitimate son. In the latter instance he would have been the half-brother of Alexander. Regardless of either possibility, Ptolemy, a few years older than Alexander, had been his intimate friend since childhood, and later became one of Alexander's closest generals, and one of the seven bodyguards who protected him.

Ptolemy's life was one of continuous action and adventure. He accompanied Alexander during his earliest Asian campaigns, and was one of the major protagonists in the later Afghanistan and India campaigns. Alexander had him at his side when he visited the Oracle in the Siwa Oasis, where he was proclaimed a son of Zeus.

When Alexander died in 323 BC, Ptolemy was appointed satrap of Egypt, and he quickly mobilized to subjugate Cyrenaica. Foreseeing succession struggles, Ptolemy went at great length to carry the body of Alexander to Memphis, Egypt. Burying his predecessor would strengthen his claim of succession and weaken the claim of his rival, Perdiccas, the imperial regent. In effect, in the year 321 Perdiccas set out to invade Egypt. Ptolemy mounted a successful defense, and his rival was subsequently murdered by two of his subordinates.

In the year 318 Ptolemy occupied Syria and extended a protectorate over Cyprus. However, his occupation was short-lived. Alliances continuously shifted and peace was precarious. In 309 BC Ptolemy commanded a fleet that occupied the towns of Lycia and Caria in western Anatolia, then took possession of Corinth, Sicyon and Megara in

Greece. In a reverse of fortune Cyprus was attacked by Demetrius, at the service of the satrap Antigonus, and lost to Ptolemy. In the winter of 306 BC, Antigonus attempted the invasion of Egypt. Ptolemy successfully resisted. After this time Ptolemy concentrated his efforts within Egypt. The above are but a few signposts of a very outwardly oriented life.

Ptolemy I died in 283 BC at the age of eighty-four at the helm of a well-organized kingdom. He managed to bring stability and progress to his lands and became known for his liberality and his support for arts and knowledge. Egypt benefited from Ptolemy's sound political and administrative policies, as well as from his cultural choices. He moved the capital to Alexandria to escape the influence of the old religion in Memphis. Close to the Mediterranean Sea, it was better suited to preserve the connection to Greece, rather than to old Egypt. And in effect, Greek became the official language for both government and commerce.

It was Ptolemy who founded the Great Library of Alexandria. The sovereign turned the town into the intellectual center of the Mediterranean, and attracted great minds from the whole area for a few centuries to come, among them Euclid and Archimedes. Ptolemy himself wrote a history of Alexander's campaigns. Though it has not survived, it was considered objective and praised for its honesty and sobriety.

Ptolemy took personal interest in the great mathematician Euclid, whom he sponsored personally. Although interested in Euclid's work, he could not find his way into his most important opus, the *Elements*. The philosopher Proclus reports that Ptolemy asked for an easier way to master its concepts. The mathematician's reply was "Sire, there is no royal road to geometry."

Ptolemy died in 283 BC. The dynasty he created ruled Egypt for almost three hundred years, until Julius Caesar conquered it.

Ramon Lull

Ramon Lull was a mystic, philosopher, preacher and missionary to the Arabs, and lived from 1232 to 1315. Steiner spoke of him in 1924. Lull was a wealthy young man, who lived a carefree life until he had visions of the Crucified One. After that he devoted his life to Him and wrote many books. His most famous was the *Ars Magna*, a sort of revelation of the Logos. This writing played an important role in Medieval thinking, even though it appears rather abstract. Agrippa of Nettesheim, Giordano Bruno and Nicolas Cusanus were touched by it.

Majorca had been part of Arab territory until James the Conqueror added it to Catalonia, Christianized it, and enslaved the local Muslim population. Ramon's father had received land from the crown, and Ramon Lull became the Seneschal (the administrative head of the royal household) to the future King James II of Majorca, who was a relative of his wife.

Ramon Lull formed a family, but he lived what he would later call the carefree and wasteful life of a troubadour of sorts. This changed in the year 1263 thanks to a series of visions, which Lull recorded. In his life as troubadour, Ramon was used to composing gay songs and poems. One night he was looking for inspiration for writing a song in jest to a lady whom he sought; while beginning the song, he saw to his right, as if suspended in mid-air, Jesus Christ on the Cross. This vision returned five times, inducing his choice to leave his family, work, and possessions in order to serve God. He had three goals in mind: to convert Muslims to Christianity, to promote the founding of religious institutions for the teaching of foreign languages, and to write a book that would be effective in converting skeptics to Christianity. Lull became a Franciscan tertiary, and returned to Majorca, where he purchased a Muslim slave from whom he learned Arabic.

For the next nine years, until 1274, he immersed himself in continuous study and contemplation. He read what he could from both Latin and Arabic literature, in order to master Christian and Muslim theological and philosophical thought. During this time he wrote a compendium of the Muslim thinker Al-Ghazali's logic and the *Book on the Contemplation of God*, a guide to finding truth through contemplation.

His major work, *Ars Generalis Ultima,* or *Ars Magna*, addressed the goals he stated at his conversion. The book was intended as a debating tool for converting Muslims to Christianity through logic and reason. He wanted readers to be able to inquire into any argument or question expressed in terms of Christian beliefs, and use visual aids and a book of charts to bring together various ideas and generate statements, which would provide an answer.

In the *Ars Magna* Ramon Lull tried to express the way in which man relates to the godhead through a series of sixteen divine qualities, inspired by the tree of the Sephiroth. These qualities were arranged four by four around a certain sound. Emanuel van Emmichoven continues: "The intention, in fact, was to meditate on such a schema, quality by quality; and do this in relation to another schema, in which another sound (e.g. S) would be surrounded by three soul qualities or seven virtues and an equal number of vices."[285] Lull wanted to resort to the use of a number of basic, undeniable truths, believing that one could understand most of any field of knowledge by studying combinations of these elemental truths. He hoped that Jews or Muslims would agree with these attributes, and would therefore be led to understand and accept Christianity. Though elaborate and ambitious, this attempt fell short, because the concepts were insufficiently developed, especially when one compares them to the contemporary Aquinas and the Scholastics.

Lull also wrote a novel, *Blanquema*, which was famous at the time. Among its chapters it counted *The Book of Lovers and Beloveds*. The book extolled the power of love of the lover who loves his beloved unconditionally. The lover was by extension the fervent Christian, and God was the beloved. One of its stanzas said: "The heart of the lover raised itself to the heights of the beloved, so that it was not hindered from love in the depths of this world."[286]

Lull's life still carried adventuresome aspects; they addressed one of his other vows: converting Muslims to Christianity. His first mission to North Africa in 1285 ended with his expulsion from Tunis. He returned to North Africa in 1304, and again in 1308, confident that the conversion of Muslims could be carried out spiritually, without the need for military force. In 1314 Lull traveled again to North Africa and was stoned by an angry crowd in the coast town of Bejaia in present-day

---

[285] E. van Emmichoven, *Willem Zeylmans van Emmichoven*, 240.
[286] Ibid, 241.

Algeria. He was rescued and brought back to Majorca, where he died at home in the following year.

Summing up

The youth of van Emmichoven echoed at times the lives of Ptolemy and Lull. In his youth the Dutch doctor had dreamt of leading armies. He had been fascinated by the characters of Napoleon, Alexander the Great, Julius Caesar. And he had supported the Boer War, though later he was appalled by the horrors of modern warfare and started to understand the political background to war. On the other hand, his mystical leanings and romantic aspirations seem to echo what lived in the soul of the troubadour turned mystic and scholar, Ramon Lull.

Much of the social skill that had found a place in the life experience of Ptolemy, took on another form in van Emmichoven. The consummate politician that was Ptolemy was now present in other ways. The doctor was skilled at looking at the qualities of his opponents. He was able to summarize at the end of conferences everything that people had contributed, and therefore was asked to give the concluding address. Son and biographer Emanuel too offers the image of the eagle that circles above and sees everything, and he concludes: van Emmichoven was a "man of the middle," "someone capable of encompassing and combining the most painful contradictions and oppositions" and able to mediate solutions.[287] "He always found the right word to say, and human difficulties melted away in the presence of his genial wisdom. He was exceptionally capable of being all things to all men, yet he always remained eminently himself." And further, "Everyone felt that he would be able to see the matter from all sides."[288]

It was almost as if the world at large intuited his great qualities. Van Emmichoven himself was surprised at the response to his public lectures all over the world. Certainly, his credentials as a doctor who had founded an institution were apt to raise interest. But one is bound to see something more at work here, the grace of the Ptolemy incarnation

---

[287] Emanuel Zeylmans, *Willem Zeylmans van Emmichoven*, 139.
[288] Ibid, 142.

at work. During that incarnation the ruler had had a central role in the world culture of the time, of which Alexandria was the capital. Culture flowed to Alexandria from all over the Mediterranean thanks to the sovereign's liberality. And van Emmichoven spread anthroposophical culture from the Netherlands worldwide, finding a ready reception in all places.

In Zeylmans van Emmichoven we have a representative of the Aristotelian stream, though one far from a prescribed stereotype. To begin with he accompanied Alexander and Aristotle's cultural revolution in the Near East, primarily as a man of action and a politician. He ruled Egypt with wisdom and sponsored the new culture, the legacy of Aristotle. He aspired to this culture himself, as is witnessed by the founding of the Alexandria library and his own literary striving. He could not however penetrate fully into Hellenistic thinking, witness his historical exchange with Euclid, recorded by Proclus.

Ramon Lull lived at the time of the Scholastics of Aquinas. And he strove in the same direction in which they did. He was, however, at the periphery of this effort, and found a home in the Franciscan order that was much more devoted to deeds of the heart than to intellectual striving. Yet Lull was far from a typical Franciscan, and he was only a tertiary, who had the leisure to devote his life to study. In this sense he pursued what an Aristotelian of the time intended to achieve. Moreover, he was engaged in different terms in Aquinas' intellectual fight against cultural Islam. Similarities notwithstanding, his karma did not offer him the tools for the sharpening of the intellect that Scholasticism had fashioned. His attempt, nevertheless, was aimed in the same direction, and found a completion in the twentieth century, when once again he joined his spiritual master.

With good reason does Lievegoed say that van Emmichoven had a very intense inner life, and that he went straight to the essential. To Lievegoed, van Emmichoven looked a lot older than he was, and gave the impression of a "truly ancient soul." This has nothing to do with the notion of "old souls" or "young souls." Rather, it may be related to how Steiner portrays the Aristotelian Strader in contrast to the Platonist Capesius in his Mystery Dramas, particularly in The Portal of Initiation.

Strader, though younger in years, is portrayed as older; Capesius is portrayed younger. Strader, as a man of thinking, has the quality of old age; Capesius, more prone to outer enthusiasm and to awakening others through warmth, has a quality of youth even in his old age.

Lievegoed continues, "Within the anthroposophical movement, [van Emmichoven] was an original thinker. His whole stature was saturnine, in his face the skeleton dominated. He was a spiritual eagle that hovered far above the earth. With the people to whom he gave his confidence, he had a relationship of deeply hidden warmth and absolute loyalty. In such a relationship, time became something infinite: when you had a profound conversation with him it could suffice for a couple of years."[289] Van Emmichoven was a true spiritual investigator who could live with questions for a long time, confident in the help of the spiritual world. On occasion, upon awakening from sleep he would receive pictures, from which he could form inner judgment, and build inner certainty.

Things stood quite otherwise with Bernard J. Lievegoed. No two close anthroposophists have ever described such a distinct polarity, nor have they brought their collaboration to such fruitful heights. We turn to the younger doctor next.

Bernard Lievegoed

Lievegoed was present at a 1926 international pedagogical conference organized by the Dutch anthroposophists. The young man had red hair and a fiery temperament, and looked younger than his age. His fellow students called him "fire-ball." He was introduced to van Emmichoven, then thirty-three, and twelve years his elder. The younger man appreciated that "Despite his young years he [van Emmichoven] seemed a mature person." The elder man, hearing what the friends were calling Lievegoed, approached the youth very directly: "Now then, how do things stand with you—will you willingly sacrifice yourself to the dragon...?" Lievegoed was puzzled and moved, and the question kept circling in his mind. He concluded: "During the next months I came to

---

[289] An Interview with Jelle van der Meulen, *The Eye of the Needle: Bernard Lievegoed*, 34.

see that I must ask Zeylmans how I might find the way to my own self. That was the beginning of an intimate friendship and pupilship that was to last thirty-five years."[290]

Whereas van Emmichoven wrote his biography in the third person under the pseudonym of Bender Bole, Bernard Lievegoed chose to do it in an interview conducted over three days with Jelle van der Meulen and published in 1991, the year previous to his death. Elements of his biography appear here and there through self-disclosures he offers in lectures. This is another small but significant contrast between the two Dutch doctors.

Jelle van der Meulen opens the book by underlining two characteristics of the work of Lievegoed: his orientation towards the future, and his way of working "with conviction and without timidity, [placing] the contents of spiritual science in the bright light of public life." In fact, the doctor posed as condition for the interview, his wanting to discuss urgent themes of importance for the coming years.[291] These statements by van der Meulen are a very succinct way of encapsulating much of what Lievegoed's being encompassed.

A Melting Pot of Cultures

Bernard Cornelis Johannes Lievegoed was born in Medan, on the island of Sumatra, on September 2, 1905. The young child went to grade school and made friends with people of different religions. At age ten he spent two years in Amsterdam before moving to Java. There he completed high school, returning to The Hague to present his final pre-university exam.[(41)]

As a child Bernard was used to riding on boats on rivers where alligators roamed; going around almost naked, except for a hat; guiding a boat through rapids; going on long mountain hikes and reaching the summits; descending into the crater of a volcano when the weather allowed it; or viewing performances of the Hindu Mahabharata epic

---

[290] Emanuel Zeylmans, *Willem Zeylmans van Emmichoven: An Inspiration for Anthroposophy: A Biography*, 113.
[291] Lievegoed, *The Eye of the Needle*, 7.

cycle. His exposure to the local culture made him realize how vastly different its values were from what he experienced at home. Consider that in his school he had only two other European boys, seven of Chinese origin and five Javanese, plus one black. He came thus to experience fully the Indonesian culture and understand how the locals viewed Westerners.

By the time he was sixteen he had moved to his ninth house, and had been practically obliged to understand all social and religious customs. And in these he was deeply interested. However, at the soul level, he lived in inner loneliness, with questions that did not interest those around him. His mother, a very dedicated feminist, was the president of the Association for Women's Suffrage in the Dutch East Indies. From her he received the constant injunction of doing something useful, which the child found oppressive. His father fought all his life against the excesses of colonialism. He had a strong feeling for justice, and wanted to separate reality from emotion in order to act in a dispassionate way. He had no interest in political ideologies. But the child could not find answers from his parents about his inner quests. What he heard from a Catholic clergyman in response to his desire to know the soul could not satisfy him.

Lievegoed experienced illnesses and personal losses at key moments in his biography. At age four he developed acute cholera, with high fever and dehydration. Of nine children who contracted the disease, only he and another one survived. The illness left him with paralysis on his right side, and he had to learn to walk again. He recovered almost fully, but maintained a slight disorder of the right arm afterwards, root cause of very bad handwriting. As a further consequence he could not participate in sports because he didn't have good balance. This pushed him to withdraw within himself, and gave him the feeling of being somewhat weaker than others.

In his early twenties Lievegoed fell in love at first sight with a very introverted girl, Truus. He was engaged for four years, and married her in 1931; she died in 1932 after the birth of their first child. At that time Lievegoed had become a physician, and had been drawn into anthroposophical work. For a time his involvement with anthroposophy was partly a flight from the pain of the loss. After the death of Truus, a new intense relationship with her best friend, Nel Schatborn, blossomed. It led to a marriage of fifty-five years, blessed by six children.

Premonition and Encounter with Anthroposophy

As a child, Lievegoed had a recurring dream of a wooden temple on top of a mountain, and he knew that he needed to get up there. He dreamt that he would begin to climb but never reached the top. With heavy building blocks he erected a miniature Greek temple, and kept it atop a table for months and months until his mother removed it. Years later, in relation to his sister being sick, he heard from a family friend in The Hague that in Basel, a temple for the anthroposophists had been built on top of a hill, and that the Catholics had burned it. He commented in the interviews of the book: "… during his story the shivers ran over my back, from the top down and from the bottom up."[292] This was his first encounter with anthroposophy, but only later did he understand that the man had been talking about the Goetheanum. He was then eighteen years and seven months old, the time of his first moon node. When Steiner came to Holland in the same year, Lievegoed was busy with his high school exam, and never had another chance to see him. From these circumstances he gathered the feeling of having come too late.

The young man had an attraction towards the scientific world. Originally he wanted to study electro-technology. He remembers having wires connected all over his room. For a period he was also interested in chemistry, but was reluctant to spend his life in a factory. The choice of medicine was providential, since he felt it left him free to decide later on a more specific direction.

In 1924 Lievegoed started his medical studies in Groningen. He did research on cancer cells, finding out how mutations developed in their proximity. He received his medical degree in 1930; later he returned to complete a doctorate, and wrote a thesis on "Fundamentals of Therapeutic Use of Musical Elements" in 1939. He commented that becoming an MD allowed him "to be able to feel at home in an official

---

[292] Lievegoed, *The Eye of the Needle*, 23.

way in the world of psychiatry."[293] Another parallel track to the world of van Emmichoven.

In the spring of 1926 he had received from Els Joekes, a close family friend, the book *Fundamentals of Therapy* by Steiner and Wegman. And he had an immediate sense of recognition. However, he decided to postpone the study of anthroposophy until completing his exams.

In 1926 he attended the anthroposophical pedagogical conference in The Hague mentioned above. There, he met van Emmichoven, Herbert Hahn, W.J. Stein and Eugen Kolisko. In 1928 or 1929 he saw a performance of *The Guardian of the Threshold* at the Goetheanum, together with his father, who also became an anthroposophist. Soon after came his first visit at Ita Wegman's clinic in Arlesheim. He felt immediately at home and had his first conversation with Ita Wegman, with whom he had in common the experience of growing up in the East Indies. He was impressed by her personality because she was both most spiritual and very practical. It was after this visit that he decided to join the Anthroposophical Society.

Upon meeting with anthroposophy, Lievegoed began a very intensive course of study. He devoted great interest in the qualities of the seven planets and in the concept of development, particularly from *Occult Science* and *True and False Paths in Spiritual Investigation*. The way in which he entered into anthroposophy is quite remarkable. It is better told in his own words concerning his relationship with *The Philosophy of Freedom*. "I experienced much of the first part as something which I, as a good pupil, simply had to learn, just as one sometimes has to learn rather boring things in school—it didn't appeal to me very much but this section [moral imagination and moral technique] sprang out from the page, in bold print, as it were, and I thought 'Yes, that is precisely what you are looking for, that is your life's task.'"[294]

By the time he established his work with developmentally disabled children, he knew that curative education involved the therapeutic aspect, the lifestyle, the medicines, etc., to which Steiner had made many contributions. But, a whole other realm was that of suitable social

---

[293] Lievegoed, *The Eye of the Needle*, 26.
[294] Bernard C. J. Lievegoed, *Developing Communities*, 10.

forms that would be appropriate for each phase of the organization. Here Steiner had not made direct contributions, since that had not been a question or a felt need when institutions were only in their infant stage. Lievegoed saw that moral technique would be very important in the search for these new social forms. Development and moral technique formed in fact the two touchstones of his whole work and literary output.

During the years after he met both Wegman and van Emmichoven, Lievegoed soon got involved in the development of the anthroposophical movement in the Netherlands. He was part of organizing the De Stakenberg international youth camp with van Emmichoven. The very novel initiative was criticized by many anthroposophists, even before it happened. And it set a precedent: consider hundreds of young anthroposophists coming from all over Europe and camping, and up to five hundred people doing eurythmy in the open air at one time.

During the time of the expulsions from the General Anthroposophical Society, Lievegoed was going through the loss of his first wife, and around him he was witnessing the ascendancy of Nazism. The younger generation wanted to build a strong Society while avoiding being burdened by the inner conflicts.

Moral Technique and The Needs of the Times

What happened as soon as Lievegoed got deeply involved in the Dutch Society corresponds to the Michael call of the times. The doctor created the institute for curative education "Zonnehuis Veldheim/ Stenia," the NPI (Institute for Organizational Development) and the Free High School (a one-year course for students preparing for university), and worked at the refashioning of the First Class of the Dutch Anthroposophical Society. In addition he wrote numerous books, including *The Developing Organization; Phases of Childhood; Phases: The Spiritual Rhythms in Adult Life;* and *Man on the Threshold: The Challenge of Inner Development.*

Zonnehuis and Personal Crises

Soon after the de Stakenberg camp, Lievegoed decided to start working on curative education. He had the ambitious goal of treating the disabled as part of a family, rather than inmates of an institution. It was rather vague and it did not receive much support from the people to whom Lievegoed spoke. One day Lievegoed had the opportunity of visiting a curative institution in Jena, because he had gone to an anthroposophical meeting and had been assigned to visit a home for "backward children." There he was part of a music appreciation class, and realized how differently things could be done. This was what he called a "coincidence." To the anthroposophist Pache, he asked if this would be possible in the Netherlands, and the latter said: "Yes, of course—just go and start."[295] This led to the initiative of the Zonnehuis in 1931, and the birth of the first curative educational institute in the Netherlands. In organizing the place Lievegoed realized he had to break new ground in anthroposophical knowledge and practice.

The war years were to bring a test to the nation and to the young doctor. During the war he contracted scarlet fever, accompanied with erysipelas and kidney problems, and he came close to dying. He had visions, and witnessed what was happening in Russia, particularly at the battle of Uman. He was experiencing the retreat of the German army, and saw a German soldier dying and a great figure of light approaching him. The latter experience was very strong.

After the war the Zonnehuis grew from sixty to some two-hundred-thirty children. It accepted both developmentally disabled and socially handicapped children; finding appropriate social forms became more important than ever. Lievegoed experienced another deep crisis when his son, Diederik, died of diphtheria at age five. At times he became desperate and wondered what his life was about. He asked himself why he had to lose two close family members. In addition he had the feeling of not having found his destination yet.

---

[295] Bernard C. J. Lievegoed, *Developing Communities*, 6.

Birth of NPI (Institute for Organizational Development)

Lievegoed remembers that preceding the important initiative of NPI was an experience, which "arose—by chance, as people say." The question came out of the surrounding world: "Could I help in a situation where trainees were causing difficulties when they finished their apprenticeship?"[296] The situation arose in light of the fact that the factory[what factory? This is not clear. Explanatory sentence needed] had a training workshop, in fact a whole separate factory, in which one hundred apprentices operated semi-independently from the whole. When, at the age of eighteen, they came under the supervision of the older foremen, there were highly explosive situations, which resulted in the majority of the ex-apprentices leaving. Apart from the social conflicts, this was a major financial drain for the firm. Having no previous experience of industrial life, Lievegoed spent a lot of time listening. He does not tell us how the experience ended, but it probably had a positive outcome, since new developments happened in the succeeding years.

Wim Schukking, Secretary of the Association for Industry and Commerce, looking for someone who could say something sensible about the industrialization of the Netherlands after the war—and particularly about what would have to change in education for this to happen—called on Lievegoed. The doctor gave a lecture which was a great success. He was in effect becoming more and more familiar with problems of growing organizations.

Lievegoed continues: "To my great astonishment there then came a request from our University in Rotterdam, from the Faculty of Social Economics, for me to take over a professional chair for Social Psychology, later Social Pedagogy."[297] It was a completely new field of inquiry and he declined it at first, only to accept it two years later. In 1954 the doctor was involved in the founding of NPI, and became professor of Social Pedagogy at the Netherlands School of Economics in Rotterdam. He accepted, provided he could call it Social Ecology, and that he could teach from experience. The NPI had been established for that purpose, and connected with the faculty chair at the School of Economics. The institute was supported by companies such as Shell, Philips, Unilever

---

[296] Bernard C. J. Lievegoed, *Developing Communities*, 13.
[297] Ibid, 10.

and AKZO, and it was built from the start as a purely anthroposophical initiative. It was independent from the university, though it had links to it.

Lievegoed was strongly driven to make anthroposophy part of European culture, and to make it visible by developing an anthroposophical view on social problems. That vision resulted in the book *The Developing Organization*. Lievegoed tells us another "coincidence" had been building up. There were some twelve to fifteen students who had graduated in 1947-48 from social science studies and were now using their talents in different fields, while attempting to use their anthroposophical knowledge as well. Many of these students were willing to let go of their professions and join their colleague for an uncertain, pioneering experiment.

NPI made contact with anthroposophy possible when people asked questions about the deeper aspects of its work. Moreover, everyone knew that NPI co-workers were anthroposophists. In addition, Lievegoed wanted people who worked for the NPI to have the springboard of their vocation in the work of the First Class of Spiritual Science. He wanted anthroposophists to be in touch with the real problems of people and be able to offer something out of anthroposophy. The most important thing was to be able to offer something specific out of a concrete situation. As he would say, "The good always takes place in a situation."[298]

NPI worked in Switzerland, Germany, England, South Africa and Holland. All of its work was based on the idea of development according to Steiner. This idea has been fleshed out in [sorry but the meaning of that is not clear] "the concept of development of a person in the great culture-epochs, the concept of development of a person through the many rhythms of the years, the concept of development of the Ego through karma and reincarnation." And further: "Therefore, we also picture to ourselves that moral technique and development are very closely connected, and in fact the whole Social-Pedagogical Institute (NPI) was founded on the concept of development."[299] The first step taken by the institute was the re-shaping of the Dutch technical colleges, which counted some 156 schools.

---

[298] Bernard J. Lievegoed, *Towards the Twenty-First Century: Doing the Good*, 66.
[299] Lievegoed, *Developing Communities*, 16.

Lievegoed, and a certain Fintelmann, gave lectures and developed the curriculum together, with the objective of retraining all the teachers. From Monday to Saturday groups of teachers came for weeks in succession. The development of the curriculum arose from a discussion back and forth between those who had the technical knowledge and those with pedagogical insights (NPI co-workers). This went on for five years, and the idea of development meant that hardly two courses were alike. Over a week's time, things started shifting around on the third day, and upon leaving many teachers were moved; they were open to the new.

For Lievegoed NPI issued out of the curative movement, which was devoted to the sick child; now it turned to sick society. And other initiatives followed in the same direction.

Other Initiatives

In 1963 Lievegoed became dean of the Department of Corporate Science at the School of Technology in Twente, another new faculty created for the purpose. In 1971 he was part of starting the Free High School in Driebergen, over which he presided until 1982; it was a preparatory year for undergraduate students. Just as with NPI, he also wanted to bring together the deepest exoteric work with the innermost esoteric disposition. Lievegoed's overall work had quite an effect on Dutch culture at large. In recognition of this, the Royal Dutch Publishers Association awarded him the Golden Quill in 1983.

In 1948, van Emmichoven asked his younger colleague to take on class work in Amsterdam, and to become a class reader. Lievegoed accepted and took on an intensive study of the nineteen lessons of the First Class. The whole effort allowed him to experience the images of the lessons more directly. This led him in two directions. On one hand he wanted to develop a basis for understanding the esoteric work of doctors; on the other, he set himself the challenge of being able to see beings in social life in the same way as a doctor should see beings in the remedies he uses. He concludes, "I began to live with these beings in the same way you live with realities you can see with your eyes."[300]

---

[300] Lievegoed, *Towards the Twenty-First Century*, 63.

Lievegoed's Books and Social Work

We will now turn to two emblematic interests of Lievegoed: one in relation to the soul, which will be compared directly to van Emmichoven's approach; the other concerning group work. The first is more theoretical; the second one shows in many ways Lievegoed the man of action.

Lievegoed wrote three books about the soul. We will refer to his latest and most mature work: *Man on the Threshold: The Challenge of Inner Development*, in which he distilled his ideas about "biographic psychotherapy." We will then turn to *Developing Communities*, which includes a cycle of lectures and a manuscript, respectively *Forming Curative Communities* and *The Organizing of Cultural Institutes*, to look at the dimension of Lievegoed's group and organizational work. In addition we will also draw from *Towards the Twenty-First Century: Doing the Good*.

We offer the Table of Contents of *Man on the Threshold*, which the reader can compare with van Emmichoven's *Anthroposophical Understanding of the Soul* in Appendix 5. At the time of the book Lievegoed was interested in psychotherapy. His own approach to it he called "biographical psychotherapy." Development became central to his approach. He wanted to show the laws at work in the course of human life, particularly in relation to its seven-year cycles, and illustrate that many problems are normal at certain stages of development. Overall, he wanted to place development as a result of overcoming resistance to inner experiences that are not understood, experiences that differ at each stage of life.

The first part of the book describes aspects of human development compared to the image of man and the world conception of anthroposophy. The second part covers the fundamentals of biographical psychotherapy. Therefore, key words of the book are human development, biography and therapy.

Humanity is crossing the threshold. Taking this as the premise of the book, Lievegoed describes the boundaries that the soul meets: the "observational boundary" into the phenomenal world, and the inner boundary into the soul, behind the mirror of memory: cosmos outside and metabolism inside. These are the two boundaries that materialism cannot overcome.

The Way of the Soul

Lievegoed goes on to contrast the Egyptian Mysteries with the Northern Mysteries. He characterizes the first Mysteries as the path inward, a "path backward in time" which led to hallucinatory experiences of one's own organic forces. The pupil understood that what worked as a disturbance in his ether body was connected with the forces that were laid down during his previous life, in the ether body he had then. In this path one met the Lesser Guardian of the Threshold.

The Northern Path, which extended over all of Europe, Southern Russia and even old Persia, led to ecstasy, to being one with the cosmos. The pupil had to be protected from being torn by the elements, and courage was central to his schooling. He perceived the beings of the elements, and he became aware of the presence of the adversary beings. In this path one met the Greater Guardian of the Threshold, and met with the dead.

The path inward and the path outward form a thread throughout the book. A theme that is added immediately after is that of the importance of the ego and its role in biographical development. The author looks at how the ego unfolds from childhood onwards, and how it drives the voice of conscience and the drive for development.

The path between death and rebirth is briefly mentioned. Then we are shown how the higher ego works from the spiritual world, and how it influences biographical development from the sphere of the spirit at the time of the moon nodes.

After giving us a recapitulation of the main esoteric paths of development from ancient India to Rosicrucianism, Lievegoed introduces the path of anthroposophy proper. And he characterizes the so-called "doubles," which he divides in seven groups:

- hereditary tendencies in constitution, temperament, character
- upbringing (comparable with our persona)
- undigested remnants from previous lives

- unredeemed nature beings
- certain geographic forces (leading to the geographic double)
- incarnation as man or woman
- Guardian of the Threshold

Lievegoed, as a doctor, can now bring the planetary processes as they appear in organ formation and in soul development. He introduces us to the "double-planetary processes" which he first worked out in relation to the study of the biodynamic preparations. These are Saturn and Moon; Jupiter and Mercury; Mars and Venus. The Sun stands on its own, and is also present as a mediator in the three other pairings.

The path inward and the path outward, the sheaths of the soul and the double-planetary processes are now brought forward in the matter of the development of the sentient, intellectual and consciousness souls: the Venus/Mars polarity in relation to the Sentient Soul; the Mercury/Jupiter polarity in relation to the Intellectual Soul; the Saturn/Moon polarity in relation to the Consciousness Soul. And special attention is given to the irregularities of development of the three soul sheaths, and how they express themselves.

The theme of the double is looked at in relation to the path inward and the path outward. Especially on the path inward, the link is drawn between the symptoms of the unconscious crossing of the threshold, and how it manifest in abnormalities: neuroses that turn into reversible psychoses and eventually get fixated in irreversible psychoses. Lievegoed the doctor shows how constitutional types follow four diverse courses of developments due to the double, according to the predominant influence of kidney, lung, liver or heart.

At the ending of the first part Lievegoed mentions the therapeutic approaches that can be followed in each instance. Thus, the book naturally moves to Part 2, in which he provides an outline of anthroposophical care of the soul, including some of the most common soul challenges in our time.

A theme weaving through the whole, though not specifically in one chapter or the other, is karma and reincarnation, which is central to all that Lievegoed develops.

Van Emmichoven has given us, as it were, a map of the soul, a sharply clear understanding of how the soul connects us to world and body, with an understanding of how consciousness evolves from these premises, and how we can develop imagination, inspiration and intuition. He looks only briefly at deviations from the norm (e.g. schizophrenia, paranoia) just to indicate how soul functions should work in a state of balance. His effort forms a great textbook advancing a completely different view of the soul in contrast to official materialistic science. It can be understood by anyone with a solid scientific training and an open mind. It cogently advances a coherent and articulate view of the human being.

Consciousness and its transformation in its higher stages are not examined by Lievegoed. On the other hand, he does look at the crossing of the threshold that happens in modern human beings. Lievegoed places at the center what is peripheral to van Emmichoven's approach. He is not setting out to demonstrate a whole new understanding of the soul. He is looking first and foremost at the development of the therapeutic approach. His goal is laying the foundations of "biographical psychotherapy." To that end, he espouses an eminently developmental emphasis. He looks at the sheaths of the soul (sentient, intellectual and consciousness souls), which are not developed in van Emmichoven.

As much as van Emmichoven chisels very precise details, Lievegoed paints with broad brushstrokes. When one looks more closely at the details, it is obvious that the work is unfinished. But that is not what matters. Lievegoed has managed to connect the role of the planets, physiology, and the paths inward and outward with an understanding of what anthroposophical therapy can offer, in addition to what is known and already done in the field. It is interesting that he refers very often to Jung, as if with the intent of bringing forward the latter's work. And he offers a view of the future in his very short presentation of the training of the anthroposophical psychotherapist. Addressing what the future calls from us is, as we have seen, central to Lievegoed's outlook in life.

The elder doctor sows the seeds for a future culture, by challenging present-day assumptions and offering a paradigm change. Embracing his message means turning one's back on old assumptions. The second doctor offers ideas to continue and improve what is already present in the world. He answers particular needs of the times. This is all the more so in the other book we will turn to: *Developing Communities*.

Group Work and Moral Technique

Lievegoed lamented that in regard to *The Philosophy of Freedom* a great deal is said in relation to pure thinking, moral intuition and moral imagination, but very little about moral technique. And he was aware that this was the pioneer work of NPI. "In the 1950s an institute was founded with a view to implementing such a technique."[301]

Moral imaginations are built by the individual's effort in relation to ethical matters. These are acted out in greater or lesser strength according to the moral technique that one possesses. And moral technique can be learned. In *The Philosophy of Freedom* this is expressed thus: "Moral action, then, presupposes, in addition to the faculty of having moral ideas (moral intuition) and moral imagination, the ability to transform the world of percepts without violating the natural laws by which these are connected. This ability is moral technique. It can be learnt in the sense in which any kind of knowledge can be learnt. Generally speaking, men are better able to find concepts for the existing world than to evolve productively, out of their imagination, the not-yet existing actions of the future."[302] In communities or organizations Lievegoed assessed that "the task among co-workers is, actually, how to develop the moral technique that makes it possible to seek continually new social forms of the organization, in such a way as not to encroach upon the freedom of any member. An extraordinarily difficult task."[303]

In the realm of moral technique, applied to the creation of social forms, Lievegoed saw no absolute models. He took his start from important premises. The Consciousness Soul is antisocial; from this derives the need to create external forms, which can make social life possible today. Hence the need for the external framework of threefolding within society; but threefolding can only be introduced at the macro-level, not

---

[301] Lievegoed, *Towards the Twenty-First Century*, 201.
[302] Lievegoed, *Developing Communities*, 9
[303] Ibid, 19.

in single organizations. At the meso-level of organizations the three spheres correspond to the culture of the organization (parallel to the cultural), its social life (parallel to the political life) and the sphere of work (parallel to the economic). It is particularly the middle sphere that Lievegoed addressed.

Organizations are subject to developmental laws. The understanding that the author offers on the laws of development (individual and organizational) is paramount so that when there are difficulties one can see things objectively, and stop blaming one or the other person. One can recognize systemic problems and identify what steps can be taken to correct a deficit or face a challenge.

The first link between individual work and group work lies in the development of skills for empathy, the ability to listen in such a way that one feels in oneself what is happening in the other person. Through this social empathy one is able to understand how things happen in the inner world of the other person, without feeling the need to pass judgment. In effect, there is no point in trying to convince each other in relation to the world of objects. The only thing that makes sense is to consider the other person's world of significance in relation to an object, since the same object has very different significance for different individuals.

Once we move to group work, moral technique evolves: it becomes "procedure." Through interaction people work together to form a common image. To reach that end more effectively, procedure is needed. It is through a discriminating procedure that one can handle differing ideas, temperaments, emotions and directions of will. Procedure is the outline of group work and how it comes about in phases. The four phases of group work that Lievegoed recognizes are:

-   formation of the group: who should be part of it and who not; the right number of people; and how the group can achieve its aim. This corresponds to a warmth stage, corresponding to the warmth ether.

-   stage of image-building: it involves information and clarity about goals. It is the stage of building of the light ether and one of the most important phases of work.

- formation of judgments: this is based on new criteria and boundaries added to the conversation. The group builds in the chemical ether.

- decision-making, with periodical review; grounding decisions in reality. This corresponds to the shaping of the life ether.

Lievegoed outlines above something that is now more and more well known in the world of "social technology" and participatory facilitation. He can certainly be counted as one of the pioneers in the field.

Group work can lead organizations to the experience of what Steiner calls their "new group souls." Here too, Lievegoed's work had much of a pioneer quality. When groups learn to work together and really listen, a moment can arise in which "the group suddenly becomes interesting for the spiritual world."[304] This will remain so only as long as these special conditions are preserved. And people should make a point of remembering such moments.

The social tendency of the Consciousness Soul can be compared to the germinating power of the seed. The soul can perceive the future as a seed-like force. It senses what lies ahead in the social realm. And here is expressed in concrete terms the aspiration of Lievegoed to work for the future, to hear what the future is calling us into. This is also the whole gesture of his life in listening to what to others may seem detours of fate. It is to these, which he calls "chance" or "coincidences," that he calls our special attention in his lectures, while showing us that the kind hand of destiny is at work. Such were the events that led Lievegoed to start the Zonnehuis or build the NPI.

Nowhere is the idea of being open to the new, to what is completely different, as clear as in the expression of a new kind of leadership that Lievegoed propelled. Charismatic leadership held sway in the third post-Atlantean epoch (Egyptian and Sentient Soul); the pharaoh was the envoy of the spiritual world. In recent times has arisen bureaucratic leadership, which corresponds to the needs of the Intellectual Soul. The bureaucratic leader is only an authority in his field of expertise.

---

[304] Lievegoed, *Developing Communities*, 85.

In the Consciousness Soul leadership is bound to a specific situation; it becomes what Lievegoed calls "free wandering leadership." It is a function that moves between people. This type of leadership is taken in such a form that the leader does not act for the group, but helps the group find its way, taking the others and not him- or herself as the starting point. It is an adult educational activity. In our time we need to form "hierarchies of trust." And in an integrated organization the responsibility of the hierarchies of trust can be carried by a circle.

Lievegoed perfected this idea of leadership in his work at NPI. Every co-worker in the institute could take responsibility for a project in which he had competence and became the leader, then freely associated with others whom he had chosen or accepted. He in turn would work as a colleague under the leadership of another individual leading his own project. And each co-worker would seek to specialize more in one direction than another.

Lievegoed had outlined a whole new way to work socially through the practices established by NPI: "The practical exercises in the NPI courses are also designed to facilitate the mastery of moral technique. Their essential element is that whilst one participates fully and actively in them one is also a spectator. And this is the condition of the Consciousness Soul."[305] And further "the only way to defeat Ahriman is from inside. Inside, in so far that we see what he is doing. As we are trying to work out of anthroposophy we cannot stand outside. ... We have to know how our social life is manipulated, because only by knowing how this is done can we defeat Ahriman. That is the reason why we can stand alone and have that feeling of we happy few and the bad outside world."[306]

We will conclude this section by quoting words that reflect what was of most relevance to Lievegoed in the way anthroposophy could offer answers to people in need. Referring to working in social life, Lievegoed tells us: "An answer out of the real situation alone counts. That means entering into the life of the other one. ... The real task is to bring sensible, reasonable social concepts according to the situation at hand, not according to our predilections of foreknowledge." And further, "We

---

[305] Lievegoed, *Towards the Twenty-First Century*, 129.
[306] Ibid, 21.

have to create an in-between world. We have to come down from ideas so that they can come up from social reality. Then they can say: 'We are speaking with someone who knows our social reality on the one side and can bring us social concepts which can help us to solve our problems.'"[307]

Lievegoed/van Emmichoven: a Contrast

Both Lievegoed and van Emmichoven fulfilled some of the express wishes of Rudolf Steiner in the Netherlands. Their spiritual master had warned against sectarianism in the Society, and neither doctor could ever be accused of it. Steiner had also indicated that the Society would increasingly need the therapeutic aspect for its work. And Zeylmans, a doctor and great diplomat, passed the baton to another doctor with specific social therapeutic skills. Not surprisingly, it was from the Dutch Society, and more specifically from van Emmichoven, that arose the possibility of healing the rift that had been opened with the expulsions of prominent anthroposophists and national societies from the Anthroposophical Society in 1935.

The younger doctor operated in ways quite dissimilar from the elder, and for a good and significant part of his work, indeed dissimilar from much that had been done anthroposophically before him. At the time of Steiner only a rare few Platonists had incarnated; the Society was by and large Aristotelian to its core. Was Lievegoed one of the first Platonists coming after Steiner's time? What indicates this possibility is the fact that he did work in ways similar to many other Michaelites of the present, whose work comes clearly from a Spirit Recollection perspective rather than from a Spirit Beholding angle: witness his constant reference to moral technique, or his urging us to act by being involved while seeing things as a spectator, which Steiner first introduced in his description of the Moon Path. He was a pioneer within anthroposophy, and he also broke ground for much that has been further developed in the present. These current trends were presented in *Karl Julius Schröer and Rudolf Steiner: Anthroposophy and the Teachings of Karma and Reincarnation*, Chapter 7.

---

[307] Lievegoed, *Towards the Twenty-First Century*, 48-49.

We may never know much about Lievegoed's incarnational paths, but he seems to offer us some pointers, both from the way he works, and from what he says about the Platonists. Referring to the year 2000 and the so-called "culmination," this is what he has to say: "They [Aristotelians] will work together with the great Platonists, who are people of enormous will for the good in social life. Platonists are not people with feeble wills, and where this will is, it will be for good in social life."[308] And if something is certain about Lievegoed it is his overabundance of will forces, and how he used them for the "good in social life." The doctor truly began his work when he joined with the twelve to fifteen anthroposophists who had studied social sciences to found the NPI.

The introduction of anthroposophical work in the Netherlands followed an almost perfect sequence; one that opened up many possibilities. Van Emmichoven paved the way for medical work through a novel and successful institution. He organized the Dutch Society, gave it direction and stability. He was a recognized authority far beyond the immediate circles of the Society. He gave a face and recognition to the cultural contribution of anthroposophy. As an Aristotelian he could only work bringing forward clearly articulated sets of concepts anchored in anthroposophy. He had to show that there was a coherent thought world that could stand on its own, as an alternative to dominant materialistic science. His books could only be anthroposophical. Anthroposophical thought cannot borrow from or amalgamate with materialistic sciences. It can recognize what has validity in science, but has to offer a wholly other foundation for thinking. No compromise is possible in this situation.

Lievegoed could and did write both for anthroposophists and non-anthroposophists. He lectured for both audiences as well. And he wrote purely anthroposophical books, doing novel anthroposophical research.

His approach differed from van Emmichoven's pursuits. He found his place in life when he was able to answer the call of the times, and understand what the future was calling him to in seeming detours of fate, coincidences, chance events. He had a keen capacity to listen

---

[308] Lievegoed, *Towards the Twenty-First Century*, 10.

to the future. To these connections of destiny he repeatedly calls our attention in *Developing Communities*. Lievegoed's gift was the ability to sense what he would be called to do, jump into completely uncharted territory, and offer answers that came completely from the need of the moment. Often, these answers were born out of a collaboration, as in the case of NPI. The NPI co-workers had an educational approach; they were meeting people with their own field of expertise, one most often foreign to the work of NPI. Together they had to find answers. Anthroposophy provided answers through Lievegoed and his peers, though the people they served were free to pursue these answers to the source, or rest content with the external aspects of the solution. Thus to the firm establishment of the anthroposophical world that the elder doctor accomplished, followed the full engagement of anthroposophy in relation to the needs of the time made possible by Lievegoed.

Lievegoed's central tenets of development and moral technology meant primarily doing the good out of anthroposophy. They meant adapting anthroposophy to the need of the moment, and presenting it in the particular way in which a given group of people could receive it; it was eminently tied to an external context. Van Emmichoven lived in a world of imaginations that he could only offer faithfully. He struggled to formulate new answers directly from the spiritual world. He primarily pursued purely cultural questions, and these he had to offer within the full context of their source.

The two men had established a way of working that fully honored their strengths and differences. Lievegoed's work stands out primarily for the courage to place anthroposophy in the crucible of experience and to offer concrete answers to pressing problems. Though a doctor, he shone first and foremost as a social facilitator. He also offered an extended body of anthroposophical thought. Here, people may point with justice to some inaccuracies, especially when the doctor extended his gaze to much more general issues than his immediate field of action. Some of Lievegoed's theses are very broad, or not supported enough by a cohesive line of reasoning. That is the case for example with his assertions on Manu in *The Battle for the Soul*, where he links the initiate with the Mani of the third century AD with little precise background to support his views.[309] Those who have researched the matter more extensively know that Manu formed a line of incarnation that continued in Melchizedek, the Sun priest of the Bible, whereas Mani's earlier incarnations took place in Egypt and at the time of Christ.

Lievegoed probably knew that he had to hone his thinking skills, the ones that seemed "boring" when he was tackling the first part of *The Philosophy of Freedom*. This is something that he did certainly challenge himself to do, and it is probably for that reason that he considered himself a pupil of van Emmichoven for as long as the elder friend lived.

The strength of Lievegoed, much as was the case in German idealists, came from the spiritual inheritance of "idea-experiences." In him, as in Dr. Bach, we can detect the power of ideas that live in the soul with primeval force, and that have been implanted there from the grace of previous lives. Bach called it "just knowing." In both cases it is as if the soul sought to recapture these idea-experiences, and render them active in the world. It is this inner knowledge that awakened at times of Lievegoed's life the inner dissatisfaction that told him that he needed to do something else out of the core of his being, and that only external needs and circumstances, and an openness to them, would tell him what this something could be.

Even though Lievegoed looked up to his colleague in gaining surety of thought, the relationship between the two doctors was not an unequal one. Van Emmichoven could see the strength of his friend. He could see that many of the social problems that the Dutch or international Anthroposophical Society faced were problems of moral technique and social skill, and that someone like Lievegoed was better equipped to tackle them than he was, hence his decision to name him his successor.

The dynamic of the work between the two towering figures of Dutch anthroposophy has a lot more to teach us, and we will return to them at the end of our explorations. For now we will turn to two complementary ways of looking at the life of the soul, more particularly in relation to the matter of forgiveness.

---

[309] Lievegoed, *The Battle for the Soul: The Working Together of Three Great Leaders of Humanity*, 82-83.

Forgiveness: One Question, Two Approaches

The following exploration has taken many years of my life. It is placed at the intersection of a research question and a life-practice and discipline. Prokofieff's *Occult Significance of Forgiveness* has offered much fodder for thought in the first endeavor; Marshall Rosenberg's *Nonviolent Communication: A Language of Life* has spurred me to change deeply engrained lifelong habits. I have explored the first book and studied it several times on my own over twenty years, and returned to it in a study group format just two years ago. The practice of Compassionate Communication has accompanied me through exposure to extensive trainings, and continued practice in the last eleven years. I will look at what both authors have to offer in their respective fields, then compare their approaches. This comparison does not include a biographical component.

Prokofieff: The Occult Significance of Forgiveness

Forgiveness takes on deepening steps according to which sheath of the human body is worked upon by the ego. It moves from accepting the other human being to taking on responsibilities on his behalf, and beyond that to taking on the redemption of spiritual beings.

In permeating the sphere of the senses, the ego infuses the human being with the ability to have greater tolerance and empathy; in acting one step deeper into the etheric, the ego enables the act of forgiveness proper. In reaching into the astral body, the ego brings about the ability to take on other people's karma. And finally, when working consciously upon itself, the ego can carry the karma of humanity upon itself. Rudolf Steiner's biography underlines time and again this last aspect. Other stages of forgiveness will not be considered here, as they lie in the far future of humanity and concern the redemption of Lucifer and Ahriman.

In the first stage of the path, the ego brings consciousness into the perception of the senses. Do we fully perceive another person, or do we simply allow the subconscious interplay of sympathies and antipathies to color our sense impressions, positively in the case of sympathy, negatively in the case of antipathy? In one instance that part of ourselves that we call the "double," or everything of an unredeemed nature in our being, bypasses the ego and reinforces our natural tendencies. When we truly perceive with the ego we are able to suspend judgment, and then impressions can awaken in us after-images, which offer us deeper insight.

A historical example of this kind of tolerance led Marie Steiner to write her "Appeal for Reconciliation." The document, written in 1942, addressed the situation in the General Anthroposophical Society. In her plea Marie Steiner describes the perils of reacting to antipathies and sympathies before forming fuller pictures of reality, or correct imaginations of other human beings. She points to the role of rumors in the formation of "specters, not realities." And further, she attacks the edifice of self-righteousness to which we can succumb when we are facing matters of great weight: "We never have it [truth] completely. What a lot of self-deception and delusion pours forth over it even when we think we are wholly in possession of it! How it is again and again torn into shreds through passion, self-righteousness, vanity and ambition."[310] No words could better present the havoc that an unrecognized double in our soul can wreak with all our social relations. And Marie Steiner concludes by inviting her colleagues to forgive: "What can we do to rescue our moral substance? We can forgive! Everyone can forgive what lies within him to forgive. We can forget what ought to be forgotten instead of rummaging about old injustices."

The forgiveness to which Marie Steiner invited her colleagues is "potentized tolerance," so to speak. When tolerance is brought deeper into the will—at the level of the etheric body—a degree of withdrawal of the ego becomes possible. Whoever forgives knows the moment of utter powerlessness, a feeling of annihilation or fear of loss of self. To achieve this stage and touch the will at such a deep level, inner discipline in the form of meditation, prayer or exercises is paramount. The Spirit Self alone can allow us to forgive; it is this sheath of the human being that offers us the certainty that we still are an eternal individuality, no matter what the offending act seems to have taken from us. Historical examples

---

[310] Sergei Prokofieff, *The Occult Significance of Forgiveness*, Appendix 1.

238

of exceptional cases of forgiveness, produced as if spontaneously in the moment, indicate the strong presence of a Spirit Self, fruit of the grace of previous lives.

Work of forgiveness that reaches into the etheric body has the power of dissolving structures formed there by our double. Aspects of the double are in effect like islands of etheric and astral substance in our soul to which the ego has little access. The act of forgiveness helps dissolve these structures. The results of such work upon the etheric bear immediately upon the soul's capacity to perceive into the etheric. On the basis of examples like that of Bill Cody, of which more will be said below, Prokofieff concludes, "The path of forgiveness is the most direct and surest path whereby the spiritual forces of the etheric Christ may flow into modern earthly civilization, while the person himself is sooner or later enabled to gain a clairvoyant experience of Him."[311]

Bill Cody came to the attention of George Ritchie, who had himself a certain measure of receptivity to the Christ in the etheric, having had a near-death experience at a time in which he turned to Christianity. Ritchie met Bill Cody, not his real name, in a liberated Nazi concentration camp in 1945. The survivors had reached the limits of starvation, scores of them unable to recover even after they had been freed. In the midst of such devastation, one person attracted special attention, an individual who seemed to have been shielded from the effects of Nazi atrocity. "His posture was erect, his eyes bright, his energy indefatigable," in spite of having lived in the camp for six years. He offered his interpreter services in five languages and worked up to fifteen-sixteen hours per day, without showing any loss of energy. The explanation for such a contrast between Bill Cody and the others was offered to Ritchie when the Polish Jew disclosed his biography.

Bill lived in the Jewish section of Warsaw. When the Germans captured the Jewish population of the ghetto, Bill saw his wife and five children killed in front of him. He was spared because he spoke German, and could be used as an interpreter. Expanding on the turning point that changed his life, Bill Cody commented, "I had to decide right then, ... whether to let myself hate the soldiers who had done this. It was an

---

[311] Sergei Prokofieff, *The Occult Significance of Forgiveness*, 54.

easy decision really. I was a lawyer. In my practice I had seen too often what hate could do to people's minds and bodies. Hate had just killed the six people who mattered most to me in the world. I decided then that I would spend the rest of my life—whether it was for days or many years—loving every person I came in contact with."[312] Prokofieff points out the important fact that the decision to forgive was paired with the decision to love.

In moving further on the path, forgiveness metamorphoses into the ability to take on other people's path of destiny. When this happens the ego acts upon the astral body, transforming it. This is possible through the influence of the Life Spirit. Two instances, at least, appear quite clearly in Steiner's life. In the first one he took up Schröer's life task at an early age. Of this much has already been said in this book and in *Karl Julius Schröer and Rudolf Steiner: Anthroposophy and the Teachings of Karma and Reincarnation.*

Later in life Steiner came across the destiny of Nietzsche, and saw the grandeur and fragility of his soul. He had succumbed to his one-sidedness and to the clutches of Ahriman to such a degree that his *Ecce Homo* was, Steiner tells us, written by Ahriman himself. And yet, about him, Steiner could say that he was a fighter for freedom, and for that reason he wrote *Friedrich Nietzsche, Fighter for Freedom* in 1895.

Steiner could detect in Nietzsche the absolute courage to follow a path that would lead him to the barren soil of modern scientific undertaking, and reject the pat security of a faith that had lost all substance. This was what Nietzsche followed to the end, though in an extremely one-sided fashion. When such a person encounters this fate something is lost to humanity, and this justified Steiner's considerable detour in attending to Nietzsche's legacy and offering a fuller assessment of his accomplishments to a culture that would have judged him solely by his epilogue. Consider that there was nothing more foreign to Steiner's worldview than the extreme anti-Christian positions of the late Nietzsche. And Steiner had to accept being called a nihilist, and face the disbelief and hostility of his contemporaries. By immersing himself completely in the impulses that lived in Nietzsche, Steiner was able to

---

[312] Sergei Prokofieff, *The Occult Significance of Forgiveness*, 23.

redeem them and offer them as building blocks leading from the natural sciences to the science of the spirit.

Assuming another person's karma means forgiving her for what she could not achieve, but it also goes a step further. The one who forgives forgets what has been done against himself. The one who takes on someone else's karma, continues someone else's intentions and brings them to their intended fruition. It means relinquishing one's own life task for a time. This is very clearly stated by Steiner in Schröer's case in the Hague conversation he had with W.J. Stein in 1922: "I resolved at the time to live Schröer's destiny as my own and relinquish my own path of destiny."

When the ego acts consciously upon itself, the forces of Spirit Man are at play. This is something that can only happen in the instance of an initiate, and it allows him to bear the karma of humankind. Steiner was the initiate attempting with all his energy to counter destructive forces bringing the whole of culture on a path of decline. His endeavor to lead humanity on an upward path was met with all degrees of hostility from the world around him. His darkest night of the soul came in the time preceding the Christmas Foundation Meeting. Here, in a decisive soul trial, he had to commit to carry the karma of the Anthroposophical Society upon himself for the benefit of the progress of humanity. At this stage of the path the initiate attains the revelation of Christ in the higher spiritual world. He perceives Christ out of his own ego, as the very archetype of this ego.

Prokofieff's study of the occult foundations of forgiveness has touched thousands of individuals worldwide. What he expresses from the perspective of the four sheaths of the human beings offers us an incentive for a new understanding of the ideal of forgiveness and its implications at microcosmic and macrocosmic levels.

We will now turn to an approach that takes its start from language and communication and the phenomenological apprehension of four levels of communication: observation, expression of feeling, expression of needs and requests. This phenomenological approach is the work of Marshall Rosenberg. It is known as Nonviolent Communication, NVC, or Compassionate Communication. The latter term offers us the fuller characterization of Rosenberg's approach to communication. We will therefore refer to it as NVC or Compassionate Communication.

Marshall Rosenberg and Nonviolent Communication

Compassionate Communication is a dynamic perspective centered on a clear and succinct expression of self, paired with a focused understanding of the reality of the other human being. These have been called, respectively, honesty and empathy. Improving the quality of the communication we have with others, or with self, leads to an increased sensitivity towards the reality of what lives between human beings. From the repeated effort at mastering honesty and empathy we evolve self-empathy or self-connection, the heart of the practice of NVC.[313]

NVC Basics

Based solely on phenomena, NVC divides communication into four steps:

- observation: what we see in the world, expressed in terms as objective as possible; these are the conditions that influence the following levels

- feelings: the reaction of sympathy or antipathy that is called forth by environment and events in our inner world

- needs: the universal terms that define our intentions in the world, that align us with our values and aspirations, and our day-to-day concerns, hopes, aspirations, etc.

- requests: what we ask from self or others in order to bring intentions to another step of their expression

Can we really see what meets us in the world? How do we avoid coloring our perceptions with our likes and dislikes? How can we avoid

---

[313] Marshall B. Rosenberg, *Nonviolent Communication: A Language of Compassion.*

interpreting what meets us? Here are some common traps: generalization (you are always late; you never listen, you don't respect me...), vagueness (I feel well, I feel OK, I feel bad, it's good...), stereotypes (Japanese, French, other nationalities, women, politicians do or don't do this, they eat so and so, they have these tendencies...), evaluative verbs that imply a judgment (s/he delays, hurries, procrastinates, ignores...), and other pitfalls. We can avoid generalizations by recourse to memory: three times out of four, 80% of the time in the last six months, is more accurate than "always" or "never." Vagueness can be replaced by more exact assessment: I feel inspired, excited or happy instead of I feel good; I feel overwhelmed or sad instead of bad. Stereotypes should be avoided by referring to experience: the Japanese people I know..., I heard that some people in Cuba..., 80% of Republicans in Congress... Evaluative words should be replaced by more value-neutral words: when I asked him to do his chores, he went to his room first, and did not answer my question (instead of procrastinating or ignoring). Even without going further into other categories of false observations, we can realize that truly seeing is a step not to be taken for granted.

The world of our feelings can cause us inner difficulty. In addition, culture and habit may tell us that it is too private to share. However, feelings color everything we do or say, and we may be unaware of them at our own and other people's expense. Becoming aware of them begs the question of how best to express them in order to offer valuable information and ease communication. Here two pitfalls exist. The first is assuming an automatic link between events in our lives and resulting feelings. Don't we often hear expressions like "You make me angry" or "If only this had happened, my life would be so different and I would be happy." Compassionate Communication invites us to distinguish between stimuli (everything that meets us in the external world that causes natural movements of sympathy and antipathy) and causes (our inner reaction to the stimuli), and focus mostly on the latter. A clear understanding and expression of feelings is paramount to an objective apprehension of events and assessment of needs, be they our own or those of others.

Another trap in the expression of feelings consists in coloring these feelings with a judgment. A typical example is the use of passive verbs:

I feel manipulated, judged, abandoned, loved or unloved... In the guise of feeling we are in reality expressing a judgment (I believe you are manipulating me, judging me, abandoning me, etc.), and therefore alienating the listener.

The expression of needs forms the heart of Compassionate Communication and what distinguishes it from approaches that have similar goals. Needs animate everything we say or do, much more so than our feelings. They are, however, a step more difficult to recognize. Often an understanding of needs depends on clarity in our life of feelings. Since the latter is often unclear, needs do not surface to our consciousness with any clarity. Needs are expressed in universal terms in what we know as values: freedom, choice, autonomy, companionship, intimacy, growth, spirituality, etc. When I truly express a need I am speaking in terms that everybody can understand and appreciate without having to deny my experience. The needs another person expresses are present in me, no matter how vaguely. And the need a person expresses cannot go against the needs of another person. My need for freedom can live with your need for order; my need for companionship is not negated by my need for privacy, and so on. Needs are expressed in terms that are universal. What is not expressed universally becomes a strategy, such as "I need you to do this for me"; "I need you to give me more money"; "I need you to listen to me", etc. A strategy expressed as a need poses an obstacle to clear communication.

Not understanding or not expressing our needs comes at a price in our lives and in our relationships. Coming to an understanding of them brings us closer to connection with others and to self-connection. And understanding the needs of others is the most difficult but most important step, in forming truly lasting connections. From the above we can understand that we are going up a progressively more difficult ladder when we move from observation to feelings and to needs. However, establishing the earlier steps firmly makes expression of the following steps easier.

Every impulse of will needs to find a way to manifest in the world, take a form and move forward. This is what we mean by requests. The disconnected self makes demands, not believing that there is a way to meet needs of self and others at the same time. We either live in what is a finite world of resources and possibilities, or we come to believe that there are many more resources available than we are generally aware of, that the only limit really lies in a lack of flexibility and strength of imagination. A request differs from a demand when the person who requests is truly willing to hear "no" as an answer, and remain engaged in looking for solutions together with the other person.

The practice of Compassionate Communication awakens in those who take it up the awareness of a continuous choice between two terms that present themselves to our souls. For didactic purposes the two alternatives are playfully called "giraffe" and "jackal." The giraffe is the emblem of the higher self, because of all land mammals, it is the one with the largest heart; it is a gentle creature, able to have a perspective from on high. The jackal offers a more self-centered perspective. Continuing the analogy further, we can recognize in the jackal the expression of the double, and in the giraffe the expression of our ego, when it is inspired by our spirit self.

Referring to the jackal does not imply demonizing part of our soul. On the contrary; though the uninhibited jackal will lead us to poor communication and life choices, his voice is far from useless. So-called "jackal messages" coming to our soul carry vital information about our feelings and needs, if we can listen attentively. The jackal, like the double, can only be transformed with our patient and continuous efforts. After all we can only be respectful of others if we learn to honor and respect ourselves, and for that we need to come to know the working of our jackal/double.

From these basic premises we can now attempt to approach the phenomenon of forgiveness, which in personal practice seldom appears in black or white outlines. The boundaries between who needs to forgive or be forgiven are seldom obvious.

NVC and Forgiveness

There is hardly a mention of forgiveness in NVC, and that is the case for more than one reason. Forgiveness simply acquires another level of reality when connection to others and connection to self are strengthened. We will therefore approach this topic from the perspective of regrets or mourning, terms that are more often used in Compassionate Communication.

The word is the most powerful tool for good or for ill. Hundreds of times a day we offer it to others in blessing or curse, and everything in between. Very often we have cause for regret and/or learning. Something we say or do not say, together with what we do or don't do, may come back to our mind as a life-learning situation.

Why do we regret or mourn at present something done or said in the past? A way to explain regret is to look at it from the perspective of a conflict of needs. What we regret was done to fulfill some immediate needs. One or more additional needs may have been ignored, because they were neglected in the choice of strategy that met only the initial needs. Regretting means realizing that in facing a complex situation with various layers of needs, we acted from an incomplete perception of our own and other people's needs. Recollecting the events and looking at feelings and needs offers us a better perspective of all needs involved. In a typical situation I may have acted out of the need to ensure my own physical or psychological safety. I may have done so at the expense of someone else's safety, or lacked consideration for their need to be heard, to be respected, to exert choice, etc.

Regretting will lead one to mourning the choice. When I mourn I will look at needs that I have met, and consider needs that I did not perceive clearly at the moment of my choice. I will perceive more clearly both my needs and the needs of the other person, especially when I discuss the situation with the other party. I will discern at the same time what other strategies may have fulfilled all my own and the other person's needs.

Very often, regrets may be expressed by both parties. Both will formulate requests of what they would do differently, or what they would like the other person to do differently. Ultimately, after mutual exploration, agreement will be reached in a series of steps to take in future similar situations, whenever possible.

The above process for expressing regrets has completely bypassed the notion of forgiveness. Rather, we simply have resolution, with mutual agreements. The situation could be more complex. The process, however, remains archetypally similar.

Let us suppose that something particularly traumatic has been perpetrated against the self, something that causes irretrievable losses, in which the responsibility lies completely with one person: a reckless car accident, a theft, a crime. In this instance we can either process the incident between individuals, or process it inwardly.

The first instance is best illustrated in the case of restorative justice. Someone may have committed a crime and is brought face to face with his victim, using the NVC approach. In this instance the victim will listen to the perpetrator express his feelings and needs, and with the help of an NVC mediator, assure that the perpetrator acknowledges feelings and needs. The mediator will also offer the perpetrator the chance to express the perspective that led to the crime in the same way one would offer regrets: feelings, needs met by the action, and needs not met. This would lead to a deepening connection through the victim letting the other party know the depth of her anguish, and the perpetrator expressing more and more of his regrets. Eventually, and probably over a length of time, the victim will open his heart to the perpetrator and this will lead to forgiveness. The perpetrator generally offers compensation, to the victim or to society, through an action that allows him to lessen his regrets and increase his self-awareness.

Real forgiveness is the approach that is needed in absentia. If a victim experienced in the process of Compassionate Communication needs to process her inner response to a demeaning action by a person not willing to face her/him, the same process will be repeated inwardly. The victim will regularly take the opportunity to honestly express himself and honor feelings and unmet needs. This leads to the concept of self-empathy, the ultimate goal of NVC. Our needs can be met inwardly when there is no possible external solution. This is a long, laborious process, depending on the gravity of the offense received. Eventually, the victim will be led to understand the feelings, needs, and whole outlook of the perpetrator. She will inwardly accept to receive healing from this continuous process, until over time, the effects of the wrong suffered will no longer press upon the soul, and only the memory will endure.

Subtle Aspects of NVC

We will now follow a process that is not inherent to Compassionate Communication. We will review the experience of Compassionate Communication as a whole and let its phenomena guide us towards a higher understanding of the laws it reveals. This can only be done with the help of ideas we receive from anthroposophy. We will first look at the experience of needs: our hopes, desires, concerns, aspirations, values in life. We will then turn to the whole expression of NVC.

What we express as needs are in reality expressions of the will, something that lives in us below the level of awareness of the ego. Steiner indicates that the will acts at the level of the sheaths of the body and evolves with these[314] (see Table 8). At the level of the physical body we have instincts, such as hunger, thirst, safety, procreation, which are weak in the human being and much stronger in animals. In the latter, the animal's form is an image of what the instinct is in the will. If we move a step further, in the etheric we have drives, in which instinct becomes more inward. Under this category fall needs such as comfort, rest, relaxation, nurturing, protection. In the astral the will takes the form of desires. These are not only more inward, but also more conscious. Desire is also more transitory than drives or instincts; it is created by the soul anew each time. Examples would include needs that sustain our life of soul: order, stability, reliability, efficiency, consistency, continuity, acceptance, support, fairness, companionship, intimacy, privacy, etc. The ego expresses itself in motives, which are unique to the human being; the animal still has desires, but it has no motives. Only in the human being can desires become motives of the will. Motives are those impulses of will that give a specific direction of intention to each human being. Such self-expression is found in the needs for choice, freedom, honesty, integrity, significance, dignity, respect, truth/wisdom, beauty, goodness, etc. Each of these values will have a relative importance, and the totality of these will form the life of motives of each human being. No two human beings will express this reality in the same manner.

The expression of the list of needs, the ones mentioned and others, cannot lead us further into the higher bodies of the human being. Above

---

[314] Rudolf Steiner, *The Study of Man*, lecture of August 25, 1919.

NEEDS AND EXPRESSION OF THE WILL

Needs are listed in relation to the expression of the will as it moves and metamorphoses in the human sheaths. This list is not 'exact' nor exhaustive!

INSTINCTS (physical)
Sustenance: food, water, air, shelter
Physical safety
Sex and reproduction

DRIVES (etheric)
Comfort
Space
Rest, relaxation
Nurturing
Protection
Security
Play

IMPULSES (astral)
Order, stability
Reliability, honoring agreements
Healing
Stimulation
Ease, efficiency
Information
Consistency, continuity
Appreciation
Acceptance
Warmth, caring, support
Fairness
Belonging
Fun
Enjoyment
Variety
Adventure, discovery
Companionship, intimacy
Privacy

MOTIVES (ego)
Choice
Freedom, autonomy
Coherence
Honesty, integrity
Awareness

Openness
Clarity
Communication, input, feedback
Self-connection
Self-expression, creativity
Challenge
Humor
Balance, harmony
Flexibility
Peace
Inspiration
Meaning, significance
Dignity
Respect, consideration
Acknowledgment, recognition
Inclusion, participation
Mutuality
Gratitude, wonder, inspiration
Hope
Mourning
Connection, communion
Empathy, understanding
Contribution, accomplishment
Celebration
Wholeness
Truth/Wisdom
Beauty
Goodness
Love

Above motives there are no new needs;
rather a deepening of motivation

WISH (Spirit Self)
Mourning and resolve to improve

INTENTION (Life Spirit)
Far future

RESOLUTION (Spirit Man)

Table 8: Needs and Expressions of the Will (table compiled by the author)

this level, the lived experience of the life of needs does not change. It intensifies. We have already found the expression of what Steiner calls "wish" in the Spirit Self. This is simply the ability to regret and the desire to improve. NVC has expressed this in the process of regret or mourning. The Life Spirit expresses the will in intentions, which bring the simple desire a step further into the will. A wish, become more concrete, is an intention. Whereas the first lived more closely to the stage of mental picture, the intention is more focused on the importance of the feeling and will elements. At the stage of Spirit Man, the will takes on the form of resolution, or the complete wedding of will with the thinking, the near inability to do what we know is not right. Resolution is not possible in the will until the soul is freed from the body.

We can now come to understand why needs are central to NVC. It is in the expression of needs that we touch the uniqueness of the individual. In the will are expressed the pre-birth intentions we carry from the spiritual world. These intentions live within us unconsciously, driving our karma towards fulfillment. When we understand more closely a person's needs, when we form an idea of the range and extent of this person's needs and how these color the life of feeling, we are sharing in the world of these pre-birth intentions. We are coming much closer to an understanding of the other person's being than what we can seek in the expression of his/her thoughts.

As van Emmichoven reminds us, willing is an older force than pure feeling; however, willing is more unconscious than feeling. We know less about our willing than about our feeling.[315] Our feelings form an avenue to the expression of our will, but it takes practice in order to bring our needs to awareness, and it is all the harder if we cannot reach our feelings, which lie closer to the surface of consciousness than our will. By understanding the expression of the will in relation to the expression of the life of feelings, we enter into the ability of forming imaginations of a human being. Every human being will present himself to our field of experience differently from any other. If every experience is an opportunity to reflect on the quality of events, the tenor of the

---

[315] F.W. Zeylmans van Emmichoven, *The Anthroposophical Understanding of the Human Soul*, 61.

feeling life, and the expression of the will, the real image of the other human being will form over time through continued inner discipline. And the same will be true of ourselves, since we will gather information and understanding about how we operate, how we react to events of destiny, and what really matters most in our choices and in the ultimate direction of our lives.

Progress on the path of Compassionate Communication goes hand in hand with a deepening of intention and attention. By intention we mean focus on purpose, and awareness of our needs at any given moment, added to the ability to direct our will to what matters most in the moment. Attention means capacity to observe and be present to the quality of our relationships. It also means ability to direct our focus without being distracted by strong feelings and emotions, recurrent or undesired thoughts. Greater attention means increased ability to observe and keep emotions at bay. When attention and intention are mastered to a higher degree than is the norm, everything that comes towards us can receive greater understanding; we can more fully observe what comes from our environment, other human beings and our inner world. We can therefore understand more subtly how we operate, what are our personal triggers, shortcomings and difficulties. In the final instance we will be able to master life lessons that may long have troubled us, and master new challenges more readily.

In Steiner's archetypal social phenomenon we are told that when we interact in human dialogue, the speaker gradually puts the listener in a condition similar to sleep. This lasts until the listener awakens, becomes the speaker and the roles are reversed. This is the case because we are antisocial in our waking consciousness. On the other hand, we are social in our sleep. In this condition we share our inner world with everybody else in our life; here, however, we are not conscious. Since this is an inescapable human condition of present times, Steiner points out that the only way around this dilemma is our own deliberate effort to develop imaginations of the other human being. We have given examples of these exercises in Chapter 5. The examples given there concerned the ability to look at a person who has contributed to our life and present well-being, by bringing back to mind everything that touched us in the life of the senses, feelings and will, and creating a living portrait of the person in our mind's eye, in effect developing an imagination. In other places Steiner goes a step further in asking us to look at those who may have harmed us, wanting us to leave aside personal sympathies and preferences. In the order of karma such distinctions of sympathy/antipathy cease. Many determining events in our lives have arisen from opposition we have received. Therefore, the above can be repeated in the same way with people we do not look upon with favor, people who have countered us, or those we believe have hurt or hindered us. We will gain a different perspective about them from the practice of such exercises.

An exercise that Steiner offered in conjunction with the above consists in looking upon our lives as objectively as possible. We are asked to look at a time in our lives and portray it so vividly that we are viewing it as if we were strangers to ourselves. This can be done by looking at the last two, three or four weeks, but the same can be done over a year or longer time spans. Here too we start to develop an imagination.

There is no reason to believe that Steiner's exercises are the only exercises possible in developing an imagination of other human beings. The exercises are themselves the expression of larger archetypes. Compassionate Communication draws from these very same archetypes, and offers us another expression of them. In deepening the practice and understanding of conversation we come upon a different perspective of the other human being. Normally, when we meet something in the world, we immediately return to ourselves and formulate sympathies and antipathies. These only reinforce themselves with time, unless we face unpleasant experiences or blows of fate that force us to challenge our assumptions. Compassionate Communication opens up the space of reaction that is usually very brief between perception and response to events in our lives. It does so through a discipline of very clear questions, which could be summarized thus: "What do I see in the world and in me?"; "What is happening in the feeling realm in me and in the other person(s)?" "What is it that I, and others, really need? What do we want to achieve?" When used to its fullest capacity, NVC is a tool for moving away from a moralistic worldview to an inner morality of the higher self, to a self-determined morality. From this vantage point there is no need for either/or, good or bad, winner or loser perspectives. The only question worth asking is "How can this situation turn to the benefit of all people involved?" NVC is an invitation to take responsibility for our lives, which we can entertain only when we abandon harsh judgments of self and others.

Prokofieff/Rosenberg: Comparison and Conclusion

What Prokofieff offers from a more Aristotelian perspective, finds a complement in a more Platonic and experiential approach to forgiveness in Nonviolent Communication (NVC). In the first instance we are shown the steps that lead us to forgiveness and further beyond it. We are shown the consequences of the act of forgiveness upon our souls, upon the soul of the person forgiven, and the larger macrocosmic consequences. In the second approach we are asked to put into practice relatively simple notions by seeing and expressing with clarity four levels of communication. Translating these notions into habits may take months or years, according to inner capacity. Changes will only occur in the measure of the earnestness of our efforts. In this light we can recognize that NVC is simply another expression of moral technique, and an approach that would not be considerably different from the one followed by Lievegoed.

What the two approaches have in common is a movement away from dogma or tradition. They observe the phenomena, and the phenomena only. Prokofieff analyzes the phenomena as if from the outside, referring to anthroposophical concepts of the threefold human being. He invites us to see the threads that weave between our inner life and the life of the cosmos. Rosenberg offers us his building blocks of communication from the lived experience of language; he has recourse to repeated experience, which has modified the expression of his ideas, and finally given it the shape of Nonviolent Communication. We may learn more from one approach or the other. Based on my repeated study of the book and years of practice of Compassionate Communication, it is my conviction that the two fructify each other.

We will now turn to natural sciences by looking at two renowned scientists: Rudolf Hauschka, an anthroposophist to whom we owe groundbreaking scientific discoveries and the innovative method that produced the Wala medications. His life and work will be contrasted to that of the Englishman Edward Bach, famous for the flower remedies that bear his name.

CHAPTER 8

ARISTOTELIANS AND PLATONISTS
IN THE NATURAL SCIENCES

We will now set aside psychology and enter into the field of natural science. And once again we will first look at an individual who worked at the time of Steiner and in his immediate circles, Rudolf Hauschka. We will later turn to someone who worked in a diametrically different way from the first, Dr. Edward Bach. We will then look at the larger contrast between the two.

Rudolf Hauschka

Rudolf Hauschka tells us in his autobiography that his earliest memory was of a clap of thunder at age two and a half. He was frightened and his grandfather said, "The Heavenly Father speaks." The expression stayed with him long after.[316]

Childhood

Rudolf's father married in 1890, and Rudolf was born in 1891 in Vienna. The father, a blacksmith, came from a very simple background: one grandfather a shepherd, the other a blacksmith. Rudolf grew up

---

[316] Rudolf Hauschka, *At the Dawn of a New Age: Memoirs of a Scientist.*

fascinated by the work in the smithy, where his father had set up shop, with a metal grindery and galvanizing equipment.

In Rudolf's early years, after he was vaccinated for smallpox, his health was fragile. His mother decided to treat him with cold-water therapy, followed by warming up in bed. He gradually recovered, and later spent time visiting a thermal spring rich in iron. His mother took great pioneering initiative by changing the family's diet away from the usual coffee and rolls, to herb tea with whole-meal bread and honey. She introduced new vegetables and fruits.

Rudolf spent summer vacations on a relative's farm, befriended all the domestic animals, and gradually acquired an understanding of farm operations and crop rotation. But the city cast an equal spell on his soul. The thirst for world experiences drove him to the railroad station to see the Orient Express.

A World of Elements and Imaginations

Rudolf's parents directed him towards the technical professions and enrolled him in the *Realgymnasium*. At age fourteen he was exposed to what he called "extremely interesting subjects": mathematics, geometry, physics. But language and grammar had also awakened his interest.

In mathematics he was particularly drawn to spherical trigonometry. There he met for the first time the concept of infinity in a study of conic sections. He stood in awe at the fact that in a hyperbola, just as one branch disappears into infinity, the other becomes visible on its return journey. Here his words are worth quoting in full: "And in between lies an area of invisibility, of inaudibility, of perhaps unattainability in terms of our thinking. But I felt there must be a way to broaden consciousness that, at least in some dim sort of way, one might be in a position to grasp the nature of infinity. I made efforts, I practiced, *I identified with the hyperbola and had further trouble with remaining within myself.* Then an artistic experience came to my aid. During a Bruckner symphony I heard for the first time a most singular thing. I was struck by the many and *long pauses in the music and, as I listened attentively, they seemed to me to be filled with a wonderful music*--rather like resonance before and after in audible music, and I imagined that it could have been something like this that Plato meant when he spoke of the music of the spheres. The music of Bruckner seemed to *lift itself out of audibility into the realm of infinity*, to linger there for some moments, and then come back once more into earthly audible music. I thus became firm in my conviction that, over and above this world we perceive with our senses, there is a higher world to which, in the future, we will have one day to find an entrance" (emphasis added).[317]

In his studies the boy eagerly learned free drawing and color perspective according to Goethe. Some of his paintings in fact received recognition by his teacher and were displayed in the school hall. Another memory stood out to the later Hauschka, of writing an essay: "Man should be noble, helpful and good." In the discussion that resulted from it he advocated "that it was physically necessary to care for the earth in order for the sake of human progress, to evolve yet further."[318] On another occasion he wrote an essay on the theme: "The best thing that arises out of history is the enthusiasm that it excites in us." In it he described old parts of Vienna and its history, and finished with a reference to a patriot, Kolschitzky, who fought against the Turks and also processed coffee and established the first coffee house in Vienna. It was a clever and imaginative way to link history to the geography and traditions of the city. The essay earned him the nickname "poet."

Hauschka's religious leanings were not as strong as his scientific ones. He questioned dogma with good reason. Upon the urging of his mother he had to take on confirmation, but he resisted committing to a denomination. Such was the tension in his soul that he brought his inner dilemma to the priest at the point in which he was going to back off from the ceremony. In response he received the poem *My Heavenly Kingdom* by Peter Rosegger. The poet argued for the cycle of birth and rebirth in nature as in man, and pointed to the mystery of reincarnation (through the idea of resurrection of the individual), arguing for the continuation of being and of consciousness. The image of the hyperbola, and the experience of eternity in the music of Bruckner, naturally came

---

[317] Hauschka, *At the Dawn of a New Age: Memoirs of a Scientist*, 12.
[318] Ibid, 13-14.

back to the adolescent's mind, allowing him to "endure the confirmation service." Secretly he thought to himself "The Heavenly Father speaks."

The youth's future self spoke already in the way his soul resonated in the experience of chemistry, and in the way he later described it in his autobiography. He felt he had "a personal relationship with the elements." And further, "My experience of the elements was of intelligences which, in order to observe, I approached in awe. Soon, however, I came to familiar terms with them. I felt I was in a fairytale land where trolls, goblins, gnomes, elves and pixies worked behind the substance, revealing themselves in the interaction of elements."[319] His capacity for developing imagination, in a way similar to his Vienna essay, is best illustrated in the description of his favorite element, antimony: "...this metallic substance behaved like a child; in its molten state in the form of tiny globules, it raced gaily around, ... and then, all rolled up, put on a white fur of crystal needles...; then again, in tartar emetic, it hid between the big, grown up substances. Finally, when dropped into an electrode, it exploded, and how like a naughty child, who scratches and bites when you wish to take him by the hand!"[320]

An Answer to His Questions

The youth's love of chemistry led him to the next stage of his university studies. There he was attracted to organic chemistry, particularly the chemistry of carbon. "What kind of cosmic secret is it that hides behind carbon, that enables it to continually build up new substances in millionfold variation ..."[321] He soon was attracted to color chemistry and to the role of oxygen and hydrogen. He saw that oxygen caused color to become visible, and that hydrogen had a polar-opposite behavior, spiritualizing substance. Having acquired such a level of fine perception, it was only natural that at the time doubts were arising in his soul whether synthetic substances could really be equivalent to their natural counterparts.

---

[319] Hauschka, *At the Dawn of a New Age: Memoirs of a Scientist*, 18.
[320] Ibid.
[321] Ibid, 20.

Hauschka gradually encountered anthroposophy. He had heard about it at first from Karl Schubert--a future Waldorf teacher--in his student days. But he felt he could not respond to it yet. In his professional years, shortly after the war, his colleague Dr. Chwala had put him in contact with pupils of Steiner. But he remembers not being able to overcome his skepticism: "I heard mere words and was unmoved. I was not mature enough. I had not learned yet to distinguish the Grail from its bearers."[322]

Another opportunity arose when his daughter started going to the Neuwachtschule in Köln, not an official Waldorf school, but "run along the lines of the Waldorf schools." Through his daughter's teacher, Frau Ebersold-Förster, he finally felt that he had been exposed to anthroposophy before. "The words she found were not words merely, but carried a spiritual force which re-established for me a contact with what is experienced before birth." Everything else that had left a mark on his soul was reawakened: the hyperbola of his youth, the music of Anton Bruckner, the poem of Peter Rosegger at the time of his confirmation, and even the first impression of thunder in his earthly life, "The Heavenly Father is speaking." He felt he could unite himself with his pre-birth intentions and remembered "the mission of transformation to be my task on earth, the transformation of myself, the transformation of nature and of the earth," themes reminiscent of one of his earliest essays.[323]

Starting with this important moment, his destiny came towards him more strongly. In 1924 he wanted to participate in a summer conference in Arnhem, Holland despite the obstacles caused by the French occupation. There he ran into Rudolf Steiner again and again, and had brief but rich conversations with him. In a lecture in which Steiner spoke about the destiny of the Anthroposophical Movement, he remembers, "I found corroborated my intuition concerning a pre-birth experience," assuredly a recurrent theme for Hauschka. In light of this memory he asked Rudolf Steiner a question that was close to his heart:

---

[322] Hauschka, *At the Dawn of a New Age: Memoirs of a Scientist*, 35.
[323] Ibid, 12.

"What is life?" Steiner told him to study rhythm. "The hyperbola came once again into my mind."[324]

Once again, Hauschka's daughter directed him to the next step. Because she had bronchial troubles, he brought her to the Arlesheim clinic, then run by Ita Wegman. In Arlesheim he was told that Steiner had meant to invite him to the Weleda laboratories next door to the clinic. Unfortunately Steiner had fallen ill and was no longer able to receive visits; negotiations for Hauschka to join Weleda failed.

Having failed to find a professional outlet in Dornach, Hauschka accepted the adventuresome invitation of his friend, Ehrenreich, to go to Australia and start a shark enterprise, using various parts of the animal: producing leather from shark skin and putting shark meat into commercial production by removing all traces of the oily smell. A yacht called "Istar" was fitted for the enterprise, but the project failed, not least because of intense commercial commercial opposition.

It is fascinating to hear Hauschka's very precise observations about the sharks' physical characteristics and movements in his own words. He points to the exposed gills and the shark's inability to move backwards, among other things. The animal's area of distribution corresponds to Ancient Lemuria; there are sharks that live elsewhere, but they are "scavengers and renegades," leading an independent existence. Sharks have a long life and an enormous appetite, coupled with a massive digestive capacity and liver, and a great fertility rate. Hauschka compares them to a demonically hardened picture of the conditions of evolution of Lemurian times.

Encountering His Life Task

At the time that the shark adventure was faltering, Hauschka had a chance to participate in an anthroposophical world conference in London, and there he talked to Ita Wegman, who alerted him to the need for people to work in anthroposophical science. She invited him to set up laboratories at the institute of clinical therapy in Arlesheim. As the shark adventure collapsed further, Hauschka felt free to move

---

[324] Hauschka, *At the Dawn of a New Age*, 13-14.

into the path of his destiny. Another attempt to work with Weleda failed, and Hauschka opened Wala Laboratories in 1935. What made Wala unique was the procedure for preserving medicines without the use of alcohol: the doctor had recourse to the polarities of light and darkness, warmth and cold, movement and rest for extracting the active ingredients of medicinal herbs. Through these rhythmic alternations, natural preservation could be extended for many years with no need for alcohol or other preservatives.

The following are some of the areas Dr. Hauschka worked in, not necessarily in chronological order. In the years after his response to Ita Wegman, Hauschka undertook long studies of formative forces. With Ehrenfried Pfeiffer he turned his interests to the elemental world. In observing hoarfrost (ice crystals produced on windows at temperatures below freezing), he noticed that those produced in front of a flower shop were quite different from those at a butcher shop. He turned to photographing the crystals generated by different plant juices, and identifying the patterns produced by different plants.

From this first line of inquiry he moved to the study of crystallizing salts. Through these he could also demonstrate the formative tendencies in blood and use this tool to diagnose illnesses. Hauschka also developed "capillary-dynamic" analysis (now called chromatography) and started looking at so-called "rising pictures" (Steigbilder). Using the capillary-dynamic method he was able to detect the cancer configuration that precedes cancer itself. His cancer research continued with the elaboration of mistletoe remedies, which are effective in its cure.

Based on his experience, Hauschka recognized that the formative forces work through the zodiac constellations and the planets. He could also discern these forces at work in the creative word through the larynx. He could make this visible to others by speaking against a flame, and seeing the characteristic forms generated by the sounds. This interest in the creative word illuminated many aspects of Hauschka's research.

Continuing his work on formative forces, Hauschka joined Günther Wachsmuth in studying how these forces act in vitamins. He thus identified the forces of warmth ether in Vitamin A, of light ether in Vitamin C, of chemical ether in Vitamin B, of life ether in Vitamin D. From here it was only a short step to becoming interested in the question of nutrition. In fact, nutrition and the study of substance, or matter itself, formed the mainstay of Hauschka's scientific work.

Steiner had recommended that bread rise with salt and honey, rather than yeast. Hauschka, working on this, discovered that it could be done only with freshly ground biodynamic flour; the best was a mix of four grains (wheat, barley, rye and oats). Continuing his work on nutrition, he turned to the production of "elixirs," fruit juices that would preserve aroma, taste, quality, and wholesomeness. He achieved this with wild fruits and berries rather than the more widespread cultivated varieties. These were the first Wala elixirs.

In reading *The Riddles of Philosophy*, Hauschka was struck by the mention of the work of Baron Albrecht von Herzeele. He did what he could to track his work down and replicate it. Von Herzeele had studied the germination of seeds grown in distilled water and sealed from their immediate environment, and shown that their mineral constituents registered an increase of 30 to 100 percent during germination, concluding that in organic life the generation of elemental substances is a daily occurrence. Results similar to those of the baron had been corroborated by the work of a French scientist working on algae, who noted the emergence of iodine and potassium, as if from nowhere. After becoming acquainted with him, Hauschka turned to the study of Rosicrucian alchemy. His comprehensive explorations, and the ideas of space and counter-space presented by George Adams, brought him to a deep understanding of the formative forces, and strengthened his connection with the passion that had awakened in his youth.

Hauschka's World of Imaginations

We will now review Hauschka's world of living ideas and his way of working as expressed in the book *The Nature of Substance: Spirit and Matter*, arguably his most important literary legacy. This will be an abridged overview of the main points of the book. We can say from the start that the book forms a very large imagination built on many levels of smaller imaginations. In fact, what Hauschka states at the very end of the book could be a fitting introduction: "We have attempted to show here how it is possible, while maintaining scientific exactness, to feel one's way towards the living laws of the world; to find and unravel the threads which lead from earthly matter to its origin in the creative forces in the cosmos. This book was meant to be a contribution to discerning the pulse-beat of the cosmic organism."[325] And such it is.

The author takes his departure from the organic world and moves to the inorganic world and the metals. For each of these worlds he first builds imaginations of single chemical elements, such as oxygen, carbon, silica, calcium, sulfur, iron, gold, etc. He then relates each of them to the influences of the zodiac or to the action of the planets, and builds first a zodiac wheel of the elements and later the sevenfold correspondence between metals and planets. Finally, he offers the imagination of a new Periodic Table of the Elements, which he calls the "spiral of creation." Let us now look at this step by step.

Hauschka starts his work by repeating the experiments of Baron von Herzeele, which demonstrated transubstantiation of the elements. These had been important to Hauschka in his early scientific explorations. He then moves on to the plant, starting from the creation of starch in the plant's middle zone, and questioning the chemical equation of its formation as a definite explanation of this wonder. He introduces the idea that something much larger than what conventional science acknowledges accounts for the formation of starch: the action of light and air and water. From his conclusion, "Starch is a bewitched rainbow drawn down into matter by the plant's vital activity," the reader realizes that this will be no ordinary book on chemistry. We will return later to this image and its genesis.

Starting from the organic world, Hauschka makes a patient effort to lead the reader to an understanding of a zodiacal circle of the elements. His premise is that plants came first, and the soil and inert chemical elements later. Having looked at the formation of starch, he leads us into its metamorphoses in the various parts of the plant: sugars, cellulose, etheric oils, fatty oils. In this way he introduces us to the first three gases of the atmosphere: carbon, hydrogen and oxygen. And because he weaves an understanding of these elements from his vast storehouse of observations, new imaginations emerge and culminate in the offering

---

[325] Hauschka, *The Nature of Substance*, 233.

of new names: *pyrogen* for the hydrogen in relation to its connection to the fire element; *biogen* for oxygen in relation to the part it plays in promoting life, and *geogen* for carbon, the element of form of all living organisms.

One element remains to be considered, the gas most prevalent in our atmosphere: nitrogen. But in order to do this, Hauschka first leads us into the exploration of another part of the living world: the animals, and all that is most animal-like in the animal and plant world in which nitrogen plays a role, namely proteins and the alkaloids (natural plant poisons). With nitrogen, re-baptized *aerogen*, (carrier of the element of movement), Hauschka completes the so-called "atmospheric cross," in which nitrogen/aerogen stands in polarity to carbon/geogen and hydrogen/pyrogen stands in contrast to oxygen/biogen. And he places the influences of the elements' processes into the constellations: Libra for hydrogen; Aquarius for oxygen; Scorpio for carbon; Taurus for nitrogen.

Hauschka now leads us to an apparent detour, the study of vitamins. By looking at the nature of vitamins and studying the effect of their deficiencies (avitaminoses) he arrives at the previously mentioned correlation between vitamins A, B, C and D and the ethers: warmth ether for Vitamin A; chemical ether for vitamin B; light ether for vitamin C; form ether for vitamin D. He indicates that vitamins should be seen as universal shaping forces, rather than chemicals, as we are used to thinking of them. The theory is put to the test by creating artificial laboratory conditions for avitaminoses, to prove that vitamins are not chemical compounds but primary cosmic formative forces. This is done by excluding either chemical activity (Vitamin B), light (Vitamin C), warmth (Vitamin A) or gravity through creation of a vacuum (Vitamin D). Here Hauschka introduces crystallization images of yeast cultures exposed to vitamins, and of cultures shielded from one of the four influences. The crystallization method involves a saturated potassium nitrate solution that produces visual forms, one could say imaginations. Normal crystallization of yeast cultures exposed to vitamins produces regularly radiating crystals. Cultures in which one cosmic element is excluded produce stunted images with minimal crystal patterns. Hauschka has now introduced us to a more imaginative way of thinking about the cosmic origin and action of natural substances.

Having offered us images of what is alive, the author offers us an overview of the scientific development of synthetic substances from coal tar, the world of "mirror images," in which artificial substances mimic natural substances. This is the world that has given rise to the huge development of synthetic drugs. The production of carbon compounds in the plant that was previously explored is now mirrored in synthetic drugs. For every level of the plant's hydrocarbons (starch, sugar, essential oils, fatty oils, cellulose) there is a reflection, as it were, below nature. And the question naturally arises, "How do these twin sets of substances differ?"

To get to the next step, and the heart of the book, the principles of homeopathic dilutions are introduced. Matter emerges from an idea; the process ends in a chemical element. Matter that has lost the aliveness of the idea can be returned to its primal state through potentization, as it is practiced in homeopathy. "The potentizing method is an inspired emulation of this natural process [of plants withering and forming a seed]. It is simply a conversion of matter from appearance into being."[326]

We now move to comparing the potencies of natural and synthetic benzoic acid and their respective potency curves, measured in relation to the production of carbonic acid produced by yeast exposed to either substance. It is not possible to potentize synthetic substances (i.e., intensify them to become more active) since the force is absent. With a synthetic substance, smaller amounts of substance yield decreased results, and higher homeopathic dilutions have no detectable influence, whereas organic substances can show increased results with smaller amounts of matter in progressively higher potentized doses (D1 to D2 to D3, etc.). In the latter instance, when the matter no longer acts, the force/idea present in the substance continues to produce effects. On the other hand, synthetic substances are deprived of force because they have been severed from the cosmos.

Hauschka thus demonstrated that "Life overrides the law of the conservation of matter." And further, quoting Herzeele, "The earth does not manufacture plants by some physical-chemical process: it is

---

[326] Hauschka, *The Nature of Substance*, 112.

the plant that creates the soil by coming into material manifestation out of the universe."[327]

When plants burn, they leave mineral residues in the form of ash: among the most important are silica and calcium, aluminum and phosphorus. Hauschka turns to these next in order to build the imagination of the "mineral cross." It is silica as a macrocosmic force or process that has shaped the whole Earth. Calcium is the element "related to the statics of building the firmness of our physical frames." Furthermore silica is an acid, whereas calcium is a base.

To the first polarity is added that of aluminum and phosphorus. Clay is an aluminum silicate, and forms 20% of the Earth's crust. Aluminum has an "amphoteric nature": it can be both an acid and a base. Phosphorus is thinly scattered over the Earth's crust, contrary to aluminum; it is everywhere in minute quantities. Aluminum has an important part in the blood processes, phosphorus in the nerve processes. Hauschka now adds the mineral cross to the atmospheric cross previously constructed: silica, connected to Aries, calcium to Libra, aluminum to Capricorn and phosphorus to Cancer.

Hauschka has first looked at the atmosphere and the realm of the living (the atmospheric cross), then at the Earth's crust and the minerals. He turns now to the oceans' expanses. The oceans are the largest source of salt (3% or more dissolved). There is as much salt in the sea as there is solid rock on land. Alkalis (e.g. sodium, potassium, lithium) and halogens (e.g. chlorine, fluorine, bromine, iodine) are those that produce salts in the ocean.

Alkalis or bases like everything that is hospitable to life; they are passive, support-giving, receptive; they have an affinity with water and oxygen. Alkali salts form colloids in which solid substance is finely suspended in liquid. Alkaline processes work at the up-building that has to do with growth and nutrition. Halogens/acids, on the other hand, attack other substances aggressively. They are positive and active. They curdle colloids. Halogens press towards the conclusion of some train of action, "rounding off our destiny." Alkalis can be associated with the constellation of Virgo; halogen processes originate from the constellation of Pisces.

---

[327] Hauschka, *The Nature of Substance*, 119.

Sea salt contains an average of 16% magnesium sulfate. This proportion of magnesium is sufficient to build a whole continent. Magnesium turning into magnesia (magnesium oxide) produces a blinding light. The "alpine glow" of the Dolomites is due to the presence of magnesium in dolomitic limestone, containing magnesite. In the author's words, "It is magnesium that thrusts light into the dense materiality of starch and cellulose."[328] Magnesium process are at work in the deposits of bone-building material in the skeleton.

Sulfur deposits are found in regions of volcanic activity. This mineral has great affinity to warmth. And chemically speaking, sulfur is very sociable; it is a natural "mixer" of substances. The sulfur process supports digestion; it brings more life into the metabolic processes. Magnesium is under the influence of the constellation of Sagittarius; sulfur under that of Gemini.

Hauschka has now led us from the atmosphere and living organisms to the surface of the Earth and the depths of the oceans. The circle of the zodiac is now completed with the atmospheric, mineral and oceanic crosses. Although there are twelve elements around the circle, many others fall under the main representative of the group—all except the metals, which will be mentioned later. Hauschka summarizes his synthesis thus: "The substances that make up the atmospheric cross and work on the air mantle of the Earth create the forms of organic nature; the substances of the mineral cross go to the formation of the Earth's hard core; the substances of the oceanic cross fill the oceans with salts."[329]

In order to complete the Periodic Table of the Elements, Hauschka now turns to the metals. This he does by contrasting metals and minerals. Minerals (quartz, marble or crystals) are composed of the materials found in the region where they occur. In contrast, metal ores occur in narrow veins, independent of their surroundings. The relation of metals to man is completely different from that of minerals. Unlike minerals, metals are warm, responsive, mobile and lively, and are highly conductive of warmth and electricity. Unlike minerals, metals enter into intimate

---

[328] Hauschka, *The Nature of Substance*, 150.
[329] Ibid, 156.

relationships. The metals, Hauschka concludes, should not be placed in the same table as the other elements of the zodiac wheel. He tells us that in this table there is no proper place for the metals, and recommends eliminating them, thereby reducing the Periodic Table of the Elements to seven series, instead of eleven. He therefore initiates a wholly new imagination in relation to the metals, of which there are seven primary archetypes, rather than twelve: the planets, rather than the zodiac.

Hauschka arranges the metals according to resonance, luster, warmth and electrical conductivity, and their capacity to be cast and forged. Lead and tin (least conductive and resonant) can be cast but not forged. Iron, gold, mercury can be cast and forged. Copper and silver (most conductive and resonant) can be forged but not cast. Relating the qualities of the metals to the planetary spheres, Hauschka concludes, "We see, then, that planetary movement is metamorphosed into the properties of earthly metals. The impetus of the planets appears in a metamorphosed way as conductivity."[330]

Hauschka now orders the metals in relation to their properties. The higher the conductivity, the more the metal is related to a planet close to the Earth. Thus lead's properties make it a Saturnian element; tin is connected with Jupiter, iron with Mars, gold with Sun, mercury with the planet Mercury, copper with Venus and silver with the Moon. Gold occupies the same central place among the metals that the Sun occupies among the planets; its properties are placed halfway between lead and silver. Hauschka completes his analysis of the planets by looking at the polarities that arrange themselves around the Sun/gold axis: iron-mercury, tin-copper and lead-silver. Gold stands on its own, as the mediator among the other three polarities.

Hauschka then examines the three polarities through many phenomena: relationships with water; ores produced and their crystallization patterns; predictable or unpredictable behavior; complexity of chemistry; physical properties; and so forth. He rounds off the picture by looking beyond the metal to the archetypal process that finds its final expression in the physical metal.

The book culminates in the most ambitious of all Hauschka's

---

[330] Hauschka, *The Nature of Substance*, 163.

imaginations: his attempt to transform the static Periodic Table of the Elements into the dynamic "Spiral of Creation." This is how he explains the step he wants to take: "The Periodic Table might justifiably be thought of as the final expression of the creative cosmic symphony, which can be experienced in a more living way as it sounds through the spiral of creation. The Periodic Table could be described as a static abstraction. In the creative spiral, on the other hand, the succession of events in time is expressed."[331]

Hauschka has already indicated that chemical elements combine in single and multiple proportions, and that all of the ratios in which they combine are contained within the octave (from 1:1 to 1:7). He now arranges the zodiac wheel with twelve elements at its periphery and seven rings of the metals in the inner part of the circle; the Earth is at the center, with silver closest to it, and Saturn, with lead, closest to the periphery. This is quite reminiscent of the way in which the twelve senses are often portrayed in relation to the seven life processes. The graph reiterates that the formative influences that work on the three crosses originate in the zodiac; those that work in the metals, in the planets.

Hauschka compares the law of gravity, and the acceleration of falling objects (after 1 second a stone falls 5 meters, after 2 seconds 20 meters, after 5 seconds 125 meters, after 9 seconds 405 meters), to the process of formation of substances "falling" from the cosmos to Earth. He finds support for this in the embryology of the human fetus. The acceleration of growth and differentiation from the first to the ninth month is directly proportional to the acceleration of a falling object due to gravity, according to the values expressed above.

The result of his creative thinking builds up the imagination of a spiral of creation, in which formative impulses from the cosmos are tempered by planetary impulses. This spiral reflects the evolutionary reality of smaller cycles inscribed within larger ones in the course of a Platonic year. Silica, which forms the beginning of the spiral of creation, can serve as an example: "… a Saturnian tempering was given to the Aries impulse. Earthly silica was the result."[332]

---

[331] Hauschka, *The Nature of Substance*, 229.
[332] Ibid, 227.

Hauschka's World of Imaginations

We have given a succinct and far from exhaustive overview of Hauschka's momentous work, just to elaborate on how he fashioned his work of science and art. Among the first imaginations challenging the mind of the reader is the one already quoted: "Starch is a bewitched rainbow drawn down into matter by the plant's vital activity." As if to anticipate the reader's surprise, or confusion, Hauschka counters quite extensively:

> Picturing a plant against the background of the rainbow is not just poetic license: it is simple realism. And it touches on the deepest questions of the origin of matter.
>
> We often spend years mulling over some idea too vague as yet to find expression. Gradually it takes on contours, becomes clear and transparent, reaches a stage where it can be spoken or written down. Now it is ready for others to examine it. Every artist is familiar with this progression from idea to finished creation. And those who come to know the artist's work resurrect his crystallized thought in their appreciation of it. A culture is nothing more nor less than the realm of human thought made visible.
>
> Must we not think of the creations of the great artist, nature, as works of entirely similar origin? Must not the wealth of forms about us, built by nature according to laws which we are only just beginning to investigate, have issued from a cosmic activity akin to thinking? What happens when a higher than human being thinks, and what effect do such thoughts have?[333]

We are fortunate to have Hauschka's explanation concerning the genesis of the starch/rainbow imagination in his book on nutrition. Here he explains that the rainbow bridges the poles of light and darkness through the action of air, light and water, and starch too is formed in the middle pole of the plant, between Earth and Sun, through the

---

[333] Hauschka, *The Nature of Substance*, 22-23.

action of light, air and water. And he continues, revealing the birth of that insight. He had been pondering the question for a while during an ocean voyage to Australia, when a monsoon hit the ship. The day was bright and sunny, and the ship was enveloped by a fine spray of mist. "The whole visible world became a rainbow-colored bowl." Struck by the beauty of the experience, Hauschka formulated the insight that starch is the result of the collaboration of air, light and water in the plant. And he concluded, "A person who realizes that virgin starch is a condensed rainbow comes to a new sense of kinship with plant creation."[334]

As in the instance of van Emmichoven, we are led to realize what power lies in the personal effort to enliven thinking from its very sources so as to move beyond the surface of perception, from the phenomena to the living archetypes that are at their source.

The reader may remember that Hauschka, not unlike van Emmichoven, was called a poet by his teacher. This means that he had developed imaginative qualities from very early on. In his autobiography, thinking back to his youth, Hauschka describes antimony as a "metallic substance [which] behaved like a child." Decades later, from a more mature perspective, having lived with this imagination for a long time, he can say "this infant, antimony, is always longing for its cosmic home, for a return to the unborn condition." Here what he was able to perceive in relation to pure phenomena is brought to bear in relation to the behavior of an element that cannot quite reach the stage of a metal. It seems to retain the metallic qualities of earlier periods of Earth evolution, during which metals were as yet undifferentiated. And the author can offer the image in yet another way thus: "It is a cosmic infant suddenly transported into Earth conditions to which it has not yet had time to adapt itself."[335]

Let us look more fully at the development of an imagination: Hauschka's portrayal of the alkalis (sodium, potassium, lithium, rubidium, cesium, etc.), which is but one of dozens of efforts at building up imaginations in the book. Let us retrace four steps:

---

[334] Hauschka, *Nutrition*, 75.
[335] Hauschka, *The Nature of Substance,* 217-18.

1. <u>Description of physical properties</u>. Alkali salts (metal salts dropped into an alkali solution) form colloids. Alkalis tend to form enclosing sheaths, and all human bodily fluids are colloids (chyle, lymph and blood serum), as is plant sap. Potassium is the typical alkali that is present in these processes.

2. <u>Transitioning from properties to qualities</u>. Alkalis form soaps with fats and oils, and soap envelops and increases surface tension. Soap is a colloid that allows a great increase in surfaces. Oils are condensed cosmic warmth and soaps (formed from oils) act as enclosing warmth.

3. <u>Building up of an imagination</u>. "Silica is itself a cosmic sheath, whereas alkalis are simply earthly sheaths that enclose whatever comes into their domain. If one searches for an appropriate picture to express artistically the nature of alkalis' enclosing gesture, we come upon the pictures of maternal organisms giving shelter to the child-to-be. What is meant here can be experienced by contemplating the Sistine Madonna. ... We feel in the gesture her deep connection with the heavenly powers for which she has provided earthly shelter."

4. <u>Completing the imagination and linking it to a cosmic archetype</u>. "In ancient times, when no one doubted that the terrestrial is always a housing for the spirit, this truth was felt to be pictured in the constellation of Virgo, the virgin. Here could be experienced the sheath-forming power, whence forces of ripening and fertility rayed down to earth. ... We might say that an apple can be seen as a picture of brimming sap confined within a form by the Virgo forces active in the alkali."[336]

We have completed a tableau of Dr. Hauschka's biography and life's work. The doctor's name is linked to the innovative use of anthroposophical medicines, which no longer use alcohol as a preserving agent. We can now turn to the work of another pioneer in the medical field: Dr. Edward Bach, who stimulated the rebirth of homeopathy at a new level, through his work on the now famous Bach Flower Remedies.

---

[336] Hauschka, *The Nature of Substance*, 144-46.

The reader may not need to assess the whole of the English doctor's life and work before realizing that we stand before two scientists who work in radically different ways.

Dr. Edward Bach

Nothing is quite conventional in the life of Dr. Bach. Neither is the way in which he pursued his revolutionary approach to medicine, nor the way in which flower remedies made their entrance into the medical field. The flower remedies have now been abundantly tested for their efficacy, but much work is needed in elucidating how they work and what happens in the so-called sun method of plant preparation, or in the boiling method.

Childhood and Early Career

Edward Bach was born in Moseley, near Birmingham, United Kingdom, on September 24, 1886. As a boy he was both cautious and imaginative, and already displayed a headstrong and resolute character. His "helper" instinct was visible in the care he offered his younger sister, as well as other people in need. Part of this may have stemmed from the fact that at an early age his health was already a matter of concern.

The child displayed amazing determination and intensity of purpose. He could concentrate on some object of interest, allowing nothing to distract him. He had a great fondness for everything that came from Wales, where his family line originated, and the intuitive nature and love of beauty that are often a trademark of the Welsh. Such was his passion for fresh air that he removed the glass from his bedroom window in order to enjoy it more fully.

When deciding on a vocation, he vacillated a long time between studying theology or medicine.[22] This is a theme that returns throughout his life. Having studied to become a medical doctor, he first became a "casualty house surgeon" before realizing that such a profession was too taxing for his fragile health. He later set up his own practice and also began microbiological research as assistant bacteriologist at the University College Hospital of London.

Observations showed him early on that the same treatment did not cure all patients who had the same disease, and that the proportions of the uncured could be very high. He also realized that individuals with the same temperament would often respond well to the same remedy, whereas others needed a different one. He concluded that personality type was a more important determining factor than physical symptoms in the treatment of illness. However, he grew progressively disappointed seeing both those whom he could not cure, and those whose health he could not maintain. Like Hahnemann—the founder of homeopathy— before him, he found that orthodox medicine failed to give lasting healing to his patients.

In 1917 Bach was hospitalized. The cause, according to Mechthild Scheffer, was a tumor in his spleen.[337] When he was admitted to the hospital the surgeons operated at once, doubting that they could save him. He had a severe hemorrhage and lost consciousness during the operation, and was told he had only three months to live. He went back to work with great energy, having most likely grasped the subtle relationship between illness and mental attitude; and with reason, when one looks more closely at the doctor's life at the time. Bach's first wife was Gwendoline Caiger, whom he married in 1913. In 1916 his daughter with Kitty Light was born, and in April 1917 Gwendoline died of diphtheria. In May of the same year he married Kitty Light, separating from her in 1922. His illness, we can surmise, was the culmination of a soul state that generated choices and events that were difficult to integrate in the doctor's life.

Homeopathy

The revived Bach was starting a second life. He had already approached vaccine therapy, a specialized field of medicine, the closest in kind to homeopathy's famous tenet that "like cures like." It is no surprise, therefore, that in 1919 Bach started working as a pathologist in London's Homeopathic Hospital. Here he started using the homeopathic method for making vaccines in compresses and pills. He had developed seven

---

[337] Mechthild Scheffer, *Encyclopedia of Bach Flower Therapy*, 13.

kinds of "nosodes," vaccines that he related to types of bacteria in the intestinal flora and to an individual typology. It is rare to find more than one of the seven kinds of bacteria in any given individual; Bach had begun to observe that he could recognize the right nosode to administer just by looking at an individual's body type, behavior, posture, and way of walking. He gathered observations that showed him that individuals with phobias of fire, heights, crowds or traffic almost invariably had a predominance of paratyphoid bacteria; tense, restless individuals prone to anxiety had a dominant Proteus population; and so on. He also ascertained that the dominant bacterial population remains remarkably constant in the individual, no matter what the patient's history may be. The nosodes led Bach to the rediscovery of toxemia that Hahnemann, the founder of homeopathy, had called Psora, those conditions relating to chronic illnesses tied to intestinal poisoning.

Bach had come to accept homeopathy's view that it is not the illness alone that needs the physician's attention, but the whole patient. His ultimate dream was to develop a simple therapy that could be self-administered, and to move from bacterial nosodes to plant remedies that could be more easily produced and personally administered. He was conducting research with plants that never appeared as flower remedies, but realized that he could not obtain the results he hoped for because of what he called a "problem of polarity." He surmised that "The remedies of the meadow and of Nature, when potentized, are of positive polarity; whereas those which have been associated with disease are of the reverse type, and at the time it seems that it is this reverse polarity which is so essential in the results which are being obtained by bacterial nosodes."[338] Bach Flower Remedies later overcame what Bach called the problem of polarity.

The Flower Remedies

In his typically radical fashion, Bach left his laboratory and practice—although he was a successful and esteemed physician—and wandered into the Welsh countryside in search of plant remedies. He was wandering

---

[338] Nora Weeks, *The Medical Discoveries of Edward Bach Physician*

in nature as he had done as a child, but now with a remarkably single-minded focus. The step he was taking was truly enormous. It was not unlike Hahnemann's departure from allopathic medicine, years before he discovered the potentizing method that led to homeopathy. In fact, the doctor had his predecessor's work at heart when he said:

> It is obviously fundamentally wrong to say that "like cures like." Hahnemann had a right conception of the truth, but expressed it incompletely. Like may strengthen like, like may repel like, but in a true healing sense, like cannot cure like. This is not to detract from Hahnemann's work; on the contrary, he pointed out the great fundamental laws, the basis ... we are merely advancing his work, and carrying it to the next natural stage... Another glorious view then opens out before us, and here we see that true healing can be obtained, not by wrong, but by right replacing wrong; good replacing evil; light replacing darkness. Here we come to the understanding that we no longer fight disease with disease; no longer oppose illness with the product of illness; no longer drive out maladies with such substances that can cause them [one of the principal tenets of homeopathy]; but, on the contrary, to bring down the opposing virtue which will eliminate the fault.[339]

Bach was not seeking a departure from homeopathy, rather an enhancement of it. For that to happen, the last major breakthrough was needed. Both his future discoveries—the "sun method" and "boiling method," of which more will be said below—came in flashes of sudden inspiration, much as the idea of potentizing through "succussion" came to Hahnemann. Bach had developed a refined degree of "intuition" from

---

[339] Edward Bach, *Ye Suffer From Yourselves* quoted in Barnard, *Patterns of Life Force: A Review of the Life and Work of Dr. Edward Bach and His Discovery of the Bach Flower Remedies*, 63.

training in the scientific method and from observing his patients in countless hours of practice.

Few examples have been preserved of the way Bach proceeded in the discovery of his floral remedies. We have two in Gorse and Heather, two of the "seven helpers"— remedies produced with the sun method. In the first case Bach tells us that an inner message came to him; immediately afterward, he noticed the Gorse flower. The discovery of Heather was preceded by a question he asked a self-centered woman: "What do you think is the most beautiful sight in the world?" Her answer, "The mountains covered with heather," led the doctor to the choice of that plant. Although this way of proceeding may seem superficial at first, it denotes Bach's ability to listen to everything the world had to offer him. This insight alone would clearly amount to nothing were it not for the tedious work of examination and confirmation of the plants' effects on patients.

What led Bach to the sun method was the intuition that in a dewdrop on a leaf, lies encapsulated an energetic essence of the plant, an extract that is potentized in a way both similar to and different from homeopathic remedies.[340] This intuition was possible because Bach's senses were quickened, particularly his sense of touch, through which he could feel the properties of a plant. He just needed to hold a petal or blossom, or place it on his tongue, to feel its healing properties. He had in effect become his own mobile laboratory.

The first nineteen flower remedies were prepared using the "sun method"; the other nineteen, except for one, using the "boiling method." We could visualize the sun method as a large-scale production of dewdrops: flowers of the desired plant are placed in a glass bowl and completely covered with spring water. There are a host of specific conditions that accompany the process. The flowers must be harvested on a sunny day without clouds, and be exposed to the sun for two hours before being harvested at the time when dew would be produced; they must have reached the peak of blossoming just prior to pollination.

---

[340] About the differences between homeopathic and flower remedies, see: Richard Katz and Patricia Kaminski, *Flower Essences and Homeopathy: An Article Exploring the Relationship between These Two Allied Therapies.*

The advantage of the sun method lies in the fact that there is no loss of potency due to drying, transportation or processing of the plant. Everything is done on-site, up to the preparation of the mother tincture. The boiling method uses flowers harvested with six inches of twigs, which are boiled for half an hour; all other conditions are the same as in the sun method.[341]

After finding the first nineteen remedies, Bach thought his task accomplished. The second series of nineteen was found in a completely different way: for a few days before the discovery of each remedy, the doctor suffered intensely from the state of mind that the flower essence would later cure. He suffered to such a degree that those around him marveled at how he was able to stand such pain and retain his sanity. During the hottest part of the summer, when looking for one (unspecified) remedy of the second series, Bach's body was covered by a virulent rash, which burned and irritated constantly; for weeks his legs were ulcerated, raw from knee to ankle; his hair fell out and his eyesight almost failed. Before he found the remedy, his face was swollen and extremely painful; he had a severe hemorrhage that did not cease until the plant remedy was located.[342]

The first decisive proof, or the most tangible, of the efficacy of the remedies was offered by the use of the so-called "Rescue Remedy." This is a composite of five flowers—originally three. Dr. Bach first applied it in its original form in 1930 to revive from shock a man who had survived a great storm at sea. He and a mate had been holding on to the mast of a boat for many hours before lifeboats rescued them; they were

---

[341] Dr. Bach did not say why he used the second boiling method. He discovered the second group of nineteen plants from March to July 1935. At that time he was undergoing the state of mind that the remedy would later cure. It has been speculated that the boiling method was devised in order to treat woody species, but this argument fails to justify the presence of herbaceous plants such as Mustard and Star of Bethlehem among the second group of nineteen. Rather, J. Barnard finds justification in Bach's remark that the sun-boiled remedies act at a deeper level, therefore the need to extract their healing quality with a more radical means than the sun method. The second group of nineteen plants addresses the great trials of life that submit the individual to great pressure, intense emotions and pain.
[342] Weeks, *The Medical Discoveries of Edward Bach Physician*, 116.

both unconscious at the time of the rescue. Bach was able to minister to one of the two as soon as he was carried into the lifeboat. The man had completely recovered upon reaching the hotel following his rescue. The remedy—now made from Impatiens, Star of Bethlehem, Cherry Plum, Rock Rose and Clematis—has since been successfully used in all situations involving shock.[343]

In the winter of 1930 Bach started treating many patients with the new flower remedies, with encouraging results. Among the first was a forty-five-year-old alcoholic woman. Five weeks after the treatment, she was drinking in strict moderation; her craving had passed. She had maintained this state three years later.[344] Another patient had survived a severe motor accident which had paralyzed his left trapezius muscle; he could not raise his arm above the shoulder. There was a marked physical improvement three months later, and his worry and anxiety were gone.[345] Over the years, Bach cured patients who had seemed hopeless and diseases that had persisted for years.

In three cases—one of asthma, the others of alcoholism and paralysis—the patients were given chiefly Agrimony because they all belonged to the same type.[346] Among those primarily treated with Clematis were patients suffering from asthma, cysts, and aftereffects of so-called "sleepy sickness," a form of encephalitis.[347] The above illustrates Bach's discovery that although the patients suffered from the same disease, a different remedy was needed in each case. The same remedies work only for people displaying the same character type.

Bach's career proceeded in a movement of recapitulation and refinement—from surgery to vaccine therapy to homeopathy, and finally to flower remedies. Let us find our way into the doctor's mind to see what made this possible.

---

[343] Philip M. Chancellor, *Handbook of the Bach Flower Remedies*, 237-242.
[344] Weeks, *The Medical Discoveries of Edward Bach Physician*, 71.
[345] Ibid, 72.
[346] Ibid, 73.
[347] Ibid, 75.

"Healer Know Thyself"

Bach's path of discovery consisted of having to overcome intense psychic and physical pain. He confided to Nora Weeks—for many years his closest collaborator—that he had been suffering physical pain practically all his life. As we saw above, in 1917 the doctor was operated on for cancer and told he had three months to live. His remission was complete; nevertheless Bach struggled for another twenty years with his deteriorating body.

Bach was both a thorough scientist and a soul with a metaphysical bent. His most famous and most financially successful work, *Heal Thyself,* is one of the first modern books in which medicine is treated from a spiritual perspective, by Bach the theologian, as it were. It is far from being well structured and supported, but provides us with a blueprint of Bach's inner journey of discovery of ideas that were revolutionary at the time, and are becoming more commonplace at present. At times, the doctor's enthusiasm pushed him to proclaim radical principles in rather simplistic terms. Only later in life did he moderate them and become more discriminating in his approach.

A look at Bach's soul life is also very indicative of the way in which his scientific mind shared the soul of a semi-mystic. We will offer just a few examples. Bach possessed the gift of healing touch. On several occasions he felt impelled, especially during the beginning of his research into flower essences, to lay his hand on a patient's arm or shoulder, and the patient was instantly healed. The doctor felt at once a tremendous compassion and a desire to be of help, and "would feel the healing life flow from his hands into the patient, who immediately was well."[348] On one occasion, Bach laid hands on a woman who had suffered a sudden hemorrhage and was vomiting blood. Bach told her that she would soon be well, and the bleeding ceased, Nora Weeks relates.[349]

Later in Bach's life, his power of healing became even stronger, and others could sense, upon seeing him, a surge of life flowing through them.[350] A woodsman had told Bach of a problem with his mouth and

---

[348] Weeks, *The Medical Discoveries of Edward Bach Physician,* 43.
[349] Ibid, 83.
[350] Ibid, 108.

tongue that made him unable to eat, drink, smoke or talk comfortably. Bach healed him by putting his hand on his shoulder.[351] Likewise, Bach cured his collaborator, Nora Weeks, of severe bronchitis by just passing his hands over her back.[352]

Toward the end of his life, Bach was able to foretell events. Nora Weeks remembers that he was able to warn fishermen of a coming gale. On another occasion, he dreamed of a fisherman friend in great danger during a storm. In the dream, Bach saw his friend and another man asleep, and told the second to wake up. Bach then awoke, startled by the dream, and went down to the shore. There he discovered the boat he had dreamt of. His friend confirmed that they had indeed been in danger and that his mate had suddenly awakened him, saving his life.[353]

It is now hardly surprising that Bach remembered some details of his previous lives, although these meant little to him, nor to hear his ideas about the impending spiritual revolution occurring in our time. He stated in 1933: "For the next coming of Christ, there is a band of people who, to welcome Him, should be able to transcend their physical natures and realize their spirituality."[354]

His above attitude bled into his scientific research. Bach declared his distrust of the intellect, which led him to work from his intuition.[355]

---

[351] Weeks, *The Medical Discoveries of Edward Bach Physician*, 108.

[352] Ibid, 182.

[353] Ibid, 106-07.

[354] Howard and Ramsell, *The Original Writings of Edward Bach*, 77.

[355] In Bach's book *Free Thyself* we see this quote:

> "Health is listening solely to the commands of our souls; in being trustful as little children; in rejecting intellect (that knowledge of good and evil); with its reasonings, its 'fors' and 'againsts', its anticipating fears; ignoring convention, the trivial ideas and commands of other people, so that we can pass through life untouched, unharmed, free to serve our fellow-men."

Further in the same chapter we read: "Truth has no need to be analysed, argued about, or wrapped up in many words. It is realized in a flash, it is part of you. It is only about the unessential complicated things of life that we need so much convincing, and that have led to the development of the intellect. The things that count are simple, they are the ones that make you say, "Why, that is true, I seem to

Obviously, as a scientist with many years of laboratory experience, he had a vast store of knowledge from which to draw in the collection of his observations and the elaboration of his concepts. Bach may have been intuitive, but Nora Weeks reminds us that he spent a great deal of time checking everything about his plants: the way they grew, propagated, reproduced; soil conditions, humidity, environmental conditions, and so forth.

Bach Flowers and Healing

One of Bach's fundamental premises is that we come to earth with the task of learning one—or maybe two or three—main lessons. These lessons are both earthly and spiritual: they are unique in their individual articulation, but archetypal in their essence. Examples include overcoming pride, learning to deal with fear, acquiring patience, developing discernment, becoming more compassionate, and so on.

Bach determined from his observations of human typology that there were twelve primary life lessons. In the book *Free Thyself*, he indicates twelve great qualities (such as joy, courage, forgiveness, wisdom). These qualities are to be attained in order to learn the meaning of love, by fighting the conditions that cloud the qualities (grief hiding the dimension of joy, terror or fear hiding courage, ignorance hiding wisdom). Illness befalls the personality that refuses to learn these soul lessons. Illness is caused primarily by an imbalance between the higher self and the personality, or lower self. However, illness has a

---

have known that always," and so is the realization of the happiness that comes to us when we are in harmony with our spiritual self, and the closer the union the more intense the joy." (Edward Bach, *Heal Thyself*, chapter 3, in *The Original Writings of Edward Bach: Compiled from the Archives of the Dr. Edward Bach Healing Trust Mount Vernon, Sotwell*, edited by Judy Howard and John Ramsell.

From the above in light of Bach's biography his "reject of the intellect" becomes more circumstantiated. It reflects Bach's journey in the expression of his self and the rejection of fears that had cramped his youth and early adulthood. Suffice to remember the three years from age 16 to 19 when he worked in the family's brass foundry before mastering the courage to make known his desire to be a doctor. It also applied to the tumultuous life of feelings in his relationships and marriage.

forward-moving thrust that invites us to overcome our negative personality traits when our conscious personalities don't want to accept the lessons life brings us. Illness indicates not only the need for change, but also the way leading to change. This is not a heartless statement, coming from somebody who had extensive firsthand knowledge of what he was talking about. In retrospect, one can say that accepting his illnesses gave Bach the strength not only to continue living, but also to fulfill his destiny. He barely kept his illnesses at bay until he completed his mission in 1936.

Bach believed that illness is the ultimate "like cures like": disease prevents our wrong thoughts and feelings to be carried too far in the world. He was confident that disease disappears when the lesson is learned, and went so far as to say that there is no incurable disease. Observations from among his patients give weight to this assertion: some patients recovered much faster from severe, acute conditions than others did from much milder chronic complaints.

As a doctor specializing in vaccine therapy, Bach had learned that the immune system preserves the memories of previous microbial infections and therefore knows how to master them a second time around, if necessary. In the same way, when we have mastered a life lesson, we acquire qualities that render us immune to our previous fears, shortcomings and life challenges. This realization led him to the conclusion that certain soul states are pathological and intrinsically generate an illness before it is physically carried into the body by a pathogen.

Different therapeutic substances offer help at different levels: physical, energetic/etheric or emotional. Bach moved from the etheric/energetic level most commonly dealt with in homeopathy to the emotional level that is treated by flower remedies. As a doctor, he saw his role in trying to strengthen the spirit of the patient. From these premises he elaborated a medicine that takes care of emotional illness before it moves on to the etheric plane and later congeals as physical illness. However, as we saw, Dr. Bach also used the flower essences for all types of physical illness, both acute and chronic.

Using the Bach Flower Remedies

In reviewing Dr. Bach's legacy, the last word should address the use of the flowers themselves, which, unlike most other remedies, can be self-prescribed. And this can be done, broadly speaking, in two ways.

The first requires becoming familiar with the soul states each flower addresses. The simplest way to do this is to proceed through the list of flowers, checking both negative states of mind and the sought-after positive state of mind. After some time of using these repertories, we will find the task simplified because we will start to remember the therapeutic function of many flowers. Helpful in this approach are *Dictionary of Bach Flower Remedies: Positive and Negative Aspects*; *The Bach Remedies: A Self-Help Guide*; and *New Bach Flower Therapies: Healing the Emotional and Spiritual Causes of Illness.*[356] In going through the plants, it is generally recommended to choose no more than five or six remedies.

A second approach consists in completing a questionnaire to help select the remedies, for example the *Double Questionnaire and Final Choice Checklist* or the *Questionnaire for the Self-Determination of the Correct Bach Flower Combinations.*[357] The first questionnaire looks at three sets of larger questions. The first is the *Present situation questionnaire*, addressing "How am I reacting to my current problem?" The second is a *Character questionnaire,* asking "What are the negative behavior patterns that keep me from implementing my goal?" The third is a *Final Choice Checklist* asking "What is most bothersome right now?"

The *Questionnaire for the Self-Determination* addresses in sequence "Me and my present situation," "Me and my difficulties: me and my environment" and "Me and my past."

Both from my personal experience and from the experience of others who have used the remedies, discerning what is needed at a certain point

---

[356] Leslie J. Kaslof, *Dictionary of Bach Flower Remedies: Positive and Negative Aspects*; T. W. Hyne Jones, *The Bach Remedies: A Self-Help Guide*, and Dietmar Krämer, *New Bach Flower Therapies: Healing the Emotional and Spiritual Causes of Illness.*

[357] Scheffer, *Encyclopedia of Bach Flower Therapy,* and Mechthild Scheffer, *Mastering Bach Flower Therapies: A Guide to Diagnosis and Treatment.*

in time requires asking oneself to look back at the immediate past and seeking to recognize what states of mind have engulfed us. Some of them may not be continuous, but nevertheless reappear regularly. In other words, using the Bach Flower Remedies requires an effort of spirit recollection. Since it requires an objectivity that cannot fully be reached for oneself, it is justifiably recommended to use another trusted person as a mirror or helper.

In yet other ways, the flowers call us to an exercise of spirit recollection. When a state of soul is discerned, many individuals who are used to the flower remedies know that half the effort of transforming it has already been reached, especially if what is discerned is a rather superficial state of mind, or something that has already been tackled before. Thus, over time the use of the flowers becomes an aid in developing skills of spirit recollection.

The legacy of Bach in the medical field is rather unique. The flowers are, practically speaking, a tool for enhancing self-consciousness. They support from without what an individual can do, at least partly, for himself from his own inner resources. After all, the way in which Bach went about finding the flowers addressed both the awareness of an inner state and the recognition of an etheric force that matched the soul state. And the doctor left us much more precise descriptions about the soul state than he did about the qualities of the plants, and the reason for his choice.

That Bach's intuitive approach had limits is obvious when we look at the efforts of his successors. These, not having Bach's level of intuition, inherited a complete line of products but without the body of knowledge that would allow them to conceptually elaborate on it and further it. A successful attempt in this direction—Flower Essence Remedies—uses the Goethean and spiritual scientific approach to determine new flower remedies beyond the thirty-eight discovered by Bach.[358] We will return to it.

---

[358] The Flower Essence Society continues the research for the introduction of new flower remedies. It publishes the *Flower Essence Repertory: A Comprehensive Guide to North American and English Flower Essences for Emotional and Spiritual*

Explaining Bach and Continuing his Work.

A plethora of questions can be asked about Bach's legacy. How can we understand the action of the flower on the emotional or mental imbalances it helps to heal? What is at work in the sun method? In the boiling method? How can the flowers be used for all ranges of physical ailments?

Julian Barnard has systematically attempted to answer the first question from a phenomenological and Goetheanistic approach in relation to all thirty-eight flower remedies. Let us see how he approaches Impatiens—Bach's main type—and shows us how the plant illustrates the path from soul illness to healing.[359]

Impatiens is the plant of Dr. Bach and of many initiators and innovators. The doctor was a very self-motivated individual who preferred to work alone without given schedules, norms or regulations. On occasion, as Nora Weeks remembers, he would purposely do things to shock or be rude toward those solely motivated by curiosity about him. He disliked hypocrisy and often refused to meet with people of whom he disapproved. Interestingly, he was annoyed if he had to wear a hat and made little sudden gestures as if to remove it. Following his intuition he made quick decisions and was annoyed by slow people. He could become angry very quickly, but would just as quickly forget his temper. It is not surprising in this overview to realize that Bach was a heavy smoker.

The Impatiens soul type is choleric, impatient and sensitive to criticism. People of this type tend to sit on the edge of their chair, ready to produce outbursts of energy that they use to influence the outer world. When under stress, this kind of person is likely to be rather vocal. In order to resolve a difficult situation or conflict, the temptation to use force is great. In fact this type often harbors, in the depth of his soul, a vein of cruelty. Bach goes so far as to attribute to this type the traits of the inquisitor.

Impatiens Glandulifera, native of the Himalayas, is an annual that can reach more than six feet in height. It lives between 6,000 and 13,000

Well-being, Patricia Kaminski and Richard Katz, The Flower Essence Society, Nevada City, CA.

[359] Julian Barnard, *Bach Flower Remedies: Form and Function*, Chapter 2, 32-36.

feet in altitude, loves damp soil, and develops well when close to a source of animal manure. The heavy seeds form thick colonies that choke all other growth when they germinate, thanks to a rapid growth of almost an inch per day. A pasture colonized by this plant is permanently degraded for animal use. The unique and exotic flower form that has inspired the name "poor man's orchid" is fertilized by cross-pollination. The flower, finely balanced on top of the stem, is indicative of the grace, spontaneity and compassion that were found in Edward Bach and the Impatiens type. For therapeutic purposes Bach deliberately chose the mauve flowers of the plant rather than the red ones that are far more common. The color mauve has a soothing and delicate quality not present in the red flowers. The traits of the flower contrast with the rigid gesture and tension that appear in the pods which, once ripe, explode and propel seeds out of the plant like projectiles. No doubt this gesture prompted the designation Impatiens. The tension visible in this gesture is clearly indicative of the Impatiens type. The floral remedy makes the person "less hasty in action and thought; more relaxed, patient, tolerant and gentle towards shortcomings of others and upsetting conditions."[360]

Similar to this characterization of Impatiens, Julian Barnard offers invaluable research into all thirty-eight Bach flowers. Following the Goethean approach, Richard Katz and Patricia Kaminski are now extending the range of remedies by the constant addition of new flowers, using common species and plants from California and the American West.[361] The same is being done in other parts of the world.

In Katz and Kaminski's view, Bach's flowers work with characteristics both similar and contrary to psychological imbalances, as is visible in the gesture of the plant itself—in the realm of archetypes that lie beyond the realm of duality. They reach the conclusion that the flowers evolve, according to the alchemical principle of metamorphosis and the union of opposites, into a new synthesis.[362] The Bach remedies can

---

[360] T. W. Hyne Jones, *Dictionary of Bach Flower Remedies: Positive and Negative Aspects.*

[361] Patricia Kaminski and Richard Katz, *Flower Essence Repertory: A Comprehensive Guide to North American and English Flower Essences for Emotional and Spiritual Well-Being.*

[362] Katz and Kaminski, *Flower Essences and Homeopathy,* 12

thus reach the emotional realm. Unlike homeopathic remedies, they work in accordance with the freedom of the individual. Potentizing the flower remedies makes them effective but in a compulsory way, thus presenting the problem of side effects that can result from use, or misuse, of homeopathic remedies.[363] All of the above was intuited by Bach. He envisioned his flower remedies as medications "flooding our bodies with beautiful vibrations of our Higher Nature in the presence of which disease melts like snow in sunshine."[364] He also stated that the remedies "bring more union between our mortal and spiritual self."[365] For this reason he could assert that the remedies were "more spiritualized than all the previous remedies."[366]

Why are we using the sun method to potentize the plant? At this stage the question can be broken into two sub-questions. Why are we using the flower? And what is present in the dew that allows for a potentizing effect? Katz and Kaminski address the first question with the help of the studies of George Adams and Olive Whicher. The flower brings to completion the maturation of earthly substances towards the cosmos. In the flower the plant reaches cosmic light, and the interplay of cosmic and earthly forces is revealed in "color, fragrance, subtle texture, and stellar geometry."[367]

The importance of the dew in the process of the sun method can be understood from the work of Guenther Wachsmuth. In the forming of the dew, something is rendered visible and made usable that is related to the breathing in and out of the ethers of the Earth.[368] The Earth exhales and inhales once in the course of each day. It exhales the chemical ether into the light ether zone (the atmosphere) and then draws it back into the solid Earth. The exhalation occurs during and after sunrise. When

---

[363] Katz and Kaminski, *Flower Essences and Homeopathy*, 10.

[364] Howard and Ramsell, "Ye Suffer From Yourselves" in *The Original Writings of Edward Bach*, 62.

[365] Ibid, 68.

[366] From a letter of Dr. Edward Bach quoted in "Ye Suffer From Yourselves" in Howard and Ramsell, *The Original Writings of Edward Bach*, 106.

[367] Katz and Kaminski, *Flower Essences and Homeopathy*, 7.

[368] Guenther Wachsmuth, *The Etheric Formative Forces in Cosmos, Earth and Man: a Path of Investigation into the World of the Living [Vol. 1]*, 49-51.

dew is formed, the chemical ether expands from the center of the Earth outwards and meets the light ether. This process of cosmic breathing is made usable in the sun method. What was a simple act of human potentizing in the case of Hahnemann's homeopathic remedies is now elevated to a process of potentizing involving the whole Earth organism in relation to the cosmos. This explains that though the flowers can be considered very low potencies in relation to conventional homeopathy, they can actually touch soul conditions that homeopathic remedies can only affect at quite high potencies.[369]

To my knowledge nothing has been written about the boiling method, and what it adds to the sun method. However, Dietmar Krämer has started to inquire into the differences between the nineteen flowers of the first group and the nineteen flowers of the second.[370] Krämer has outlined twelve "tracks" starting from one of the twelve initial types, which we can presume—as Bach did—to correspond to the signs of the zodiac. Krämer calls the flowers of this type "communication flower." He then distinguishes "compensation flowers," which correspond to typical neurotic reactions: e.g. showing off the virtue we lack in a carefully willed or studied manner. This state of mind cannot be maintained for long and it finally leads to the states addressed by "de-compensation flowers," which correspond to psychopathological end-states (psychosis). These emotional states need to be treated before the more reversible ones, because they affect the body or threaten to do so. Most of the flowers of the last type correspond to flowers extracted with the sun method, whereas most of de-compensation flowers are obtained with the boiling method. It seems that the boiling method may add potency to the flower.

Hauschka and Bach: Comparison and Conclusion

We have in Hauschka and Bach two ultimate examples of great accomplishments in the scientific field, and breakthroughs that can stimulate research for decades to come, if not more. The work of the two

---

[369] Katz and Kaminski, *Flower Essences and Homeopathy* 7.

[370] Dietmar Krämer, *New Bach Flower Therapies: Healing the Emotional and Spiritual Causes of Illness.*

overlapped in their medical research; however, here the similarities stop, and a fascinating world of differences arises.

Dr. Bach lived a stormier and more adventuresome life. He was able to take on sudden new directions, based on dim inspirations dictated by the voice of his conscience; inspirations that he knew he could not ignore. And everything in his life had an air of drama: his near death at the hand of cancer; his sudden professional changes; his striking discoveries of one plant after another (each with unusual stories of its own) or the never-ending illnesses that pushed him to search for the second series of nineteen remedies. He was eminently able to follow his inner voice, no matter what the personal cost: sacrificing successful careers and reputations, undergoing severe physical trials.

Edward Bach is known today for the set of thirty-eight plants which he proved could be used to assuage psychological states that precede illness, or cure the illnesses themselves once they have reached physical manifestation. His inspirations led him to discoveries that he could only corroborate later in time. The idea of moving from bacterial nosodes to plants, of using the power of the dewdrop for medicinal purposes, of moving on from the "sun method" to the "boiling method," and many others, were generally correct. His biography (for instance, what was said to him by people he met) and even his body (his illnesses) were instruments of research. In most, if not all, instances, inspirations led him to find the remedy, in the act of matching the "vibration" of the plant to the "vibration" of the illness—an undoubtedly poor scientific terminology.

It is surprising, to say the least, that in all his work with the thirty-eight plants that now form the Bach flower repertory, the doctor never gave us an explanation as to why the particular plant was chosen, nor a description of the plant or its physio-chemical properties. In speaking of the plants, Dr. Bach seems much more a high priest of antiquity, inspired by sources beyond himself. His conventional scientific worldview could not build an epistemological bridge to his scientific innovations. Much like the German idealists, we could say that Bach took his departure from the "idea-experience," an idea that lived with primal force within his soul, an idea that first manifested unconsciously and that led him to the goal, acquiring firmer ourtlines in the process. In *Heal Thyself*, Dr.

Bach gives us an idea of how this "idea-experience" lived in him: "Truth has no need to be analysed, argued about, or wrapped up in many words. It is realized in a flash, it is part of you."[371] We could speculate about what Bach could have achieved had he met and accepted spiritual science. After all, he was a Mason and deeply interested in occultism.

Dr. Bach acted at a level not dissimilar to Goethe, though his research had less of a theoretical and more of a practical goal. Even more than with Goethe, healers and scientists that are following Dr. Bach will have to understand and render understandable what Bach knew instinctively, below the threshold of consciousness, to render his discoveries truly and fully usable for posterity.

What a different world was occupied by Dr. Hauschka: another fully coherent biography, but another track, so to speak. We can understand Dr. Hauschka to a high degree through his books and what he says about his way of working. In contrast, Dr. Bach becomes understandable when we draw both from his work and his life. The notable threads in Hauschka's life are questions that carry him from childhood on: his first question about infinity through the hyperbola; the silences in the Bruckner symphony; the poem of Peter Rosegger at the time of his confirmation with its intimations of immortality and reincarnation; the memories of his pre-birth intentions; his perceived mission of transforming self, nature and the Earth.

Dr. Hauschka's life unfolds fairly regularly: nothing is highly dramatic, whereas with Dr. Bach almost everything is. In Hauschka's life everything can be understood on the basis of a steady progress, though with intensification and metamorphosis. At an early age his inquisitive mind can look at his town, or at the chemical element antimony, with deeply imaginative insights. He is a master at building, or rather we should say, living in the world of imaginations and describing them. He has reached imaginative consciousness. His book on *The Nature of Substance* is a continuous building of imaginations. The imagination of an element takes life in its polarity with another. To one polarity he

---

[371] Edward Bach, *Heal Thyself*, chapter 3, in Howard and Ramsell, *The Original Writings of Edward Bach*.

adds a second one. To the polarity of hydrogen and oxygen is added that of carbon and nitrogen. And this forms what he calls the "atmospheric cross." These imaginations are completely lawful; nothing is left to a caprice of the moment. Nothing is forced into place. Finally, the whole work itself is a grand imagination, composed of many smaller imaginations. Hauschka lets the imaginations reveal to him the being of the elements he loved from early youth. He saw the imaginations; he portrayed them and made them understandable to others who are willing to make an active effort to grasp them.

Bach set the course for a few centuries ahead. The inspirations he received are like signposts or road maps; they have not been filled in. The work is only outlined, and many others will have to step in to fill in the gaps, complete the edifice, offer the body of imaginations that build his new science of healing. The doctor died exhausted by a task that acted as a slave driver. He reached the goal line and passed away. Others like Hauschka can now work their way backwards and tell us what Dr. Bach meant, what he himself could not have said.

Dr. Bach has much of the soul-type that characterizes a Platonist. His way of working, highly intuitive, parallels that of Goethe, the quintessential Platonist. His strong observational skills led him to the recognition of the seven patient types. Later, through leaps of intuition, he came to the formulation of the sun method and the boiling method. Each new remedy of the thirty-eight was found through a new inspiration. Since he refused the tools of the intellect as a way to organize his body of thinking, he was utterly unable to develop imaginations about the plants he worked with. He was unable to tell why a plant was the remedy to an illness he wanted to counter. However, he could proceed to test his inspirations.

Some of Hauschka's soul affinities are worth mentioning here. He felt very attracted to and impressed by the Celtic Mysteries (Hibernian Mysteries and Celtic Christianity). No doubt, here is a soul attracted to the role of Christ as lord of the elements.[372] And the fact that he was a contemporary of Steiner indicates with a high level of probability that he was an Aristotelian.

---

[372] Hauschka, *At the Dawn of a New Century*, 63.

In a couple of areas of these scientists' work, we can observe some interesting overlap. Both doctors were very familiar with homeopathy: Hauschka could understand the principles at work; Bach could intuit, verify and physically sense that they were far superior remedies to those of allopathic medicine. The two doctors worked at detecting the early stages of an illness: Bach by looking at the soul stage that precedes illness; Hauschka by looking at the physical-etheric changes that accompany the soul states leading to cancer. It's as if the two scientists were looking at the same question from two opposite sides: Bach from within, through the soul states themselves, which were characterized in the prescription of the remedy; Hauschka from the outside, through the subtle changes occurring at the bodily level.

Dr. Hauschka is the quintessential example of the scientist of the future. He cautiously and carefully builds observation after observation, and integrates these with Steiner's indications and a grasp of everything that spiritual science has to offer which is pertinent to his research topic. No doubt inspirations played a role in his life and in his scientific work. Overall, however, it was his capacity to live in imaginations and convey them to posterity that is his trademark legacy. People like Dr. Bach continuously infuse their culture with what appear to be contributions nobody could have foreseen, strokes of genius. These are great contributions, and yet unfinished. It is people like Hauschka that we can expect to shed light on the discoveries of Bach, if they accept and recognize the greatness of such contributions. Dr. Bach may be able to look further into the future. People like Dr. Hauschka can make that future more accessible for the use of all.

CHAPTER 9

ARISTOTELIANS AND PLATONISTS IN THE SOCIAL SCIENCES

In this section we will look at two alternative ways of seeing or approaching the social question, and articulate the idea of the threefold membering of society. The first will be an overview of what Steiner characterized as the threefold social order, building it up concept after concept. The second is the result of collective inquiry into new ways of affecting social reality, built through reflection on experience. It led to the elaboration of the "social processes triangles," a pragmatic way of recognizing and working with the three spheres of society. This formulation came about through the work of the Institute of Cultural Affairs (ICA) in the USA. The overall analysis we will now embark upon will remain impersonal, since on the one hand it brings forth universal imaginations conveyed to us by Steiner, and on the other hand it features the work of ICA, in which no individual names are ever given, nor are they necessary to our survey.

The first analysis, which may be known to many of my readers, will be a simple presentation of Steiner's ideas of threefolding. To understand the second we will have to look not only at the models developed by ICA, but to the social dynamic that made them possible.

Threefolding from the Realm of Ideas

Ever since the Industrial Revolution we have faced choices between the purely pragmatic approach of a capitalism devoid of any new ideas, and the generous but impractical views promoted by socialistic thinking.

Culture under the capitalist system has evolved in two directions. The first simply addresses the requirements of political and economic life. The other turns to man's deeper aspirations but has no more connections with practical life, nor the ability to foster spiritual renewal. Much of culture is carried directly from the past, or re-echoes past impulses without finding a new impetus of its own.

Socialism rightly perceived how capital extended control over social life and over the individual. Its solution was state control over the means of production, and the abstract motivation of work done for society. Ultimately, socialism simply continued the work of capitalism and deepened its materialistic trend. Socialism made of culture a mere superstructure reflecting economic reality. The line of thinking goes something like this: Capitalism has erected a certain culture that reflects its own values; socialism will build up a culture that reflects its own aims. This is the reason for choosing the word "superstructure." In short, no autonomous reality is offered to the sphere of culture. The only tangible realities originate from the economy and politics; culture reflects the interaction of the two. Socialism further devalued the role of culture and drove it away from the public scene, placing great obstacles to its pursuit by the individual.

The dependence of both capitalism and socialism upon the scientific, naturalistic outlook of our time is reflected in the split between inner and outer lives, the continuation of the old dilemma of knowledge versus faith that has accompanied the Western World since the Middle Ages.

Ultimately, Steiner points out, humanity will grow soulless in the social order that is the result of present-day industrialism. A symptom of it appears in the divorce of vocation from human needs and aspirations. Apart from often barely satisfying their material needs, workers find no social and spiritual motivation from their jobs. The rich grow richer and hardly stop to think for what purpose they are amassing capital beyond any possible notion of satisfaction of personal needs. The only alternative to this state of affairs lies in the rise of a truly independent cultural life. The modern soul's aspiration to democracy and economic justice will find its place as a natural consequence of threefolding, with its present emphasis on the strengthening of the cultural sector.

Integrating the Three Spheres

Threefolding sees the landscape of the human being a little as one would a diversified farm. Each part of the landscape—fields for crop production, pastures, orchards, ponds, etc.—must be treated according to its nature, without losing sight of the whole. Each function of the social organism must be kept in balance by the others. The division into three areas of social life will not endanger the ultimate unity, since each human being has interests in all of the areas. This harmonization will be entrusted to specific institutions bringing forth the necessary dialogue.

The cultural sphere founds its wellspring in the life of the spirit. The political life addresses that which is common to all men, that which makes them equal in the realm of soul. The economy addresses the satisfaction of the needs rooted in our bodily nature. Through the membering of social life, the threefold social order (TSO) seeks cultural freedom; democracy and equality under the law; and a feeling for brotherhood in the economy.

The TSO takes for granted the reality of the division of labor and social function that is essential to modern life and cannot be suppressed in the name of a return to the past. As much as the results of the division of labor could be decried in the present state, we should not forget that in the necessity to satisfy other people's needs and have our needs satisfied by a multitude of other members of the economy, lies a potent seed for overcoming egoism. Undoubtedly, however, the division of labor is accompanied by an inescapable consequence: the weakening of interest in one's work. Without interest, a man cannot work; or he will do so only for a time, with a terrible sense of emptiness. The necessary interest will be stimulated from the political arena and from a renewed culture. The cultural life will animate us with the realization that our skills and uniqueness as individuals play a vital function in society. This interest will also derive from being part of a life of rights, which we will help to build. At present, our only gauge of the usefulness of our life lies in monetary compensation. In the TSO it is the unfolding of human faculties and their harmonious cooperation that gives a standard for success. Increase of capital will follow as the natural consequence of the above, not the reverse.

The TSO gives recognition to both conservative and progressive thinking, but lies above political thinking alone. It reconciles the false dilemma of capitalism and socialism at a level that lies higher than either. The TSO is also the only view that gives economy and culture an independent role in the social process by completely emancipating both from the political process. Thus the administration of economic life should be conducted solely upon economic grounds. The administration of cultural concerns, be they schools, universities, museums, churches, spiritual groups would likewise be removed from the political sphere. Let us look more closely at what the membering of the social order tries to achieve.

An Independent Cultural Life

Cultural life is alone able to give meaning, spread new values and be the source from which originates our desire to contribute to social life. Culture is what helps us develop our faculties of judgment and our life of feeling—the supports for true ethical individualism. The state and the economy tone down the development of individualism. Political life brings us together in everything that manifests our commonalities as human beings, not our individuality.

Cultural life cannot be submitted to the will of the whole. A culture subjugated to the criteria of democracy thwarts the development of what is unique in each human being, and therefore deprives society of the continuous innovation and renewal springing from its individual contributions. Education entrusted to the state can only introduce abstract cognitive, aesthetic and moral values into civilization. This is why culture needs to be self-administered along its own lines of interest.

The result of a free cultural life will be individuals that will develop independent cognitive, aesthetic and moral values and will be able to find their place in society by aligning themselves with the dictates of their inner being. Valuable, unique contributions and innovations will thus reach society for the benefit of all. At present schools ask themselves how the individual can best fit into the current order of affairs, into the structures of state and economy. "What can we teach him that will fit him to the job market?" is an often-heard parameter of education. The questions an independent cultural life can ask itself are: "What can each individual contribute that is truly unique, and that would offer society the greatest benefit? And how could we foster that?"

The person who truly evolves within an independent cultural life will not docilely fit into a pre-established plan, into the cogs of a mechanism. In this we can see how the striving for an independent cultural life conflicts with views that ultimately distrust the free contributions of the individual or want to subordinate him firmly to the central authority of the state. It is not surprising that this was, and is, the view of totalitarian regimes. However, in democracies the adverse role of state-controlled education, which works in this very same direction, is rarely perceived and questioned at present.

Cultural life will also have another important role in promoting the vision of a community's development, its quality of life. The cultural life should rightfully determine to what ends land and capital are to be devoted. At present, considerations of capital return, scarcely mitigated by social and ecological considerations, determine land use. In the other scenario cultural interests determined by a community—such as rates of urban growth, quality of the environment, kinds of industrial activity promoted and allowed—may be legitimate grounds for limiting capital returns. Growth based on higher return criteria alone often hurts a community's quality of life.

The role that naturally falls to the state concerns the sphere of rights and everything that serves to protect the integrity of the individual, and all that preserves national integrity from external threats. This is the area that is most readily understood at present. The political sphere brings us together in what is universally human, in what makes us all equal, regardless of cultural background, ethnicity or social standing. Much that is today left to the economy is in reality the concern of the political arena. Thus, human remuneration, hours and length of work, in short anything that concerns labor, lies beyond the rightful reach of the economy. The whole matter of human remuneration was of central interest to Steiner, who saw in the commodification of labor the root of man's estrangement from his work. For Steiner, when the question of labor is equated with wages rather than human needs, the human being is alienated from the forces of karma, which guide our lives on earth.

In the present social order the economy often oversteps its bounds. If the economy steps into legislation, then what comes out of it are only disguised economic decisions that will not take into account the rights of all. A manager of a business is not the best person to ascertain and determine what the legal relationships with his workers should be.

Likewise the political arena can only legislate what ultimately leads to rights, even if it aspires to the welfare of all. All it will ultimately do is protect; it cannot promote or guide production through legislation, nor operate to redistribute wealth. Decisions for the good of all can only be taken in such a way that legal dispositions are completely divorced from business interests, and economic decisions fall away from the sphere of government.

It is in the economic realm that Steiner's ideas on threefolding are truly revolutionary. From what has been said of the cultural and political life derives the realization that an economy true to its nature need concern itself solely with production and circulation of goods.

A truly vibrant economy cannot be subordinated to the political realm, since it responds to its own laws and processes. The economy needs to be run on the basis of individual competence, through the ability to engage in contractual agreements derived from free initiative and conceived for the benefit of all. And much of future economic life should revolve around the creation of new associations.

The Economy and Its Associations

Steiner foresaw that meaning and value will have to flow into the economy from the political and cultural life through the key idea of associative economics. In the new economy, the association will play the role that the individual played in the relatively easy economy of the Middle Ages. Associations are groupings of particular economic sectors bringing together consumers, distributors and producers in order to regulate production, distribution, resource allocations, movement of labor, and so on.

However, associations alone do not purvey the values and meaning that the individual needs in his work. Since it cannot be found in one's occupation alone, given its fragmented nature in the global economy, inner satisfaction derived from work will have to come from a vibrant cultural sphere that imbues the individual with spiritual values. An active participation in political life will enliven our participation in an economic life where our individual rights are upheld. The desire to work will follow more easily when people know that their work is done in a way that guarantees them a dignified human existence.

Associations act a little like a group soul in the economy, a realm whose complexity no individual mind can comprehend. In the economy we truly act out of a will that is mostly unconscious. Associations are like organs of awareness, both informing the individual and raising his sense of integration within the given sector, and his responsibility towards the whole.

Naturally, an association in a sector of the economy will tend to act one-sidedly in its own interests, because the members' perception of reality cannot encompass the whole. This can be tempered when the process is repeated in the other sectors of the economy, and higher-level associations are created for the goal of balancing out the interests of the different sectors and provide an accurate image of the will of the whole.

The justification for economic associations stems not from a humanitarian standpoint, but purely from an economic one. We could say that Steiner favored free trade, although within much stricter parameters than what we intend today as free trade. Steiner realized that although profit-making is an egotistical aim, this is not an argument that can be used for its elimination. Profits are actually what indicates whether a commodity should be produced or not, whether a project is feasible and should be supported. The individual profit motive can only be replaced by the working of economic associations that can coordinate production and consumption and assess real needs, rather than let these assessments take place through the dictates of supply and demand, the cycle of booms and busts in the market. In the threefolded state the profits generated from economic activity—national or international— will benefit all, not just the few as in the capitalist economy.

Land, Means of Production and Credit

Money, in our present financial markets, has become independent from the economy. Money emancipated from human needs supports its own growth, regardless of human aspirations. This consideration leads us to a final important aspect of the work of the economy and its relationships with cultural and political life.

The impetus towards the separation of the spheres of social life gives a new meaning to the idea now considered a holdover of indigenous humanity, that land and means of production are not commodities. Here too, this will not be an attempt to return to the past. In a threefolded society the management of capital assets lies outside the economy. It cannot be assured through heredity, but can only be attributed to an individual or group on the basis of their ability to ensure the optimal performance of assets and capital for the good of all. When an individual no longer works for the good of the whole, the job needs to be transferred to another party with the ability to perform the tasks. The movements of capital will be determined in the sphere of rights and in cultural life.

Finally, the same is true of credit. Under present conditions credit is based upon the likelihood of return on capital. Individual ability becomes secondary to the imperatives of capital. In the TSO, credit will be given for the use of land or means of production to those individuals who can best administer them in response to the goals outlined by the cultural and legal spheres, ascertaining the priority of human needs in a community. The present working of capital obscures human needs through recourse to abstract impersonal notions of supply, demand, market, credit rates, etc. In a threefolded society, someone who receives credit will have to be connected to the local community through the associations, and through them to the whole economic sphere. Associations thus allow the individual to develop a larger sense of responsibility in the economy.

Closing the Cycle

Having seen the importance of the three spheres, we can now "close the cycle" of their relationships. An important idea that Steiner offered is the realization that the economy continuously generates surpluses. In the present view of things, these are said to have their source in capital, or in the resourcefulness of the entrepreneur. The reality is that these belong to the inherent resourcefulness of the human spirit. It is from culture—through research, innovation, education—that we receive the continuous renewal from which derive economic surpluses. This is why the return on capital should flow back into supporting cultural renewal and the individual development that ensures it.

At present, since surpluses cannot disappear, they are invested in products that will create destruction, or that will themselves be destroyed. Such is the case, on one hand, of the whole armaments industry. On the other hand, we have the spread of planned obsolescence, which ensures that products have a shorter lifespan and faster turnover. In the same vein are products that cannot be repaired, recycled or used for other purposes. The alternative of Steiner's scenario—distant as it may be from modern common sense—offers the only possible sustainable future for humanity.

To reach the ideals of a threefolded society, incentives will have to be offered for capital to flow into the arena of culture without strings attached. A vibrant economy will always produce surpluses. For these surpluses not to be a burden on the environment or on social harmony, gifts will have to be given to the arena of culture, which cannot generate its own capital. The above cycle forms what some call a "virtuous cycle." The economy is built up from the realm of culture in ways which, however obvious, are masked from current economic thinking. An economy that only builds itself works as a parasite on the body social. For surpluses to work in a sustainable way, they will have to flow back into the commonwealth, promote education and innovation, and be directed to the development of individual capacities and talents that meet the challenges of the future.

All of Steiner's opus represents the effort to re-enliven culture in the effort to reintroduce a universal spiritual understanding and language that honors humanity's aspirations at the time of the Consciousness Soul. Steiner offered the whole of anthroposophy as a gift that would reconnect a humanity divorced from its spiritual roots to a new source of meaning and values. Many today intuitively know that renewal has to flow into social life from the fountainhead of the spirit, but lack an understanding of how this very same spirit can be more than an abstract repository of meaning and become a concrete, practical tool for societal renewal. The threefold commonwealth tells us that spirit lies at the base of social renewal, while allowing us to see how it does that.

However, the TSO is not per se the guarantee of social happiness, but rather a vision of the conditions under which the spheres of society can be brought to healthy collaboration, to what Steiner called the "healthy social organism." The vision of a healthy social organism can only provide the prerequisites necessary for all that human beings must nurture and develop through their own abilities and needs. Trusting the process of the TSO means doing away with the blind trust in institutions or parties that pervades modern culture, and realizing that whatever the structure, it can be used antisocially. To counteract this we have to rely on the vitality of the cultural realm, which will allow us to correct antisocial tendencies as they develop.

The ideas that concern the threefolding of society offer us clarity about what steps should be taken for making freedom, equality and brotherhood a reality in their respective fields of action. Of greatest importance is the realization that the human being needs to reconnect again to his/her pre-birth intentions. For that purpose there must be a separation between one's role in the economy and financial remuneration. Individual needs must be assured through the associations and legislated in the political body, not determined through pay rates that are derived via the market.

Threefolding awakens a perception of karma and reincarnation. But the contrary is also true. An active and personal understanding of the forces of karma, and ultimately of the reality of reincarnation in our daily lives, is a potent motor for bringing about threefolding. Reconnecting the individual with the forces of his/her destiny strengthens society for the attainment of threefolding. Whenever individuals can take responsibility for their lives through a recognition of their own role in shaping their biography and their communal endeavors, immense creative forces are released and made available that can be used for creative social renewal. We will look at an expression of this reality in the history and work of the Institute of Cultural Affairs.

Threefolding from the Ground Up

What follows relates to the destiny of a group of people who have offered American society a strong impulse for renewal. There are many such groups; however, it is generally difficult to gather enough written information to be able to detect trends and themes of their history. The author was able to gather information and insight about the Institute of Cultural Affairs (ICA) and its ways of working by virtue of having taken a Mastery in Technology of Participation, offered by the Institute. This has given him a direct experience of the social methodology that ICA has produced over decades. One of these methodologies has come surprisingly close to formulating an empirical form of threefolding. It bears the name of "social process triangles."

The Institute of Cultural Affairs and Fifth City

In 1954 the World Council of Churches met in Evanston, Illinois. On that occasion Christian businessmen founded the Evanston Institute of Ecumenical Studies.[373] At the same time, a group of Christian students and staff of the University of Texas (called "The Christian Faith and Life Community") started to research the relationship between faith and contemporary life. Under the direction of Dr. Joseph W. Matthews, the group designed a curriculum for students and laity, the so-called *Religious Studies I.*

In 1962 the Ecumenical Institute appointed Dr. Matthews its new dean, and he brought seven families from Texas with him, who carried on a comprehensive life of Christian worship, study, and service. At this time the initial, small group started the so-called Order: Ecumenical (sic), formed primarily by families of volunteers. The order was modeled after known religious family orders. The mission the order gave itself was church renewal and community development. Three directions

---

[373] The history of ICA is taken from Stuart Umpleby and Alisa Oyler, "A Global Strategy for Human Development: The Work of the Institute of Cultural Affairs," published in *Systems Research and Behavioral Sciences,* vol. 24, # 6, November-December 2007, 645-653, and R. Brian Stanfield, *The Courage to Lead: Transform Self, Transform Society.*

were consistently followed from this moment on: education, research and implementation. The pioneering curriculum emphasized whole-system models. And the Institute's "Fifth City"—a bold and successful experiment in comprehensive community development—was the first major step of implementation.

Between 1962 and 1964, the Institute started offering its courses in Chicago. Its cultural curriculum component presented cutting-edge ideas in cultural disciplines and social structures, with a focus on whole-systems models. The idea was to create models of reality, knowing full well that a model is only relative, yet it should be internally consistent and able to honor traditional wisdom, rather than merely focus on passing fads. There were twelve courses in all: six theoretical and six practical. From 1964 to 1967, some 20,000 people in North America passed through the trainings, which were offered also in Asia, and Australia. Later the curriculum evolved into two parts: one focusing on religious and theological dialogue courses, the other on contemporary social trends.

In 1965 the first Annual Summer Research Assembly took place, and that is where the first practical methods were developed, such as the Focused Conversation, of which more will be said below. From 1971 until the mid-80s, the Global Research Assemblies were convened, gathering in one place up to a thousand or more people from all over the world. By 1968, there were about one hundred people on the Institute's staff.

The original seven families had moved from Texas to Chicago in 1963, where they chose a ghetto neighborhood, with a total of sixteen blocks on the West Side, predominantly African-American. This area later became known as Fifth City, and the Institute of Ecumenical Studies established itself in the heart of the city. The newcomers approached the local population with door-to-door interviews and neighborhood meetings, through which they gained an overall view of the residents' main concerns, and with them, began to design strategies of intervention. This comprehensive approach covered everything from early childhood education and programs for youth, adults and elders to health care, housing and economic revitalization.

The following were some of the approaches:

- Reaching out to teenage gang members, and to teenagers in general, through a fifteen-week course; this was considered important for the future leadership of Fifth City.

- Offering cultural programs for the neighborhood.

- Moving eighteen suburban families, both black and white, back into the city; among them a doctor and a businessman.

The group started rehabilitating apartments and a community center, opened a shopping center that hosted five businesses, and inaugurated an auto service center and a car wash. Fifth City owned equipment with which it could communally improve the infrastructure and the landscape. All this activity attracted the new Bethany Hospital and the CTA Bus Garage, for a total of $40 million in investment; the two organizations employed a total of more than one thousand people in the adjacent neighborhoods. Many partnerships were formed between Fifth City and businesses, local government, and other non-profit organizations, highlighting a tri-sector approach to social development.

Social Process Triangles and the Birth of ICA

Begun as an effort for church renewal and community development, the Ecumenical Institute spread worldwide at the end of the 60s. It took on the name of Institute for Cultural Affairs (ICA) in 1973, to distance itself from the fading ecumenical element, and to acknowledge its global cultural dimension. The decision to change its name was a direct result of an effort undertaken two years earlier, in conjunction with the birth of the "Social Process Triangles." The so-called "Corporate Reading Research Project" was conducted through a comprehensive literature review involving all the Institute's offices throughout the world. This project took one year and covered the study of 1,500 seminal books that explored all aspects of the social question. The work was narrowed down by a core group of about thirty people meeting every weekend during the winter and spring of 1971. This culminated in the summer of 1971 with a gathering of 1,500 people coming to Chicago with the aim of understanding how to look at the issues engaging global society.

The data sifted from the books was used to create a triangular model of the social process. The major insight emerging from the study was that social questions were usually framed in reference to either economic or political dimensions, with health and education services added on. The result of the team effort was the discovery that culture could be added as a third category to politics and the economy, encompassing health and education services, but also much more. Social questions could thus be articulated through the contributions of economic, political, and cultural "commonalities." The understanding of the underrated role of culture was later affirmed in the choice of a name for the renewed organization: the Institute of Cultural Affairs.

The interrelationship of the three commonalities was conceived in this way:

> The ideal (rarely found) is a balanced tension between the economic, the political and the cultural. When this happens, society is in a healthy state. When these three processes of society are not held in balance, society gets sick. When we are deprived of the means of adequate livelihood, political chaos and rioting can result. When we are deprived of participation in the political process, our livelihood is likely to suffer while masters grow rich on the resources denied us. When our culture is taken away from us, we easily become political and economic victims, or find our lives devoid of meaning.[374]

And further:

> To be a social human being is to be inexorably involved in issues of sustenance and survival (economic); of ordering and organizing society to overcome chaos (political); and of education, family and community,

---

[374] Brian Stanfield, *The Courage to Lead*, 151.

and the celebration of life and death (cultural). These three, together with all the particular processes that make them up, create the whole system that we call society, or the social process. Because the social process is systemic, any malfunction in any one part will reverberate through the whole system. The same goes for the good things going on in any one part. In addition, if there is not some kind of basic balance between the three major processes, the whole social process suffers.[375]

Underlying the forces at work in the social field, three drives were defined:

The three major processes of society—economic, political, and cultural—are based on three basic drives found in all humans and in all societies. The first is the *drive for survival, for resources, livelihood, and money*—the economic dimension of life—the "that-without-which" there can be no decision-making and no consciousness.... The second is the *drive for order*, for the organization of society through law-making, and law-enforcing bodies so that there is security and justice for all—the political dimension of society.... Third is the *drive for meaning*, that bleeds significance into both the economic and political dimensions of society. This is the cultural dimension.[376]

Two other models were developed from the Social Process Triangles: Social Process Dynamics and Social Imbalances.[377] All the tools thus developed played a key role in ICA research, training and consulting. The triangles can in effect be applied at every level of reality, from the community to the national and international levels.

---

[375] Jon C. Jenkins and Maureen R. Jenkins, *The Social Process Triangles*, 8.

[376] Ibid, 9.

[377] Ibid, Chapters 5 and 6.

The first-level triangle (Table 9) quite simply introduces the reality of the three commonalities, but it also brings out something beyond the obvious.

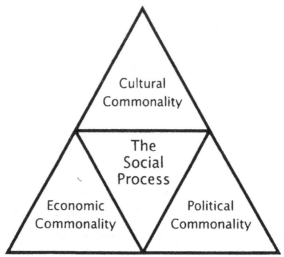

Table 9: Social Process Triangles, first level
(Source: Stanfield, *The Courage to Lead*, 149)

In this triangle we can see the relationships of three parts, which are respectively:

1. Foundational (bottom left): the economy. Without the economy the other two poles cannot go on.

2. Ordering or organizational function (bottom right): "The communal pole, which pertains to the relationship of power and decision-making in the midst of any social group. ...[it] counteracts people's fundamental tendency to destroy each other by creating a social contract."

3. Sustaining meaning-giver (top): culture. "This is the dynamic which dramatizes the uniquely human in the triangle; it is the spirit which makes participation in the social process worthwhile. This is the arena of the symbols, style, and stories which give significance to the whole."[378]

---

[378] Jenkins and Jenkins, *The Social Process Triangles*, 24.

Placing the cultural arena on the top of the triangle is a statement attesting to the determining place it occupies in relation to the other two areas. It is not surprising that ICA also offered one of the earliest global conferences on the emergence of Civil Society in 1996 in Cairo.

Something else emerges from the triangles. Each of the three processes limits, sustains, and creates the other two. Each of the three processes can be broken into its components at deeper levels, and there one would find again the tension between a foundational process (economic component) at the bottom left; a connecting process (political component) at the bottom right; and an informing process (cultural component) at the top.

Let us see what a triangle looks like at the second level. The second level (Table 10) shows how each pole of the triangle repeats the threefold ordering present on the first level. At the second level in the economy we have resources (economic component); production (political component); and distribution (cultural component). At the level of the political commonality we meet corporate order (capacity to enforce the law, providing security for a functional culture); corporate justice (upholds individual rights, ensures equitable structures, providing links between bureaucratic structures and the grassroots); and corporate welfare (assuring that rights and responsibilities serve all citizens, and providing motivation for cooperation).

We can look further at just one example of the third-level triangle. At the third level of the political commonality, in what corresponds to the U.S. national government, we have: executive (economic component); legislative (political component); and judicial (cultural component).

The triangles allow us to place any of the smaller processes in society into a comprehensive context, showing how they are connected to the other areas of the social organism, enabling one to assess the health or imbalance of any given social unit. They can serve to visualize what patterns are at play in any given situation, thus throwing light on where the leverage points are. If action were taken at these points, positive effects would ripple throughout the system.

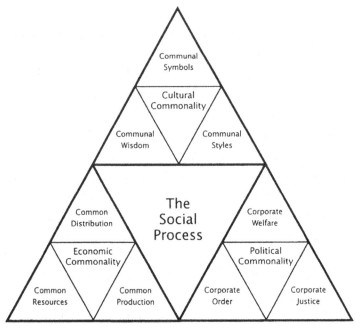

Table 10: Social Process Triangles, second level
(Source: Stanfield, *The Courage to Lead*, 149)

Armed with its whole-systems analysis and the Social Process Triangles, ICA tested its ideas worldwide. After 1975, the Institute established worldwide demonstration community projects, on the pattern of Fifth City—one project in every time zone, twenty-four in all.[379] Each project was meant to be highly accessible to all and staffed by skilled pioneers in economic, social and cultural renewal; it tackled all local issues and involved all local stakeholders. Many an initial project stimulated replication efforts in neighboring communities. This soon amounted to three hundred projects in twenty-five nations.

The projects brought together all stakeholders of the community, voluntary consultants from the public and private sectors and ICA staff. In a week-long conference involving highly participatory processes designed for developing consensus, the partners designed a comprehensive four-year plan of local development. An average of three couples on the ICA payroll remained in the community to teach their

[379] Umpleby and Oyler, "A Global Strategy for Human Development: The Work of the Institute of Cultural Affairs," 2.

whole-system approach to development and offer leadership trainings for an average of four years. Further development was left in the hands of the local community.

Technology of Participation

Prior to seeing the fruits of the work of ICA, a hypothesis had formed in my mind that, given truly participatory processes and inclusion of all needs and all perspectives (covering the three social spheres), threefolding could emerge in the larger social arena outside of anthroposophy, in a form similar to what Steiner formulated from an esoteric perspective. However, I did not know how this hypothesis could be verified, until the Social Process Triangles appeared for my consideration. The history of ICA seems to prove this hypothesis; one would be hard pressed to find Steiner's ideas in any of the achievements of ICA.

I do not mean to imply that the Social Process Triangles render explicit in all aspects the ideas of threefolding; for that, Steiner's concepts become essential. Practical discoveries cannot turn into clearly articulated imaginations, which alone can make threefolding into the living reality that Steiner envisioned. Nor would I imply that Steiner's ideas are not necessary for achieving threefolding in optimal ways.

We will now turn to the other aspect of our investigation. How did ICA awaken a sense for the forces of destiny in its members and affiliated communities? How did it render the life of "the whole" alive, in the sense that Steiner propounds when he speaks of associations?

ICA developed a whole set of facilitation tools which are now branded "Technology of Participation" (ToP). This was a collective elaboration. No individual names are attached to any of these processes: Focused Conversation, Consensus Workshop, Participatory Action Planning, and Participatory Strategic Planning, among others.

What all these processes have in common are four key steps that become more and more complex at higher levels of decision-making. The metamorphosed levels cannot be intellectually determined, from the simpler techniques (Focused Conversation) to the more complex ones (Action Planning, Strategic Planning). Only trial and error could determine them. The higher-level processes incorporate the lower-level processes of Focused Conversation and Consensus Workshop.

A Focused Conversation can be used to study some subject, for informal social purposes, or for decision-making on simple, non-controversial matters. It allows a group to raise issues, expand perspectives, gather data from a large group, and get to the heart of the matter. Practical applications include exploring a topic and seeing the whole picture; reviewing documents/presentations; reviewing events; investigating a far-ranging topic; exploring topics without having to come to a consensus.

The following are the four levels of a Focused Conversation:

- Objective (O) level (perception): questions about facts and external reality.

- Reflective (R) level (inner response): internal response to the data; feelings, moods, emotions, memories, images and associations.

- Interpretive (I) level (judgment): questions to draw out meaning, values, significance and implications.

- Decisional (D) level (decision): to elicit resolution, bring the conversation to a close and make resolves about the future.[380]

Let us move a step further to another participatory process, the Consensus Workshop.[381] A Consensus Workshop works best when there are real decisions to make and real problems to solve; the more concrete the concern and the more pressing the need, the better. It is used for planning, problem-solving, summarizing a group's insights, coming to consensus on a resolution. At the level of the Consensus Workshop the four levels become:

---

[380] Stanfield, *The Art of Focused Conversation: 100 Ways to Access Group Wisdom in the Workplace*.
[381] Stanfield, *The Workshop Book: From Individual Creativity to Group Action*.

1. <u>Brainstorming the ideas</u>: gathers all relevant data. Parallel to objective phase (O) of Focused Conversation (FC).
2. <u>Clustering the ideas</u>: puts similar items together in clusters. Parallel to reflective phase (R) of FC.
3. <u>Naming the clusters</u>: offers a comprehensive picture of the order of all ideas. Parallel to interpretive phase (I) of FC.
4. <u>Resolving to implement the results</u>: moves the group into action, using the Focused Conversation questions. Parallel to decisional step (D) of FC.

The Consensus Workshop includes Focused Conversations, especially at the preview and review stages.

Following the progression upward, the Consensus Workshop is continued in so-called Action Planning, which is also patterned in four steps, and includes elements of both Focused Conversation and Consensus Workshop. It is typically conducted over four to eight hours. And finally, the most complex of the ToP methodologies is Participatory Strategic Planning, which ideally requires from two to three days.

ICA was one of the early pioneers of what is known today as "social technology." Other approaches to social technology have become known of late. Among these are World Café, Open Space Technology, Appreciative Inquiry, Consensus Decision-Making, Conversation Cafés, and others.

Understanding Social Technology: Theory U

Let us build an understanding of what is at work in social technology by adding another step which makes the transition to a theoretical understanding easier. The above processes were discovered and elaborated through years or decades of trial and error. What is remarkable is that they correspond to the first five or six stages of what today is called the "U," as it has been made popular by Otto Scharmer.[382]

In Scharmer's terminology the steps of social technology are:

---

[382] Otto Scharmer, *Theory U: Leading from the Emerging Future; The Social Technology of Presencing.*

- downloading
- seeing
- sensing
- presencing
- crystallizing
- protoyping
- performing

For a summary of the above see Table 11.

We will first look at the terminology as it is presented by Otto Scharmer in his Theory U, then see larger patterns emerge as we touch back on Focused Conversation and Consensus Workshop.

Finally we will show the greater archetype at work behind the "U."

Theory U recognizes seven steps that lead to a complete organizational transformation: one that encompasses head, heart and will. Table 11 refers to the working of an organization (a public agency, business, corporation, non-profit organization or network of organizations), when new processes of dialogue, participation and decision-making are allowed to find expression. In such an entity are both internal stakeholders—those who work within the organization or are financially invested in it—but also all external stakeholders who have a stake in its work. Stakeholders for a corporation that manufactures chemicals are not only its employees, management and suppliers, but also consumers, people who live around the factories, countries that supply raw materials, municipalities and political entities located where the factories operate, NGOs that work with environmental issues, and so forth.

People in normal cultural conditioning do what Otto Scharmer calls "downloading." They reproduce spoken and unspoken cultural patterns: they know what they can talk about and what is off limits; they know how to talk about it, and whom to talk to. In short, they have adapted to a culture that to some degree is resistant to change from within. This is a pattern that social technology aims at modifying.

The first step of transformational dialogue encourages true conversation in which people can soberly assess reality without hiding any of it. At this stage people can start to see the complex web of events, relationships and processes that form their reality. This is the stage of truly seeing, and it is achieved through what is called the "Open Mind." The group will start to see patterns of harmony and progress, and places where conflict and dissonance exist. Reality will appear in all its complexity, showing participants the one-sidedness of their previous judgments. This stage may be overwhelming, but it is a precondition for loosening previous perceptions and allowing the new to form. It calls to mind the interviews that took place in Fifth City, where some five thousand problems were detected. The Ecumenical Institute (later ICA) was not deterred, certain as it was of the reliability of its systems-thinking approach.

Social Technology: Theory U

Table 11: The Steps of Theory U

From the first level of the Open Mind, the participants can start to see patterns emerging and realize that they have unconsciously been part of dysfunctional dynamics as well as of forward-moving processes. Individuals and groups are then encouraged to take responsibility for their part in the collective patterns. Each stakeholder group can understand with empathy the perspectives of the other stakeholders. This is what encourages connection between stakeholders at the level of feelings, and what Scharmer calls the work of the Open Heart. Only after this stage has been experienced can visions and options for action emerge more organically.

When the process is completed, a shift is perceived and the participants acknowledge a common ground from which they can operate, allied with a new enthusiasm and desire for moving into concerted action. Going through the Open Will means being able to let go of predetermined solutions or favored outcomes.

The Open Will sets the stage for something new that has been called "Presencing" (from presence and sensing). Presencing is a space in which the past is put on hold, and the participants can collectively listen to the future that wants to emerge. Letting go makes room for a process of allowing, or in Scharmer's words, "letting come."

Presencing is an experience that suspends all our earthbound perceptions and concepts. It is expressed in as many ways as there are individuals. Here are some samples. "When I am part of a social field that crosses the threshold at the bottom of the U, it feels as if I am participating in the birth of a new world. It is a profound, quieting experience; I feel as if I've been touched by eternal beauty. There is a deep opening of my higher Self," offers Betty Sue Flowers. For Joseph Jaworski, "...moving through the bottom of the U is becoming aware of the incredible beauty of life itself, of becoming re-enchanted with the world.... When the sort of commitment you are talking about happens, you feel as if you're fulfilling your destiny, but you also feel as if you're freer than you've ever been in your life. It's a huge paradox." Otto Scharmer echoes: "For me, the core of Presencing is waking up together—waking up to who we really are by linking with and acting from our highest future Self—and by using the Self as a vehicle for bringing forth new worlds."[383] Although the above testimonials border on the mystic or spiritual, the people who report them are very sober-minded individuals, used to dealing with big business decisions.

After Presencing, "on the other side of the U," the group transitions into decision-making and organizational transformation. At the stage of

---

[383] Peter Senge, C. Otto Scharmer, Joseph Jaworski, Betty Sue Flowers, *Presence: Exploring Profound Change in People, Organizations and Society*, 111, 113, 222 and 234.

crystallizing, previously generated insights acquire focus and direction. Ideas are built upon and acquire more solidity.

Prototyping, which comes next, means nurturing and sustaining pilot initiatives for testing the feasibility of new ideas at a small scale. Because these are part of a concerted effort, it is likely that they will receive all needed support in order to later be replicated. Successful pilot initiatives are then spread throughout the entire organization.

Performing, the final stage of the U, means integrating each step of the transformative process within the culture of the organization. But this word also means more; the organization that wants to "perform" will set in place structures and processes that allow it to operate in a new way at each step of the way. Such an organization will develop organs/structures for seeing, sensing, presencing and co-creating.

Working with the New Group Souls

What appears in the U is something that Steiner has familiarized us with: the seven life processes as they unfold in time. We can now revisit the diagram of the U with the seven life processes in mind, as they have been presented in Chapter 5.

The following are the correspondences we can detect between the stages of the U and the seven life processes:

- downloading (*breathing* in Steiner's life processes terminology): more precisely we should be speaking of suspending downloading
- seeing (*warming*)
- sensing (*nourishing*)
- presencing (*secreting*)
- crystallizing (*maintaining*)
- protoyping (*growing*)
- performing (*reproducing*)

In the act of suspending downloading, we form a better connection with our social environment; we relate to it. In seeing, we create relationship through warmth of interest. In sensing, this goes a step further; what was seen as outside of us is brought into living relationship with the inner life. This is what it means to be able to take responsibility for our behaviors and for our deeds. In presencing, deeper insight is generated, and made utterly individual. This is what is surprising about the ways in which any given individual will describe presencing; such a large reality can only be partially described by any individual, and no two individuals will describe it in quite the same terms. Crystallizing means creating that critical mass of energy through which an organization can step into a new reality. Prototyping leads to shaping new realities: starting at a small level what later can be replicated for the whole organization. When a group is ready for performing, it is able to create the conditions for making the cycle just described an ongoing reality of the organization. It means transforming what is a single experience into a corporate culture.

Let us look at the Focused Conversation. In terms of the seven life processes, all the steps above correspond to stages 1, 2 and 3 (Objective, Reflective, Interpretive), and the last one corresponds to stages 5 and 6 together (Decisional). The reason for the apparent gap is that the unnamed step 4 corresponds to a stage of inner activity, not externally recognizable, the stage that Otto Scharmer calls "presencing." It is the place of shift in which nothing external happens, but through which it is possible to move from the stages of preparation on the one hand to implementation on the other. Without step 4, a group would not be able to move to stages 5 and 6 of the life processes. When step 4 is mentioned in Technology of Participation it is called maieutic (from the Greek "maieutikos," relating to midwifery or, by extension, the process of helping to bring forth a person's latent knowledge). It is a step for "eliciting a sense of wonder and openness to the transcendent dimension of life. It is the skillful use of questions that enable self-reflection and an increasing awareness of collective consciousness."[384]

All of the approaches of Technology of Participation include the first three processes, and then the fifth and the sixth together. The fourth

---

[384] *Cultivating Collective Consciousness with Transcendent Self-presence. A Guided Dialogue Method*, Jean Watts, Pat Miller, PhD, & John Kloepfer, PhD, abstract available at http://www.facilitativeleader.com/pdf_files/ja_ccc_wtsp_03.pdf

step is not a "visible" one, though it is the moment of transformation that characterizes all of ToP methodologies, and of Theory U (see Table 12). Without presencing, the turning point of individualization (fourth life process: secreting), there would be no true Focused Conversation, Consensus Workshop, Action Planning, etc.

Life Processes	Focused Conversation	Consensus Workshop	Theory U
Breathing	Objective level	Brainstorming	Suspending downloading
Warming	Reflective level	Clustering ideas	Seeing
Nourishing	Interpretive level	Naming the clusters	Sensing
Secreting	Maieutic level		Presencing
Maintaining	Decisional	Generating Resolve	Crystallizing
Growing	Level	For action	Prototyping
Reproducing			Performing

Table 12: Life Processes in Relation to Social Processes

The ToP processes allowed true participatory decision-making, through which emerged the will of that which is larger than the sum of the parts. In turn, these processes molded the particular forms through which the Ecumenical Institute evolved into ICA, and through which ICA modeled its interventions globally. Processes and forms were continuously influencing and modifying each other. The ToP processes emerged from the history of ICA and informed its own growth, allowing natural threefolding, in a way that shows the interconnection of processes and outcomes, of participatory decision-making and threefolding.

In the above processes emerges the will of something that is larger than the whole. This is what we can call the "new group consciousness" or the "new group souls." And these "new group souls" speak when strong vessels of mutual trust and harmonious collaboration have been built in a human grouping. Relating this to the Anthroposophical Society, Steiner predicts: "Later [in the future] we shall live in the connections and associations that men create for themselves, uniting in groups with those of similar ideas while retaining their complete freedom and individuality. To realize this is necessary for a right understanding of something like the Anthroposophical Society. The Anthroposophical Society is intended to be a first example of such a voluntary association, although we may be well aware that it has not yet reached very far."[385]

Further in the same lecture cycle, Steiner indicates why groups that allow the working of the new group souls will be important for the future of the earth:

> But when men find themselves together in voluntary associations, they group themselves around centers. The feelings streaming in this way to a center once more give [spiritual] beings the opportunity of working as a kind of group soul, though in a quite different way from the early group souls.... These new beings, however, are compatible with man's complete freedom and individuality. Indeed, in a certain respect we may say that they support their existence on human harmony; it will lie in the souls of men themselves whether or not they give as many as possible of such higher souls the opportunity of descending to man.... The more that associations are formed where feelings of fellowship are developed with complete freedom, the more lofty beings will descend, and the more rapidly the earthly planet will be spiritualized.

The author has felt very privileged to experience this higher spiritual presence in memorable instances, when groups are led, with respect for the inherent laws of the seven life processes, to a deepening of the meaning of life experiences. Where one would normally expect to find the deepest experience of suffering, in the recognition of individual or collective shortcomings, the Easter experience of dying and becoming is

---

[385] Steiner, *The Influence of Spiritual Beings upon Man*, June 1, 1908 lecture.

made possible. It is not necessary to know about the seven life processes or to have an active spiritual life in order to be part of these collective experiences. What is absent in individual knowledge can be rebuilt through the wisdom present in the processes that allow harmonious collaboration of individuals.

Processes and forms have continuously been influencing and modifying each other in the history of ICA. The Technology of Participation (ToP) processes emerged from the history of ICA and informed its own growth. The Social Process Triangles, touching the concepts of threefolding from the ground of experience, emerged quite naturally from studies using the Focused Conversation as their touchstone practice.

The work of ICA, or of Otto Scharmer, clearly indicates that social change hinges upon recognition of the destiny forces, which unite each and every one of us. It rests on the important preconditions of bringing people to hear and know each other in ways that are hardly possible in day-to-day ordinary consciousness. Extraordinary dialogue and ways of meeting are preconditions for breaking molds of thinking, feeling and will, and the gateway to freeing the forces of destiny that call us to common endeavors. Through these the new group souls can manifest.

Integrating Threefolding Ideas and Social Processes

We have finished the analysis of two different ways of conceiving and living social reality. We first looked at a world of imaginations that were built by Steiner in a spiritually scientific way. This is a world of concepts/imaginations that sees the archetypes at work in all social reality. The archetype manifests individually in space and time, i.e. in relation to a country/territory and a particular time in history. This is a world of imaginations that each individual can recreate in his/her own soul. Each time it is born anew in an individual soul, a new contribution is offered to the world. And this effort has spiritually tangible reality; it affects the world around us.

Another path has appeared that is just as universal. It carries here the general name of Institute of Cultural Affairs, and is not linked to any given individual. What made the path of ICA unique was the continuous effort to create moments of true presence, of presencing, moments in which the higher being of a group can be felt. To achieve this state repeatedly means to bring our higher selves to converse with each other; to awaken to the reality of our common destiny; to act collectively with respect for individual freedom; to allow a result that is larger than the sum of the parts; to recognize in social reality the archetypes that form it. Going this way amounts to creating a new social reality that moves in the direction of threefolding, as was manifestly the case with the Social Process Triangles. The first path we have explored in this section is the more Aristotelian; the second, more Platonic.

We can now return to the series of biographies we have examined to see similarities and differences at work. We will first look at similarities between Aristotelian ways of working, then to similarities between Platonic ways of working. From the two will emerge a clear contrast.

Aristotelian and Platonist Approaches to Social Sciences in Perspective

Both Hauschka and van Emmichoven were called poets by their teachers. Neither one of them developed even minimally as a poet, but both had very developed imaginative capacity, and a love for the Word. The same was true of Sergei Prokofieff, who in his youth was literally an inspired poet. Between age seventeen and nineteen, Peter Selg tells us, he received poetic inspiration to write poetry about "spiritual battles and apocalyptic events."[386] Selg evokes the image of the young man being awakened at night by powerful inspirations and rushing to capture the images that flooded his soul, often "putting on paper a poem that had arisen fully formed in [him]."

At around age twenty-one Prokofieff set out to transform anthroposophical ideas "into images filled with life, into imaginations— or at least pre-imaginations." Hearing the words of the Foundation Stone Meditation, he felt deeply touched by the sound of the German

---

[386] Peter Selg, *Sergei O. Prokofieff's Life Work: Memorial Address Held in the Goetheanum Carpentry Building, July 29, 2014*, Anthroposophy Worldwide No 9/14.

words, and was strongly determined to learn it. "Language and content revealed themselves to me for the first time in their inseparable unity."[387] He felt German was the language of the Mysteries of modern times, and it became the language of his spiritual life.

The three individuals mentioned above had a very clear and conscious relationship to the Word; they knew the power of the Word and the tragic reality of the fallen Word in the present time. Hauschka's prose delivers one imagination after another in one of the most poetic works of science that may ever have been produced. Van Emmichoven builds imaginations of the soul with a much more sober language and way of proceeding. Likewise, he guides us through image after image of the Goetheanum building, showing how his soul was transported by the colors and forms of the first Goetheanum in a chapter aptly titled *The Goetheanum as Revelation of the Cosmic Word*.[388] Hauschka sees the processes of the chemical elements; van Emmichoven the processes of the soul in their mobility. The same is also true if we live in the imaginations of the threefold social order as they have been communicated by Steiner and summarized above. In this way we can characterize the Aristotelian pole.

How different the worlds of Edward Bach and Lievegoed, or of ICA! How much more important for them it is to act out of "intuition," or more correctly, Inspiration. What made the Welsh or Dutch doctors unique was their capacity to listen to what the future required of them, and to take steps that weren't quite predictable, nor foreseeable. Dr. Bach gave up one career after another, seemingly just in order to roam the countryside in search of some remedy or another out of common flowers. Dr. Lievegoed wandered far off his profession to listen to the needs of industry, or to evolve curricula for different kinds of schools. Both individuals were able to trust their inner voice and step into completely new territory. They were able to first experience and give themselves to a call, and later to offer answers to questions asked by their environment. Only with hindsight would they realize what had set them in motion; the end goal seems to have been pulling them forward.

---

[387] Peter Selg, *Sergei O. Prokofieff's Life Work*, 4.

[388] F. W. Zeylmans van Emmichoven, *The Foundation Stone*.

Lievegoed was able to elaborate a body of knowledge behind his experiences, whereas the work of Dr. Bach has now begun to be elucidated by his successors. ICA was born as an endeavor to place faith at the heart of one's life and work in the world. It developed a systems-thinking curriculum and set the precedent of community development in Chicago's Fifth City. From there the work took the direction of facilitation tools on one hand, and models of development on the other. And finally, it led to the realization of the importance of culture and the power of civil society. The willingness to create collective spaces of openness let the group unfold in a dynamic and organic way towards successive discoveries.

In self-disclosure, during a lecture, Lievegoed tells us that his major moments of learning most often occurred through relationships in conversation, in lectures he gave which were received earnestly by participants, or in work done with others.[389] This learning had arisen from without, rather than from the inner images that Hauschka or van Emmichoven could produce in their active struggling with spiritual scientific ideas. It is interesting to note that the same was true for Dr. Bach: witness the numerous clues he received from his patients, and from the encounter with the being of the plant. Both Lievegoed and Dr. Bach, or the members of ICA, were adepts on the path of Spirit Recollection. Because of anthroposophy, Lievegoed could also tread the path of Spirit Beholding and offer his discoveries in the language of spiritual science. Thus, he could both develop his work and then make its steps accessible and understandable through spiritual scientific concepts. Without the benefit of anthroposophy, one could surmise, he would have acted in a much more similar way to Dr. Bach.

Dr. Hauschka was a true and pure scientist. What he had to say he could elaborate entirely from the field of natural science. Bach and Lievegoed were doctors, and certainly mastered their field of knowledge. Yet both operated at the intersection of natural sciences and the humanities. In *Heal Thyself,* Bach's soul sounds strangely at home within the field of metaphysics. And Dr. Lievegoed's greatest contributions to posterity lay in the field of social sciences.

---

[389] Lievegoed, *Developing Communities,* 35.

At the heart of the Platonic way of experiencing the world are two elements. The first is a deep immersion in one's field of knowledge. The second is the ability to listen to what the future wills into being, and to be a conduit for it. In Lievegoed's characterization, this is a path in which action or resolve of will precedes knowledge; it rests on the ability to live experientially in a question that life poses us. Results and a clear knowledge about the path pursued will depend on individual ability, and may come long after the initial resolve of will is taken. Lievegoed was able to a large extent to elaborate a coherent body of knowledge based on the work he accomplished in the social field. Dr. Bach was not concerned about it; he was content with offering mankind a new body of homeopathic remedies. His life was a testament to his inner faithfulness to his calling.

Let us see what the Aristotelian/Platonic polarity has to offer to social life and to the renewal of culture.

Social Life in the Views of van Emmichoven and Lievegoed

The different ways of working upon the social world are clearly recognizable in the perspectives of van Emmichoven and Lievegoed. Both of them were quite cognizant of Steiner's injunction of knowing to which stream they belonged. Van Emmichoven had awakened to the reality of his previous lives, triggered by his first encounter with Steiner. Lievegoed had the courage to introduce a way of working which was quite new, precisely because he wanted to bring the impulses of his stream to the fore. He seems to have been indirectly cognizant of the Platonic stream, and what he says about it closely corresponds to his soul make-up.

How did the two doctors see the different paths or streams? Characteristically, they expressed themselves in diametrically polar ways on the subject: van Emmichoven from the depth of his understanding of the Foundation Stone Meditation, Lievegoed out of his experience with innumerable groups of people, or at the hand of his diverse life endeavors.

In a general sense, van Emmichoven believed that sacrifice is crucial for a healthy social life. In his book *Hygiene of the Soul*, the doctor has many fictitious characters offer ideas on various matters. As concerns social life, it is quite indicatively the character of the doctor who speaks what is closest to van Emmichoven's heart. "'Sacrifice,' said the doctor, 'is the only true basis of social life. It is inherent in the mystery of the human "I." The "I," the core of our personality, does not really come forth until it has made the sacrifice of offering its whole being out of love of mankind.'"[390] And further, "'Just as the "I" had to grow first *in* and *through* the community, now a new community will have to be born out of our "I." *That* is the great task before which the human "I" is placed. Like a ferment, the power of the "I" will have to permeate the whole of social life and guide its vital growth.'"[391]

To attain the larger social goal, van Emmichoven asks that more and more conscious individuals take up the development of the I and exert an influence over their fellow men. And this is what can be achieved through exercises and meditation. The calls of the Foundation Stone Meditation outline this very path to self-sacrifice.

The theme of the Christmas Foundation Meeting and the Foundation Stone Meditation occupied van Emmichoven for many years, and he gave numerous lectures on the theme. He was in fact one of the first anthroposophists to draw attention to Steiner's use of the rhythms of the Foundation Stone Meditation. He had meditated on them since 1923. It is worth quoting him at length in the work of his son and biographer: "'Practice spirit remembering' not only means that we learn how our own 'I' is part of God's 'I'—no, out of cosmic heights we hear resound: 'From the divine, humanity takes its existence,' the humanity together with which we must come to a brotherly, social community. Thus 'Practice spirit reflection' (Spirit Mindfulness) is a path of schooling for meeting the being of Christ, the cosmic ego, the 'I' of humanity, to which in the far-distant future all human beings can find their free relationship. The third task set us, 'Practice spirit vision,' is ultimately the path from natural science to spiritual science, from anthropology to anthroposophy."[392]

---

[390] F. W. Zeylmans van Emmichoven, *Hygiene of the Soul*, 177.

[391] Ibid, 177-78.

[392] Emanuel Zeylmans, *Willem Zeylmans van Emmichoven: An Inspiration for Anthroposophy. A biography*, 249.

Notice that van Emmichoven recognizes in Spirit Remembering (Recollection) the path leading to "a brotherly social community." In his book on the Foundation Stone, van Emmichoven further elaborates on this theme and refers to one of the first exercises in *Knowledge of Higher Worlds*: looking back over the day's experiences as a spectator. Then he refers to other exercises, such as looking back at particular phases of one's life, concluding "it should really be possible, after several years of these exercises, to look back on one's whole life as a detached observer."[393]

At the center of Spirit Mindfulness van Emmichoven places everything of the nature of meditation, which centers around meditation itself but is also much more. On one hand, it means recognition of the laws of destiny, through which the individual can feel his own I in the World-Ego of Christ. On the other hand, it addresses the study of anthroposophy, which can start to acquire a more meditative quality and become more than reading with the head.[394] And Spirit Beholding would be "The whole path of knowledge which Rudolf Steiner described... and, indeed the whole of anthroposophy, is a path of spiritual practice."[395]

In effect, even though he mentions practices rather than specific paths, van Emmichoven outlines the very same different attitudes that Lievegoed derives from below, as it were. Lievegoed was used to the practice of letting spiritual scientific ideas fade into the background and seeing them re-emerge from experience. He, too, does not refer specifically to Aristotelian and Platonist streams, but to paths. Lievegoed recognizes two paths:

- a path through clarity of thought, through which one can perceive reality more clearly and live according to the insights that are derived from it.

- a "path of intervention in the reality of the world through the will in which man initiates, works and is effective."[396]

---

[393] F. W. Zeylmans van Emmichoven, *The Foundation Stone*, 42-43.

[394] Ibid, 44.

[395] Ibid, 45.

[396] Lievegoed, *Developing Communities*, 117.

In effect, we have the path of Spirit Beholding in the first, Spirit Recollection in the second. It is the second path that Lievegoed, more than anybody else, introduced into anthroposophy. A third path is also mentioned in the same lectures, to which we will return later.

Referring to the first two paths, Lievegoed concludes: "Thus we have on the one hand the path of the individual who strives mentally and, on the other, the path of the individual who works socially into the earthly foundation process."[397] Taking the example of philosophical matters, Lievegoed points out that here things must be precisely defined, and he thus refers to the first path. "However, in the social realm... one will make no progress in such a way; it is impossible and would be a violation of social life. It leads to an overly strict and inappropriate application of principles in which the drive to form [of the cultural sphere] takes precedence over the living reality."[398] The above basic attitude is, according to Lievegoed, important in the path of the will, "for will-impulses conflict with each other most drastically of all."[399]

The path of the will is one that cannot be taken on one's own; it is the path of community. This is the path that brings us to karmic groups and enables us "to compensate for one another's deficiencies, where each person's Intuition is protected by the others."[400] In these Mysteries we can decide to form a karmic group, not out of the past, but in view of the future. However, nobody can make progress on this path if they do not make progress on the other (the path through clarity of thought). And he judges that the reverse is true: that nobody on the individual (cognitive) path will make progress unless they work socially and deliberately with others, in listening to what is needed from the future and sensing what is coming from our pre-birth intentions. Here Lievegoed shows himself in agreement with van Emmichoven's repeated assertion that the soul works as a unity, meaning that all its processes need to be honored to attain a state of balance and health.

Following the contrast between the practices of the first and third

---

[397] Lievegoed *Developing Communities*, 118.
[398] Ibid, 120.
[399] Ibid, 120.
[400] Ibid, 147.

panels of the Foundation Stone Meditation that is at the center of this book, we could say that Spirit Recollection is the more direct set of practices towards social change; Spirit Beholding can potentially have the deepest effect when a growing number of people engage in it with full determination. Directness and immediacy in one, depth and intensity on the other: this is how the two paths can complement each other in affecting social reality. This is also how Lievegoed complemented van Emmichoven.

According to Lievegoed, the individual path strives towards Imagination, Inspiration and Intuition, in that order. It is the path that every human being takes after death "in order to participate Inspiratively in the 'conversation of the Hierarchies.'"[401] The other path begins with Intuition, which one awakens within the other, then moves to Inspiration and Imagination. And this is a process which places us in the stream of karma, and cannot be navigated alone.

In between the two paths, Lievegoed also places the "path of soul-perception," which is also the artistic way. One who walks this path feels pain whenever a concept becomes fixed. He is also unable to participate in intellectually clever conversations. For a person who primarily follows this path, the soul always experiences new situations, which are fully justified for the individual. And, in the soul, each person is individually unique.

Van Emmichoven was a pioneer, as he shows in his *The Foundation Stone Meditation*, in his understanding of Spirit Recollection. Lievegoed understood the importance of strengthening his own faculty of Spirit Beholding. One can wonder to what degree this work of coming closer to a fuller recognition of the different paths was the result of a long friendship and mutual learning. Lievegoed faced the difficulty of introducing a way of working that was new for the Anthroposophical Society. After all, Platonists were hardly present at the time of Steiner, and what they were going to bring was bound to create surprises. No doubt van Emmichoven himself may have been surprised by the way his colleague operated. He may not have fully understood him; but it

---

[401] Lievegoed, *Developing Communities*, 190-91.

goes to his credit that he felt the need of moving into the future with trust. Lievegoed fully understood the necessity of integrating Spirit Recollection with Spirit Beholding, and thus deepening the kind of knowledge which he had felt to be "boring" when he first approached *The Philosophy of Freedom.*

What the two doctors offered us in their vision of the sources of social change cannot be viewed as alternatives, as either/or. Once again, it is out of such meetings of minds and integration of perspectives that we can see a fuller picture emerge. The greatness of Lievegoed's collaboration with van Emmichoven is such that it allows us to form a picture that is larger than that of each individual contribution. It is a both/and rather than an either/or.

Aristotelians, Platonists and the Culmination in the New Millennium

Steiner's famed and elusive "culmination" at the end of the twentieth century is only possible when Aristotelians and Platonists come together with their different ways of working in the sciences, arts and humanities, and in the social field. Whereas Platonists and Aristotelians can work with a certain independence in their respective strongest fields— Platonists in the humanities, Aristotelians in the sciences—no such thing is possible in the social art. No outcomes will be possible without conditions bringing the whole of the Michaelic movement together. Unless this is made possible, threefolding will hover far above social reality. The limits and failures of either purely Aristotelian or Platonic approaches have appeared on the global stage with clarity. Little has been achieved in the field of threefolding from insisting on the perspective of ideas alone. The promoters of such ideas hold on to a treasure that they may find hard to share with humanity. What ICA achieved through the Social Process Triangles was remarkable; it is sobering to realize that it has all but disappeared from consciousness. Very few know or apply the ideas of the Social Process Triangles at present, and the book has not been republished.

It should be clear from the above analysis that threefolding revolves around both ideas and processes; it is both science and art, theory and practice. It can be reached both from the realm of ideas and from the ground of experience, and best from both. Each individual, and each Michaelic stream, will reach it from their favorite end. But both ends need to meet each other for what is to be a culmination of the Michaelic movement in the third millennium.

Steiner approached the theme of cultural and social renewal with the *Threefolding Memorandum* and books and lectures ever since 1917. Only after that year could he articulate the idea of threefoldness in the social realm, because he had previously discovered and studied threefoldness in the human being. But in 1913 he was already showing social and cultural renewal on stage in *The Souls' Awakening*. In that play, four individuals who have come to know each other through their personal efforts in spiritual development, and through their friendship, embark on the ambitious proposition of placing their spiritual knowledge and personal growth at the service of humanity. Hilary, who takes them aboard his manufacturing enterprise, has the hope of converting spiritual impulses into reality by offering culturally determined, artistically designed articles, and by changing the nature of working relationships within his enterprise, to place it so to speak at the service of the time spirit, Michael.

When the TSO did not yet exist as an idea, individuals on stage were showing the spiritual processes of working together (the Social Mysteries) that made possible the expression of a new social reality. Steiner was already showing in 1913, in an artistic and Platonic way, what he could only later develop with Aristotelian scientific clarity of concepts in 1917. The anthroposophist interested in social work can learn to integrate what is said by Steiner in his books on threefolding, and to see social reality in movement as it is portrayed in his Mystery Dramas, thus bringing together science and art. Something equivalent will have to happen on the social stage, locally, nationally and globally.

CONCLUSIONS

In describing the evolution of philosophy and worldviews from Platonism to Aristotelianism, from Chartres to the Dominicans, from classical German culture to anthroposophy, we are showing a progression that inexorably tends to the Aristotelian schooling of the mind, to the schooling of the senses and to the furthering of Goethean phenomenology into spiritual science. Ultimately all sciences or arts of the future will have to be pursued in fuller consciousness, and scientists or artists will be able to retrace all their steps and make their process completely understandable and usable to those who will follow.

On the basis of the above, a certain confusion may arise. We may become completely focused on the absolute value of truth and its attainment, at the expense of a truly evolutionary view of history. The truth may be set in contrast and opposition to the good that is mapped out by the course of history, or at least that immediate future that has been mapped out in clear understanding by Steiner. Aristotelians and Platonists have continued to evolve their worldviews throughout history and have always incarnated in alternation, with rare exceptions. At present, for the first time, they are incarnating together. Our challenge lies in accepting our differences, and in the fact that the attainment of a more Aristotelian path of the future still requires us to accept the ways in which we all work at present. Otherwise, the good that human collaboration requires in the name of the renewal of culture will stand at odds with a sense of truth too narrowly and too prematurely interpreted.

The above need to move towards Aristotelianism is most completely true in the realm of the natural sciences. We have shown how Dr. Bach's intuitive way of working is both immensely valuable as an addition to homeopathic medicine, and greatly challenging for his successors. Still, it is exactly his example that shows us clearly how a more Platonic style of research (which can undoubtedly not be replicated) can avail itself of an Aristotelian clarity of thought in the research of people like Julian Barnard, Patricia Kaminski and Richard Katz, or Dietmar Kramer, who have furthered the work of the Welsh doctor. Isn't this an example of how the streams can work together?

A decidedly Platonic way of working is paving great avenues in the arena of human development. Here the Platonic outlook, turning to pure phenomena, has offered great results to the world. We have explored at length the work of Marshall Rosenberg and his Nonviolent Communication. At present it has become a science and art that has offered many individuals invaluable self-understanding and progress in tackling and integrating challenging life experiences. Much the same could be said about the work of Alcoholics Anonymous and Twelve Step, Bert Hellinger's Family Constellations, Elizabeth Kübler-Ross's hospice work, and so on. These have been explored at length in *A Revolution of Hope.*[402] All of these approaches have in common with those that owe their origin to anthroposophy a complete departure from tradition and dogma, and an almost exclusive reliance on phenomena. The work that has developed from the above authors and groups has a validity of its own; it is already fully operational. The Aristotelian complement can offer a spiritual- scientific understanding that increases self-consciousness; it can add a body of thought that elucidates what is at work in general principles, and in the countless experiences that individuals have had over decades.

Matters stand differently when we explore the social sciences. Here art and science stand in balance, and the work of the Platonists naturally complements what the Aristotelians have to offer. Here too, much of what has been offered to the world through trial and error, and intuition, can be raised to the light of a new understanding. Much that has been done instinctively can now be elucidated, further understood through spiritual science, improved or modified. The work of Otto Scharmer has

---

[402] Luigi Morelli, *A Revolution of Hope: Spirituality, Cultural Renewal and Social Change*, Chapter 6.

laid a theoretical foundation for much that American social innovators have done in the last forty years, starting with organizations like the Institute of Cultural Affairs. It is only natural that in the social sciences, more than anywhere else, we will depend on a fuller cooperation of the twin impulses if we want to reach the necessary renewal of culture that the Earth needs in the new millennium.

Steiner's Mystery Dramas offer us an artistic understanding of what it means to move towards the culmination in our time. Individuals of every possible inclination and stream (including Manicheans and Rosicrucians) work side by side. They are challenged to integrate far larger differences than the ones we have spoken about in this book. These individuals work in ways that cover not just what we see most in our circles, but what we often find outside of them. Suffice it to mention the seer Theodora, or the spiritual recluse Felix, who play an important role throughout the plays. Steiner met individuals of this kind in his own life. They played a role in his development and he led many of them to anthroposophy. In the plays Benedictus, who is much Steiner's counterpart, educates them and lets their own gifts benefit his whole circle. The various individuals may converge towards more uniform ways of working in future lifetimes; meanwhile they are still strikingly different, and unpredictably so. The integration of such a disparate group of people presents challenges upon challenges over the course of the four plays. However, they are called together by destiny, and only the integration of their different gifts can produce the "culminations" that the Mystery Dramas exhibit on stage.

When we look at organized anthroposophical circles of the present, it seems that Aristotelians can more easily find themselves at home. Their presence within anthroposophical circles comes almost as a matter of fact; the doors can open for them more easily. They can also more easily and fully articulate the uniqueness and the contributions of spiritual science. Platonists within anthroposophy often allow people to benefit from the fruits of anthroposophy more indirectly. They can more easily blend with the larger culture and speak its language. They tend to resist the thorough education of the intellect, and it is more natural for them to express their knowledge in broader terms closer to popular culture. Lievegoed did this in a conscious manner. He could, as it were, speak two languages: "high anthroposophy" with his colleagues within the Society or its movements, and "popular anthroposophy" with those who had no exposure to spiritual science. In his own words, he offered "sensible social concepts" to those who asked him for some new ideas. These were nothing else than socially accessible anthroposophical concepts couched in the language and context of the recipient.

Bernard Lievegoed was a pioneer of the work of moral technique, starting from the 1950s. Before him, only the work of Alcoholics Anonymous and Twelve Step in the 1930s had fully developed other aspects of moral technique. And it was only after him that phenomena like Nonviolent Communication or social technology and Theory U emerged. The art of the Dutch doctor has become evident in his successors, though these developed completely independently from Lievegoed's work. Nonviolent Communication and social technology are further developments of the work of moral technique and an expression of Spirit Recollection, and they bring the work of Lievegoed further. They are the expressions of modern Platonism.

Twelve Senses and Seven Life Processes

We have touched in the previous chapter on one important difference in the work of Aristotelians and Platonists. We can now present it in a new form. The Aristotelians look primarily at the education of the twelve senses, which is essential for Spirit Beholding; the Platonists work more deeply with the seven life processes, which are found underneath all the work of Spirit Recollection, and which can be found behind every single expression of it. In our previous explorations we have referred to how the U graph corresponds to the work of Nonviolent Communication (NVC), Twelve Step or social technology (Theory U). It is symptomatic that Steiner, working mostly with Aristotelians, fully developed the work of the senses, and only offered outlines of what it meant to work with the seven life processes. In his time little was done with them.

Through the twelve senses the Aristotelian individual looks out at the world of phenomena, elaborating concepts and, ultimately, developing imaginations. The Platonists develop the inner skills through the seven life processes. They are at home in soul processes and in everything that is human development. Moral technique is a particular expression of this.

Naturally, the above is only true in a very schematic sense. As van Emmichoven would remind us, the soul operates as a unity. There are no twelve senses without seven life processes. Emphasizing one at the expense of the other generates first one-sidedness, then soul imbalances. So as anthroposophists it is as much our work to develop a science of observation leading to the right concepts, as it is to familiarize ourselves with processes, development and moral technique and to acquire a feeling for what destiny is bringing into our lives. This will allow us to look at the world of phenomena with a fuller understanding, but also awaken an understanding for how karma operates in our circles, and allow us to unite our wills in concert with the spiritual world.

Integrating the Twelve Senses with the Seven Life Processes

Let us look closely at the work of Coenraad van Houten to have an idea of what this integration of work with the senses and life processes could be. The Dutch researcher, very much inspired by Lievegoed, has brought together the perspective of the twelve senses and the seven life processes, and offers an integration of these, though certainly from a more Platonic perspective.

In Adult Learning, Coen van Houten shows how anthroposophical learning is conditioned by the seven life processes. (See tables 13 and 14) The seven life processes are breathing, warming, nourishing, secreting/individualizing, maintaining, growing and reproducing. In Adult Learning they become observing, relating, digesting, individualizing, exercising, growing new faculties, developing new creativity.[403]

In breathing/observing we take in the external world through the gateway of the senses. The education of the senses forms an important premise to all subsequent work, and it is taken for granted and not developed in depth in van Houten's work. Warming/relating adds a qualitative

---

[403] Coenraad vanHouten, *Awakening the Will: Principles and Processes in Adult Education.*

relationship to our working with the senses. Ego warmth awakens interest and creates a personal connection with the object of our learning.

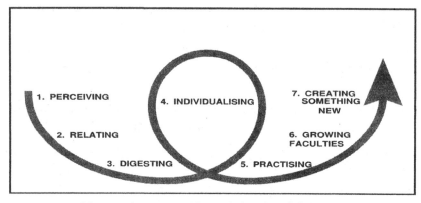

Table 13: The Seven Life Processes in Adult Learning
(From Coen van Houten, *Awakening the Will*, p. 40)

Nourishing/digesting and secreting/individualizing can be taken to mean "intellectual nutrition." We should not take the world in passively; we can observe it carefully, question it, compare what we receive with our store of experiences. This is an analytical process, very similar to what is done in materialistic science. However, we need to move further than this step of nourishing. Through the forces of our ego we unite with what we have assimilated and begin to make it our own; this is the fourth step of individualizing our learning. True knowledge is more than just assimilation of external material; it puts into motion the forces of will. Therefore it effects a change in our being. And this makes Adult Learning different from conventional learning.

Individualizing is a turning point, after which comes the step of maintaining/exercising. To deepen our understanding of a topic we can use rhythm and repetition, and adopt new ways to approach it. After that we can also go to the next step of stimulating new faculties. New capacities can be developed by designing sets of practices and exercises that address the primary challenges we encounter in our learning. Do we feel we need to strengthen our observation skills? Or is it our aesthetic judgment that needs help? Do we experience blockages in any of the seven life processes? Once a goal is discerned, we can devise exercises to help us reach the goal. When this is accomplished, we will be better learners the next time around.

The name given to the seventh and last stage is reproduction/creativity. It means attaining the ability to re-elaborate what we have taken from the environment and our inner activity. Reproducing means creating something completely new out of our inner activity. We are now able to bring forth from within what we had acquired from without; we can approach and expose the subject without the need for books or external references. The three processes before individualizing are similar in some degree to the scientific/analytic approach; the last three processes are stages of higher synthesis.

Adult Learning is primarily the activity of educating our senses, of strengthening our observation skills, coupled with the ability to form ideas from the phenomena and flee the temptation to formulate theories. We may think that emphasizing these premises alone and following a clear methodology could be a sufficient prerequisite for the work in and of itself. An individual like Hauschka was probably eminently suited to enter this modality of learning by the grace acquired in previous incarnations. He was in fact a master at observing and elevating concepts derived from phenomena into imaginations. This could also be the case for many who have received a Waldorf education. However, it may not be a given for everybody.

Our education may have hindered our observation skills, our aesthetic or moral judgment; or our personality may present us with inherent challenges. Whatever the reason, the reeducation of our learning faculties will benefit from the work that Coen van Houten recommends through knowledge of the seven life processes. Approaching the matter this way awakens the consciousness of our strengths and challenges in "learning to learn"; it allows us to form a corrective plan of study, and to awaken the will in the direction that is needed. Once the most important lessons are assimilated, we can in effect just work with the skills we have acquired, or occasionally brush up on them.

We could say that Adult Learning is primarily the activity of the twelve senses, assisted and strengthened through the seven life processes. Much more could be said about it specifically concerning the education of the senses, which van Houten quite simply takes for granted.

Things stand in different terms with Destiny Learning, or "learning from life." What is given below as one sequence is more often than not the work of various Destiny Learning events (See Table 14: Destiny Learning in relation to Adult Education and Spiritual Research).[404] It will most likely not be as linear as it is made to appear below, and may take months or years. What we are presenting serves more as a possible archetype that can be realized in many variations.

Destiny Learning too, like Adult Learning, starts from the activity of the senses. The first step of "breathing" consists in looking at a significant event in our biography as clearly and objectively as possible. The setting, the individuals involved, the details of the environment, as well as feelings, sensations, thoughts, and everything experienced inwardly are remembered vividly. This is a way of "breathing in" the event. In the second step, warming, we place this event in the flow of our biography. We give the event a place in our biography, and realize how it has contributed to shaping our life. Very often the event is one of many similar events in our life, and we now start to recognize a gesture common to all of them. The next step is that of nourishing, and it leads us to surmise the common origin of the events and the learning task that emerges from them. In this step we try to reach the deeper, originating causes in a previous life; we wrestle for self-knowledge. The first question may be "What are the deeper causes of events in my destiny?" The second one requires an inner taking of responsibility: "What is this event trying to tell me, and what inner capacities do I need to develop in order to transform challenge into opportunity?"

Individualizing/accepting our destiny, the central step of the process, implies great will effort, since it requires complete identification with the event. At this stage it is no longer possible to waver and hold on to regrets. We now have to recognize and accept the way the double hides itself from us, be it in guilt and denial, anger and violence, or anything in between. We will either meet Luciferic doubles that estrange us from our real task through love of self, or Ahrimanic doubles that chain us to the reality of the five senses, to fixed concepts and acquired

---

[404] See van Houten, *Practising Destiny: Principles and Processes in Adult Learning* and *The Threefold Nature of Destiny Learning*

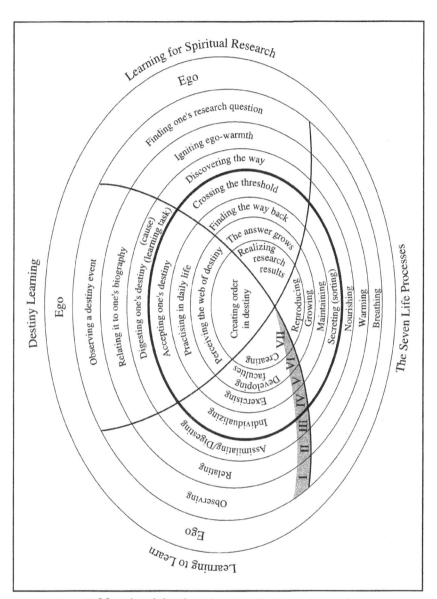

Table 14: Adult Education, Destiny Learning and
Spiritual Research in Relation to the Seven Life Processes
(From C. van Houten, *Practising Destiny*, p. 15).

habits. Behind these doubles looms our higher self, which orchestrates the events of our life.In the next step, we will work at transforming the double we have just recognized. Through specially designed exercises and assignments, we will first have a clear view of how our double limits our freedom in meeting new situations.

Transforming our double can only be done in small increments, with what we can call "freer deeds," small steps that we can accomplish daily that are commensurate to our inner strength. This can be started in the realm of thinking, e.g. modifying the way in which we think of a person. To this change of mind can be added small deeds: saying something cordial, offering greetings, setting a time to talk with the person, taking a step out of our ordinary routine, etc. Any such step will certainly prompt an inner reaction from our double. We can turn to journaling to gain an understanding of our patterns of behavior and acquire insights as to how to transform them.

The next steps lies in the far future for most of present-day humanity. It means developing faculties of karmic perception, and bringing order into one's karma. All the steps we have taken so far will help us awaken the ability to sense the forces of destiny. Our double, having become more familiar to us, gradually acquires the role of guide, indicating to us what could be the next steps we should take.

When entering the last two stages we become agents for social change. We will be able to have deeper insights into what a situation calls for; and we can work effectively outside of our past karmic ties, our "moon karma." We now know true freedom and can create new "sun karma."

As we may have sensed from what is said above, there is a marked contrast between Adult Education and Destiny Learning. This is because Destiny Learning makes primary recourse to the activities of reviewing, evaluating and previewing. These occur primarily through the seven life processes, secondarily through the twelve senses. Accurate observation and precise thinking serve as a support in looking at the destiny event and in confining oneself to the facts, avoiding interpretation. For the rest, learning follows the activity of the will. Learning is generated from within since something has to be set in motion before we can see its effects in the world, review it, evaluate it, and conceive of a next step.

Through Destiny Learning we become more aware of the element of development; of how we grow from looking back at various events in our lives and see relationships between events; of how gestures emerge that are unique to our karmic being. It is quite natural to move into the stages of observing/thinking, to feeling and will. The same is true when we look at social technology such as Technology of Participation. A group that works harmoniously has to develop common insights and come to common decisions by walking through the steps of Open Mind, Open Heart, Open Will, by descending into the life processes through the so-called "U."

Uniting Senses and Processes in Spiritual Research

To repeat van Emmichoven, the life of the soul is a unity. We cannot favor one soul activity at the expense of another without suffering consequences over the medium and long term. This is expressed most clearly in the last path that Coen van Houten sees as a step further than Adult Learning and Destiny Learning: Spiritual Research (See Tables 14 and 15).[405] Here the term Spiritual Research stands as a particular expression and method of the much larger field of spiritual research.

Spiritual Research is the culmination of the other two paths. We are only able to conduct Spiritual Research when we have made the fruits of anthroposophy our own, when we have thoroughly grasped and individualized some part of anthroposophy, when it lives in us independently of external supports; ideally we can "reproduce" it because we have perfected our adult education in the field. However, another precondition is also needed.

Spiritual research is utterly personal. The same question, developed by two distinct individuals, carries different connotations and needs be developed in utterly individual terms. Our questions are personal because they are linked to our biography, and not only our earthly biography. Unless grace has equipped us with strong self-determination, we need to develop a sense for our being in time, an ability to transcend our life challenges so that the questions we ask are not colored, influenced

---

[405] van Houten, _Creative Spiritual Research: Awakening the Individual Spirit._

and conditioned by our life experiences. The responses need to be universal, after all. The researcher needs to reach objectivity. In other words, we cannot do spiritual research out of curiosity, nor out of our raw life questions. We can do spiritual research based on our pre-birth intentions and assisted by our understanding of anthroposophy, once we have mastered a certain topic, and cleared the obstacles that karma has placed in our way. Here we see how the more Aristotelian approach of Adult Learning assisted by the more Platonic Destiny Learning helps us reach the goal of Spiritual Research, through which anthroposophy is enriched by new individual contributions.

Life processes	Learning processes	Spiritual research path
1. breathing	Observation	Encounter and recognize my research question (a questioning observation)
2. warming	Connecting	Creating research warmth through free ego activity
3. nourishing	Spiritual digesting	Finding and going on the path. Method and schooling become one
4. secreting	Individualizing	The answer breaks through out of the other world, and will be researched through independent encounter
5. maintaining	Exercising	Finding the way back to this world and being able to express in words
6. growing	Developing new faculties	An answer grows in this world, becomes earth ripe, checking, applying, making operational
7. reproducing	Creating	Realizing the research results

Table 15: An Overview of Spiritual Research
(From Coen van Houten, *Creative Spiritual Research*, p. 31)

How Can Aristotelians and Platonists Help Each Other?

From the above we can start to surmise how some Michaelites can serve the others. Aristotelians can teach Platonists to cultivate the rigor of thought, to acquire method and discipline in learning. They can teach them not to extrapolate or form hazardous hypotheses. They can train them in the rigor of the word. Lievegoed learned much of this at the feet of van Emmichoven.

Platonists can teach Aristotelians to integrate life experiences, to use them as the basis for their research questions. They can familiarize them with the necessity of individual processes, and offer discrimination in that realm. Most of all, they can help them take the steps from moral imagination to moral technique. This is probably what van Emmichoven intuited when he passed the baton of the Dutch Anthroposophical Society to his younger "brother."

It remains to be seen how the smaller group culminations can become the culmination in our time. How can we bring the above ideas to fertilize our working together in groups, branches, institutions, organizations, and in the Anthroposophical Society itself? To borrow the terminology that Steiner used with W. J. Stein, "How can we bring together anthroposophical thought with anthroposophical life?" And how can these encourage the convergence of the twin streams in social life? It goes without saying that what is said here is only very general, an indication of directions of force.

Many Small "Culminations"

We often live in a false dilemma: the idea that differing on ideas necessitates creating further separation among ourselves; or that a certain social peace can only be superficial and be carried out at the expense of the integrity of anthroposophy, that in order to have peace we cannot really say what we think. The two aspirations are really not exclusive.

We need not dilute the force of our ideas in order to find social peace. Attaining certainty in matters of knowledge cannot be submitted to a democratic vote, or be reached through a compromise. And at times this will mean standing in a minority in defense of anthroposophy. However, things stand differently when we are trying to work together. In this instance ideas can be used as a shield for justifying personal opposition. It is much easier to hide behind some Steiner quote than to admit to others, or even to oneself, that the problem lies elsewhere. Striving for the right ideas is essential to anthroposophy. It is a work that we all need to carry individually. Here, what van Emmichoven says about the role of the individual for social change is central. Individuals who strive to seek the truth, and who are ready to sacrifice their fully formed I for the common good, are the leaven of a social future.

So what would Lievegoed add to this? When we meet each other and strive to do work together (not to discern eternal truths), there is no such thing as the absolute reality of an object, and no possibility of convincing each other about it. The same object has very different significance for two or more people. The only thing that makes sense is to consider the other person's world of significance in relation to an object. This means approaching the reality of working together from a vantage point that is the polar opposite to the first. We can meet the world of ideas with our force of thought. We can only meet the inner worlds of other people by knowing their expressions of will and feelings first, and of thought last of all. This requires the moral technique of empathic listening, and other moral tools that allow us to dialogue, deliberate and take action.

From the above we can arrive at the conclusion that we need to pay equal attention to ideas and processes, to the "what" as much as to the "how." The "what" is most easily addressed at the individual level, each on our own before we attempt it collectively. The "how" becomes crucial if we want to reach the good that "through our hearts we may found and through our heads direct with single purpose."

Anthroposophy has rarely, if ever, lost the capacity to look at the "what." It can strengthen it, but it will not lose it. However, the idea of paying attention to the "how" has lived within our circles with varying success. It can be reintroduced or strengthened at all levels.

At the levels of organization of all sizes, paying attention to the "how" means looking at processes, and making possible the presence of new group souls, which will only unite with human beings who live and work in harmony. Such is the striving necessary to embody this reality, that the new group souls will bless groups of people working together for short moments in time, and then retreat. However, the conditions and practices must be present to allow such hierarchical beings to bless human activity again and again.

What is described here is a very large field of human reality. It applies to all levels of social reality. At the simpler level, it means for individuals to be able to recognize their places in the web of destiny, to have a sense for their biographic and karmic being. In personal relationships it means being able to know each other intimately and communicate consciously and productively. At the organizational level, this translates into allowing the form of leadership that is in keeping with the consciousness soul, which Lievegoed called "wandering leadership." At another level, Spirit Recollection extends to the understanding of the phases of development of individuals and organizations. And history is to the larger communal body what biography is for the individual.

Below are some of the goals we may want to address at group and organizational levels:

- pay attention to the way we communicate to each other, in order to strengthen understanding and render conflict productive;

- strengthen organizations through clear goals and a strong reality of inclusion for all members;

- in organizations, use participatory processes of decision-making that allow the stage of presencing to be reached;

- move toward the embodiment of the fundamental sociological law,[406] that organizations are made for people, and not the reverse, in the time of the Consciousness Soul;

[406] Published by Steiner in two articles and now collected in GA 31 of 1898: for a presentation of it see Dieter Brüll, *The Mysteries of Social Encounters*.

- have meetings that give equal importance to connection and to results; doing both at the same time actually improves both connection and results;

- do the same with conferences: tend to content as well as to quality of connection and breathing quality of the whole;

- increase the appeal of anthroposophy through the conjunction of strong ideas and strong heart spaces;

- lessen the feeling of a difference between our anthroposophical circles and an "outside world";

- approach the re-founding of the General Anthroposophical Society as an undertaking that rests both on understanding of anthroposophical truth and the ability to form strong vessels for the new group souls: the ability to bring together anthroposophical thinking and anthroposophical life;

- develop a feeling for the stream to which we belong, and the curiosity to understand people of the other stream; when we become aware of our stream, a feeling of one-sidedness should ensue, together with a drive to completion that naturally moves us to seek the other stream.

Deepening our personal sense for the truth cannot come into conflict with strengthening the perception of the forces of destiny that bring us together. Both things are equally important. And both were equally important in Steiner's life. If standing for the truth had been the only concern Steiner had in regard to Friedrich Nietzsche, all he would have had to do would be to write an inflammatory article against the philosopher, and distance himself from him as much as possible. After all, why risk his scientific reputation once more upon one the world considered a "loser"? Let us not forget that what Steiner said about Nietzsche, he rarely said about anybody else. He called his *Ecce Homo* and his *Antichrist* the work of Ahriman, no less. And yet, on the other hand, he took considerable time to dispose of his literary estate and restore the reputation of a man who had turned insane, at the heavy expense of his own personal reputation. This culminated in Steiner's book *Nietzsche, a Fighter for Freedom*.

Nietzsche was not just an individual who had gone astray. He was much more than that: he was an important individuality with a mission to carry for the good of humankind. On it depended many other individuals and the course of European civilization, to some extent. Attacking some of his ideas was necessary, and Steiner did not shrink from that; he did it with the utmost honesty. He did not attack the individual, however, because he could perceive the importance of his eternal self and the multiple links of destiny that converged upon him. What Aquinas did with Averroes in the time of the Intellectual Soul— unconditionally attack the individual's thought without concern for a personal connection with Averroes's soul—can no longer be justified in the time of the Consciousness Soul, when it actually works against doing the good, which is central to our epoch.

We need to give equal importance to both aspects of Steiner: the fighter for truth, and the individual endowed with the utmost capacity to discern the forces of destiny and allow each individual to remain free. And something else is possible at the social level, something that concerns threefolding itself, which we have already broached in the previous chapters, and which we can revisit and amplify here.

And the Larger Culmination

Threefolding is both a science and an art. The concepts of threefolding live in imaginations, and they are the basis for the "artistic science" aspect of it. The processes which will allow us to embody threefolding in the particular context of our environments form the "scientific art." This second one lies in the living apprehension of the reality of karma and reincarnation, in the ability to work with the life processes at any given level of social reality.

Let us look at one possible example of what is described above. Two authors have offered sizeable contributions to the impulse of threefolding in the modern world: Nicanor Perlas with *Shaping Globalization: Civil*

Society, Cultural Power and Threefolding (2000) and Otto Scharmer with *Theory U: Leading from the Future as it Emerges* (2007). It is certainly beyond this author to want to pigeon-hole either author as Aristotelian or Platonist; rather to outline the tendencies at play in their work. The following has simply emerged organically from a deep study of the two books mentioned.

In the first book, Perlas offers us a new way of seeing global social reality, of turning the challenge of economic globalization into an opportunity. We know that threefolding is a natural aspiration of the human soul of the present. It may not be realized consciously; even so, conditions move under the surface of social reality in that direction. Perlas has had the courage to face a present of apparent despair to wrest from it a new understanding that creates the conditions for change and for hope. It is Perlas who has underlined the cultural role of global civil society and the existing possibility of a revolution of values that can serve society and move it towards a threefold membering. He has outlined where cultural power lies, and how it can emerge to full self-consciousness; he has explored the emerging tri-sector partnerships and how they can create a new social reality, if civil society will not merely let itself be co-opted by the other two sectors. In short, he has brought us a new understanding of threefolding, one that follows what Steiner could see in his time, a century earlier. Nicanor Perlas's work offers us the "artistic science" aspect of threefolding.

Of equal importance is Otto Scharmer's *Theory U: Leading from the Emerging Future; The Social Technology of Presencing*. It shows us how so-called "social technology" can allow us to move away from external engagement in politics into fully participatory processes; how we can move beyond the discourse of social utopias, of pure free market or state interventionism, to the inclusion of all social actors and social needs in processes that call us into the future that wants to emerge. In effect, Theory U, and many other similar approaches, serve to reestablish the primacy of the cultural over the political; the primacy of "what is" over what we like to believe; of social reality over ideological readings of it. The practice of Theory U illustrates how organizational and social change follows lawful processes, and how we can avail ourselves of this knowledge in conducting a true social paradigm shift. Theory U speaks of the Open Mind, Open Heart and Open Will as premises for the experience of presencing, upon which hinges the possibility of hearing what the future is calling us into. An organic unfolding of reality takes the place of ideology.

The work of Scharmer renders concrete the possibility of aligning the work of organizations, communities and networks with the new group souls who want to inspire their progress. When all stakeholders are included in a participatory process, members of the three sectors will be present, and the needs of the three spheres will be expressed through them. From these premises the movement towards threefolding can emerge organically. Scharmer's social art forms a complement to Perlas's scientific and living understanding of reality.

Bringing together a new perception of global reality—the "what" that Perlas explores—with the processes that allow social transformation—the "how" that Theory U outlines—builds a bridge between threefolding and the unfolding of the larger forces of destiny that can make threefolding a living reality, between anthroposophical thought and anthroposophical life. The two aspects of social change need to go hand in hand.

Two books, two authors, and the work they have promoted in the world, are offered as an image of where the present and coming future of the convergence of Aristotelian and Platonic streams may lead us. With the above comparison and with the rest of this work I do not intend to point to ultimate solutions: rather to illustrations and examples of a possible future.

APPENDICES
AND
BIBLIOGRAPHY

RUDOLF STEINER'S 1922 CONVERSATION WITH WALTER JOHANNES STEIN IN THE HAGUE

(Translated by John Barnes)

In his *Autobiography*, Rudolf Steiner said that his own path led to spiritual vision. What stood before his soul was what had developed as his destiny from earthly life to earthly life. His mission was to develop this further in concrete ways. But the world first required something else of him, namely the transformation of natural-scientific thinking. The germinal thoughts that are to be found in Goethe first needed to be brought to life. In truth, however, this was Karl Julius Schröer's task, and not his. Thus Steiner decided for the time being to relinquish his own task in order to do what the world needed; he took on Schröer's mission.

"By coming to that decision at that time, I experienced true freedom. I was able to write my *Philosophy of Freedom (The Philosophy of Spiritual Activity)* because I experienced what freedom is." By pointing to this, Rudolf Steiner gave us a key to his destiny. Two forces hold sway in his life. On the one hand, there is all that he took on as his destiny by accepting Schröer's unsolved task as his own. On the other, there is everything that was included in his own destiny. Whoever reads the descriptions in his *Autobiography* with an awareness of this duality will frequently find references to it. When he compared his own views with those that formed themselves in Schröer's spirit, Rudolf Steiner found more than the difference between the thinking of two individuals. He saw the individual standing within the great relationships of historical streams, and he recognized Goethe's spiritual "type" as that of the Platonic school. Just as Goethe thought about the primal plant, so Plato had thought about the ideas that underlie sense-perceptions as their spiritual essence. And Rudolf Steiner found that Schröer, who, as a scholar of Goethe, lived in the realm of Platonic ideas, was no longer capable of finding the bridge that led from the realm of ideas to reality. He saw in Schröer the lonely heights of this super-worldly soul disposition. And that became for Steiner a greater problem for humanity; he felt that finding this bridge was a necessity.

Such were the thoughts that stimulated him to occupy himself with Goethe's *Fairy Tale of the Green Snake and the Beautiful Lily*. He saw the realm of the lily, that is, of the spirit, as existing within the Platonic stream in such a way that contact with the present time could not take place in a living way. He saw the Green Snake, whose task is to form the bridge between the world of the spirit and the world of the senses, driven to the decision to sacrifice herself. The thought of this sacrifice lived in his soul. "The mood in which I entered life in Weimar," so he says in his *Autobiography*, "was colored by my previous deep occupation with Platonism. I believe that this mood helped me orient myself in my work at the Goethe and Schiller archives. How did Plato live in the world of ideas, and how did Goethe? This question occupied me on my walks to and from the archives. It also preoccupied me when I pored over the papers in the Goethe archive." Increasingly, Rudolf Steiner recognized that the gulf between natural science—indeed between science in general—and art and religion, was to be traced back to the one-sided effects of Platonism. He expressed clearly how he understood this relationship in his book *Goethe's World View*. In it he pointed to Aristotle. He says Plato led humanity on a detour into a one-sided overvaluation of the world of ideas. Bacon then created the inverse of Platonism by failing completely to understand the importance of ideas, and basing knowledge exclusively on the sense world. Rudolf Steiner realized that reality lies in the harmonious balance of both; and that Aristotle had shown the way to this balance.

I asked Rudolf Steiner how he saw the place of his own philosophical view within the history of philosophy. He answered, "I have united two elements. From Johann Gottlieb Fichte I learned the deed of "I"-activity, which is withdrawn from the outer world. But from Aristotle I took the fullness of an all-encompassing empiricism. Only one who knows how to complement Fichte with Aristotle will find the whole of reality; and that was my way."

Schröer, however—and with him his whole age—did not find this way (Aristotle's way) to reality. Rudolf Steiner saw Schröer as a symptom of his time. The Dionysian and Apollonian principles were no longer able to find their way to one another. Nietzsche's calamity later showed this to be true. No one had formulated this problem more brilliantly than Nietzsche himself in his *Birth of Tragedy*. Nietzsche saw both of these elements in tragedy. And Rudolf Steiner recognized why Aristotle had given the true definition of tragedy, and Plato had not. Thus Rudolf Steiner's path was clearly indicated: his task was to find a modern continuation of Aristotle's path, a path which, in the present time, could not end with Thomas Aquinas. In scholasticism, reality was given through belief and thinking.

The age of natural science, however, demanded spiritual vision and thinking. In the last chapter of his *Riddles of Philosophy*, Rudolf Steiner emphatically identified the task of the present as finding this path to spiritual vision.

Thus, two streams of history were interwoven in Rudolf Steiner's life; one that came through his own destiny, and one that was represented by all that lived in Schröer's individuality. It was precisely by freely choosing to sacrifice the one for the other that "Anthroposophy" arose in Rudolf Steiner. He said:

"Three elements are interwoven in every experience of freedom. To immediate experience, they appear as a unity; but with the passage of time, they can enter into consciousness as separate entities. One experiences what one is going to do as an inner picture that arises through the free activity of Moral-Imagination. Because one loves it, what one decides to do appears as a true Imagination. The second element that is woven into this unified experience, is that higher powers admonish us to follow the impulse that is arising within us. 'Do it,' the inner voices say, and becoming aware of this is a perceptible Inspiration. Yet there is still a third element woven into this unified experience: Through this free deed one places oneself within outer arenas of destiny into which one would otherwise never have entered. One encounters other people, is led to other places; what was first grasped inwardly through Intuition now approaches one externally as new destiny. This occurs when true Intuition unfolds...You see, these three experiences that are interwoven into one are later separated out, come to consciousness in isolation, so that Imagination, Inspiration, and Intuition become conscious as acts of cognition.

And this subsequent becoming-conscious of what was experienced in the moment of his free deed in relation to Schröer, when Rudolf Steiner took Schröer's destiny upon himself, this is Anthroposophy. "Anthroposophy," he said, "is a human being: the human being that was created through this act of freedom."

I then asked Rudolf Steiner: "After thousands of years have passed, what will still remain of your work?" He answered, "Nothing except *The Philosophy of Spiritual Activity (The Philosophy of Freedom)*. But everything else is contained within it. When someone actualizes the deed of freedom depicted there, he will find the whole content of Anthroposophy." I said, "When you wrote *The Philosophy of Spiritual Activity*, were you already aware of the hierarchies that you describe in your *Outline of Occult Science* and in other places?"

I was conscious of them, [said Rudolf Steiner] but the language I used at that time offered no possibility of articulating that consciousness. That came later. But through *The Philosophy of Spiritual Activity* one can raise oneself to the perception of the human being as a purely spiritual being. And although *The Philosophy of Spiritual Activity* only depicts this, it is still true that one who penetrates to the experience of freedom then perceives the hierarchies in the environs of the spiritual human being. For they are all in the human being, and for spiritual sight, everything that is within the human being arises as spiritual surroundings. Hence, although they are not described in the book, they are nevertheless contained within *The Philosophy of Spiritual Activity.*

I asked further: "What then is the difference between natural-scientific and historical-literary knowledge?" Steiner answered:

The actual knowledge in these domains is this: Natural science comprehends ghosts with its thoughts. You only have to take the word in its original sense. What the cosmos spins, what the planets weave, this is what natural-scientific thinking comprehends. Historical thinking, on the other hand, comprehends "demons," but this word also taken in its noble sense: in the way that Socrates speaks of his *daimonion*, as a guiding spirit, a spirit such as Plutarch speaks of as a good star that men can follow. Each historical fact is a demon in the sense of the Greeks. And when one grasps these two forms of knowledge together, approaches both in their most noble form, then a path opens up. Yes, a true path. Historical thoughts are tentative thoughts, thoughts of an experimental nature. One must ask the world of spiritual beings to ensoul them. Then they correct themselves and become truth over the course of time. And natural-scientific thoughts are also thoughts that are thought by way of experiment. One must present them to the cosmos; then they become artistic pictures, Imaginations. And then, when one treads both these paths simultaneously and achieves natural-scientific Imagination and historical Inspiration, then life itself undergoes change; destiny is transformed.

Then, sacrificing, and celebrating one's destiny, one places oneself into the stream. That is the path, that is anthroposophic knowledge, that is anthroposophic life."

(From: Walter Johannes Stein, *Rudolf Steiner, Dokumentation eines wegweisenden Zusammenwirkens : W.J. Steins Dissertation in ihrem Entstehungsprozess und in ihrer Aktualität; mit Briefen und Aufzeichnungen Rudolf Steiners Korrekturen und Ergä nzungen sowie dem "Haager Gespräch" von 1922,* Thomas Meyer editor, Verlag am Goetheanum, 1985)

UNDERSTANDING OF THE SPIRIT AND CONSCIOUS EXPERIENCE OF DESTINY

(Letter to members # 17 of July 6, 1924)

This week something will be given in the communications addressed to members in these columns, which may serve to bring us to a further understanding of the weekly 'Leading Thoughts'.

The understanding of Anthroposophical truth can be furthered if the relation which exists between man and the world is constantly brought before the human soul.

When man turns his attention to the World into which he is born and out of which he dies, he is surrounded in the first place by the fullness of his sense-impressions. He forms thoughts about these sense-impressions.

In bringing the following to his consciousness: 'I am forming thoughts about what my senses reveal to me as the world', he has already come to the point where he can contemplate himself. He can say to himself: In my thoughts 'I' live. The world gives me the opportunity of experiencing *myself* in thought. I find myself in the thoughts in which I contemplate the world.

And continuing to reflect in this way, he ceases to be conscious of the world; he becomes conscious of the 'I'. He ceases to have the world before him; he begins to experience the self.

If the experience be reversed, and the attention directed to the inner life in which the world is mirrored, then those events emerge into consciousness which belong to our life's destiny, and in which our human self has flowed along from the point of time to which our memory goes back. In following up the events of his destiny, a man experiences his own existence.

In bringing this to his consciousness: 'I with my own self have experienced something that destiny brought to me', a man has already come to the point where he will contemplate the world. He can say to himself: I was not alone in my fate; the world played a part in my experience. I willed this or that; the world streamed into my will. I find the world in my will when I experience this will in self-contemplation.

Continuing thus to enter into his own being, man ceases to be conscious of the self, he becomes conscious of the world; he ceases to experience himself, he becomes feelingly aware of the world.

I send my thoughts out into the world, there I find myself; I sink into myself, there I find the world. If a man experiences this strongly enough, he is confronted with the great riddles of the World and Man.

For to have the feeling: I have taken endless pains to understand the world through thinking, and after all there is but myself in this thinking-this gives rise to the first great riddle. And to feel that one's own self is formed through destiny, yet to perceive in this process the onward flow of world-happenings-this presents the second riddle.

In the experience of this problem of Man and the World germinates the frame of mind in which man can so confront Anthroposophy that he receives from it in his inner being an impression which rouses his attention.

For Anthroposophy asserts that there is a spiritual experience which does not lose the world when thinking. One can also live in thought. Anthroposophy tells of an inward experience in which one does not lose the sense-world when thinking, but gains the Spirit-world. Instead of penetrating into the ego in which the sense-world is felt to disappear, one penetrates into the Spirit-world in which the ego feels established.

Anthroposophy shows, further, that there is an experience of destiny in which one does not lose the self. In fate, too, one can still feel oneself to be active. Anthroposophy points out, in the impartial, unegoistic observation of human destiny, an experience in which one learns to love the world and not only one's own existence instead of staring into the world which carries the ego on the waves of fortune and misfortune, one Ends the ego which shapes its own fate voluntarily. Instead of striking against the world, on which the ego is dashed to pieces, one penetrates into the self, which feels itself united with the course of events in the world.

Man's destiny comes to him from the world that is revealed to him by his senses. If then he finds his own activity in the working of his destiny, his real self rises up before him not only out of his inner being but out of the sense-world too.

If a person is able to feel, however faintly, how the spiritual part of the world appears in the self, and how the self proves to be working in the outer world of sense, he has already learned to understand Anthroposophy correctly. For he will then realize that in Anthroposophy it is possible to describe the Spirit-world, which the self can comprehend. And this will enable him to understand that in the sense-world the self can also be found-in a different way than by diving within. Anthroposophy finds the self by showing how the sense-world reveals to man not only sense-perceptions but also the after-effects of his life before birth and his former earthly lives.

Man can now gaze on the world perceptible to his senses and say: It contains not only color, sound, warmth; in it are active the experiences passed through by souls before their present earthly life. And he can look into himself and say: I find there not only my ego but, in addition, a spiritual world is revealed.

In an understanding of this kind, a person who really feels-who is not unmoved by-the great riddles of Man and the World, can meet on a common ground with the Initiate who in accordance with his insight is obliged to speak of the outer world of the senses as manifesting not only sensible perceptions but also the impressions of what human souls have done in their life before birth and in past earthly lives, and who has to say of the world of the inner self that it reveals spiritual events which produce impressions and are as effective as the perceptions of the sense-world.

The would-be active members should consciously make themselves mediators between what the questioning human soul feels as the problems of Man and the Universe, and what the knowledge of the Initiates has to recount, when it draws forth a past world out of the destiny of human beings, and when by strengthening the soul it opens up the perception of a spiritual world.

In this way, through the work of the would-be active members, the Anthroposophical Society may become a true preparatory school for the school of Initiates. It was the intention of the Christmas Assembly to indicate this very forcibly; and one who truly understands what that Assembly meant will continue to point this out until the sufficient understanding of it can bring the Society fresh tasks and possibilities again.

THE KARMA OF MICHAELIC
SOULS IN MODERN TIMES

NOTE: in what follows "anthroposophists" should be understood in a wider sense than card-carrying members, or individuals active in the anthroposophical movement. The term covers all those souls who would have the capacity to recognize anthroposophy, whether this has already been the case or not.

The fall of Intelligence into the human realm took on a new dimension with the onset of the Consciousness Soul at the beginning of the fifteenth century, because then new temptations were possible in the human soul. By the end of the nineteenth century, the age of Kali Yuga came to an end. This did not mean a sudden turn for the better. In fact, many of the habits of the previous epoch are still very strong, and still working in a far more evil and counter-productive way than they used to be.

Ahriman is striving to acquire the Intelligence that is coming within reach of humanity, to snatch it for himself, to take hold of this Intelligence from the lowest forces in his dominion. For this purpose, he will keep human intelligence from being anything other than personal intelligence. Over and against that, Michael wants this Intelligence to be the domain of all humanity, an Intelligence that benefits everyone.

The Working of the Michaelic Forces upon the Human Being

Michael's forces work from the spiritual world into the soul nature, and from there into the physical body, and they have strong formative effects upon karma. This means that for human beings who have worked in times past within Michael's impulses, their karma can only be understood in relation to the stream of Michael. They bear a "supra-personal" karma. The fact that Michael's forces work into the physical body means that they affect the Michaelite down to his health and well-being. "…it is Michael who brings the karma of men nearest of all to health and to disease."[407] Finally, this means that the Michaelites have a very strong feeling for the battle that is going on between good and evil.

Michael's work in the physical world is just one aspect of his influence; at another level, he wrests the human being away from the connections of the physical, enabling her to feel the earthly connections of hereditary and blood-bonds more loosely than others would. We know that Michael is the cosmopolitan spirit who is breaking the bonds of blood, race, and religion. Being taken hold of by his impulse means the individual will seek what is universally human. Michael forces have the strongest community-building impulses for those who feel called through him by a cosmopolitan impulse. By the same token, we cannot approach Michaelic human beings, and in particular the Anthroposophical movement, without our karma being deeply affected.

For human beings who find their way to anthroposophy, it is as if they hear the voice of their own karma telling them, "Behold, my karma is somehow moved and taken hold of by this Michael message which is sounding into the world. I, through my own karma, have to do this."[408] In effect, as anthroposophists on earth, we awaken a recollection of the great supersensible cultus in which we, and many others, were present. For many, this call of Michael is heard on one hand as a call to personal salvation; on the other hand, it may be a source of struggle, for the soul may also be influenced by Ahriman, and not be able to choose. This is because our karma is often very complex; we are closely united

---

[407] Steiner, *Karmic Relationships*, Volume 3, lecture of August 3, 1924.
[408] Ibid, lecture of August 1, 1924.

to those in the Michael stream; as closely united as we are to others who are not in that stream, but with whom we have formed karmic connections. The difference between the two groups of people is of the greatest import for the future. When an anthroposophist stands in close connection with a non-anthroposophist, this may be for the settling of old karma on the part of the anthroposophist; or it may serve the non-anthroposophist, to create new karmic connections for her future. Only these two possibilities exist; there are no intermediary ones.[409] And this is so because we stand at the parting of the ways, the time of great decision of which all the sacred traditions have spoken.

The karma-forming consequences of the Michael impulse will have even more bearing in our next incarnations. From our time onward, the Michaelic human being will appear divorced from any true connection with the race and nation in which he will incarnate. "People will say: Where does he come from? He is not of any nation, he is not of any race, he is as though he had grown away from all races and nations."[410] And Michael forces will have further race-creating effects, but the word "race" is not meant in the narrow sense in which we use it today. We can ascribe physically-forming power to the Michael impulse, of which more will be said later.

At the soul level other effects are to be expected. The Michaelite does not "fill in" the body as fully as others do; hence there is a feeling of not being able to come to terms with the world, and a struggle to do so fully. This is simply because an individual united with powerful spiritual impulses enters less deeply into the physical constitution, and actually enters it with a certain reservation. There will be a looser integration of the spiritual-astral with the physical-etheric components. The reverse is true; those who cannot approach anthroposophy are more at home in their bodies and in the world. They relate to their own intelligence as a matter of course, because it is active in them by virtue of their physical constitution, so they need not concern themselves as deeply about the consequences of their thinking.

---

[409] Steiner, *Karmic Relationships,* Volume 3, lecture of August 3, 1924.
[410] Ibid.

The above facts have more than one consequence for the Michaelite. On one hand, she will have many more opportunities to choose from than another human being; but she will also grow tired of the very things that others will naturally continue to work with. Observing this, Steiner was moved to compassion for the newer generations. "Perhaps we see it nowhere with such remarkable intensity as in the youth, and notably the youngest of the youth."[411] This condition in relation to the karma of anthroposophists requires them to form inner initiative and purposefulness; to develop the ability to make decisions out of their deeper soul impulses. Their happiness will depend on this.

Inner obstacles besiege the anthroposophist because of this inner constitution of soul, and those can become excuses for failing to act on inner initiative. Steiner compared the anthroposophist with a bee afraid of using its own sting at the right moment. That fear can arise from wanting to avoid the danger of the Ahrimanic temptation, a certain "fear of life." And instead of developing our inner initiative, the temptation can arise to put a lot of energy into refuting the tenor of our times; that is, the materialistic and intellectualistic elements. To avoid this movement of retreat requires an acceptance of the task to make oneself familiar with materialism (where it holds power) and dive into it. One example may suffice. Steiner formulated his Occult Science after assimilating the views of the German scientist Haeckel on evolution; what Steiner offered was a response to what Haeckel had brought, one-sidedly. Nevertheless Haeckel's contribution was essential as a starting point; Steiner was then able to modify it and evolve it into what became Occult Science. On the other hand, we have the example of what recoiling from approaching intellectualism did for Karl Julius Schröer; it affected him even at the physical level in his later days. In Schröer, everything that Steiner speaks about as the danger for the anthroposophist finds an embodiment.

The double tension (at both the physical and soul levels) is such that the anthroposophist will experience a harder karma than most; wanting to avoid its impact would only lead to illness or accident. So that leaves him with the necessity to bring order into his life and karma. And that

---

[411] Ibid, lecture of August 4, 1924.

necessity is the ultimate consequence of Michael's influence upon the Michaelite.

These truths correspond to something larger; they concern not just the human soul, but affect the destiny of our angels, continuing the movement that already appeared in the eighth and ninth centuries. "It is happening now, that the comparatively single and uniform kingdom of the Angeloi is being turned into a twofold kingdom of Angeloi: a kingdom of Angeloi with an upward tendency into the higher worlds, and one with a downward tendency into lower worlds."[412] This division started in the eighth and ninth centuries, but the consequences are fully felt only at present, when the Consciousness Soul has fully entered into humanity.

In the future incarnations of Michaelites and non-Michaelites, the separation of the angels will have far-reaching consequences. At first the estrangement between human beings, common in our time, will be all the more pronounced. Steiner indicated that Michael also works down into the realm of sympathies and antipathies. In light of the fact that some angels have remained faithful to Michael, whereas others have become earthly angels, Michael can help humanity to restore order in karma, since that is how deeply his influence works on the human being. "...Michael himself is bringing the power which is to bring order again into the karma of those who have gone with him. Thus we may say: What is it in the last resort that unites the members of the Anthroposophical Society? It is that they are to bring order again into their karma. This unites them."[413] And further, "This is the cosmic ray that pours through the Anthroposophical Movement, clearly perceptible to him who knows. It is the restoration of the truth in karma."

The questions of our relationships with those outside of the Michaelic Movement, and of Michael's race-forming impulse, are closely interwoven and will be manifested in future incarnations. Steiner invites us to receive deeper impressions of what it means to stand side by side with human beings who cannot receive spiritual impulses in this present life, maybe in our most immediate family relationships, and especially

---

[412] Steiner, *Karmic Relationships,* Volume 3, lecture of August 4, 1924.
[413] Ibid.

for those individuals who may be very gifted. This is important not just for their own karma (because if in this life they cannot find a connection to the spirit, they will also suffer in the next); it is important for the karma of the anthroposophist herself. "It should touch us and move us with a sense of tragedy. Until it does so, we shall never come to terms with our own karma."[414]

In future times, when the Michaelites return to befriend their loved ones who could not approach the spirit, they will be recognizable by their physiognomic features, for such is the race-forming power of Michael. They will stand in front of materialists as a living, concrete example of how the spirit affects matter positively. They will stand as a "materialistic proof" of the power of the spirit over matter; the materialists will perceive that their friends have become who they are in the physical body because of their spiritual propensities. At that point, the previous karmic connections will have stopped playing a role, except for the fact that the materialist will then pay attention to the Michaelite. "Those who were materialists today will in the future have to look continually upon those who came to the things of the spirit. This will have been left of karma."[415] And the materialist will thirst for an understanding of life that comprehends the ideas of karma and reincarnation. The above highlights the importance of a fuller evaluation and understanding of Steiner's revelations about karma and reincarnation.

Other Aspects of the Michaelites' Struggle Between Ahriman and Michael

The condition of soul of being caught between Ahriman and Michael was particularly strong soon after 1879. The spiritual world was for many directly perceptible, or concealed behind a very thin veil. Ever since that time, similar phenomena can reveal very different influences at play, bringing human destiny in line with Michael or Ahriman's purposes.

It is little known that Michael counts on the cooperation of the

---

[414] Steiner, *Karmic Relationships*, Volume 3, lecture of August 4, 1924.
[415] Ibid.

Luciferic spirits to overcome Ahriman, and the human beings stand in the middle of this battle. This is because ever since the fifteenth century, great numbers of Luciferic spirits have taken part in the School of Michael, and Michael enlists their cooperation in order to counter Ahriman's plans. "Thus the men of Michael are placed into the very midst of the battle, or if we may not call it so, the surging waves of interplay, of Luciferic impulses and Ahrimanic."[416]

Around the time in which the Michael age began, the influences of the progressive Luciferic spirits came over human consciousness to divert them from their original intentions; this was apparently to protect human beings and influence their karma to move toward Michael. This happened because Michael needed to enter into world events through the consciousness of particular human beings. Steiner offers the example of an individual (presumably a professor) who, in the late 1890s, was to study a personality who lived at the time of the Renaissance and Reformation in the usual scholarly fashion of his time. But this study did not happen, because "he fell into a kind of sleep from which he could not awaken, and was thus prevented." The impression that he was to receive from studying the historical figure was transformed in his soul, through the sleep state in which he lived, into a capacity to apprehend the Michael impulse in a living fashion. This was one way in which the man could be brought more closely to the Michael impulse. Another example can be found in The Guardian of the Threshold, Steiner's third Mystery drama. The character Capesius goes through a state of absence from his day consciousness, through which his soul is rendered able to digest and transform painful memories from a previous earth life, before returning to an active life at the side of Michael.

In other situations, the reverse could happen. Although an individual might not be brought closer to the Michael impulse, he could be prevented from moving away from it. Thus, an event might be part of something karmically predestined for an individual, but which would also threaten to create distance from the Michael impulse; a friend could take that individual away at the right time to another place, and prevent the distancing. Steiner called both conditions illustrated here a "veiling of consciousness."

---

[416] Steiner, *Karmic Relationships,* Volume 3, lecture of August 4, 1924.

Ahriman, however, also has increased access to the human soul. In the most radical instance this manifests in what Steiner called a "fainting fit" that could last for a protracted time, during which Ahrimanic forces approach the human being. This lot falls most commonly upon a human being who is highly gifted and also at home in his body. These are the human beings to whom Ahriman has the easiest access in their states of lowered consciousness. In those moments, Ahriman can insert in the human being an intelligence far superior to anything that they possessed before. This was the case with Nietzsche. Steiner indicated that this happened through an Ahrimanic angel Intelligence that incorporated in him. Through that entity, Ahriman became an author for the first time in history.[417] And this was true of two of Nietzsche's late works, *Ecce Homo* and *Anti-Christ*. In *Anti-Christ* a passage in the original edition equated Christ to an "idiot," even though at the time Nietzsche even had leanings toward Catholicism. And the book concludes by equating Christianity with the greatest curse of humanity.

Nietzsche was besieged since childhood with many disruptive illnesses. Among other things, he suffered violent indigestion, spells of shortsightedness leading to near-blindness, and migraine headaches. These persisting conditions may have been aggravated by an 1868 riding accident, and further diseases in 1870. To these, we can add the rage that lived in Nietzsche's soul at being denied university employment because of his strong anti-Christian stance. And it is quite revealing that things only worsened after the writing of those two crucial books authored by Ahriman. Nietzche was in Turin in January 1889, when he caused a public disturbance in one of the city's main squares, and had a mental collapse. Accounts of the time indicate that he had seen a horse being whipped, and had intervened in order to protect it, before collapsing to the ground. Soon after, Nietzsche sent short writings (known as the "Madness Letters") to various friends. Among other things, he claimed having had Caiaphas jailed; having been crucified himself; having asked that the German emperor be shot in Rome; and having summoned the European nations to take arms against Germany. In Nietzsche, Steiner saw the tragedy of an individual who had the courage to abandon all that in culture had served its time; he had turned to materialistic science without being able to find the way from the latter to the spirit.

---

[417] Steiner, *Karmic Relationships,* Volume 3, lecture of August 8, 1924.

F. W. ZEYLMANS VAN EMMICHOVEN, *THE ANTHROPOSOPHICAL UNDERSTANDING OF THE HUMAN SOUL*, TABLE OF CONTENTS

Table of Contents

BERNARD LIEVEGOED, *MAN ON THE THRESHOLD: THE CHALLENGE OF INNER DEVELOPMENT,* TABLE OF CONTENTS

Contents

BIBLIOGRAPHY

Edward Bach, *Heal Thyself: An Explanation of the Real Cause and Cure of Disease* (Saffron Walden, UK: C W Daniel, 2003).

Barnard, Julian,

- *Patterns of Life Force: A Review of the Life and Work of Dr. Edward Bach and His Discovery of the Bach Flower Remedies* (Hereford, U. K.: Bach Educational Programme, 1987).

- *Bach Flower Remedies: Form and Function* (Hudson: Lindisfarne Books, 2004).

Ben Aharon, Jesaiah, *The Supersensible Experience of the Twentieth Century* (London: Temple Lodge, 1993)

Bock, Emil, *The Life and Times of Rudolf Steiner*: Volume 1: *People and Places* and Volume 2: *Origin and Growth of His Insights* (Edinburgh: Floris Books, 1961).

Brüll, Dieter, *The Mysteries of Social Encounters* (Fair Oaks, CA: AWSNA Publications, 2002).

Chancellor, Philip M., *Handbook of the Bach Flower Remedies Positive and Negative Effects* (Saffron Wakden, UK: C W Daniel, 1980).

Dunn, Carol, *Plato's Dialogues: Path to Initiation* (Great Barrington, MA: Portal Books, 2002).

Geldard, Richard, *Remembering Heraclitus* (Great Barrington, MA: Lindisfarne Books, 2000).

Hauschka, Rudolf,

- *At the Dawn of a New Age: Memoirs of a Scientist*, Rudolf Hauschka (Vancouver: Steiner Book Centre, 1982).

- *The Nature of Substance: Spirit and Matter* (Forest Row, UK: Sophia Books, Rudolf Steiner Press, 1983).

Hauschka, *Nutrition: A Holistic Approach* (Forest Row, UK: Sophia Books, 2002).

Howard, Judy and Ramsell, John editors, *The Original Writings of Edward Bach: Compiled from the Archives of the Dr. Edward Bach Healing Trust Mount Vernon, Sotwell* (Saffron Walden, U. K.: C. W. Daniel Co., 1990).

Hiebel, Frederick, *The Gospel of Hellas: the Mission of Ancient Greece and the Advent of Christ* (New York: Anthroposophic Press, 1949).

Jenkins, Jon C. and Jenkins, Maureen R., *The Social Process Triangles* (Groningen, Netherlands: Imaginal Training, 1997).

Jones, T. W. Hyne, *The Bach Remedies: A Self-Help Guide* (Saffron Walden, U. K.: C. W. Daniel Co., 1989).

Kaminski, Patricia and Katz, Richard,

- *Flower Essences and Homeopathy: An Article Exploring the Relationship between These Two Allied Therapies* (Nevada City, CA.: Flower Essence Society, 1983).

- *Flower Essence Repertory: A Comprehensive Guide to North American and English Flower Essences for Emotional and Spiritual Well-being* (Nevada City, CA.: Flower Essence Society, 1994).

Kaslof, Leslie J., *Dictionary of Bach Flower Remedies: Positive and Negative Aspects* (New Canaan, CN: Keats Publishing, 1988).

Krämer, Dietmar, *New Bach Flower Therapies: Healing the Emotional and Spiritual Causes of Illness* (Rochester, Vt: Healing Arts Press, 1989).

Lievegoed, Bernard C. J.,

- *Towards the Twenty-First Century: Doing the Good* (Toronto: Steiner Book Centre, 1972).

- *Man on the Threshold: The Challenge of Inner Development* (Stroud, UK: Hawthorn Press, 1985).

- *Developing Communities* (Derby, U.K.: Hawthorn Press, 1991).

- An Interview with Jelle van der Meulen, *The Eye of the Needle: Bernard Lievegoed; His Life and Working Encounter with Anthroposophy* (Derby, U.K.: Hawthorn Press, 1991).

- *The Battle for the Soul: The Working Together of Three Great Leaders of Humanity* (Stroud, England: Hawthorn Press, 1993).

Lille, Alain de,

- *Anticlaudianus or The Good and Perfect Man*, translated and commented by James J. Sheridan (Toronto: Pontifical Institute of Medieval Studies, 1973).

- *The Complaint of Nature*, translated by Douglas M Moffat (New York: Henry Holt and Co., 1908).

Meffert, Ekkehard, *Les Cisterciens et leur impulsion civilisatrice: L'ecole de Chartres, Alain de Lille*, (Basel: Triskel Verlag, 2007).

Meyer, Thomas H.,

- W.J. Stein/Rudolf Steiner, *Dokumentation Eines Wegweisenden Zusammenwirkens*, edited by T. Meyer, (Dornach: Philosophisch-Anthropososophischer Verlag, 1985).

- *Rudolf Steiner's Core Mission: the Birth and Development of Spiritual-Scientific Karma Research* (Forest Row, UK: Temple Lodge, 2010).

Morelli, Luigi,

- *A Revolution of Hope: Spirituality, Cultural Renewal and Social Change* (Victoria B.C., Canada: Trafford, 2009).

- *Karl Julius Schröer and Rudolf Steiner: Anthroposophy and the Teachings of Karma and Reincarnation* (Bloomington, IN: I-Universe, 2015).

Perlas, Nicanor, *Shaping Globalization: Civil Society, Cultural Power and Threefolding* (Quezon City, Philippines: Center for Alternative Development Initiatives, 2000).

Morizot, Pierre, *The School of Chartres* (Spring Valley, NY: Saint George Publications, 1987).

Prokofieff, Sergei O.,

- *Rudolf Steiner and the Founding of the Mysteries* (London: Temple Lodge, 1986).

- *The Occult Significance of Forgiveness* (London: Temple Lodge, 1991).

- *The Foundation Stone Meditation: A Key to the Christian Mysteries* (London: Temple Lodge, 2006).

- *May Human Beings Hear It: The Mystery of the Christmas Conference* (London: Temple Lodge, 2004).

Rosenberg, Marshall B., *Nonviolent Communication: A Language of Compassion* (Encinitas, CA: PuddleDancer Press Book, 2003).

Otto Scharmer, *Theory U: Leading from the Emerging Future; The Social Technology of Presencing* (Cambridge, MA: Society for Organizational Learning, 2007).

Scheffer, Mechthild,

- *Mastering Bach Flower Therapies: A Guide to Diagnosis and Treatment* (Rochester, Vt: Healing Arts Press, 1996).

- *Encyclopedia of Bach Flower Therapy* (Rochester, Vt: Healing Arts Press, 2001).

Sease Virginia and Schmidt-Brabant, Manfred, *Thinkers, Saints and Heretics: Spiritual Paths in the Middle Ages* (London: Temple Lodge, 2007).

Selg, Peter, *Sergei O. Prokofieff's Life Work: Memorial Address Held in the Goetheanum Carpentry Building, July 29, 2014*, Anthroposophy Worldwide No 9/14.

Senge, Peter; Scharmer, C. Otto; Jaworski, Joseph and Flowers, Betty Sue, *Presence: Exploring Profound Change in People, Organizations and Society* (Cambridge, MA: Society for Organizational Learning, 2004).

Stanfield, R. Brian,

- *The Art of Focused Conversation: 100 Ways to Access Group Wisdom in the Workplace* (Gabriola Island, Canada: New Society Publishers, 2000).

- *The Courage to Lead: Transform Self, Transform Society* (Toronto: The Canadian Institute of Cultural Affairs, 2000).

- *The Workshop Book: From Individual Creativity to Group Action* (Gabriola Island, Canada: New Society Publishers, 2002).

Stein, Walter Johannes, *Rudolf Steiner's Life and Work,* (New York: St. George Publications, 1987).

Steiner, Rudolf,

- *Intuitive Thinking as a Spiritual Path: A Philosophy of Freedom*, 1894 (New York: Anthroposophic Press, 1995).

- *Goethe's World View*, 1897 (Spring Valley, NY: Mercury Press, 1985).

- *Christianity as a Mystical Fact and the Mysteries of Antiquity*, 1902 (Great Barrington, Mass.: SteinerBooks Anthroposophic Press, 2006).

- *How to Know Higher Worlds*, 1904 (Hudson, NY, Anthroposophic Press, 1994).

- "Origin and Goal of the Human Being," Lecture of May, 4 1905 at http://wn.rsarchive.org/Lectures/GA053/English/UNK2014/19050504p01.html

- *Freemasonry and Ritual Work, the Misraim Service: Letters, Documents, Ritual Texts, and Lectures from the History and Contents of the Cognitive-Ritual Section of the Esoteric School: 1904-14* (Great Barrington, MA: Steiner Books, 2007).

- *The Influence of Spiritual Beings upon Man*, 1908 (Spring Valley, NY: Anthroposophic Press, 1982).

- "The Theory of Categories," lecture of November 13, 1908 at http://wn.rsarchive.org/Lectures/19081113p01.html

- *The Principle of Spiritual Economy*, 1909 (London: Rudolf Steiner Press, 1986).

- *The East in the Light of the West*, 1909 (Blauvelt, NY: Garber Communications, 1986).

- *The Mission of Folk-Souls in Connection with Germanic-Scandinavian Mythology*, 1910 (Blauvelt, N. Y.: Spiritual Research Editions, Division of Garber Communications Inc., 1989).

- *Background to the Gospel of Saint Mark*, 1910 (London: Rudolf Steiner Press, 1968).

- *Occult History: Historical Personalities and Events in the Light of Spiritual Science*, 1910 (London: Rudolf Steiner Press, 1982).

- *The Reappearance of Christ in the Etheric World*, 1910 (Spring Valley, NY: The Anthroposophic Press, 1983).

- *The Mission of Folk-Souls in Connection with Germanic Scandinavian Mythology*, Rudolf Steiner, 1910 (New York: Garber Communications, 1989).

- *Four Mystery Dramas*, 1910-1913 (London: Rudolf Steiner Press, 1997).

- *Wonders of the World, Trials of the Soul, Revelations of the Spirit*, 1911 (Whitefish, MT: Kessinger Publishing's Rare Mystical Reprints, 1929).

- *From Jesus to Christ*, 1911 (London: Rudolf Steiner Press, 1973).

- *Esoteric Christianity and the Mission of Christian Rosenkreutz*, 1911-12 (London: Rudolf Steiner Press, 2000).

- *Reincarnation and Karma*, 1912 (Great Barrington, Mass.: Anthroposophic Press, 2001).

- *Self-Education: Autobiographical Reflections: 1861-1893*, 1913 (Spring Valley, NY: Mercury Press, 1985).

- *Secrets of the Threshold*, 1913 (Hudson, NY: Anthroposophic Press, 1987).

- Rudolf Steiner *The Riddles of Philosophy*, 1914 (Great Barrington: Steiner Books, 2009).

- Rudolf Steiner, *The Riddle of Man: from the Thinking, Observations, and Contemplations of a Series of German and Austrian Personalities: What They Have Said and Left Unsaid*, 1916 (Spring Valley, NY: Mercury Press, 1990).

- *Earthly Death and Cosmic Life*, 1918 (London: Rudolf Steiner Press, 1964).

- *The Challenge of the Times*, 1918 (Spring Valley: Anthroposophic Press, 1941).

- *Ancient Myths: Their Meaning and Connection with Evolution*, 1918 (Toronto: Steiner Book Centre, 1971).

- *A Sound Outlook for To-day and a Genuine Hope for the Future*, 1918 (Typescript of unpublished English translations of 7 lectures, from GA 181).

- *From Symptoms to Reality in Modern History*, 1918 (Rudolf Steiner Press, 1976).

- "Social and Anti-social Forces in the Human Being," lecture of December 6, 1918 (Spring Valley, N.Y.: Mercury Press, 1982).

- *Inner Aspect of the Social Question* 1919 (London: Rudolf Steiner Press, 1974).

- Steiner, *Ideas for a New Europe: Crisis and Opportunity for the West,* 1919 (Sussex: Rudolf Steiner Press, 1992).

- *Study of Man: General Education Course*, 1919 (London, Rudolf Steiner Press, 2004).

- *Ideas for a New Europe: Crisis and Opportunity for the West*, 1919-1920 (Sussex: Rudolf Steiner Press, 1992).

- *The Redemption of Thinking: A Study in the Philosophy of Thomas Aquinas*, 1920 (London: Hodder and Stoughton, 1956).

- *The Search for the New Isis, Divine Sophia*, 1920 (Spring Valley, NY: Mercury Press, 1983).

- *Polarities in the Evolution of Mankind: West and East, Materialism and Mysticism, Knowledge and Belief*, 1920 (London: Rudolf Steiner Press, 1987).

- *Awakening to Community*, 1923 (Spring Valley, NY: Anthroposophic Press, 1974).

- *Earthly Knowledge and Heavenly Wisdom*, 1923 (Hudson, N.Y.: Anthroposophic Press, 1991).

- *World History and the Mysteries in the Light of Anthroposophy*, 1923 (London: Rudolf Steiner Press, 1997).

- *Anthroposophical Leading Thoughts: Anthroposophy as a Path of Knowledge; The Michael Mystery*, 1924 (London: Rudolf Steiner Press, 1998).

- *The Easter Festival Considered in Relation to the Mysteries*, 1924 (London: Rudolf Steiner Press, 1968).

- *True and False Paths in Spiritual Investigation*, 1924 (Whitefish, Montana: Kessinger, 2003).

- *The Constitution of the School of Spiritual Science; Its Arrangements into Sections*, 1924 (London: Anthroposophical Society in Great Britain, 1964).

- *Autobiography: Chapters in the Course of My Life: 1861-1907*, 1924 (Hudson, NY: Rudolf Steiner Press, 1999).

- *Rosicrucianism and Modern Initiation*, 1924 (London: Rudolf Steiner Press 1982).

- *The Roots of Education*, 1924 (Hudson, NY: Anthroposophic Press, 1997).

- *Karmic Relationships*, Volumes 1 to 8, 1924 (London: Rudolf Steiner Press, 1977).

Tradowski, Peter, *Kaspar Hauser: The Struggle for the Spirit; A Contribution Towards an Understanding of the Nineteenth and Twentieth Centuries* (London UK: Temple Lodge, 1997).

Umpleby, Stuart and Oyler, Alisa, *A Global Strategy for Human Development: The Work of the Institute of Cultural Affairs*, published in *Systems Research and Behavioral Sciences*, Vol. 24, # 6, November-December 2007.

Wachsmuth, Guenther, *The Etheric Formative Forces in Cosmos, Earth and Man: a Path of Investigation into the World of the Living*, Volume 1 (London: Anthroposophic Press, 1932).

Weeks, Nora, *The Medical Discoveries of Edward Bach Physician* (Saffron Wakden, UK: C W Daniel, 1977).

Zeylmans, Emanuel *Willem Zeylmans von Emmichoven: An Inspiration for Anthroposophy; A biography* (Forest Row, UK: Temple Lodge 2002).

Zeylmans von Emmichoven, Willem,

- *Hygiene of the Soul* (Whittier Books, 1955).

- *The Foundation Stone* (London: Rudolf Steiner Press, 1963).

- *The Anthroposophical Understanding of the Human Soul* (Spring Valley, NY: The Anthroposophic Press, 1982).

van Houten, Coenraad,

- *Awakening the Will: Principles and Processes in Adult Learning* (Forest Row, UK: Adult Education Network, 1995).

- *Practising Destiny* (London: Temple Lodge, 2000).

- *The Threefold Nature of Destiny Learning* (London: Temple Lodge, 2004).

von Manen, Hans Peter, *Twin Roads to the Millennium: The Christmas Conference and the Karma of the Anthroposophical Society* (London: Rudolf Steiner Press, 1988).

Watts, Jean, Miller, Pat, & Kloepfer, John, *Cultivating Collective Consciousness with Transcendent Self-presence. A Guided Dialogue Method*, abstract available at http://www.facilitativeleader.com/pdf files/ja_ccc_wtsp_03.pdf

Printed in the United States
By Bookmasters

\